PARLIAMENTARY S

ONE WEEK LOAN

Thi:
tuti
there
(2) an ana   s of Parliament's ab
exercise of its own authority, including   vis.   ey's con.
of sovereignty, a repudiation of the doctrine of implied repeal an
proposal of a novel theory of 'manner and form' requirements for la
making; (3) an examination of the relationship between parliamentary
sovereignty and statutory interpretation, defending the reality of legislative intentions and their indispensability to sensible interpretation
and respect for parliamentary sovereignty; and (4) an assessment of the
compatibility of parliamentary sovereignty with recent constitutional
developments, including the expansion of judicial review of administrative action, the Human Rights and European Communities Acts and
the growing recognition of 'constitutional principles' and 'constitutional
statutes'.

JEFFREY GOLDSWORTHY holds a Personal Chair in the Faculty of Law
at Monash University in Melbourne, Australia, where his major interests
are legal philosophy and constitutional law, theory and history.

CAMBRIDGE STUDIES IN CONSTITUTIONAL LAW

The aim of this series is to produce leading monographs in constitutional law. All areas of constitutional law and public law fall within the ambit of the series, including human rights and civil liberties law, administrative law, as well as constitutional theory and the history of constitutional law. A wide variety of scholarly approaches is encouraged, with the governing criterion being simply that the work is of interest to an international audience. Thus, works concerned with only one jurisdiction will be included in the series as appropriate, while, at the same time, the series will include works which are explicitly comparative or theoretical – or both. The series editors likewise welcome proposals that work at the intersection of constitutional and international law, or that seek to bridge the gaps between civil law systems, the US, and the common law jurisdictions of the Commonwealth.

Series Editors
David Dyzenhaus, *Professor of Law and Philosophy,
University of Toronto, Canada*
Adam Tomkins, *John Millar Professor of Public Law,
University of Glasgow, UK*

Editorial Advisory Board
T.R.S. Allan, Cambridge, UK
Damian Chalmers, LSE, UK
Sujit Choudhry, Toronto, Canada
Monica Claes, Tilburg, Netherlands
David Cole, Georgetown, USA
K.D. Ewing, King's College London, UK
David Feldman, Cambridge, UK
Cora Hoexter, Witwatersrand, South Africa
Christoph Moellers, Goettingen, Germany
Adrienne Stone, Melbourne, Australia
Adrian Vermeule, Harvard, USA

PARLIAMENTARY SOVEREIGNTY

Contemporary Debates

JEFFREY GOLDSWORTHY

Monash University

CAMBRIDGE UNIVERSITY PRESS
Cambridge, New York, Melbourne, Madrid, Cape Town, Singapore,
São Paulo, Delhi, Dubai, Tokyo

Cambridge University Press
The Edinburgh Building, Cambridge CB2 8RU, UK

Published in the United States of America by Cambridge University Press, New York

www.cambridge.org
Information on this title: www.cambridge.org/9780521884723

First published 2010

Printed in the United Kingdom at the University Press, Cambridge

A catalogue record for this publication is available from the British Library

Library of Congress Cataloguing in Publication data
Goldsworthy, Jeffrey Denys.
Parliamentary sovereignty : contemporary debates / Jeffrey Goldsworthy.
p.   cm. – (Cambridge Studies in constitutional law)
Includes bibliographical references and index.
ISBN 978-0-521-88472-3 (hardback)
1. Great Britain. Parliament.   2. Legislative power–Great Britain.
3. Legislation–Great Britain.   4. Law–Great Britain–Interpretation and
construction.   I. Title.   II. Series.
KD4210.G65 2010
342.41′052–dc22
2010022336

ISBN 978-0-521-88472-3 Hardback
ISBN 978-0-521-14019-5 Paperback

CONTENTS

DETAILED TABLE OF CONTENTS

ACKNOWLEDGMENTS

Six of the chapters in this book are revised and updated versions of essays published previously. Chapters 3, 4, 6 and 8 have been only lightly revised, while Chapters 2 and 5 have had significant new material added to them. The other chapters are new, but include some material that appeared in previously published essays. I thank the following for permission to republish the following essays, or material that appeared in them:

Cambridge University Press, for 'The Myth of the Common Law Constitution', in D. Edlin (ed.) *Common Law Theory* (Cambridge: Cambridge University Press, 2007), and for some material in 'Questioning the Migration of Constitutional Ideas: Rights, Constitutionalism and the Limits of Convergence', in Sujit Choudhry (ed.) *The Migration of Constitutional Ideas* (Cambridge: Cambridge University Press, 2006).

Oxford University Press, for 'Legislative Sovereignty and the Rule of Law', in Tom Campbell, Keith Ewing and Adam Tomkins (eds.) *Sceptical Essays on Human Rights* (Oxford: Oxford University Press, 2001); 'Homogenizing Constitutions' *Oxford Journal of Legal Studies* 23 (2003) 483–505; and 'Judicial Review, Legislative Override, and Democracy', in Tom Campbell, Jeffrey Goldsworthy and Adrienne Stone (eds.) *Protecting Human Rights, Instruments and Institutions* (Oxford: Oxford University Press, 2003).

Hart Publishing, for 'Abdicating and Limiting Parliamentary Sovereignty' *King's College Law Journal* 17 (2006) 255–80.

The New Zealand Journal of Public and International Law, for some material in 'Is Parliament Sovereign? Recent Challenges to the Doctrine of Parliamentary Sovereignty' *New Zealand Journal of Public and International Law* 3 (2005) 7–37.

LexisNexis, for some material in 'Parliamentary Sovereignty and Statutory Interpretation', in R. Bigwood (ed.) *The Statute, Making and Meaning* (Wellington: LexisNexis, 2004).

Federation Press, for '*Trethowan's* case', in G. Winterton (ed.) *State Constitutional Landmarks* (Sydney: Federation Press, 2006), and some material in 'Manner and Form Revisited: Reflections on *Marquet's* Case', in M. Groves (ed.) *Law and Government in Australia* (Sydney: Federation Press, 2005).

Ashgate Publishing, for some material in 'Legislative Intentions, Legislative Supremacy, and Legal Positivism', in Jeffrey Goldsworthy and Tom Campbell (eds.) *Legal Interpretation in Democratic States* (Aldershot: Ashgate/Dartmouth, 2002), pp. 45–65.

The original versions of these essays record my indebtedness to many colleagues and friends who provided helpful comments while they were being written. I will not repeat my thanks to them here. But I do thank Richard Ekins for very helpful comments on a draft of Chapter 8. I also thank my daughter Kate Goldsworthy for her meticulous proofreading, and Juliet Smith and Emma Wildsmith for their assistance in preparing the manuscript for publication.

I dedicate the book to my wife Helen, with gratitude for all her love and support.

1

Introduction

I

This book is a collection of essays with four main themes. The first is criticism of the theory known as 'common law constitutionalism', which holds either that Parliament is not sovereign because its authority is subordinate to fundamental common law principles such as 'the Rule of Law', or that its sovereignty is a creature of judge-made common law, which the judges have authority to modify or repudiate (Chapters 2, 3, 4 and 10). The second theme is analysis of how, and to what extent, Parliament may abdicate, limit or regulate the exercise of its own legislative authority, which includes the proposal of a novel theory of 'manner and form' requirements for law-making (Chapters 5, 6 and 7). This theory, which involves a major revision of Dicey's conception of sovereignty, and a repudiation of the doctrine of implied repeal, would enable Parliament to provide even stronger protection of human rights than is currently afforded by the Human Rights Act 1998 (UK) ('the HRA'), without contradicting either its sovereignty or the principle of majoritarian democracy (Chapters 7 and 8). The third theme is a detailed account of the relationship between parliamentary sovereignty and statutory interpretation, which strongly defends the reality of legislative intentions, and argues that sensible interpretation and parliamentary sovereignty both depend on judges taking them into account (Chapters 9 and 10). The fourth is a demonstration of the compatibility of parliamentary sovereignty with recent constitutional developments, including the expansion of judicial review of administrative action under statute, the operation of the HRA and the European Communities Act 1972 (UK), and the growing recognition of 'constitutional principles' and perhaps even 'constitutional statutes' (Chapter 10). This demonstration draws on the novel theory of 'manner and form', and the account of statutory interpretation, developed in Chapters 7 and 9.

II

The English-speaking peoples are reluctant revolutionaries. When they do mount a revolution, they are loath to acknowledge – even to themselves – what they are doing. They manage to convince themselves, and try desperately to convince others, that they are protecting the 'true' constitution, properly understood, from unlawful subversion, and that their opponents, who wear the mantle of orthodoxy, are the real revolutionaries.[1] They appear certain that their cause is not only morally righteous, but also legally conservative, in that they are merely upholding traditional legal rights and liberties.

Today, a number of judges and legal academics in Britain and New Zealand are attempting a peaceful revolution, by incremental steps aimed at dismantling the doctrine of parliamentary sovereignty, and replacing it with a new constitutional framework in which Parliament shares ultimate authority with the courts. They describe this as 'common law constitutionalism', 'dual' or 'bi-polar' sovereignty, or as a 'collaborative enterprise' in which the courts are in no sense subordinate to Parliament.[2] Or they claim that the true normative foundation of the constitution is a principle of 'legality', which (of course) it is ultimately the province of the courts, rather than Parliament, to interpret and enforce.[3] But they deny that there is anything revolutionary, or even unorthodox, in their attempts to establish this new framework. They claim to be defending the 'true' or 'original' constitution, 'properly understood', from misrepresentation and distortion.[4] And they sometimes accuse their adversaries, the defenders of parliamentary sovereignty, of being the true revolutionaries.[5]

---

[1] This happened during the civil war of the 1640s, the Glorious Revolution of 1688, the American Revolution of 1776, and the secession of the southern States of the US in the 1860s. See for example R. Kay, 'Legal Rhetoric and Revolutionary Change' *Caribbean Law Review* 7 (1997) 161; R. Kay, 'William III and the Legalist Revolution' *Connecticut Law Review* 32 (2000) 1645.

[2] Philip A. Joseph, 'Parliament, the Courts, and the Collaborative Enterprise' *King's College Law Journal* 15 (2004) 333 at 334, discussed in Chapter 10, Section II, Part D, below.

[3] S. Lakin, 'Debunking the Idea of Parliamentary Sovereignty: the Controlling Factor of Legality in the British Constitution' *Oxford Journal of Legal Studies* 28 (2008) 709.

[4] D. Edlin, *Judges and Unjust Laws, Common Law Constitutionalism and the Foundations of Judicial Review* (Ann Arbor: University of Michigan Press, 2008), p. 177.

[5] Judicial repudiation of parliamentary sovereignty 'would not be at all revolutionary. What is revolutionary is talk of the omnipotence of Parliament': R.A. Edwards, 'Bonham's Case: The Ghost in the Constitutional Machine' *Denning Law Journal* 63 (1996) 76.

Claims like these are familiar ones in the development of the unwritten British constitution over many centuries. How, for example, did the common law subordinate what were once called the 'absolute prerogatives' of the Crown? By strenuously asserting that those prerogatives had, all along, been creatures of and therefore controlled by the common law. When we read the constitutional debates of earlier centuries, we see on all sides the pervasive tendentiousness of legal thinking pursued by those who care so passionately about practical outcomes that objectivity has become impossible. This was noted by A.V. Dicey:

> The fictions of the courts have in the hands of lawyers such as Coke served the cause both of justice and of freedom, and served it when it could have been defended by no other weapons … Nothing can be more pedantic, nothing more artificial, nothing more unhistorical, than the reasoning by which Coke induced or compelled James to forego the attempt to withdraw cases from the courts for his Majesty's personal determination. But no achievement of sound argument, or stroke of enlightened statesmanship, ever established a rule more essential to the very existence of the constitution than the principle enforced by the obstinacy and the fallacies of the great Chief Justice … The idea of retrogressive progress is merely one form of the appeal to precedent. This appeal has made its appearance at every crisis in the history of England and … the peculiarity of all English efforts to extend the liberties of the country … [is] that these attempts at innovation have always assumed the form of an appeal to pre-existing rights. But the appeal to precedent is in the law courts merely a useful fiction by which judicial decision conceals its transformation into judicial legislation.[6]

Today, the sovereignty of Parliament is the target of attempted innovation disguised as an appeal to pre-existing rights. Whether 'the cause both of justice and of freedom' would be advanced by clipping Parliament's wings is debatable. But even if it would be, it cannot plausibly be maintained that there are 'no other weapons' to achieve this than artificial, unhistorical fictions. 'Sound argument' candidly aimed at formal legislative or even constitutional reform is surely preferable to surreptitious judicial law-making.

In an earlier book, I set out to refute various philosophical errors and dispel several historical myths concerning the doctrine of parliamentary sovereignty.[7] Prominent among these errors and myths are the beliefs that

---

[6] A.V. Dicey, *An Introduction to the Study of the Law of the Constitution* (10th edn), E.C.S. Wade (ed.) (London: MacMillan, 1959), pp. 18–19.

[7] J. Goldsworthy, *The Sovereignty of Parliament, History and Philosophy* (Oxford: Clarendon Press, 1999).

the doctrine of parliamentary sovereignty: (a) is a relatively recent development, no older than the eighteenth century; (b) supplanted an ancient
'common law constitution' that had previously limited Parliament's
authority; (c) is a creature of the common law that was made by the judges
and can therefore be modified or even repudiated by them. But it is possible, as Ian Ward has observed, that even if I was right, 'truth matters
little in a politics of competing mythologies'.[8] I take him to mean that
lawyers and judges who find the doctrine of parliamentary sovereignty
morally objectionable, and are committed to bringing about its demise,
are unlikely to be either able or willing to assess objectively the historical
evidence and jurisprudential analysis that I presented – or perhaps even
to acknowledge their existence. The mythology of common law constitutionalism is indeed very difficult to dispel. Scholarly works continue to
perpetuate it while ignoring the weighty arguments and evidence to the
contrary.[9]

The desire to clothe legal revolution in the trappings of legal orthodoxy
is not, of course, peculiarly British. Constitutional debates reminiscent of
those in Britain today took place in France between 1890 and the 1930s.
Before 1890, the French legal system was firmly based on the principle
of legislative sovereignty, which had been established during the French
Revolution and the rule of Napoleon. But after 1890, leading public law
scholars began to revive natural law ideas, arguing that the legislature
was bound by an unwritten higher law, which the judges were capable
of discerning and ought to enforce. According to a recent account, these
neo-natural law ideas were 'functionally equivalent to rule of law notions
in Anglo-American legal theory'.[10] These scholars waged a persistent
campaign to convince judges, first, 'that they were juridically required to
exercise . . . substantive judicial review', and secondly, 'that the judges had

---

[8] Ian Ward, *The English Constitution, Myths and Realities* (Oxford and Portland
Oregon: Hart Publishing, 2004), p. 185.
[9] E.g., E. Wicks, *The Evolution of the Constitution, Eight Key Moments in British
Constitutional History* (Oxford and Portland: Hart Publishing, 2006). Although some
footnotes show that Wicks knew of my book, she completely ignores the evidence it contains. She makes many unsupported claims such as that 'there was no suggestion' around
the time of the 1688 Revolution 'that Parliament should be unlimited in its legislative
powers', and that 'fundamental principles of the common law constitution . . . remained
to bind the King-in-Parliament': *ibid.*, 20. To the contrary, there were many explicit statements by eminent lawyers not only around that time, but much earlier, that Parliament's
powers were unlimited: see, e.g., J. Goldsworthy, *The Sovereignty of Parliament*,
pp. 124–34, 149–65 and 173–81.
[10] A. Stone Sweet, 'Why Europe Rejected American Judicial Review, and Why It May Not
Matter' *Michigan Law Review* 101 (2003) 2744, 2755.

already begun doing so, but apparently did not yet know it'.[11] The basis of the second claim was that a number of judicial decisions supposedly made complete sense only if higher, unwritten constitutional principles were assumed to exist. As one of these scholars argued in 1923, the judges 'without expressly admitting it, and perhaps without even admitting it to themselves, have opened the way to judicial review'.[12] This campaign was making headway until the publication of a book that explained how the American Supreme Court had stymied democratic social reform by reading laissez faire principles into its Constitution, and warned that French judges might follow suit. This book had an enormous impact, and routed the campaign in favour of judicially imposed, higher law principles.[13]

Law is an unusual discipline, in that the truth of legal propositions is not independent of people's beliefs about them: indeed, it depends on whether enough of the right people believe them. According to H.L.A. Hart, the most fundamental norms of a legal system owe their existence partly to their being accepted as binding by the most senior officials of the legal system, legislative, executive and judicial.[14] Norms that are accepted today might no longer be accepted tomorrow – so that propositions of law that are false today might be true tomorrow – if the beliefs of enough of the right people can be changed. The process by which the common law gradually evolves can be of great assistance in bringing about such changes. Obiter dicta or dissenting opinions that are false can, through sheer repetition, come to appear true; indeed, sufficient repetition can eventually clothe them with authority. For example, it can be confidently predicted that dicta in *Jackson* v. *Attorney-General*[15] challenging the doctrine of parliamentary sovereignty will be cited in this way regardless of their inaccuracies. Judges know this, which is no doubt why, as Lord Cooke of Thorndon observed, some of them have been 'inching forwards with ever stronger expressions when treating some common law rights as constitutional'.[16] As Tom Mullan says, of the obiter dicta in *Jackson*:

> The most obvious reading is that certain judges are staking out their position for future battles. They do fear that Parliament and governments cannot be trusted in all circumstances to refrain from passing legislation inconsistent with fundamental rights, the rule of law or democracy. When a case involving such 'unconstitutional legislation' arises they want to be

---

[11] *Ibid.*, p. 2757.   [12] Quoted in *ibid.*, p. 2758.   [13] *Ibid.*, pp. 2758–60.
[14] H.L.A. Hart, *The Concept of Law* (Oxford: Oxford University Press, 1961), ch. 6.
[15] [2005] UKHL 56.
[16] Robin Cooke, 'The road Ahead for the Common Law' *International and Comparative Law Quarterly* 53 (2004) 273 at 277.

in a position to strike it down without appearing to invent new doctrine on the spot. They want to be able to say that they are applying settled constitutional doctrine. *Jackson* may then be a useful precedent ... *Jackson* may [also] be viewed as a shot across the government's bows.[17]

The central claims of 'common law constitutionalism' are false, or so I argue in what follows. Most senior legal officials, including judges, still accept the doctrine of parliamentary sovereignty. Stuart Lakin has recently claimed that 'there is simply no widely accepted "core" of acceptance about the relative powers of Parliament and the courts'.[18] But this is hard to square with his admission that only 'a distinguished minority' of judges and academics currently support the idea that there are limits to Parliament's authority.[19] Among the senior judiciary, dissent from the core principle of parliamentary sovereignty is a relatively recent, minority view, inspired by the false claims of the common law constitutionalists. Recently, that dissenting view was firmly repudiated by Britain's then most senior judge, Lord Bingham of Cornhill.[20] If a majority of British judges were converted to the dissenting view, the rule of recognition that currently underpins the constitution might be undermined. But, as I will argue shortly, this would be very risky because the judges could not replace it with a new rule of recognition without the agreement of the elected branches of government.[21]

The claims of the dissenters could prove self-fulfilling if they are repeated so often that enough senior officials are persuaded to believe them. And this could happen even if these officials are persuaded for reasons that are erroneous (such as that common law constitutionalism was true all along). If that happens, original doubts about their correctness will be brushed aside as irrelevant, and the law books will be retrospectively rewritten. After revolution, as after war, history is written by the victors. If the legal revolution succeeds, it will not be acknowledged to have been a revolution. It will be depicted either as a judicial rediscovery of 'hitherto latent' restrictions on Parliament's powers that the law always

---

[17] T. Mullen, 'Reflections on *Jackson v. Attorney General*: questioning sovereignty' *Legal Studies* 27 (2007) 1 at 15–16.
[18] S. Lakin, 'Debunking the Idea of Parliamentary Sovereignty' at p. 727.
[19] *Ibid.*, p. 730.
[20] The Rt Hon Lord Bingham of Cornhill, 'The Rule of Law and the Sovereignty of Parliament', King's Law Journal 19 (2008) 223.
[21] See Chapter 2, below.

included,[22] or as the exercise of authority that the judges always had to continue the development of the 'common law constitution'.

III

This book includes further efforts to resist the legal revolution sought by the common law constitutionalists. Chapter 2 presents historical and philosophical objections, and Chapters 3 and 4 respond to arguments based on the political ideal known as 'the rule of law'. The first section of Chapter 10 is also relevant to this theme. I attempt to show that Parliament has been for centuries, and still is, sovereign in a legal sense; that this is not incompatible with the rule of law; and that its sovereignty is not a gift of the common law understood in the modern sense of judge-made law. It is a product of long-standing consensual practices that emerged from centuries-old political struggles, and it can only be modified if the consensus among senior legal officials changes. Furthermore, it ought not to be modified without the support of a broader consensus within the electorate. The recent Green Paper titled *The Governance of Britain* ends on the right note: constitutional change in Britain as significant as the adoption of an entrenched Bill of Rights or written Constitution requires 'an inclusive process of national debate', involving 'extensive and wide consultation' leading to 'a broad consensus'.[23] Such changes should not, and indeed cannot, be brought about by the judiciary alone.

If radical change is to be brought about by consensus, legislation will be required. Chapters 5, 6 and 7 discuss problems relating to Parliament's ability to abdicate or limit its sovereignty, or to regulate its exercise through the enactment of requirements as to the procedure or form of legislation. Chapter 5 reviews all the current theories of abdication and limitation, and advocates an alternative based on consensual change to the rules of recognition underlying legal systems. The theories of A.V. Dicey, W. Ivor Jennings, R.T.E. Latham, H.W.R. Wade and Peter Oliver are all subjected to criticism. Chapter 6 is a detailed account of the influential decision in *Trethowan* v. *Attorney-General (NSW)*,[24] which is often misunderstood and misapplied in discussions of 'manner and form'. This account reveals the difference between the 'manner and form' and 'reconstitution' lines of

[22] M. Elliott, 'United Kingdom Bicameralism, Sovereignty, and the Unwritten Constitution' *International Journal of Constitutional Law* 5 (2007) 370 at 379.

[23] *The Governance of Britain* (CM 7170, July 2007), paras 198 and 213.

[24] (1931) 44 CLR 97 (High Court).

reasoning that were first propounded in that case, and shows that much of the majority judges' reasoning was dubious. Chapter 7 draws on the previous two chapters to propose a novel theory of Parliament's power to regulate its own decision-making processes, by enacting mandatory requirements governing law-making procedures or the form of legislation. In passing, it discusses the somewhat different issues raised in *Jackson v. Attorney-General*,[25] which involved what is called in Australia an 'alternative' rather than a 'restrictive' legislative procedure. The novel theory of restrictive procedures that is proposed differs from the 'new theory' propounded by Jennings, Latham and R.F.V. Heuston, and from the neo-Diceyan theory of H.W.R. Wade. It rejects a key element of Dicey's conception of legislative sovereignty, and the popular notion that the doctrine of implied repeal is essential to parliamentary sovereignty. Chapter 7 concludes with the possibly surprising suggestion that a judicially enforceable Bill of Rights could be made consistent with parliamentary sovereignty by including a broader version of the 'override' or 'notwithstanding' clause (s. 33) in the Canadian Charter of Rights, which enables Canadian parliaments to override most Charter rights. Chapter 8 examines this topic in more detail, analysing the relationship between the judicial protection of rights, legislative override, legislative supremacy and majoritarian democracy.

Chapter 9 is a detailed account of the relationship between parliamentary sovereignty and statutory interpretation, which argues that legislative intentions are both real and crucial to avoiding the absurd consequences of literalism. It also describes and criticises the alternative 'constructivist' theories of interpretation defended by Ronald Dworkin, Michael Moore and Trevor Allan. It acknowledges the frequent need for judicial creativity in interpretation, including the repair or rectification of statutes by 'reading into' them qualifications they need to achieve their purposes without damaging background principles that Parliament is committed to. The intentionalist account is further developed in Chapter 10, where it is shown to be crucial to the traditional justification of presumptions of statutory interpretation, such as that Parliament is presumed not to intend to infringe fundamental common law rights, and also crucial to the defence of parliamentary sovereignty against other criticisms.

Chapter 10 is a lengthy defence of parliamentary sovereignty against recent criticisms that it was never truly part of the British constitution, or

---

[25] [2005] UKHL 56.

is no longer part of it, or will soon be expunged from it. The Chapter begins with some historical discussion, and then considers at length the consequences of recent constitutional developments, including the expansion of judicial review of administrative action under statute, the operation of the *European Communities Act* 1972 (UK) and the HRA, and the growing recognition of 'constitutional principles' and possibly even 'constitutional statutes'. It argues that none of these developments is, so far, incompatible with parliamentary sovereignty.

IV

The once popular idea of legislative sovereignty has been in decline throughout the world for some time. 'From France to South Africa to Israel, parliamentary sovereignty has faded away.'[26] A dwindling number of political and constitutional theorists continue to resist the 'rights revolution' that is sweeping the globe, by refusing to accept that judicial enforcement of a constitutionally entrenched Bill of Rights is necessarily desirable. To be one of them can feel like King Cnut trying to hold back the tide.

This book does not directly address the policy questions raised by calls for constitutionally entrenched rights. For what it is worth, my opinion is that constitutional entrenchment might be highly desirable, or even essential, for the preservation of democracy, the rule of law and human rights in some countries, but not in others. In much of the world, a culture of entrenched corruption, populism, authoritarianism, or bitter religious, ethnic or class conflicts, may make judicially enforceable bills of rights desirable. Much depends on culture, social structure and political organisation.

I will not say much about this here, because the arguments are so well known. I regret the contemporary loss of faith in the old democratic ideal of government by ordinary people, elected to represent the opinions and interests of ordinary people.[27] According to this ideal, ordinary people have a right to participate on equal terms in the political decision-making that affects their lives as much as anyone else's, and should be presumed to possess the intelligence, knowledge and virtue needed to do

---

[26] T. Ginsburg, *Judicial Review in New Democracies: Constitutional Courts in Asian Cases* (Cambridge: Cambridge University Press, 2003), p. 3.

[27] I hope the term 'ordinary people' does not seem patronising. I cannot think of an alternative, and I regard myself as an 'ordinary person'.

so.[28] Proponents of this ideal do not naively believe that such a method of government will never violate the rights of individuals or minority groups. But they do trust that, in appropriate political, social and cultural conditions, clear injustices will be relatively rare, and that in most cases, whether or not the law violates someone's rights will be open to reasonable disagreement. They also trust that over time, the proportion of clear rights violations will diminish, and 'that a people, in acting autonomously, will learn how to act rightly'.[29] Strong democrats hold that where the requirements of justice and human rights are the subject of reasonable disagreement, the opinion of a majority of the people or those elected to represent them, rather than that of a majority of some unelected elite, should prevail. On this view, the price that must be paid for giving judges power to correct the occasional clear injustice by overriding enacted laws, is that they must also be given power to overrule the democratic process in the much greater number of cases where there is reasonable disagreement and healthy debate. For strong democrats, this is too high a price.

What explains the loss of faith in the old democratic ideal? I am aware of possible 'agency problems': failures of elected representatives faithfully to represent the interests of their constituents. In many countries this is a major problem. But I suspect that in countries such as Britain, Canada, Australia and New Zealand, the real reason for this loss of faith lies elsewhere. There, a substantial number of influential members of the highly educated, professional, upper-middle class have lost faith in the ability of their fellow citizens to form opinions about important matters of public policy in a sufficiently intelligent, well-informed, dispassionate, impartial and carefully reasoned manner. Even though the upper-middle class dominates the political process in any event, the force of public opinion still makes itself felt through the ballot box, and cannot be ignored by elected politicians no matter how enlightened and progressive they might be. Hence the desire to further diminish the influence of 'public opinion'.

If I am right, the main attraction of judicial enforcement of constitutional rights in these countries is that it shifts power to people (judges) who are representative members of the highly educated, professional,

---

[28] This position is most ably defended by J. Waldron, *Law and Disagreement* (Oxford: Oxford University Press, 1999), Part III, and 'The Core of the Case Against Judicial Review' *Yale Law Journal* 115 (2006) 1346.

[29] R. Dahl, *Democracy and Its Critics* (New Haven: Yale University Press, 1989), p. 192.

upper-middle class, and whose superior education, intelligence, habits of thought, and professional ethos are thought more likely to pro- duce enlightened decisions. I think it is reasonable to describe this as a return to the ancient principle of 'mixed government', by re-inserting an 'aristocratic' element into the political process to check the ignor- ance, prejudice and passion of the 'mob'. By 'aristocratic', I mean an element supposedly distinguished by superior education, intellectual refinement, thoughtfulness and responsibility, rather than by heredity or inherited wealth.

The obvious rejoinder is that the attraction of judicially enforceable rights has more to do with the procedures that judges follow – procedures that promote more impartial and carefully reasoned decision-making – than the personal qualities of the judges. Of course there is something to this, but I do not find it completely convincing. If the main problem were deficiencies in the deliberative procedures of elected legislatures, then the most obvious remedy would be to improve those procedures to promote more careful, well-informed and dispassionate reasoning. The theory propounded in Chapter 7 could prove very useful in that regard. Judicial enforcement of rights would be a fall-back position, to be resorted to only if such reforms were unsuccessful. Few advocates of constitutional entrenchment approach the issue in that way, although improving the deliberative procedures of the elected branches of government is a pri- mary aim of the unentrenched, statutory bills of rights in New Zealand and Britain.

The American model of entrenched constitutional rights is no longer the only alternative to a system of untrammelled legislative sovereignty. New 'hybrid' models pioneered in Canada, New Zealand and Britain allo- cate much greater responsibility for protecting rights to courts, without completely abandoning the principle of legislative supremacy based on the old democratic ideal. Judges there have not been given ultimate author- ity on questions of rights. Indeed, s. 33 of Canada's Charter of Rights, which enables legislatures to override Charter rights, 'was included in the *Charter* for the very purpose of preserving parliamentary sovereignty on rights issues'.[30] Parliaments in New Zealand and Britain were deliberately left with discretion as to whether or not to defer to judicial views of the compatibility of their statutes with rights. If an 'aristocratic' element has

---

[30] P.W. Hogg, A.A.B. Thornton and W.K. Wright, 'A Reply on "*Charter* Dialogue Revisited"' *Osgoode Hall Law Journal* 45 (2007) 193, 201.

been added to the political process, its primary function is to improve the quality of the debate over human rights, not to impose its will on the legislature by force of law.[31]

These models offer the possibility of a compromise that combines the best features of both the traditional British model of legislative sovereignty, and the American model of judicial supremacy, by authorising courts to pronounce on the compatibility of legislation with protected rights, while preserving the legislature's authority to have the final word.[32] They are experiments that may or may not work. It has been suggested that in practice, they will probably collapse (if they have not already collapsed) into something like the American model of judicial supremacy.[33] The compromise they attempt to strike between legislative and judicial authority is heartily disapproved of by advocates of constitutional entrenchment, who actively seek to bring about such a collapse. For example, common law constitutionalists are not satisfied with the enhanced protection of rights provided by the HRA, which was deliberately designed to leave Parliament with the final word. They continue to incite the courts to find fundamental common law rights entrenched within Britain's unwritten constitution, to insist that whatever Parliament may have intended the HRA establishes a strong form of 'constitutional' judicial review, and to condemn as constitutionally illegitimate any parliamentary response to judicial declarations of incompatibility other than meek acquiescence. Their views are criticised in later chapters.[34]

If enhanced judicial protection of rights is needed, I prefer the statutory bill of rights model to the Canadian one. My somewhat tentative assessment of the latter and its relationship to the old democratic ideal is outlined in Chapter 8. Although I regard it as defective – in particular, in the way that s. 33 is framed – I am not implacably opposed to possible improved versions of its basic architecture. In general, I regard the new hybrid models as important experiments in constitutionalism. Universal adoption of the American model of constitutionally entrenched rights would, in my opinion, be premature and dangerously complacent, ruling

---

[31] See Chapter 8, below.
[32] See Chapter 8, below.
[33] M. Tushnet, 'New forms of judicial review and the persistence of rights- and democracy-based worries' *Wake Forest Law Review* 38 (2003) 813; M. Tushnet, 'Weak-form Judicial Review: Its Implications for Legislatures' *New Zealand Journal of Public & International Law* 7 (2004).
[34] See the discussion of Trevor Allan in Chapter 4, and Aileen Kavanagh in Chapter 10, Section II, Part D, below.

out possibly superior alternatives. It may turn out that the old democratic ideal does not need to be abandoned in order to maintain a level of human rights protection at least as good as that achieved in the United States and other countries that have adopted the American model. In fact, I believe that the evidence already shows that this is possible.

2

The myth of the common law constitution

I Introduction

The relationship between the common law and statute law is a subject of debate. The controversy goes deeper than questions of interpretation, such as – given the doctrine of legislative supremacy over the common law – why, how and to what extent the meaning of a statute can legitimately be governed by common law principles.[1] The answers to those questions depend partly on more basic issues concerning the legal foundations of the two bodies of law, and their respective status. The orthodox view is that because Parliament can enact statutes that override any part of the common law, statute law is superior to common law. But according to an increasingly popular theory, Britain's 'unwritten' constitution consists of common law principles, and therefore Parliament's authority to enact statutes derives from the common law. Sir William Holdsworth once expressed the view that 'our constitutional law is simply a part of the common law'.[2] For Trevor Allan, it follows that 'the common law is prior to legislative supremacy, which it defines and regulates'.[3] This theory has become so popular that even the British government has endorsed it. When the Attorney-General, Lord Goldsmith, was asked in Parliament what was the government's understanding of 'the legal sources from which the legislative powers of Parliament are

---

[1] See Chapter 9, Section II A(2) and Chapter 10, Section III, Part E, below.
[2] W. Holdsworth, *A History of English Law* (2nd edn) (London: Methuen and Sweet & Maxwell, 1937), vol. 6, p. 263.
[3] T.R.S. Allan, *Constitutional Justice: A Liberal Theory of the Rule of Law* (Oxford: Oxford University Press, 2001), p. 271; see also *ibid.* at pp. 139, 225, 229, 240 and 243; T.R.S. Allan, 'Text, Context, and Constitution: The Common Law as Public Reason' in D. Edlin (ed.), *Common Law Theory* (Cambridge: Cambridge University Press, 2007), p. 185; T.R.S. Allan, 'The Common Law as Constitution: Fundamental Rights and First Principles' in Cheryl Saunders (ed.), *Courts of Final Jurisdiction: The Mason Court in Australia* (Sydney: Federation Press, 1996), p. 146.

derived', he replied, 'The source of the legislative powers is the common law.'[4]

This theory threatens to invert the relationship between statute law and common law as traditionally understood. In this context, the common law is usually characterised either in positivist terms, as a body of rules that the judges have made, and can therefore change, or in Dworkinian terms, as a body of norms that rests on abstract principles of political morality, which the judges have ultimate authority to enunciate and expound.[5] On either view, instead of the judges being clearly subordinate to Parliament, and obligated to obey its laws, they are elevated to a position of superiority over it. On the first view, they have only a self-imposed legal obligation to obey its laws – a 'self-denying judicial ordinance' – that they have legal authority to repudiate.[6] On the second view, the scope of any obligation derives from abstract principles of political morality, and is ultimately for them to authoritatively determine. Since even on the first view, judges in deciding whether they should continue to obey statutes are guided by their assessment of political morality, the two views are in this respect similar.[7] Both views amount to a takeover bid: they threaten – or promise – to replace legislative supremacy with judicial supremacy.[8] Instead of Parliament being the master of the constitution, with the ability to change any part of it (except, perhaps, for the doctrine of legislative supremacy itself), the judges turn out to be in charge. The direction in which some of them would like to develop the constitution is apparent in recent statements of Laws, L.J. In administrative law, 'the common law has come to recognise and endorse the notion of constitutional, or fundamental, rights'.[9] Parliament retains its sovereignty for now, but may lose it 'in the tranquil development of the common law, with a gradual reordering of our constitutional priorities to bring alive the nascent idea that a

---

[4] *Hansard* (HL), col. WA 160, 31 March 2004, quoted in Lord Anthony Lester, 'Beyond the Powers of Parliament', *Judicial Review* 95 (2004) at 96.

[5] See, e.g., section III below. I am using the term 'Dworkinian' in a loose, generic sense. I am concerned with constitutional theorists who are influenced by Ronald Dworkin, rather than with Dworkin himself.

[6] Justice E.W. Thomas, 'The Relationship of Parliament and the Courts' *Victoria University of Wellington Law Review* 31 (2000) 5 at 26.

[7] They differ as to whether those principles should be classified as legal as well as moral/political principles.

[8] It is welcomed as a promise in M.D.J. Conaglen, 'Judicial Supremacy: An Alternative Constitutional Theory' *Auckland University Law Review* 7 (1994) 665.

[9] *International Transport Roth GmbH* v. *Secretary of State for the Home Department* [2003] QB 728 at 759.

democratic legislature cannot be above the law'.[10] In *Jackson* v. *Attorney-General*, Lord Steyn picked up the baton, stating that the doctrine of the supremacy of Parliament

> ... is a construct of the common law. The judges created this principle. If that is so, it is not unthinkable that circumstances could arise where the courts may have to qualify a principle established on a different hypothesis of constitutionalism.[11]

Sometimes, the basic argument is extended to the authority of written constitutions, which is also held to derive from the common law. Dixon C.J., reputedly Australia's greatest judge, maintained that the common law was the 'ultimate constitutional foundation' that underpinned the authority of the Australian Constitution.[12] This was because that Constitution was enacted in a statute by the British Parliament: its authority depended on Parliament's, and therefore derived ultimately from Britain's unwritten, supposedly common law, constitution.[13] Recently, Australian proponents of unwritten constitutional principles have attempted to push Dixon C.J.'s suggestion much further than he would have approved of.[14] A similar idea is being promoted in Canada. According to Mark Walters, in several recent decisions of the Canadian Supreme Court 'the legal authority for the operative constitutional principles is said to derive from Canada's unwritten, or common law, constitution'.[15] Walters' own writings assume that there is such a 'common law constitution', whose 'structural principles' include the rule of law, the separation of powers and individual rights.[16] Trevor Allan maintains that this is true of all the constitutions in former

---

[10] Sir John Laws, 'Illegality and the Problem of Jurisdiction' in Michael Supperstone and James Goudie (eds.), *Judicial Review* (2nd edn) (London: Butterworths Law, 1997), para. 4.17.

[11] *Jackson* v. *Attorney-General* [2005] UKHL 56; [2006] 1 AC 262 at [102]; see also Lord Hope at [126], and Laws L. J. in *Thorburn* v. *Sunderland City Council* [2003] QB 151 at [60].

[12] Sir Owen Dixon, 'The Common Law as an Ultimate Constitutional Foundation' in O. Dixon, *Jesting Pilate, And Other Papers and Addresses* (Woinarski, ed.) (Melbourne: Law Book Co., 1965), p. 203.

[13] *Ibid.*, esp. pp. 203 and 206.

[14] Michael Wait, 'The Slumbering Sovereign: Sir Owen Dixon's Common Law Constitution Revisited' *Federal Law Review* 29 (2001) 58.

[15] Mark D. Walters, 'The Common Law Constitution in Canada: Return of the *Lex Non Scripta* as Fundamental Law' *University of Toronto Law Journal* 51 (2001) 91 at 92.

[16] See, e.g., Mark D. Walters, 'The Common Law Constitution and Legal Cosmopolitanism' in David Dyzenhaus (ed.), *The Unity of Public Law* (Oxford: Hart Publishing, 2004), p. 431.

Commonwealth countries, both written and unwritten: all are based on unwritten principles of constitutionalism and the rule of law, which lie at the heart of the common law tradition:[17] '[T]hese (common law) jurisdictions should, to that extent, be understood to *share* a common constitution,' whose common features 'are ... ultimately more important than such differences as the presence or absence of a "written" constitution, with formally entrenched provisions, whose practical significance may easily be overestimated'.[18] Douglas Edlin has now extended this claim to the United States Constitution: 'the written American Constitution and the unwritten English constitution are both derived directly from the common law', and 'it is a mistake to think that the Constitution is more fundamental than its common law underpinnings'.[19]

This understanding of the authority of written constitutions might have drastic consequences. Limits that the written constitution imposes on the exercise of legislative or executive powers might be supplemented by unwritten, 'common law' limits. Edlin is forthright on this point: 'wherever one finds the common law, one finds legal principles that act to constrain the abuses of state power. Wherever one finds the common law, one finds common law constitutionalism.'[20] It follows that even the power to amend the constitution might be held to be limited by deeper common law principles, which can be changed (or authoritatively declared to have changed) only by judicial decision.[21]

The term 'common law constitutionalism' is now widely used to denote the theory that the most fundamental constitutional norms of a particular country or countries (whether or not they have a written constitution) are matters of common law.[22] As previously noted, there are different versions of common law constitutionalism – including legal positivist and Dworkinian versions – built around different conceptions of the common law. Common law constitutionalism is defended on historical, as well

---

[17] See Allan, *Constitutional Justice.*

[18] Allan, *Constitutional Justice*, pp. 4–5; see also *ibid.* at p. 243. For critical discussion, see Jeffrey Goldsworthy, 'Homogenising Constitutions' *Oxford Journal of Legal Studies* 23 (2003) 483.

[19] D. Edlin, *Judges and Unjust Laws; Common Law Constitutionalism and the Foundations of Judicial Review* (Ann Arbor: Michigan University Press, 2008), pp. 188–9.

[20] *Ibid.*, 189.

[21] Allan, 'The Common Law as Constitution' in Saunders (ed.), *Courts of Final Jurisdiction*, 158 at 159 and 164.

[22] See, e.g., Thomas Poole, 'Back to the Future? Unearthing the Theory of Common Law Constitutionalism' *Oxford Journal of Legal Studies* 23 (2003) 435; Thomas Poole, 'Questioning Common Law Constitutionalism' *Legal Studies* 25 (2005) 142.

as philosophical, grounds.[23] The historical argument is that England's unwritten constitution was always a matter of common law. The philosophical argument is that its present unwritten constitution is best analysed as a matter of common law. I will first discuss the historical evidence, and then turn to philosophical analysis.

II The historical record

The historical defence of common law constitutionalism has distinguished antecedents. According to John Phillip Reid, common law constitutionalism was orthodoxy in Britain until the late eighteenth century, when it was supplanted by the relatively new theory of parliamentary sovereignty.[24] J.G.A. Pocock famously argued that in the seventeenth century, the common law was regarded by its practitioners – most notably Sir Edward Coke – as embodying an immutable 'ancient constitution' that conferred and limited governmental powers.[25] Much earlier, C.H. McIlwain claimed that in the medieval period, the common law constituted a fundamental law that bound both the King and the 'High Court of Parliament', which could enunciate, but not change, that law.[26]

McIlwain's claims have been discredited, Pocock's thesis heavily qualified, and Reid's views shown to be dubious.[27] Yet it is still widely assumed

[23] For historical argument, see Walters, 'The Common Law Constitution in Canada', 105–36.

[24] John Phillip Reid, *Constitutional History of the American Revolution: The Authority to Legislate* (Wisconsin: University of Wisconsin Press, 1991), pp. 4, 6, 24, 63, 78 and 81.

[25] J.G.A. Pocock, *The Ancient Constitution and the Feudal Law: A Study of English Historical Thought in the Seventeenth Century* (Cambridge: Cambridge University Press, 1957). Pocock modified his position in the 1987 reissue of this book, *The Ancient Constitution and the Feudal Law: A Study of English Historical Thought in the Seventeenth Century, A Reissue with a Retrospect* (Cambridge: Cambridge University Press, 1987).

[26] Charles H. McIlwain, *The High Court of Parliament and Its Supremacy* (New Haven: Yale University Press, 1910), ch. 2; Charles H. McIlwain, 'Magna Carta and Common Law' in *Constitutionalism and the Changing World* (New York: Macmillan, 1939), 132 at p. 143.

[27] See Jeffrey Goldsworthy, *The Sovereignty of Parliament: History and Philosophy* (Oxford: Clarendon Press, 1999), pp. 38–45, 60 and 62 (discussing McIlwain); J.W. Tubbs, *The Common Law Mind: Medieval and Early Modern Conceptions* (Baltimore: Johns Hopkins University Press, 2000), p. 206, n. 34 (discussing McIlwain); Goldsworthy, *The Sovereignty of Parliament*, pp. 188–92 (discussing Reid); Tubbs, *The Common Law Mind*, p. 130 (discussing Pocock); Johann P. Sommerville, 'The Ancient Constitution Reassessed: The Common Law, the Court and the Languages of Politics in Early Modern England' in R. Malcolm Smuts (ed.), *The Stuart Court and Europe: Essays in Politics and Political Culture* (Cambridge: Cambridge University Press, 1996), pp. 39–64; Johann P. Sommerville, *Royalists and Patriots: Politics and Ideology in England 1603–1640* (2nd edn) (London: Longman, 1999), pp. 103–4 and 261–2.

that England has long had a common law constitution. Brian Tamanaha, for example, writes that:

> England has had an *unwritten* constitution for centuries ... This constitution served as the functional equivalent of the written US Constitution in the sense of a law that set limits on the law-makers. Coke's decision in *Doctor Bonham's* case testified to this understanding ... The basic idea was that the common law, a body of private law reflecting legal principles, established the fundamental legal framework.[28]

Unfortunately, all these propositions except the first are wrong. England has never had a constitution that served as the functional equivalent of the American Constitution. It has been conclusively established that the common law never subjected Parliament's legislative authority to limits whose violation could warrant the judicial invalidation of a statute.[29] As I have argued at some length elsewhere, Coke's famous dictum in *Doctor Bonham's* case might be understood to suggest that he thought otherwise, although even that is very doubtful; but if he did, he was in a tiny minority, and later changed his mind.[30] The most careful and thorough subsequent analyses of Coke's language have confirmed (although for different reasons) the majority scholarly opinion that in *Doctor Bonham's* case he did not intend to assert a judicial power to invalidate statutes.[31] It is odd that his famous dictum is still regularly cited in constitutional textbooks as evidence that Parliament's law-making authority was, in an earlier era, subordinate to a controlling common law.[32] This chapter will challenge Tamanaha's final, more modest proposition that the common law 'established the fundamental legal framework' of English government.

---

[28] Brian Z. Tamanaha, *On the Rule of Law: History, Politics, Theory* (Cambridge: Cambridge University Press, 2004), p. 57.

[29] Goldsworthy, *The Sovereignty of Parliament*; Tubbs, *The Common Law Mind*, pp. 21, 27, 30, 34–5, 46, 55, 57, 77, 183 and 186.

[30] See generally Goldsworthy, *The Sovereignty of Parliament*; see also *ibid.* at 111–17 (discussing Coke).

[31] I. Williams, 'Dr Bonham's Case and "Void" Statutes' *J Legal History* 27 (2006) 111; P. Hamburger, *Law and Judicial Duty* (Cambridge, Mass: Harvard University Press, 2008), ch. 8 and Appendix I; R. Helmholz, 'Bonham's Case, Judicial Review and the Law of Nature' *J of Legal Analysis* (2009) 325. Hamburger disagrees with Williams at *ibid.*, 625 n. 7. Edlin (*Judges and Unjust Laws*, ch. 5) presents arguments to the contrary, which are discussed in Chapter 10, Section II, Part A. For another recent account of Dr Bonham's case that offers Edlin no support, see J. Allison, *The Historical English Constitution* (Cambridge: Cambridge University Press, 2007), pp. 131–48.

[32] See, e.g., P. Joseph, *Constitutional and Administrative Law in New Zealand* (3rd edn) (Wellington: Brookers, 2007), pp. 488–9; I. Loveland, *Constitutional Law, Administrative Law, and Human Rights; a Critical Introduction* (4th edn) (Oxford: Oxford University Press, 2006), p. 22.

There is no doubt that many common law principles, such as those relating to the Crown's prerogatives, have long been part of the unwritten constitution. At issue here is the broader claim that the unwritten constitution as a whole, including its most basic doctrines such as parliamentary sovereignty, is a matter of common law.[33] I will argue that the extent to which it should be regarded as being, or at any time having been, a matter of common law depends on the answers to at least three different, but interrelated, questions. Over the centuries, these questions have been answered in many different ways, some of which are as follows.

1.   What is the nature of the common law?

Does the common law consist of: (1) the customs of the community, regarded either as immemorial and unchanging, or as gradually evolving; (2) the 'common erudition,' or learned tradition, of the common law bench and bar; (3) a body of norms resting on fundamental 'maxims' or 'principles' whose identification, exposition and application involves an essentially moral 'reason' and judgment; (4) a body of judge-made rules laid down ('posited') by courts in past cases; or (5) some combination of two or more of these alternatives (e.g., the customs of the community, insofar as they are consistent with 'reason,' or insofar as they are recognised and applied by the common law courts)?

2.   What is the scope of the common law?

How is the scope of the common law best understood: (1) does it confer and impose powers, rights, obligations and liabilities only with respect to particular subject-matters, mainly in areas of private law such as land law and contract law, but including some matters of public law such as the 'ordinary' prerogatives of the Crown? On this view, powers, rights and so on with respect to other subject-matters – such as the royal succession, the 'absolute' prerogatives of the Crown, and the powers and privileges of Parliament – subsist independently of the common law (even if the common law necessarily recognises and defers to them). (2) Or is the common law omnicompetent and comprehensive, in the sense that

---

[33] For present purposes, nonjusticiable constitutional conventions, which are not regarded as 'law' at all, can be disregarded. The claim in question concerns constitutional norms that are recognised and applied by the courts.

all non-statutory legal powers, rights and so on – including the power to make statutes – are its creatures, and subject to its control?

3.   Who has ultimate authority to expound the common law?

Is the authority to expound the common law possessed by: (1) the Crown, (2) Parliament (meaning the Crown-in-Parliament), or (3) the regular common law courts?

A few observations concerning these questions may be helpful. First, they have frequently been subjects of obscurity and disagreement. In his study of common law thought in the medieval and early modern periods, James Tubbs emphasises that lawyers and judges were concerned much more with technicalities of pleading and procedure than with theoretical questions, and consequently there is little systematic discussion of general jurisprudence in the common law literature until the sixteenth century.[34] Even then, '[t]he impression one gets from reading a wide range of … reports … is of a profession with very little interest in legal philosophy, one that does not go to the trouble of attempting to formulate a coherent jurisprudence'.[35] Tubbs denies that any single conception of the nature of the common law was ever generally accepted.[36] Obscurity and disagreement continued even into the seventeenth century, when some eminent lawyers stressed the antiquity of the common law and identified it with custom, while others showed little interest in its age and emphasised its inherent 'reason'.[37] Moreover, agreement as to one of our three questions was often accompanied by disagreement about another. Sir Edward Coke and Sir John Davies, for example, held similar conceptions of the nature of the common law, but radically different opinions about its scope, especially as to whether it governed the royal prerogative.[38] Disagreement about the first and second questions continues today.

Secondly, the weight of opinion with respect to each question has shifted over time: some answers that were popular in past centuries were rejected in later ones. In the seventeenth century, it was generally accepted that Parliament had ultimate authority to enunciate and interpret the common law, but until 2009 that view could aspire to plausibility only in the tenuous

---

[34] Tubbs, *The Common Law Mind*, pp. 23 and 1, respectively.
[35] *Ibid.*, pp. 115 and 188.
[36] *Ibid.*, pp. 48, 65, 69, 70, 115, 162 and 190–2.
[37] *Ibid.*, pp. 194–5 and chs. 6–8.
[38] See text accompanying n. 98 below (discussing Coke), text accompanying nn. 116–118 below (discussing Davies).

sense that the highest court was formally the House of Lords; in reality it is, of course, a separate court and only nominally a 'committee' of that House.

Thirdly, the questions are interrelated, in that a particular answer to one may be difficult to reconcile with a particular answer to another. For example, for reasons given in the next section, if the common law is merely a body of judge-made rules, it cannot be the source or basis of Parliament's law-making authority.[39] On the other hand, if it consists of the customs of the community, this becomes more plausible, as does the broader claim that the unwritten constitution as a whole is a matter of common law.

Fourthly, apparent agreement that the unwritten constitution is a matter of common law may obscure disagreement over important details. Even if some seventeenth century lawyers believed that the most fundamental laws of the constitution were part of the common law, they may have meant something very different from superficially similar beliefs held today. They may have conceived of the common law as the custom of the realm, which the High Court of Parliament – rather than the 'inferior courts' of Westminster – had supreme authority to enunciate and expound. That view provides little support for modern theories in which the common law is conceived, on Dworkinian lines, as an evolving body of principles of political morality, which the ordinary courts have ultimate authority to identify and develop.

It is not possible, in this chapter, to provide a comprehensive account of how these three questions have been answered in each of the many centuries over which the British constitution evolved. That would require a book. All that is possible is a brief account of the main issues.

We start with the period up to the sixteenth century, which is clouded by a lack of both clear theoretical thinking about constitutional fundamentals, and written records of what thinking there was. According to Pollock and Maitland, medieval English lawyers had no definite theory of the relationship between enacted and unenacted law, or between law and custom.[40] Chrimes reports that 'the half-expressed concepts and ideas behind the machinery of government are often elusive and hard to

[39] See text accompanying nn. 200–204 below.
[40] Sir Frederick Pollock and Frederic William Maitland, *The History of English Law Before the Time of Edward I* (2nd edn) (vol. 1) (London: Cambridge University Press, 1968), p. 176.

interpret, because of the meagreness with which fifteenth-century people recorded what to them were assumptions that called for no statement'.[41]

Nevertheless, it is surely significant that in books such as Tubbs's *The Common Law Mind*, Doe's *Fundamental Authority in Late Medieval England*, and Chrimes's *English Constitutional Ideas in the Fifteenth Century*, one searches in vain for any reference to a political theorist or lawyer asserting that the major institutions of government owed their existence and authority to the common law.[42] Could this have been one of those 'assumptions that called for no comment' mentioned by Chrimes? After all, many writers starting with 'Bracton' spoke of kings being 'under the law'.[43] If they meant customary law, and if all customary law was common law, then perhaps the theory of common law constitutionalism was implicit in medieval legal thought. But these are two big 'ifs'.

It is tempting to assume that medieval and early modern lawyers regarded both the source and limits of the King's basic rights and powers as essentially customary. But in fact this is dubious. Some of those rights, powers and limits were no doubt believed to derive from divine or natural law. Others were regarded as having been laid down in the *Leges Edwardi* and *Leges Henrici*: the Laws of Edward the Confessor, and the Laws of Henry I. William the Conqueror claimed to be the lawful successor of Edward the Confessor, and Henry I in his coronation charter 'confirmed' Edward's putative laws as amended by William with the consent of his barons.[44] When the texts that supposedly recorded these 'laws' were revised in the twelfth century, apocryphal additions inserted constitutional ideas derived from scholastic political principles and the English coronation oath.[45] The baronial rebellion that led to Magna Carta was preceded by a demand for the confirmation of Henry I's charter, and was strongly influenced by the *Leges Edwardi*. The *Leges*, along with two other documents of equally dubious origin, the *Mirror of Justices* and *Modus*

---

[41] S.B. Chrimes, *English Constitutional Ideas in the Fifteenth Century* (New York: American Scholar Publications, 1966), p. xvi.

[42] Tubbs, *The Common Law Mind*; Norman Doe, *Fundamental Authority in Late Medieval English Law* (Cambridge: Cambridge University Press, 1990); Chrimes, *English Constitutional Ideas*.

[43] It is now known that William Raleigh wrote *De Legibus Consuetudinibus*, which Bracton later edited. See Paul Brand, 'The Age of Bracton' in John Hudson (ed.), *The History of English Law: Centenary Essays on 'Pollock and Maitland'*, Proceedings of the British Academy (Oxford: Oxford University Press, 1996), 78 at pp. 78–9.

[44] J.C. Holt, 'The Origins of the Constitutional Tradition in England' in Holt, *Magna Carta and Medieval Government* (London: Hambledon Press, 1985), 1 at p. 13.

[45] *Ibid.*

tenendi Parliamentum, became the core of the so-called 'ancient constitution', which in later centuries was widely thought to serve both as a shield against tyranny, and a justification for rebellion.[46]

Tubbs maintains that when Glanvil and 'Bracton' discussed the 'unwritten laws' of England, they were referring not to customary laws, but to decisions and enactments of kings, acting with the advice of their magnates, that had not been recorded in writing.[47] The most thorough recent study of 'Bracton' concludes that:

> What he meant by the idea of a king under God and the law was, in the first place, that the king ought to proceed by the judgment of the barons and, secondly, that a king ought to practice the Christian virtues. But neither notion carries with it any connotation of a body of substantive, much less constitutional, law that the king ought not to contravene.[48]

In the abbreviated version of 'Bracton', known as *Britton*, all English law was depicted as the product of royal authority.[49] The substantive common law was, as Charles Oligvie has observed, 'the child of prerogative', based on the writs of the Angevin and Plantagenet kings that were later supplemented by statute.[50] It is clear that the King's clerks and judges had no mandate to deal with the most fundamental laws governing his right to the throne (if there were any), or to question the scope of his powers. Their own jurisdiction and authority were derived from him, and 'Bracton' denied that they could hold him to account.[51] In the many disputes between kings and barons, the latter never appealed to the common law or its courts: they complained that it was the King's law, and the judges were his servants.[52] Moreover, 'there was so little substantive law that the question of legality at the level of high politics hardly arose. The answer of

[46] Janelle Greenberg, *The Radical Face of the Ancient Constitution: St. Edward's 'Laws' in Early Modern Political Thought* (Cambridge: Cambridge University Press, 2001). For the actual origins of these documents, see *ibid.* at pp. 9, 57–61, 71 and 77–8. Note that the term 'ancient constitution' is of modern coinage, an attempt to translate old ideas into a modern idiom.

[47] Tubbs, *The Common Law Mind*, pp. 3, 7, 12, 15–17 and 189.

[48] Donald Hanson, *From Kingdom to Commonwealth: The Development of Civic Consciousness in English Political Thought* (Cambridge, Mass: Harvard University Press, 1970), p. 131.

[49] Tubbs, *The Common Law Mind*, p. 187.

[50] Sir Charles Ogilvie, *The King's Government and the Common Law 1471–1641* (Oxford: Blackwell, 1958), p. 10.

[51] Goldsworthy, *The Sovereignty of Parliament*, pp. 22–3.

[52] Hanson, *From Kingdom to Commonwealth*, pp. 159, 188–90 and 214.

the great twelfth and thirteenth century law books to fundamental political questions was that such matters lay with the king and magnates of the realm.'[53]

In the fourteenth and fifteenth centuries, it is unlikely that the most basic laws on which royal government rested would have been classified as part of the common law, even if they were by then customary. Tubbs challenges the received view that the common law was, at that time, generally identified with the customs of the realm.[54] He argues that it was more frequently treated as the 'common erudition' (or in his words, the 'learned tradition') of the bench and bar of the common law courts.[55] Despite reading five thousand Year Book cases, he uncovered very little evidence that medieval common lawyers primarily understood their law to be custom,[56] and even in the sixteenth century, when it was often described as 'common usage' or 'common custom', lawyers 'nearly always mean only the usage or custom of the bench and bar'.[57] Only in the early seventeenth century did an important common lawyer, Sir John Davies, unequivocally describe the common law as the custom of the English people, and even then, his opinion was unorthodox.[58] Tubbs's conclusions corroborate Norman Doe's, who reports that 'forensic and judicial usage and learning'– and judicial rather than popular consent – were treated in the Year Books as the basis of the common law.'[59] 'Indeed, the idea that the common law was in the keeping of, or within the control of, the judges was implicit in several stock phrases ... Sometimes, the judges overtly employ the idea that a rule exists or a result is reached because they "assent" to it.'[60] This quasi-positivist conception of the nature of the common law surely had implications for its scope. It is unlikely that those who conceived of it as the 'common erudition' of the bench and bar would have thought that it

---

[53] *Ibid.*, pp. 131–2.   [54] Tubbs, *The Common Law Mind*, pp. 1–2.

[55] *Ibid.*, pp. 2, 24–5, 45–52, 56–7, 65–6, 111, 114, 130 and 193–4. The common law as 'common erudition' is a principal theme in J.H. Baker, *The Law's Two Bodies: Some Evidential Problems in English Legal History* (Oxford: Oxford University Press, 2001), Lecture Three, esp. at pp. 67–70 and 74–9.

[56] Tubbs, *The Common Law Mind*, pp. 24, 29, 45–6 and 50.

[57] *Ibid.*, pp. 191–2. See also Doe, *Fundamental Authority*, p. 26; Alan Cromartie, *Sir Matthew Hale 1609–1676: Law, Religion and Natural Philosophy* (Cambridge: Cambridge University Press, 1995), pp. 14–15.

[58] Tubbs, *The Common Law Mind*, p. 192; see also *ibid.* at pp. 130–2.

[59] Doe, *Fundamental Authority*, p. 22; see also *ibid.* at p. 32 (noting that occasionally the fiction was expressed, notably by St. German, that the community had consented to the common law).

[60] Doe, *Fundamental Authority*, pp. 23–4.

governed such fundamental matters as the royal succession, or the privileges and powers of Parliament.

The royal succession was not governed by clear, well-established rules – customary or otherwise – until the eighteenth century. The Crown was at different times claimed by hereditary right, right of conquest, and/or election affirmed by statute.[61] There was no consensus as to which of these claims had priority, or as to their ultimate basis: a claim to hereditary right, for example, could be based on either custom or the law of God. Chrimes denies that the fifteenth century had any 'accepted public law' dealing with the succession.[62] In Sir John Fortescue's lengthy defence of the Lancastrian claim to the throne, he relied on natural law, not custom.[63] In later recanting that defence, he said that in 'the laws of this land … the students learn full little of the right of succession of kingdoms'.[64] In 1460, the judges declined to express an opinion concerning a dispute over the matter, because as 'the King's justices' they were unfit to decide it; moreover,

> the matter was so high and touched the King's estate and regality, which is above the law and passed their learning, wherefore they dared not enter into any communication thereof, for it pertained to the Lords of the King's blood, and the peerage of this his land, to have communication and meddle in such matters.[65]

It is equally unlikely that the powers and privileges of the 'High Court of Parliament' – the highest court in the realm – would have been regarded as subject to the 'common erudition' of 'inferior courts'. In 1388, the Lords who prepared charges of treason against some of Richard II's associates, including a number of judges, declared 'that in so high a crime as is alleged in this appeal, which touches the person of the King … and the state of his realm … the process will not be taken anywhere except to Parliament, nor judged by any other law except the law and court of parliament'; 'the great matters moved in this Parliament and to be moved in parliaments

---

[61] Howard Nenner, *The Right to be King: The Succession to the Crown of England 1603–1714* (North Carolina: University of North Carolina Press, 1995), pp. 1–12.

[62] Chrimes, *English Constitutional Ideas*, pp. 22 and 34.

[63] Sir John Fortescue, *De Natura Legis Naturae* (New York: Garland Publishing, 1980), referred to in Tubbs, *The Common Law Mind*, p. 53.

[64] Sir John Fortescue, 'The Declaracion of Certayn Wrytyngs' in *The Works of Sir John Fortescue*, p. 532, quoted in Chrimes, *English Constitutional Ideas*, p. 22.

[65] *Rotuli Parliamentorum* (London, s.n., 1767–1777), V, pp. 375–6, quoted in W.H. Dunham and C.T. Wood, 'The Right to Rule in England: Depositions and the Kingdom's Authority, 1327–1485' *American Historical Review* 81 (1976) 738 at 750.

in the future, touching peers of the land, should be introduced, judged and discussed by the course of Parliament and not by civil law nor by the common law of the land, used in other and lower courts of the land'. This followed advice given by judges and sergeants at law that the proceedings were 'not made nor affirmed according to the order which either one or the other of these laws [common or civil] requires'.[66] In 1454, the judges acknowledged that 'the determination and knowledge of that privilege (of the high court of Parliament) belongs to the Lords of Parliament, and not to the justices'.[67] We will later encounter similar views expressed by the House of Commons in 1604, Sir Edward Coke in his *Fourth Institute*, and Sir Matthew Hale.[68] As Donald Hanson concludes:

> Obviously, the estates of the realm in parliament were quite clear that these matters of high politics were not governed by the common law. In short, the men of the Middle Ages were unwilling to attribute to the common law the constitutional bearing which modern enthusiasts have been so ready to see there.[69]

As a body of law administered by particular courts, the common law was sometimes regarded as just one branch of the *lex terrae* or 'law of the land'.[70] On this view, other bodies of law, administered by other courts, were equal in status. The issue was raised during jurisdictional disputes between the common law courts and civil law courts, that broke out in the late sixteenth century. The common law judges began to issue prohibitions against suits pending in civil law courts, which resented the loss of business that this threatened to cause.[71] The civilians could not hope for assistance from Parliament, which was dominated by common lawyers, so they appealed to the King. They argued that as he had delegated his jurisdiction as the 'fountain of justice' to all his various courts, he retained supreme authority to determine the boundaries between their jurisdictions. The argument assumed that all his courts, common law, civil law, ecclesiastical and prerogative – and the bodies of law they

---

[66] Bertie Wilkinson, *Studies in the Constitutional History of Medieval England 1216–1399* (vol. 2) (London: Longmans, 1952), pp. 280 and 282; see also S.B. Chrimes and A.L. Brown (eds.), *Select Documents of English Constitutional History 1307–1485* (London: Adam & Charles Black, 1961), pp. 146–9.

[67] *Rotuli Parliamentorum*, V, 240, quoted in Chrimes, *English Constitutional Ideas*, p. 152.

[68] See text accompanying nn. 106–108 and 162 below.

[69] Hanson, *From Kingdom to Commonwealth*, p. 215.

[70] Brian P. Levack, *The Civil Lawyers in England 1603–1641: A Political Study* (Oxford: Oxford University Press, 1973), p. 143.

[71] *Ibid.*, pp. 72–81.

administered – were constitutionally parallel and equal, all subordinate to the King, but none to any other.[72] Lord Chancellor Ellesmere complained that Sir Edward Coke desired 'to weaken the power of the Ecclesiastical Court, as if they were not absolute in themselves in jurisdictions naturally belonging to them, but subordinate [to] the judges of the common law to be controlled in things that fall not within the level of the common law'.[73] But some writers had begun to equate the 'law of the land' with the common law alone.[74] The common lawyers regarded their courts and their law as superior to the civil law and its courts. The common law alone constituted the law of England and the supreme guardian of the people's liberties, and it demarcated the jurisdiction within which civil and other laws could legitimately operate.[75] The civil law was equivalent to a special body of customary law that was accorded legal recognition for particular purposes by the common law.[76]

The civil lawyers lost this battle, partly because the Tudor monarchs needed the support of the common lawyers to impose royal supremacy over ecclesiastical courts and canon law.[77] But the common law did not achieve a similar victory in its jurisdictional struggles with courts of equity early in the next century. The Court of Chancery, unlike the civil law courts, could plausibly claim to be as ancient as the common law courts.[78] Furthermore, since Chancellors outranked common law judges, it could also plausibly claim to be the highest of the King's courts (apart from Parliament itself).[79] In addition, several writers depicted equity as a moral law deduced directly from the law of God, and therefore as inherently superior to all positive laws, including the common law.[80] These claims did not, of course, go unchallenged. Common lawyers such as Sir Edward Coke ranked courts according to the law they administered, and

---

[72] *Ibid.*, pp. 81–3.
[73] 'Observations on Ye Lord Cookes Reportes', in Louis A. Knafla, *Law and Politics in Jacobean England: The Tracts of Lord Chancellor Ellesmere* (Cambridge: Cambridge University Press, 1977), p. 297.
[74] Knafla, *Law and Politics in Jacobean England*, p. 166.
[75] Levack, *The Civil Lawyers in England*, pp. 144–5 and 122–3.
[76] *Ibid.*, pp. 145–6.
[77] *Ibid.*, pp. 125–6; John Guy, 'The "Imperial Crown" and the Liberty of the Subject: The English Constitution from Magna Carta to the Bill of Rights' in Bonnelyn Young Kunze and Dwight D. Brautigam (eds.), *Court, Country and Culture: Essays on Early Modern British History in Honor of Perez Zagorin* (Rochester: University of Rochester Press, 1992), 65 at pp. 72–3.
[78] Levack, *The Civil Lawyers in England*, p. 147.
[79] Knafla, *Law and Politics in Jacobean England*, pp. 160–1.   [80] *Ibid.*, p. 161.

since the common law was in his opinion superior to equity, its courts were 'above' the Court of Chancery.[81] Leading common lawyers denied that equity was derived directly from divine law; it was, instead, concerned with the reasons underlying positive laws, and aimed merely to prevent strict adherence to legal rules from defeating those reasons.[82] Lord Chancellor Ellesmere denied both claims of superiority: he regarded Chancery and Star Chamber as equal to the common law courts, and the laws they administered as equally part of the 'law of the land'.[83] James I accepted the view that civil lawyers had urged in the previous century, insisting that he would settle jurisdictional disputes among his courts: it 'is a thing regal, and proper to a King, to keep every court within its own bounds'.[84] He said that the Court of Chancery was 'independent of any other Court, and is only under the King ... from that Court there is no appeal'; if it exceeded its jurisdiction, 'the King only is to correct it, and none else'. He explicitly forbad the common law courts from bringing charges of *praemunire* against Chancery for allegedly exceeding its powers.[85]

The common law came to be regarded as superintending all other bodies of law administered by English judges, except for equity, which it never subordinated.[86] This development appears to have been part, and a partial cause, of broader changes in conceptions of the nature and scope of the common law. Instead of being merely the 'common erudition' of particular courts, it was increasingly portrayed as the repository of immemorial customs of the realm, including those dealing with the rights and powers of the King and Parliament. This led to what has been called the 'classic age of common-law political thought, of ancient constitutionalism' described by writers such as J.G.A. Pocock and Glenn Burgess.[87] Janelle

---

[81] *Ibid.*, p. 160.   [82] Tubbs, *The Common Law Mind*, pp. 102–3.

[83] Knafla, *Law and Politics in Jacobean England*, pp. 161 and 166.

[84] King James VI and I, 'Speech in Star Chamber 1616' in Johann P. Sommerville (ed.), *King James VI and I: Political Writings* (Cambridge: Cambridge University Press, 1995), 212 at p. 213. See also 'Speech of 21 March 1610' in Sommerville (ed.), *King James VI and I*, p. 188.

[85] King James VI and I, 'Speech in Star Chamber 1616' in Sommerville (ed.), *King James VI and I*, pp. 214–15.

[86] On other bodies of law, see, e.g., Sir Matthew Hale, *The History of the Common Law of England* (Charles M. Gray, ed.) (Chicago: University of Chicago Press, 1971), p. 4; Sir William Blackstone, *Commentaries on the Laws of England* (vol. 1) (Oxford: Oxford University Press, 1765), p. 15.

[87] Pocock, *The Ancient Constitution and the Feudal Law*; Glenn Burgess, *The Politics of the Ancient Constitution: An Introduction to English Political Thought 1600–1642* (Hampshire: Palgrave Macmillan, 1992).

Greenberg has shown that constitutional claims based on supposedly 'ancient laws', such as the *Leges Edwardi*, were commonly made long before the seventeenth century.[88] But it may have been only in the late sixteenth century that it became widely believed that the substance of these ancient laws survived only through having been absorbed by the common law, which had thereby inherited their role as the fundamental law of the land.[89]

Alan Cromartie suggests that assuming the mantle of national custom served the common law's ambitious claim to be able to resolve disputed questions of high politics: 'they needed to offer some kind of explanation why the customs observed by the bench should bind upon the nation as a whole'.[90] Many lawyers thought that the customs of the realm had, in effect, been consented to by the King and the community.[91] Coke's theory may have been slightly different, but the result was the same. As Charles Gray explains that theory:

> [t]he lawyer working exclusively through the law discovered something more than the law – the native fund of preferences and values, national character in effect … [W]ith the faith that legal thinking at its best disclosed 'the common custom of the realm', the lawyer stepped out of his 'art' while refusing to budge from it. He turned political oracle.[92]

Cromartie argues that between 1528 and 1628, there was a 'constitutionalist revolution' in English political culture that originated within the legal profession.[93] Coke, who stated that the '[common] laws do limit, bound and determine of all other human laws, arts and sciences', was

---

[88] Greenberg, *The Radical Face of the Ancient Constitution.*

[89] The thesis that the common law originated in these laws is found in the writings of Polydore, Vergil, Holinshed, Sir John Dodderidge, John Speed, Peter Heylyn, John Cowell and William Whiteway, quoted in Greenberg, *The Radical Face of the Ancient Constitution*, pp. 88, 99, 108, 135, 136, 152–3 and 156, respectively. See also the views of Hale and Vaughan, below at n. 145.

[90] Cromartie, *Sir Matthew Hale*, p. 16.

[91] *Ibid.*, pp. 12–13.

[92] Charles M. Gray, 'Parliament, Liberty, and the Law' in J.H. Hexter (ed.), *Parliament and Liberty: From the Reign of Elizabeth to the English Civil War* (Stanford: Stanford University Press, 1992), 155 at pp. 162–3. Cromartie's account of Coke's thought is somewhat different. See Cromartie, *Sir Matthew Hale*, pp. 13 and 32.

[93] Alan Cromartie, 'The Constitutionalist Revolution: The Transformation of Political Culture in Early Stuart England', (1999) 163 *Past and Present* 76, esp. at 82 (for the 1528 date) and 111 (for the 1628 date). These themes are developed in his book, *The Constitutionalist Revolution: An Essay on the History of England, 1450–1642* (Cambridge: Cambridge University Press, 2006).

particularly influential.[94] The common lawyers came to think of their law as 'the legal master science', based on natural law, which determined the respective rights of the King and his subjects with such perfect reasonableness that no resort to extraneous principles was necessary.[95] The common law allowed the King's servants to administer other bodies of law only on the condition that they remained accountable to it.[96] This principle applied not only to rival courts, but to statutory bodies such as Commissioners of Sewers that exercised discretionary powers. But it did not go unchallenged. One lawyer, Robert Callis, rejected Coke's view that all discretions were subject to the rule of common law, arguing that some statutes conferred authority 'to order business there arising in course of equity': in other words, discretion guided only by the statutory body's understanding of the law of nature.[97]

Most importantly, Coke's principle applied to the prerogatives of the King himself, which many common lawyers insisted were conferred and limited by the common law.[98] Sir Henry Finch expressed this view when he said that the King's prerogative 'grows wholly from the reason of the common law ... [o]nly the common law is the *primum mobile* which draws all the planets in their contrary course'.[99] (This Latin term – meaning 'first moveable' or 'prime mover' – had been used by Aristotle, and later Ptolemy, to denote the outermost sphere of the universe believed to cause all the other spheres to revolve around the earth. This analogy was often used in describing the ultimate source of political and legal authority.) In some quarters, the common law had come to be accepted as governing even the royal succession. In 1571, the Treasons Act declared that it was treason to maintain 'that the common law of this realm not altered by Parliament ought not to direct the right of the crown of England'.[100] And in 1610, Thomas Hedley stated that 'the common law doth bind, and lead

---

[94] Cromartie, 'The Constitutionalist Revolution', 88 (quoting Part Three of Coke's Reports in John Farquhar Fraser (ed.), *The Reports of Sir Edward Coke* (Joseph Butterworth and Son, 1826), pp. xxxviii.

[95] Cromartie, 'The Constitutionalist Revolution', 81–2. [96] *Ibid.*, p. 88.

[97] *Ibid.*, pp. 91–2, quoting Robert Callis, *The Reading of that Famous and Learned Gentleman Robert Callis; Sergeant at Law, upon the Statute of 23 Henry VIII, cap. 5 of Sewers* (London: William Leak, 1647), pp. 85–6.

[98] Cromartie, 'The Constitutionalist Revolution', 96.

[99] Sir Henry Finch, *Law, or A Discourse Thereof* (London: Society of Stationers, 1627), p. 85.

[100] Carl Stephenson and Frederick George Marcham (eds.), *Sources of English Constitutional History: A Selection of Documents from A.D. 600 to the Interregnum* (revised edn) (vol. 1) (Harper & Row, 1972), p. 352.

or direct the descent and right of the crown'.[101] He also asserted that 'the Parliament has his power and authority from the common law, and not the common law from the parliament. And therefore the common law is of more force and strength than the Parliament'.[102] If the common law was the source of the King's title to the throne, his prerogatives, and the authority of Parliament, it was indeed the constitution of the realm.

But not all common lawyers, let alone other members of the ruling elite, agreed with these views. As for the succession, Lord Chancellor Ellesmere said in 1605 that 'the King's majesty, as it were inheritable and descended from God, has absolutely monarchical power annexed inseparably to his crown and diadem, not by common law nor statute law, but more ancient than either of them'.[103] Even Coke agreed that 'the King's majesty, in his lawful, just and lineal title to the Crown of England, comes not by succession only, or by election, but from God only … by reason of his lineal descent'.[104]

Although Coke insisted that the King's prerogatives were conferred and regulated by the common law, he does not seem to have held the same view of Parliament's privileges. In his *First Institute*, in a list of fifteen 'diverse laws within the realm of England', he included – in addition to the common law itself – the *lex et consuetudo Parliamenti* (the law and custom of Parliament).[105] Later still, in his *Fourth Institute*, he discussed the relationship between the common law and the *lex and consuetudo Parliamenti*:

> And as every court of justice has laws and customs for its direction, some by the common law, some by the civil and canon law, some by peculiar laws and customs, so the High Court of Parliament *suis propriis legibus & consuetudinibus subsistit* [subsists according to its own laws and customs]. It is *lex & consuetudo Parliamenti,* that all weighty matters in any Parliament moved concerning the Peers of the Realm, or Commons in

---

[101] 'Speech on Impositions, 28 June 1610' in Elizabeth Read Foster (ed.), *Proceedings in Parliament 1610* (vol. 2) (New Haven: Yale University Press, 1966), p. 174.

[102] *Ibid.* But see the discussion of his views in Goldsworthy, *The Sovereignty of Parliament*, pp. 117–19.

[103] John Hawarde in William Paley Baildon (ed.), *Les Reportes del Cases in Camera Stellata 1593–1609* (London, 1894), 188, quoted in Conrad Russell, 'Divine Rights in the Early Seventeenth Century' in John Morrill, Paul Slack and Daniel Woolf (eds.), *Public Duty and Private Conscience in Seventeenth-Century England* (Oxford: Oxford University Press, 1993), 101 at p. 117.

[104] Hawarde, quoted in Russell, 'Divine Rights in the Early Seventeenth Century', p. 118.

[105] Edward Coke, *The First Part of the Institutes of the Laws of England* (2nd corrected edn) (Moore, 1629), ch. 1, sec. 3, p. 12.

Parliament assembled, ought to be determined, adjudged, and discussed by the course of the Parliament, and not by the civil law, nor yet by the common laws of this realm used in more inferior courts … And this is the reason that judges ought not to give any opinion of a matter of Parliament, because it is not to be decided by the common laws, but *secundum legem ad consuetudinem Parliamenti* [according to the laws and customs of Parliament]: and so the judges in divers Parliaments have confessed. And some hold, that every offence committed in any court punishable by that court, must be punished (proceeding criminally) in the same court, or in some higher, and not in any inferior court, and the Court of Parliament has no higher.[106]

Coke clearly did not regard the 'law and custom of Parliament' as an example of the local or particular customs whose application the common law sometimes authorised. He listed it separately. Moreover, local or particular customs were not authorised by the common law unless they satisfied the test of reasonableness, and it is hardly likely that judges would have dared to dispute a privilege asserted by Parliament itself, as part of its 'law and custom', on the ground that it was contrary to reason. Parliament was, as Coke acknowledged, the highest court in the realm. Cromartie suspects that Coke's discussion of the *lex et consuetudo Parliamenti* was motivated by a desire to criticise James I's conduct in the 1620s, in attempting to prevent discussion of certain matters in Parliament, and ordering the arrest of leading members of the Commons who had forcibly prevented the Speaker from adjourning debate. Coke was also warning the judges of inferior courts not to interfere with Parliament in such matters.[107] But political motivations no doubt lay behind many of his views, including his expansion of the scope of the common law in other respects. Moreover, there were good precedents for his views about the 'law and custom of Parliament'. In 1604, the House of Commons complained that James I had accepted an opinion of his judges, concerning a disputed election return, rather than a contrary determination of the House itself: 'the judges' opinion … being delivered what the common law was, which extends only to inferior and standing courts, ought [not] to bring any prejudice to this High Court of Parliament, whose power being above the law is not founded on the common law but have their rights and privileges peculiar to themselves'.[108]

---

[106] Edward Coke, *The Fourth Part of the Institutes of the Laws of England: Concerning the Jurisdiction of Courts* (4th edn) (Crooke, 1669), ch. 1, pp. 14–15.
[107] E-mail from Alan Cromartie to author, 18 March 2005.
[108] 'The Form of Apology and Satisfaction, 20 June 1604' in J.R. Tanner (ed.), *Constitutional Documents of the Reign of James I 1603–1625* (Cambridge: Cambridge University Press,

So not even Coke, the prime exemplar of the 'common law mind', consistently held that the common law was the supreme and overarching body of law, which provided the ultimate source of all legal authority and governed the scope and application of all other laws. As for other lawyers, statesmen, and political theorists, many located the ultimate source of political authority not in the common law, but in either the King, or the community represented in Parliament. Even in the fourteenth and fifteenth centuries, those who sought to account for the authority of legislation had looked not to custom or common law, but to the will of the King or the 'common consent' of the whole realm.[109] By the sixteenth century, these strands of thought had evolved into competing theories, one based on the King's divine right to rule, and the other on the consent and combined wisdom of the community.[110] Henry VIII's self-proclaimed 'imperial' kingship – deployed to justify his supremacy over the Church – entailed that he was 'under God but not the law, because the king makes the law'.[111] On this view, the King was the human source of law and political authority, and the foundation of all jurisdictions.[112] The other theory was expounded by Richard Hooker, who argued that '[t]he whole body politic makes laws, which laws give power unto the king'.[113] For many, the two theories could be happily combined to sustain the authority of the King in Parliament, but in the 1640s they were split apart with tragic consequences.

Sir John Davies is often cited as one of the two best examples – the other being Coke – of the 'classical' seventeenth century 'common law mind' that placed the common law at the core of the 'ancient constitution'.[114] The preface to Davies's *Le Primer Report des Cases [etc.]* has been described as 'the classic exposition of the common lawyer's viewpoint'.[115] He depicted the common law as the custom of the realm, refined by the accumulated

1930), 221 at 224. See also the earlier incident discussed in the text accompanying n. 67 above.

[109] Doe, *Fundamental Authority*, p. 31.
[110] Goldsworthy, *The Sovereignty of Parliament*, pp. 63–75.
[111] Quoted in Guy, 'The "Imperial Crown" and the Liberty of the Subject' in Kunze and Brautigam (eds.), *Court, Country and Culture*, pp. 67–8.
[112] Corinne Comstock Weston and Janelle R. Greenberg, *Subjects and Sovereigns: The Grand Controversy over Legal Sovereignty in Stuart England* (Cambridge: Cambridge University Press, 1981), p. 87; Goldsworthy, *The Sovereignty of Parliament*, pp. 65–7.
[113] Richard Hooker, 'Of the Laws of Ecclesiastical Polity' in J. Keble (ed.), *The Works of Mr. Richard Hooker* (7th edn) (vol. 3) (Georg Olms Verlag, 1977), p. 443.
[114] See, e.g., Pocock, *The Ancient Constitution and the Feudal Law*.
[115] David Wootton, (ed.), *Divine Right and Democracy: An Anthology of Political Writing in Stuart England* (Penguin, 1986), p. 129.

experience and wisdom of countless generations, and warned that whenever it was changed by statute, inconveniences invariably followed.[116] Yet Davies was also a royalist, who maintained that originally, the King had possessed 'absolute and unlimited power in all matters whatsoever'; that he subsequently agreed to subject his power to the positive law in 'common and ordinary cases'; but that he retained 'absolute and unlimited' power in other cases. The latter power was not conferred on him by the people or the common law: it was 'reserved by himself to himself, when the positive law was first established', his prerogative being 'more ancient than the customary law of the realm', and remaining 'above the common law'.[117] Davies compared the King 'to a *primum mobile*, which carries about all the inferior spheres in his superior course … [A]s the King does suffer the customary law of England to have her course on one side, so does the same law yield, submit, and give way to the King's prerogative over the other'.[118] He was by no means the only lawyer who held royalist views. Sir Francis Bacon said that 'the king holds not his prerogatives of this kind mediately from the law, but immediately from God, as he holds his crown'.[119] Others who agreed included Attorney-General and future Chief Justice Sir John Hobart, Chief Baron Fleming, the great antiquary William Lambarde, Lord Keeper Coventry and Serjeant Ashley.[120] James I was not alone in holding that his 'absolute' prerogative was 'no subject for the tongue of a lawyer'.[121]

The early seventeenth century was riven by constitutional disputes partly because the law of the constitution was inherently uncertain: every attempt to state it became 'tendentious as soon as it got beyond easy cases … Englishmen did not and could not know sufficiently the rules of the game in which they were players.'[122] Proponents of rival ideologies were drawn into debate over which institution was the most ancient: the monarchy, assemblies representing the community, or the common law. The

---

[116] Sir John Davies, *Le Primer Report des Cases* (Flesher, Steater, and Twyford, 1674) in Wootton (ed.), *Divine Right and Democracy*, pp. 131–2.

[117] Sir John Davies, *The Question Concerning Impositions* (Twyford, 1656), pp. 29–33. For discussion, see Tubbs, *The Common Law Mind*, pp. 133–9.

[118] Davies, *The Question Concerning Impositions*, p. 26.

[119] James S. Spedding, R.L. Ellis and D.D. Heath (eds.), *The Works of Francis Bacon* (vol. 10) (London: Longman, 1858–1874), p. 371. But see *ibid.* (vol. 14), 118, quoted in Tubbs, *The Common Law Mind*, p. 138.

[120] See Goldsworthy, *The Sovereignty of Parliament*, pp. 82–4, esp. p. 83, n. 40.

[121] Charles H. McIlwain, *The Political Works of James I* (Cambridge, Mass: Harvard University Press, 1918), p. 333.

[122] Gray, 'Parliament, Liberty, and the Law' in Hexter (ed.), *Parliament and Liberty*, pp. 191–2.

question was regarded as important because, as Corinne Weston explains, 'a derived authority was considered inferior to an original one'. William Prynne, for example, observed that 'every creator is of greater power and authority than its creature and every cause than its effect'.[123] The question was: what was the nature of England's original constitution?

Leading royalist writers found it incomprehensible that the common law could have come first, or that it could be more fundamental than the authority of the King. In his famous *Patriarcha*, Sir Robert Filmer discussed at length the necessary 'dependency and subjection of the common law to the sovereign prince':[124]

> The common law (as the Lord Chancellor Egerton teaches us) is the common custom of the realm. Now concerning customs, this must be considered, that for every custom there was a time when it was no custom ... [w]hen every custom began, there was something else than custom that made it lawful, or else the beginning of all customs were unlawful. Customs at first became lawful only by some superior power, which did either command or consent to their beginning. And the first power which we find (as it is confessed by all men) is the kingly power, which was both in this and in all other nations of the world, long before any laws, or any other kind of government was thought of; from whence we must necessarily infer, that the common law itself, or common customs of this land, were originally the laws and commands of kings at first unwritten.[125]

Not only had kings created the common law, they retained 'absolute authority' to supplement or correct it.[126] For this reason, Filmer said elsewhere, the common law 'follows in time after government, but cannot go before it and be the rule to government by any original or radical constitution'.[127] Later in the century another prominent royalist, Dr Robert Brady, criticised Coke for giving the impression that the

---

[123] Corinne Comstock Weston, 'England: Ancient Constitution and Common Law' in J.H. Burns (ed.), *The Cambridge History of Political Thought 1450–1700* (Cambridge: Cambridge University Press, 1991), 374 at p. 377, quoting William Prynne, *The Treachery and Disloyalty of Papists to their Sovereigns in Doctrine & Practice* (Cambridge University Press, 1643), pp. 35–6. But not everyone thought that the origins of government were important. See Johann P. Sommerville, *Politics and Ideology in England 1603–1640* (London: Longman, 1986), pp. 105–6.

[124] Robert Filmer, *Patriarcha, or the Natural Power of Kings* (Richard Chiswell, 1680), p. 11, quoted in Johann P. Sommerville (ed.), *Patriarcha and Other Writings* (Cambridge: Cambridge University Press, 1991), p. 54.

[125] Filmer, *Patriarcha*, p. 9, quoted in Sommerville (ed.), *Patriarcha and Other Writings*, p. 45.

[126] Filmer, *Patriarcha*, p. 11, quoted in Sommerville (ed.), *Patriarcha and Other Writings*, p. 54.

[127] Robert Filmer, 'The Anarchy of a Limited or Mixed Monarchy', in Sommerville (ed.), *Patriarcha and Other Writings*, 131 at p. 153.

common law had grown up with the first trees and grass, 'abstracting it from any dependence upon, or creation by the government'.[128] For royalists, it was obvious that kings came first, armed with divine authority, and laws followed. The common law was sometimes explained as an innovation of the Norman kings.[129] Some royalists concluded that, since all law was originally made by kings, it could be unmade or overridden by them.[130]

The royalist theory was widely regarded as a threat to the traditional rights and liberties of the people, including the powers and privileges of the Houses of Parliament. But there were different ways of resisting that threat. Johann Sommerville shows that anti-absolutists relied either on a contractual theory, according to which the powers of the King were granted and limited by a pact between him and his subjects, or on Coke's theory of an immemorial common law that stood above both king and people. He denies that everyone who regarded the King's power as limited subscribed to Coke's theory: '[T]he vocabulary of contract was almost as common as that of immemorial law.'[131]

Contractualists argued that, whenever the word 'parliament' was first used, representative assemblies had existed from time immemorial. John Selden, for example, claimed that kings, nobles and freemen had shared the power to make law from the inception of civil government in England.[132] He regarded all law and government as the product of contracts between the King and the people.[133] His views influenced his younger friends, Sir Matthew Hale and Sir John Vaughan.[134] Others argued for the same conclusion on theoretical rather than historical grounds: there must have been an original contract, whereby the community established the kingship subject to stringent conditions designed to control regal power.[135] Charles Herle stated that 'what is meant by those fundamental laws of this kingdom . . . is that original frame of this

[128] Quoted by Weston, 'England: Ancient Constitution and Common Law' in Burns (ed.), *The Cambridge History of Political Thought*, p. 407.

[129] Greenberg, *The Radical Face of the Ancient Constitution*, quoting Samuel Daniel, *The Collection of the History of England* (Simon Waterson, 1626).

[130] Goldsworthy, *The Sovereignty of Parliament*, p. 83.

[131] Sommerville, *Politics and Ideology in England*, p. 79.

[132] *Ibid.*, pp. 62–4; Paul Christianson, 'Royal and Parliamentary Voices on the Ancient Constitution c. 1604–1621' in Linda Levy Peck (ed.), *The Mental World of the Jacobean Court* (Cambridge: Cambridge University Press, 1991), 71 at pp. 83–5.

[133] Richard Tuck, *Natural Rights Theories: Their Origin and Development* (Cambridge: Cambridge University Press, 1979), pp. 96 and 99–100; Cromartie, *Sir Matthew Hale*, pp. 32, 37 and 39.

[134] Tuck, *Natural Rights Theories*, pp. 84, 113 and 134.

[135] Sommerville, *Politics and Ideology in England*, pp. 64–6 and 106–8.

co-ordinate government of the three Estates in Parliament, consented to and contrived by the people in its first constitution'.[136] It followed that the law owed its existence to the King, Lords and Commons acting together, and not to the King alone. In the 1640s, Henry Parker denied that the law was the mother of Parliament; on the contrary, Parliament was 'that court which gave life and birth to all laws'.[137] As the Earl of Shaftesbury put it much later, Parliament, rather than the King or the common law, was 'the great spring, the *primum mobile* of affairs'.[138] Many concluded that Parliament was therefore 'above the law'.[139]

Glenn Burgess argues that the doctrine of the ancient constitution broke down partly because of the impact of contractualist ideas.[140] He also describes Sir Matthew Hale as one of the few who continued the tradition of thinkers such as Coke.[141] But Hale was a contractualist. He said that 'all human laws have their binding power by reason of the consent of the parties bound'.[142] Like Selden, he regarded statute as the paradigm of law, and custom as tantamount to statute:[143] '[T]he laws of England ... are institutions introduced by ... will and consent ... implicitly by custom and usage or explicitly by written laws or Acts of Parliament.'[144] Hale surmised that 'doubtless, many of those things that now obtain as common law, had their original by Parliamentary Acts or Constitutions, made in writing by the King, Lords and Commons'.[145]

---

[136] Charles Herle, *A Fuller Answer to a Treatise Written by Doctor Ferne etc.* (John Bartlet, 1642), p. 6.

[137] Henry Parker, *Observations Upon Some of His Majesties Late Answers and Expresses* (London, s.n., 1642), p. 42, reprinted in William Haller, *Tracts on Liberty in the Puritan Revolution 1638–1647* (vol. 2) (Octagon Books, 1979). See also similar statements quoted in Goldsworthy, *The Sovereignty of Parliament*, p. 106.

[138] Earl of Shaftesbury, *Some Observations concerning the Regulation of Elections for Parliament* (Randall Taylor, 1669), p. 5, quoted in Goldsworthy, *The Sovereignty of Parliament*, p. 150.

[139] Goldsworthy, *The Sovereignty of Parliament*, p. 130; see also *ibid.* at p. 106.

[140] Burgess, *The Politics of the Ancient Constitution*, pp. 99 and 231.

[141] *Ibid.*, p. 231.

[142] D.E.C. Yale (ed.), *Sir Matthew Hale's The Prerogatives of the King* (Selden Society, 1976), p. 169; Cromartie, *Sir Matthew Hale*, pp. 23, 46, 49, 57, 67, 77 and 88.

[143] Cromartie, *Sir Matthew Hale*, p. 52.

[144] Matthew Hale, 'Reflections on Hobbes' *Dialogue*' in Sir William Holdsworth (ed.), *History of English Law* (vol. 5) (London: Sweet & Maxwell, 1945), 500 at p. 505; Yale, *Sir Matthew Hale's The Prerogatives of the King*, p. 169.

[145] Hale, *The History of the Common Law of England*, pp. 4, 6 and 44–5. Note that by 'constitutions' Hale meant particular written laws – like the so-called 'constitutions of Clarendon' – and not a constitution in our sense of the term. Elsewhere he said that 'positive constitutions ... with us are called statutes or ordinances'. See Yale (ed.), *Sir Matthew Hale's The Prerogatives of the King*, p. 169.

Because authentic records of these ancient statutes (such as parliament rolls) had presumably been lost or destroyed, their substance survived only through having been absorbed into the common law: for legal purposes, they existed 'before time of memory'.[146] Hale's friend Sir John Vaughan agreed that this was why 'many laws made in the time of the Saxon Kings, of William the First, and Henry the First ... are now received as common law'.[147] But he went further than Hale, asserting that 'most' of the common law must have originated in Acts of Parliament or their equivalent.[148]

Hale recognised that the common law could change, but also thought, in Charles Gray's words, that 'one essential thing has remained unchanged throughout: the basic political frame, or the constitutional rules by which other rules [could] be authoritatively recognised as binding'.[149] What was this 'political frame'? Hale said that the common law was:

> the common rule for the administration of common justice in this great kingdom ... it is not only a very just and excellent law in itself, but it is singularly accommodated to the frame of the English government, and to the disposition of the English nation, and such as by a long experience and use is as it were incorporated into their very temperament, and, in a manner, become the complection [complexion] and constitution of the English commonwealth.[150]

Here, Hale was using the word 'constitution' in a medical sense, to mean the commonwealth's natural state of health.[151] It is significant that he described the common law as 'singularly accommodated to' the frame of government, and not as *forming* or *embodying* the frame of government. By 'the frame of the English government,' he meant law-making by the

---

[146] Hale, *The History of the Common Law of England*, p. 4. Hale and Vaughan both understood 'time of memory' to have been fixed for legal purposes as the period after 1189, the beginning of the reign of Richard I. See Alan Wharan, 'The 1189 Rule: Fact, Fiction or Fraud?' *Anglo-American Law Review* 1 (1972) 262. Plucknett has argued that Hale was quite right to suspect that the common law often originated in legislation of one kind or another. Theodore Frank Thomas Plucknett, *Legislation of Edward I* (Oxford: Oxford University Press, 1962), pp. 8–9.

[147] *Thomas* v. *Sorrell*, (1677) Vaugh 330, 358, 124 Eng. Rep. 1098, 1101. In the full passage, Vaughan clearly uses the word 'constitution' in the same sense as Hale. See n. 145, above.

[148] *Sheppard* v. *Gosnold*, (1672) Vaugh 159, 163, 124 Eng. Rep. 1018, 1020.

[149] See Gray's introduction to Hale, *The History of the Common Law of England*, p. xxiii.

[150] Hale, *The History of the Common Law of England*, p. 30.

[151] Cromartie, *Sir Matthew Hale*, p. 63.

King, with the assent of whatever assembly from time to time represented the people.[152]

In his *Prerogatives of the King*, Hale discussed how the 'nature and extent of any government in any kingdom or place' could be ascertained. He explained that in the absence of actual records of 'the original of government' – 'the original of that pact or constitution of our government':

> we must have recourse to the common custom and usage of the kingdom ... I mean such customs as have been allowed by the known laws of the kingdom. And therefore under the word custom I take in the traditions and monuments of the municipal laws, law-books, records of judgments and resolutions of judges, treaties and resolutions and capitulations of regular and orderly conventions, authentical histories, concessions of privileges and liberties ...[153]

For example, 'by the laws of this kingdom the regal government is hereditary and transmitted by descent. This appears not only by the recognition of 1 Jac. and 1 Eliz., but by the constant usage.'[154] Evidence of the pact that established the government of England was therefore not confined to the records of common law, but included statute law as well. According to Cromartie, Hale regarded Parliament as the only place where the fundamental compact could be deliberately altered, the only place in which the 'consent of the people [and es]states of the kingdom' could be voiced.[155] That is why, when Henry VIII wished to dispose of the Crown by his last will, 'he could not make such disposal without an act of parliament enabling him'.[156] But the compact could also be altered by changes in custom and usage, which were evidence of mutual consent.[157] In that sense, Hale attributed to the common law the capacity to change the constitution, although Cromartie adds that in this respect the common law 'was conceptually equivalent to an enormous statute, on which the king and people had tacitly agreed'.[158] Hale did not think of the common law as something that could be altered by judges. He said that when the common law failed to provide a remedy for injustice, only Parliament could provide what was

---

[152] In his *Prerogatives of the King*, Hale distinguished the 'frame of government' – whether monarchical, aristocratic, democratic, or mixed – from 'the particulars of government,' which include the rights of the King and the people. See Yale (ed.), *Sir Matthew Hale's The Prerogatives of the King*, p. 6.

[153] Yale (ed.), *Sir Matthew Hale's The Prerogatives of the King*, pp. 7–8.

[154] *Ibid.* p. 13.

[155] Cromartie, *Sir Matthew Hale*, p. 50; Yale (ed.), *Sir Matthew Hale's The Prerogatives of the King*, p. 15.

[156] Yale (ed.), *Sir Matthew Hale's The Prerogatives of the King*, p. 18.

[157] Cromartie, *Sir Matthew Hale*, pp. 49 and 102.   [158] *Ibid.*, p. 49.

needed by making a new law. Not even the House of Lords, the highest ordinary court of appeal, could grant a remedy if no established law provided for one: 'for that were to give up the whole legislative power unto the House of Lords. For it is all one to make a law, and to have an authoritative power to judge according to that, which the judge thinks fit should be law, although in truth there be no law extant for it.'[159]

Hale acknowledged that the common law dealt with matters of a fundamental nature, such as 'the safety of the king's royal person, his crown and dignity, and all his just rights, revenues, powers, prerogatives and government ... and this law is also, that which declares and asserts the rights and liberties, and the properties of the subject'.[160] On the other hand, he insisted that Parliament as a whole (and not the House of Lords alone) was the 'dernier resort' – the supreme and final court of appeal – with respect to all questions of law.[161] These included questions that were too high for inferior courts, raised by cases that were:

> so momentous, that they are not fit for the determination of judges, as in questions touching the right of succession to the crown ... or the privileges of parliament ... or the great cases which concern the liberties and rights of the subject, as in the case of Ship Money, and some others of like universal nature.[162]

Hale subscribed to the belief that a representative assembly of some kind had always existed in England.[163] This became central to the ideology of the Whigs, but was strenuously denied by most Tories. As J.G.A. Pocock describes that ideology:

> it was now parliament, rather than the law as a whole, which was being presented as immemorial; and the claim to be immemorial had been virtually identified with the claim to be sovereign ... The whole concept of ancient custom had been narrowed down to this one assertion, that parliament was immemorial ... The medieval concept of universal unmade law, which the notion of ancient custom had sought to express, had collapsed.[164]

---

[159] *Ibid.*, p. 117, quoting Matthew Hale in F. Hargrave (ed.), *The Jurisdiction of the Lords House, or Parliament, Considered According to Ancient Records* (T. Cadell and W. Davies, 1796), pp. 108–9.

[160] Hale, *The History of the Common Law of England*, pp. 30–1.

[161] Hale in Hargrave (ed.), *The Jurisdiction of the Lords House*. See Goldsworthy, *The Sovereignty of Parliament*, p. 121.

[162] Hale in Hargrave (ed.), *The Jurisdiction of the Lords House*, p. 159.

[163] Cromartie, *Sir Matthew Hale*, p. 50.

[164] Pocock, *The Ancient Constitution and the Feudal Law*, p. 234; see also *ibid.* at p. 239. Corinne Comstock Weston asserts that this happened in the 1640s. See Weston,

According to Burgess, the 'classic age' of common law political thought and ancient constitutionalism came to an end in the 1640s, when loss of faith in the common law's ability to control the Crown prompted a shift to other modes of political and legal thought, relying on necessity, *salus populi*, or social contract, rather than custom.[165] Janelle Greenberg disagrees, pointing out that ancient constitutionalism and contract theory were perfectly compatible since the original constitution was widely regarded as having been established by contract. She argues that in the 1640s ancient constitutionalism took on 'a new and even more vigorous life'.[166] But Burgess may be partly right, insofar as the 'common law' version of ancient constitutionalism was thrust aside by the contractualist version.

Further developments can only be briefly sketched here. The eighteenth and nineteenth centuries were dominated by the political theory of sovereignty. Writers such as Blackstone did not derive the authority of Parliament from the common law. In discussing the application of civil and canon law by special courts, he denied that 'their force and efficacy depend upon their own instrinsic authority; which is the case of our written laws, or acts of parliament'. Instead, all their 'strength' within the realm was due either to having been 'admitted and received by immemorial usage and custom in some particular cases, and some particular courts, and then they form a branch of the *leges non scripta*, or customary law; or else, because they are in some other cases introduced by consent of parliament, and then they owe their validity to the *leges scripta*, or statute law'.[167] This assumes that the authority of Acts of Parliament was not itself derived from customary law: indeed, he asserted that it is 'intrinsic'. Elsewhere, he referred to 'the natural, inherent right that belongs to the sovereignty of a state ... of making and enforcing laws'.[168] In his view, the existence of a legislature with sovereign law-making authority was not a contingent feature of a legal system that depended on local customs. It was, instead, 'requisite to the very essence of a law': sovereignty 'must in all governments reside somewhere'.[169] It might be objected that, even if the existence of a sovereign legislature of some kind is a necessity, its

'England: Ancient Constitution and Common Law' in Burns (ed.), *The Cambridge History of Political Thought*, pp. 397–8.

[165] Burgess, *The Politics of the Ancient Constitution*, pp. 99 and 221–31.

[166] Greenberg, *The Radical Face of the Ancient Constitution*, pp. 21–2 and 157. See also the many references in her index to 'contract theory of government'.

[167] Blackstone, *Commentaries on the Laws of England*, pp. 79–80.

[168] *Ibid.* p. 47.   [169] *Ibid.*, pp. 46 and 156.

identity and composition in a particular society must be contingent, and could be determined by custom. But for Blackstone, England's legislature was established by 'an original contract, either express or implied,' entered into by 'the general consent and fundamental act of the society'.[170] Moreover, Parliament's moral authority flowed partly from the security provided by the checks and balances among the monarchical, aristocratic and democratic principles embodied in its three component elements.[171] Blackstone had no need to rely on the authority of custom.

Common law constitutionalism was alien to the classical legal positivism that came to dominate the nineteenth century. According to John Austin's influential theory,

> all judge-made law is the creature of the sovereign or state … A subordinate or subject judge is merely a minister. The portion of sovereign power which lies at his disposition is merely delegated … [W]hen customs are turned into legal rules by decisions of subject judges, the legal rules which emerge from the customs are *tacit* commands of the sovereign legislature.[172]

This theory has, of course, been shown to be flawed – most notably by H.L.A. Hart.[173] But it does not follow that common law constitutionalism was therefore the correct theory all along. As will be shown in the next section, it is not vindicated by Hart's theory of the nature of fundamental constitutional rules.[174] A.V. Dicey once wrote rather loosely that,

> the English constitution … far from being the result of legislation, in the ordinary sense of that term, [is] the fruit of contests carried on in the courts on behalf of the rights of individuals. Our constitution, in short, is a judge-made constitution, and it bears on its face all the features, good and bad, of judge-made law.[175]

But Dicey was at this point discussing what he called 'the general principles of the constitution', and as the editor of his tenth edition, E.C.S. Wade, explained in a footnote, 'it is clear from [Dicey's] examples that he is dealing with the means of protecting private rights. The origin of the sovereignty of Parliament cannot be traced to a judicial decision

---

[170] *Ibid.*, p. 52.   [171] *Ibid.*, pp. 50–1.
[172] J. Austin, *The Province of Jurisprudence Determined etc.* (H.L.A. Hart, ed.) (London: Weidenfeld and Nicolson, 1954), pp. 31–2.
[173] H.L.A. Hart, *The Concept of Law* (Oxford: Clarendon Press, 1961), pp. 46–7.
[174] See Section III.
[175] A.V. Dicey, *Introduction to the Study of the Law of the Constitution* (10th edn) (London: Macmillan, 1959), p. 196.

and the independence of the judges has rested on statute since the Act of Settlement, 1701.'[176]

There is ample evidence that Dicey did not believe that Parliament owed its authority to judge-made law. First, having stated that English constitutional law was 'a cross between history and custom', he argued that Parliament's sovereignty could be 'shown historically' by describing a number of extraordinary statutes that had been efficacious.[177] For example, he described the Septennial Act as 'standing proof', Acts of Indemnity as 'crowning proof', and repeals of statutes purporting to prohibit their future repeal as 'the strongest proof', of Parliament's sovereign power.[178] Secondly, Dicey endorsed Austin's thesis that '[j]udicial legislation is ... subordinate legislation, carried on with the assent and subject to the supervision of Parliament'.[179] Thirdly, his statement that '[t]here is no power which, under the English constitution, can come into rivalry with the legislative sovereignty of Parliament' is inconsistent with the idea that Parliament's sovereignty derives from, and therefore could be limited by, the exercise of judicial power.[180] Finally, it is doubtful that Dicey regarded even the common law as entirely judge-made: he described it as a 'mass of custom, tradition, or judge-made maxims'.[181]

Dicey seems to have regarded Parliament's sovereignty as a matter of long-standing, fundamental custom, which has the status of 'law' because the courts are obliged to accept and enforce it. He did not accept Austin's theory that there must be a sovereign power in every legal system.[182] Dicey surmised that, rather than Parliament's sovereignty being 'a deduction from abstract theories of jurisprudence', Austin's conception of sovereignty was 'a generalisation drawn in the main from English law', and 'the ease with which the theory of absolute sovereignty has been accepted by English jurists is due to the peculiar history of English constitutional law'.[183]

The notion that the common law is the source of Parliament's authority was later revived by constitutional writers such as W. Ivor Jennings in the twentieth century. But Jennings was too subtle a thinker to suggest that, in this regard, the common law was judge-made law:

---

[176] *Ibid.*, p. 195 n. 3. Jennings had previously made the same point: W.I. Jennings, *The Law and the Constitution* (2nd edn) (London: University of London Press, 1938), pp. 38–40.

[177] Dicey, *Introduction*, pp. 24 and 43.

[178] *Ibid.*, pp. 48, 50 and 65 respectively.   [179] *Ibid.*, pp. 60–1.

[180] *Ibid.*, p. 70. Hence, his assertion that 'no English judge ever conceded, *or, under the present constitution, can concede*, that Parliament is in any legal sense a "trustee" for the electors'.: *Ibid.*, p. 75, emphasis added.

[181] *Ibid.*, p. 24.   [182] *Ibid.*, p. 61.   [183] *Ibid.*, p. 72.

The most important principle [of the constitution], that of the supremacy of Parliament, is no doubt a rule of the common law. It was not established by judicial decisions, however; it was settled by armed conflict and the Bill of Rights and the Act of Settlement. The judges did no more than acquiesce in a simple fact of political authority, though they have never been called upon precisely to say so.[184]

This passage from the second edition in 1938 was repeated in the fifth in 1959.[185] But by that time, Jennings had come to question whether Parliament enjoyed complete supremacy over the common law. Emphasising that recognition of Parliament's supremacy was a practical *modus vivendi* between institutions that had once competed – sometimes violently – for power, he added that it had never been necessary to settle the precise relationship between Parliament and the common law. Therefore, whether there were some common law principles that Parliament could not repeal had not been conclusively determined, and if Parliament passed an extreme law (such as one introducing slavery) 'a judge would do what a judge should do'.[186] Some scattered passages suggest that, since this is a question of common law, the judges' decision would be authoritative.[187] But that suggestion would be incompatible with Jennings' acknowledgement that such matters are effectively settled only by the practical outcome of institutional conflict, and not by judicial law-making.[188]

In a justly famous article, William Wade wobbled on this point. He rightly said that the doctrine of parliamentary sovereignty is a common law rule only 'in one sense', because it is also an 'ultimate political fact'.[189] But he also said that the doctrine 'lies in the keeping of the courts', and cannot be 'altered by any authority outside the courts'.[190] This implies that the courts have an exclusive authority unilaterally to alter the doctrine. But that puts the cart before the horse, because the courts' authority, no

[184] W.I. Jennings, *The Law and the Constitution* (2nd edn) (London: University of London Press, 1938), pp. 38–9.

[185] W.I. Jennings, *The Law and the Constitution* (5th edn) (London: University of London Press, 1959), p. 39.

[186] *Ibid.*, pp. 160 and 157–60 for the whole argument.

[187] E.g., *ibid.*, p. 160 ('a lawyer ought to be able to say what the answer of the courts would be, and happily we cannot do so because there are no precedents'); p. 164 ('Since this is a matter of common law, this must be proved by decisions of the courts'); p. 169 ('At best they [some statutes] show what Parliament thought of its own powers, and not what the courts thought those powers were').

[188] *Ibid.*, pp. 39 and 157–8.

[189] H.W.R. Wade, 'The Basis of Legal Sovereignty' *Cambridge Law Journal* (1955) 172, 188–9.

[190] *Ibid.*, 189.

less than Parliament's, depends on 'ultimate political facts'. There is no good reason to assume that the courts, but not Parliament, can unilaterally alter the source of their own authority. Many later commentators seem simply to have assumed that, because the source of Parliament's authority cannot be statute (since that would be boot-strapping), it must be the common law, understood as judge-made law. That simplistic assumption has become very influential, but as the next section will demonstrate, it is either false or dangerously misleading.

What conclusions can be drawn from this brief historical survey? First, there is no evidence of significant, if any, support for common law constitutionalism before the seventeenth century. On the contrary, there is solid evidence that it was widely rejected. For much of the pre-modern period, the common law was regarded as the 'common erudition' of the bench and bar.[191] The idea that the authority of the judges' superiors – the King who appointed and could dismiss them, and the High Court of Parliament that could overturn their decisions – was the product of their decisions, or of their 'erudition', would have been dismissed out of hand as an absurdity. That is partly why, on several occasions, it was expressly and authoritatively denied that either the royal succession, or the privileges of Parliament, were governed by the common law.

Secondly, even in the seventeenth century, arguably the 'classical age' of common law constitutionalism, that theory was fully embraced only by a few lawyers such as Thomas Hedley.[192] Sir Edward Coke denied, at least on some occasions, that the royal succession and the privileges of Parliament were governed by the common law. He famously held that the King's prerogatives were so governed. But Sir John Davies, who shared Coke's conception of the nature of the common law, was a royalist who believed that as the human source of all legal authority, the King had retained prerogative powers that were 'above' the common law. Many lawyers, and other members of the ruling elite, agreed with him. Many others were contractualists, who believed that legal authority derived from the community as a whole, which had entered into a pact with the King that conferred and limited his powers. After the seventeenth century, the political theory of sovereignty, which maintained that there must be a sovereign legislator in every state that by definition stands above the law, became ascendant.

---

[191] See text accompanying nn. 55–61 above.
[192] The title of Chapter 6 of John Allison's *The Historical English Constitution* (Cambridge: Cambridge University Press, 2007), 'The Brief Rule of a Controlling Common Law', therefore seems inapt.

Thirdly, for most of the period surveyed here, almost everyone accepted that the High Court of Parliament was the highest court in the realm, with ultimate authority to declare and interpret the common law itself.[193] Even lawyers such as Thomas Hedley therefore accepted a version of common law constitutionalism that is very different from modern versions of the theory, which attribute ultimate authority to expound and develop the unwritten constitution to judges.

It must be conceded that, over the centuries, the ambit of the common law has steadily expanded. For example, the theory that the King possessed 'absolute' prerogatives that were above the common law eventually lost credibility. All the powers of the Crown are now creatures of either statutory or common law, and today the unwritten constitution is largely a matter of common law. Parliamentary sovereignty may be the final bastion that still resists the common law's imperial ambitions. But the common law's subjugation of other sites of legal authority does not entail that, by some kind of immanent logic, it is entitled and destined to sweep the field.

III   Philosophical analysis

I have shown that common law constitutionalism has much weaker historical credentials than is often assumed. But many lawyers accept the theory for philosophical rather than historical reasons. In the limited space that remains, these philosophical reasons will be briefly examined.

Common law constitutionalism is sometimes the conclusion of an enquiry into the source or basis of the authority of the doctrine of parliamentary sovereignty. Adam Tomkins, for example, asks:

> What then is the legal authority for the rule [of parliamentary sovereignty]? What is its source? There are two alternatives: authority might be found either in statute or in common law. The first of these options may relatively quickly be dismissed. Parliament has never legislated so as to confer legislative supremacy on itself ... The doctrine of legislative supremacy is a doctrine of the common law.[194]

Tomkins is concerned with the source or basis of the doctrine's *legal* authority, whereas other writers seem more concerned with its *moral* authority. Let us assume, for the moment, that there is a difference.

---

[193] Goldsworthy, *The Sovereignty of Parliament*, pp. 110, 118–19, 153–4 and 156–7.
[194] Adam Tomkins, *Public Law* (Oxford: Oxford University Press, 2003), p. 103.

If we are concerned with legal authority, then it is not clear that there is any need to resort to deeper principles. There cannot be an infinite regress of legal institutions or norms, each owing its authority to the next in line. There must be a basic norm or set of basic norms that is authoritative for legal purposes. These basic norms might simply be that the institutions in question possess the legal authority that is generally attributed to them. Consider written constitutions, for example. In Australia, it has become common for people to ask what the current legal foundation of the Australian Constitution is. Since the British Parliament, which originally enacted the Constitution, lost its authority to change Australian law, the answers usually given are either the common law, or the sovereignty of the people. But no good reason has been given for assuming that, for legal purposes, the Constitution must rest on some deeper legal foundation. Why cannot the Constitution itself be the ultimate foundation of the legal system, with no need for the support of deeper legal norms? And if it can, then presumably the generally accepted norms of an unwritten constitution can play the same role. In other words, constitutional doctrines such as that of parliamentary sovereignty can be legally fundamental, requiring no deeper legal support.

If, on the other hand, we are concerned with moral rather than legal authority – either for its own sake, or because positivists are wrong to think that the two are distinct – another question arises. Why would an enquiry into the ultimate source or basis of the *moral* authority of a legal institution or norm be satisfied by an appeal to a deeper *law,* such as the common law? Even if it did look to the common law, would it not insist on digging even deeper, and enquiring into the moral authority of that body of law? It is, after all, a moral rather than a legal source that is required here, and many candidates are available: necessity, prudence, justice, equality, fraternity, duty to others, fair play, consent, and so on. This is why political and legal thinkers in past centuries, when reflecting on the law's moral authority, appealed to a variety of competing principles such as divine right, natural law, ancient custom, social contract, the checks and balances of 'mixed government', the collective wisdom of the community, and the practical necessity of sovereign power.

The nature of fundamental legal norms is admittedly a subject of philosophical puzzlement. That is why we turn to thinkers such as Kelsen and Hart for enlightenment. Perhaps what writers such as Tomkins really seek, when they ask about the ultimate source or basis of the authority of constitutional doctrines, is a philosophical *explanation* of legal authority and of ultimate legal norms. But that is quite different from what they expressly ask for. Hart's theory of law, for example, helps us understand the nature and mode of existence of fundamental legal norms, and what it means to say that they are legally authoritative, but it does not provide a source or basis for their legal authority.

Common law constitutionalists might reply that, even if constitutional norms such as the doctrine of parliamentary sovereignty are legally fundamental, and do not derive their authority from deeper legal principles, it is still useful to classify them. Even if they do not rest on deeper common law principles, it may still be the case that they themselves are part of the common law.

It should be noted at this point that the common law constitutionalists' interest in classifying such norms as 'common law' is not merely taxonomical. They believe that it has an important practical consequence: namely, that such norms are 'in the keeping of the courts', which have authority either to change them, or at least authoritatively to declare that they have changed. Thus, having decided that parliamentary sovereignty is a common law rule, Tomkins infers that '[l]ike any other rule of the common law it may be developed, refined, re-interpreted, or even changed by the judges'.[195] But there is a chicken/egg problem here: is the existence of authority to change legal norms a consequence of their correct classification, or is their correct classification partly dependent on the nature and location of authority to change them? Whether we should classify unwritten constitutional norms as 'common law' surely depends partly on whether they share the distinctive characteristics of the large body of norms that uncontroversially bear that label – those of contract, property, tort, and so on. These are the characteristics that distinguish the common law from statute law. Among them is that common law norms have been developed by judicial decisions over many centuries, and that the courts have acknowledged authority to continue to develop them. But there are still major theoretical disagreements about the precise nature of these norms, and the way in which they are properly developed by judicial decisions. At least four conceptions of the nature of the common law currently compete for acceptance.

First, there is a legal positivist conception of the common law as a body of judge-made rules, which Brian Simpson in 1973 described as the 'predominant conception'.[196] Secondly, there is the conception that Simpson

---

[195] Tomkins, *Public Law*, p. 103.
[196] A.W.B. Simpson, 'The Common Law and Legal Theory' in A.W.B. Simpson (ed.), *Oxford Essays in Jurisprudence (Second Series)* (Oxford: Oxford University Press, 1973),

himself advocated, of the common law as professional custom: 'a body of practices observed and ideas received by a caste of lawyers … [and] used by them as providing guidance in what is conceived to be the rational determination of disputes …'[197] This resembles the conception of the common law as the 'common erudition' of the bench and bar, which historians have found in the fourteenth and fifteenth century Year Books.[198] Thirdly, there is Dworkin's conception of the common law as a presumptively coherent body of norms, resting on fundamental principles of political morality, which the judiciary has authority to identify and expound. This is in several respects similar to the conception held by Sir Edward Coke in the early seventeenth century.[199] Fourthly, the common law in constitutional matters can be conceptualised as customs or conventions either of the community in general, or of government officialdom. In addition, other conceptions are possible, including various 'hybrids' that combine elements of two or more of these four.

Whether unwritten constitutional norms are matters of common law depends on two questions: which of these conceptions of the common law is the most plausible, and whether those constitutional norms fit within that conception. I will attempt to answer only the second question.

Versions of common law constitutionalism based on the first and second conceptions of the common law, as judge-made law, or as the custom or 'common erudition' of the legal profession, are all implausible. As a matter of history, it is plainly false that the authority of either the King or Parliament was established either by judicial decisions or the 'common erudition' of the legal profession.[200] And philosophically, there is an incongruity between the legal doctrine that the courts are obligated to obey statutes, because Parliament is sovereign, and the theory that the courts can at any time release themselves from the obligation, because Parliament's sovereignty is their creation, and subject to their control.[201]

---

reprinted in A.W.B. Simpson, *Legal Theory and Legal History: Essays on the Common Law* (Hambledon, 1987), 359 at p. 361.

[197] Simpson, 'The Common Law and Legal Theory' in Simpson, *Legal Theory and Legal History*, p. 376.

[198] See text accompanying nn. 55–61, above.

[199] The similarities clearly emerge in Gray, 'Parliament, Liberty, and the Law' in Hexter (ed.), *Parliament and Liberty*.

[200] For Parliament, see the historical study in Goldsworthy, *The Sovereignty of Parliament*, chs. 1–8, which is summarised in ch. 9 of that book.

[201] See Thomas, 'The Relationship of Parliament and the Courts' at 26 ('The conferral of that recognition [of Parliament's sovereignty] is in the nature of a self-denying judicial ordinance.').

We would not normally agree that x is obligated to obey y, if the suggested obligation is self-imposed, and can be repudiated whenever x thinks it appropriate to do so. Such an 'obligation' would be illusory.

There is, in addition, a deeper philosophical problem. Tomkins' implicit assumption that there are only two kinds of law in Britain, statute law and common law, is demonstrably false if the common law is judge-made law. It is true that the basis of the doctrine of parliamentary sovereignty cannot be statute. No legislature can confer authority on itself by statute, because absent pre-existing authority, the statute would have to confer authority on itself, which would beg the question.[202] As Lord Lester points out, 'Parliament cannot pull itself up by its own bootstraps'.[203] But it is a mistake to jump to the conclusion that the doctrine must therefore be a matter of judge-made common law. After all, it could then be asked where the judges got *their* authority from. If it is true, as Lord Steyn insists, that Parliament's authority 'must come from somewhere',[204] it must be equally true of the judges' authority. But they, too, cannot 'pull themselves up by their own bootstraps', by conferring authority on themselves. It follows that their authority cannot come from the common law, if this is judge-made law. If it were true that all British law is either common law or statute law, their authority would then have to come from statute law – giving rise to a vicious circle in which Parliament's authority to enact statutes is conferred by judge-made common law, and the judges' authority to make common law is conferred by statute. To break the circle, someone's legal authority – Parliament's, the judges', or both – must be grounded in a kind of law that was not made either by Parliament or by the judges.

Common law constitutionalists must therefore subscribe either to the third or to the fourth conception of the common law. According to the third one, the common law is a body of norms based on fundamental principles of political morality, which the judges enunciate and expound, but have no authority to change. The identity of these principles is an objective matter: they are whatever principles provide the best moral justification of the common law as a whole. This is the conception favoured

---

[202] Note, however, that the Treasons Act of 1571 declared that it was treason to deny that Parliament had authority to regulate the royal succession.

[203] Lester, 'Beyond the Powers of Parliament' at 96. It follows that, in New Zealand, Parliament's authority cannot derive exclusively from § 15(1) of the Constitution Act of 1986 (NZ), or § 3(2) of the Supreme Court Act of 2004 (NZ), which refer, respectively, to Parliament's 'full power to make laws' and to its 'sovereignty'.

[204] 'Lord Steyn's Comments from the Lester and Pannick Book Launch' *Judicial Review* 107 (2004) at 107.

by most modern common law constitutionalists, who often depict the common law as resting ultimately on a principle of 'legality'.[205] On this view, the unwritten constitution consists of whatever fundamental principles of political morality provide the strongest moral justification of the entire legal system. These principles may therefore change if other parts of the system change. Judges do not have authority to change them, but do have authority to declare either that they have changed, or that previous understandings of them were mistaken.

Dworkin's conception of the common law seems plausible because it is consistent with the way judges develop that law. Judges do seem to believe that a constantly evolving body of fundamental principles guides them in deciding novel questions, and in overruling past doctrines that they have come to regard as erroneous. Moreover, their authority not only passively to identify and apply, but also actively to develop, these principles is acknowledged by other legal officials. Dworkin's conception can therefore form part of a plausible interpretation of the practices and understandings of legal officialdom. The problem with extending his conception of the common law to encompass the doctrine of parliamentary sovereignty is that this would not be equally consonant with official practices and understandings. There is no settled official understanding that the doctrine is merely one of a number of principles of political morality, which the judges have ultimate authority to identify and creatively develop. Common law constitutionalists assert that judges possess authority to decide whether parliamentary sovereignty has come to be inconsistent with other fundamental common law principles, and if they think it has, to modify or repudiate it. But unless this interpretation can be shown to fit general official practices and understandings, it remains a bare assertion. I have argued, elsewhere, that official practices do not justify such an interpretation.[206]

In this regard, an interpretation of the practices and understandings of legal officialdom must extend further than those of the judiciary. Let us imagine that the highest court endorses a Dworkinian interpretation of the unwritten constitution, holding it to rest on fundamental principles of political morality that confer and limit the authority of all governmental institutions including Parliament. In the absence of a broader official

---

[205] See generally the references to Trevor Allan's work in n. 3 above, and Stuart Lakin, 'Debunking the Idea of Parliamentary Sovereignty' *Oxford Journal of Legal Studies* 28 (2008) 709.

[206] Goldsworthy, *The Sovereignty of Parliament*; Goldsworthy, 'Homogenizing Constitutions'.

consensus either as to the nature of the unwritten constitution, or as to the judges' authority to interpret it in that way, their interpretation could claim no better authority than their own say-so. That would be just as question-begging and boot-strapping as the theory that the unwritten constitution is a matter of judge-made law. If the judges' claim to possess authority to interpret the unwritten constitution were itself dependent on their interpretation of it, and derived from whatever principles of political morality they regarded as morally justifying the legal system as a whole, then the theory of common law constitutionalism would ultimately rest on nothing more solid than their claim that it is morally compelling. This would hardly be likely to persuade other theorists or legal officials – in the executive government or in Parliament, for example – who have a very different understanding of the nature of the unwritten constitution and its moral justification.

Dworkin's conception of the common law, when extended to the unwritten constitution, is distinctive in that it almost merges legal and moral authority. The deepest principles of the common law confer moral as well as legal authority on all other legal norms because, by definition, they just are whatever principles of political morality provide the best moral justification of the legal system as a whole. They must therefore consist of some selection, appropriately weighted, from the principles of political morality previously listed: necessity, prudence, justice, equality, fraternity, duty to others, fair play, consent, and so on.[207] But no proposed moral justification of the law as a whole can realistically hope to secure widespread agreement. Many justifications, drawing on these diverse moral principles, have been proposed by political philosophers, and all of them remain deeply controversial. Judges are not recognised as having authority to settle this controversy. And it would be question-begging and boot-strapping if their claim to possess authority to settle it were itself dependent on their proposed settlement of it – that is, on their assessment of the deepest principles of political morality. Any other institution, such as Parliament, could with equal plausibility claim the very same authority.

As I have argued at length elsewhere, self-proclaimed moral authority – even if it is justified – is incapable by itself of sustaining law. That is why legal authority depends on general consensus, at least among the senior officials of all branches of government.[208] This leads to the fourth

---

[207] See p. 48, above.
[208] Goldsworthy, *The Sovereignty of Parliament*, pp. 254–6. Overlooking this point is the major flaw in Lakin, 'Debunking the Idea of Parliamentary Sovereignty'.

conception of the common law as judicially enforceable customs of legal officialdom, or of the community in general, which the judges did not create, and cannot change, unilaterally.[209] Mark Elliott has developed a conception of this kind, according to which the common law constitution consists of constitutional conventions that have crystallised into laws.[210] The existence of constitutional conventions requires consensus among legal officials, including politicians. If Elliott is right, the common law constitution also depends on such a consensus, and can change only if that consensus changes.

Understanding the unwritten constitution in terms of official consensus is supported by H.L.A. Hart's theory that the fundamental rules of recognition in any legal system are constituted by the practices of legal officials.[211] Such rules simply *are* whatever rules legal officials do in fact accept and follow when they make, recognise, interpret or apply law. For this purpose, 'legal officials' cannot mean judges alone, and that was certainly not what Hart meant.[212] Otherwise, his theory could not account for the authority exercised by the judges themselves. The fundamental rules of a legal system are necessarily established and maintained by a consensus among the senior officials of all branches of government. Only such a general consensus can provide both the coherence and stability that a legal system needs to survive and function effectively, and a satisfactory explanation of the authority exercised by each branch of government individually.[213]

On this view, parliamentary sovereignty, like other unwritten constitutional rules, does depend on judicial acceptance.[214] Judicial acceptance is a necessary condition for the existence of such rules, and that acceptance depends on judicial value-judgments. The judges do not passively acknowledge the existence of 'political facts', because their willingness to accept the rules – which depends on evaluative judgments – is itself a crucial ingredient of the relevant political facts.[215] But judicial acceptance

---

[209] See p. 5, above.

[210] Mark Elliott, 'Parliamentary Sovereignty and the New Constitutional Order: Legislative Freedom, Political Reality and Convention' *Legal Studies* 22 (2002) 340 at 362–76.

[211] See H.L.A. Hart, *The Concept of Law* (2nd edn) (Oxford: Oxford University Press, 1994), ch. 6.

[212] Goldsworthy, *The Sovereignty of Parliament*, pp. 240–2.

[213] *Ibid.*, pp. 6 and 240–6.   [214] *Ibid.*, p. 26.

[215] This point is seized on by Stuart Lakin, in 'Debunking the Idea of Parliamentary Sovereignty', but he overlooks the subtleties explained here, and in Goldsworthy, *The Sovereignty of Parliament*, pp. 254–9. For example, he ignores my explanation of how judicial value-judgments play a legitimate role in the settlement of 'hard cases'

is not a sufficient condition for the existence of such rules, because the acceptance of the other branches of government is also necessary. And the judges' judicial authority is equally dependent on acceptance by the political branches. This means that any attempt by the judiciary unilaterally to change the fundamental rules of a legal system is fraught with danger. Other officials might be persuaded, inveigled, bamboozled, or bluffed into acquiescing in the change. But, on the other hand, they might not. They might resent and resist the judicial attempt to change the rules that had previously been generally accepted, and take strong action to defeat it, possibly including the impeachment of 'over-mighty judges'. That might be regrettable, but the point is that if the judges tear up the consensus that constitutes the fundamental rules of the system, they are hardly well placed to complain if it is replaced by a power struggle they are ill-equipped to win. In the absence of consensus, their own authority as well as Parliament's would be up for grabs. Rules of recognition can and do change, but fundamental change in an unwritten constitution requires a change in official consensus. Judges can attempt to initiate such a change, but are well advised to make sure that the other branches of government are likely to acquiesce. If that cannot be confidently expected, they would be wise to wait for the legislature to initiate change.

This conception of the common law constitution is consistent with the nature of fundamental unwritten constitutional rules, and the process by which they are changed. But it is still problematic. The problem is that describing the unwritten constitution as a matter of common law, even in this sense, is likely to breed confusion. The vast bulk of the common law consists of substantive rules and principles, governing property, contracts, torts and so on, that are not constituted by a consensus of legal officialdom in general, and are therefore able to be changed without such a consensus having to change. Judges are now recognised as having authority unilaterally to change these rules and principles, or to declare that they have changed. They are best conceptualised as judicially posited rules, judicial customs, or Dworkinian principles.[216] To apply the same label, 'common law', to the most fundamental norms of the unwritten constitution, is likely to produce confusion, erroneous assumptions about the authority of judges to change them, and conflict between the branches of government. They are best regarded as 'sui generis', a unique hybrid of law

---

(ibid., p. 259), and also my fall-back argument that, even if a Dworkinian theory were adopted, parliamentary sovereignty should still be vindicated (ibid., pp. 254 and 271).

[216] We do not need to choose between these alternatives here.

and political fact deriving [their] authority from acceptance by the people and by the principal institutions of the state, especially Parliament and the judiciary'.[217] As one critic of the doctrine rightly put it, parliamentary sovereignty 'is at one and the same time a political fact ... a convention of the constitution and a fundamental principle of the common law'; 'the legal distribution of power consists ultimately in a dynamic settlement, acceptable to the people, between the different arms of government'.[218]

[217] George Winterton, 'Constitutionally Entrenched Common Law Rights: Sacrificing Means to Ends?' in Charles Sampford and Kim Preston (eds.), *Interpreting Constitutions: Theories, Principles and Institutions* (Sydney: Federation Press, 1996), 121 at p. 136.

[218] Justice E.W. Thomas, 'The Relationship of Parliament and the Courts' *Victoria University of Wellington Law Review* 5 (2000) 31 at 14 and 19 respectively.

3

Legislative sovereignty and the rule of law

I Introduction

Throughout the common law world, it is increasingly assumed that legislative sovereignty – legislative power that is legally unlimited[1] – is incompatible with 'the rule of law'.[2] Those who regard the rule of law as an actual legal principle sometimes argue that it necessarily excludes or overrides any doctrine of legislative sovereignty. Others, who regard the rule of law as a political ideal or aspiration, sometimes argue that it requires any doctrine of legislative sovereignty to be repealed, and legislative power subordinated to constitutionally entrenched rights.

In this chapter I will challenge the assumption, common to both arguments, that legislative sovereignty is incompatible with the rule of law. Strong opinions have been expressed for and against. It has been claimed that '[i]f parliament ... can change any law at any moment ... then the rule of law is nothing more than a bad joke'.[3] On the other hand, claims of that kind have been disparaged as 'judicial supremacist rhetoric',[4] and judicial review of legislation as a 'corrupting constitutional innovation – which [only] in vulgar jurisprudence is thought to support the doctrine of the rule of law'.[5] The disagreement is not a new one. Over fifty years ago, F.A. Hayek's argument that bills of rights enhanced the rule of law was severely criticised for confusing 'the Rule of Law' with 'the Rule of

---

[1] This can be treated as a stipulative definition of 'legislative sovereignty' for the purposes of this chapter. In addition, by 'legal limit' I will mean a judicially enforceable limit.

[2] See, e.g., F. Jacobs, *The Sovereignty of Law: the European Way, The Hamlyn Lectures 2006* (Cambridge: Cambridge University Press, 2007), p. 5; V. Bogdanor, 'The Sovereignty of Parliament or the Rule of Law?', Magna Carta Lecture, 15 June 2006, p. 20, available at http://royalholloway.org.uk/About/magna-carta/2006-lecture.pdf.

[3] G. de Q. Walker, *The Rule of Law, Foundation of Constitutional Democracy* (Melbourne: Melbourne University Press, 1988), p. 159.

[4] M. Elliott, 'Reconciling Constitutional Rights and Constitutional Orthodoxy' *Cambridge Law Journal* 474 (1997) 56 at 476.

[5] P. Morton, *An Institutional Theory of Law; Keeping Law in its Place* (Oxford: Clarendon Press, 1998), p. 371.

Hayek'.[6] The critic, Herman Finer, strongly defended majoritarian democracy, claiming that in Britain '[t]he Rule of Law is not juridical, it is parliamentary.'[7]

II Legal principle or political ideal?

The rule of law is first and foremost a political principle, an ideal or aspiration that may or may not be guaranteed by law. It can be regarded as a constitutional (but non-legal) principle, if a constitutional convention requires compliance with it.[8] If and insofar as it is judicially enforceable, it can also serve as a legal principle.

Most if not all common law jurisdictions treat the rule of law as a principle of common law, which unquestionably governs the decisions and actions of the executive and judicial branches of government. In addition, it is sometimes expressly mentioned in written constitutions, or regarded as implicit in them. Whether it is common law, constitutional, or both, the principle is sometimes said to govern the legislature as well as the other branches of government, and to be capable of overriding legislation. Trevor Allan and Sir John Laws, for example, claim that the doctrine of parliamentary sovereignty is incompatible with more fundamental legal principles, including the rule of law, which are supposedly embedded in Britain's largely unwritten constitution.[9] In Canada, the Supreme Court has often stated that the rule of law, expressly mentioned in the Preamble to the Charter of Rights, is also by implication fundamental to the Constitution as a whole.[10] According to one commentator, Supreme Court dicta support the proposition that this constitutional principle binds the legislative as well as the executive branch of government, and could therefore be used to invalidate legislation.[11] In

---

[6] H. Finer, *The Road to Reaction* (London: Dennis Dobson, 1945), ch. 4 *passim*.
[7] *Ibid.*, p. 38.
[8] Constitutional conventions are rules or principles governing the exercise of governmental powers, which officials accept as obligatory even though they are not judicially enforceable.
[9] T.R.S. Allan, *Law, Liberty and Justice: the Legal Foundations of British Constitutionalism* (Oxford: Clarendon Press, 1993), p. 16; Sir John Laws, 'Law and Democracy' *Public Law* 72 (1995) at 85 and 88.
[10] *Reference Re Manitoba Language Rights* [1985] 1 S.C.R. 721 at 750–1, quoted in P. Monahan, 'Is the Pearson Airport Legislation Unconstitutional?: The Rule of Law as a Limit on Contract Repudiation by Government' *Osgoode Hall Law Journal* 33 (1995) 411 at 421–2.
[11] *Ibid., passim*.

Australia too, the rule of law has frequently been described as a fundamental principle implied by the Constitution, and two members of the High Court have hinted that it might justify the invalidation of certain kinds of unjust legislation.[12]

Notwithstanding the importance and interest of such claims, I will be concerned in this chapter with the rule of law considered as a political rather than as a legal principle. The fundamental issue is the incompatibility of legislative sovereignty with that political principle. It is an important issue in its own right, for both political philosophy and constitutional design. Moreover, the content and scope of the rule of law as a legal principle is ultimately determined by that political principle, subject to limitations and qualifications due to other legal principles. These limitations and qualifications vary from one jurisdiction to another, and raise complex legal questions that are beyond the scope of this chapter.[13] As a political principle, the rule of law is a 'supra-national concept' of potentially universal significance, rather than a legal principle of a particular jurisdiction.[14]

It is important not to confuse two different questions. The first is whether legislatures are bound by the rule of law considered as a political principle. Few people would deny that they are, just as few would deny that legislatures are also bound by other political principles, such as equality and justice. This is perfectly compatible with legislative sovereignty, which I have defined as legislative power that is legally – not morally or politically – unlimited. In Britain, the doctrine of parliamentary sovereignty co-exists with constitutional conventions requiring Parliament to comply with many principles of political morality, including the rule of law.[15]

I am interested in a different question: namely, whether legislative sovereignty is incompatible with the rule of law – or in other words, whether the rule of law requires that legislative power be subject to legal (judicially enforceable) limits.[16] That legislative sovereignty and

---

[12] *Kartinyeri* v. *Commonwealth* (1998) 152 ALR 540 at 569 (Gummow and Hayne JJ). See also the remarks of Justice John Toohey, in 'A Government of Laws, and Not of Men?' *Public Law Review* 4 (1993) 158 at 160 and 174.

[13] Chapters 2, 9 and 10 deal with arguments to the effect that legislative sovereignty is limited by the common law. See also J. Goldsworthy, *The Sovereignty of Parliament, History and Philosophy* (Oxford: Clarendon Press, 1999), esp. ch. 10.

[14] See Norman Marsh, 'The Rule of Law as a Supra-National Concept', in A.G. Guest (ed.), *Oxford Essays in Jurisprudence* (1st series) (Oxford: Oxford University Press, 1961), p. 223.

[15] G. Marshall, *Constitutional Conventions* (Oxford: Clarendon Press, 1994), pp. 9 and 201.

[16] See n. 1, above.

the rule of law are incompatible has been assumed by critics who have accused A.V. Dicey of inconsistency for simultaneously adhering to both principles.[17] As Martin Loughlin puts it, '[h]ow can an absolutist doctrine of sovereignty rest in harmony with the idea of the rule of law? From the standpoint of mainstream contemporary jurisprudence the issue seems irreconcilable.'[18] Trevor Allan asserts that 'it is ultimately impossible to reconcile ... the rule of law with the unlimited sovereignty of Parliament ... An insistence on there being a source of ultimate political authority, which is free of all legal restraint ... is incompatible with constitutionalism.'[19] More recently, Geoffrey de Q. Walker has proclaimed 'the simple truth that parliamentary omnipotence is an absurdity and that legislative power must be balanced by the rule of law, not just as a set of procedural safeguards, but as a minimum standard for the substantive content of enacted law.'[20]

The increasing popularity of the idea that the rule of law requires even elected legislatures to be subject to judicially enforceable limits is easy to understand. It seems to involve a simple and natural extension of much less controversial requirements that on any view are close to the heart of the rule of law. If the rule of law can be reduced to a single core proposition, it is that laws should limit or control what would otherwise be arbitrary power. It is therefore uncontroversial that administrative officials, even at the highest levels of the executive branch of government, should not enjoy arbitrary power. Their decisions and acts should be governed by judicially enforceable rules or principles. But if so, it might seem that the legislative branch of government should also be denied arbitrary power – that its Acts, too, should be governed by judicially enforceable rules and principles. That is why the American system of limiting legislative power by a bill of rights is sometimes hailed as 'the elevation of the Rule of Law concept to its highest level'.[21]

---

[17] A.V. Dicey, *An Introduction to the Study of the Law of the Constitution* (10th edn), (E.W.S. Wade, ed.) (London: MacMillan, 1959).

[18] M. Loughlin, *Public Law and Political Theory* (Oxford: Clarendon Press, 1992), p. 151.

[19] Allan, *Law, Liberty and Justice*, p. 16. See also Sir John Laws, 'Law and Democracy' *Public Law* 72 (1995) at 85 and 88; F.A. Hayek, *The Constitution of Liberty* (London and Henley: Routledge & Kegan Paul, 1960), ch. 12.

[20] Walker, *The Rule of Law*, p. 359. On the other hand, Walker also says that '[i]n principle it does not matter whether these restrictions are imposed by way of written constitutional provisions and enforceable by courts, or by the dictates of custom that are enforceable by other means': *ibid.*, p. 26; see also p. 159. The second option is consistent with legislative sovereignty being subject only to non-legal constitutional conventions, as in Britain today.

[21] P.G. Kauper, 'The Supreme Court and the Rule of Law' *Michigan Law Review* 59 (1961) 531 at 532.

A full assessment of the force of such arguments requires two questions to be answered. The first is whether legislative sovereignty is inconsistent with the rule of law. The second is whether, even if it is, it is therefore unjustified. Even if it is inconsistent with the rule of law, it might nevertheless be justified on the ground that in this case the rule of law is outweighed by the principle of democracy. In this chapter, I will touch on the second question only in passing. Arguments to the effect that democracy trumps the rule of law have been made by others.[22] I believe it has been too readily conceded that legislative sovereignty is inconsistent with the rule of law. I will therefore concentrate on the first question, and argue that it is not. But the answers to both questions depend partly on the meaning and content of the rule of law as a political principle, to which I now turn.

III   The content of the rule of law

The rule of law is notoriously vague and contested. Sceptics and critics complain that it is 'often used as a mere rhetorical device, a vague ideal by contrast with which legislation, official action, or the assertion of private power is mysteriously measured and found wanting';[23] that it is 'often hazy and unclear, liable to take on any features of law which the writer finds attractive';[24] and so on.

It is generally agreed that the rule of law requires more than 'mere legality', in the sense of compliance with whatever the law of a particular jurisdiction happens to be. The rule of law requires more than the rule of the law: in other words, the law itself might not adequately protect the rule of law.[25] But how much more the rule of law requires is debatable. Proponents of 'thin' or 'formal' conceptions of the rule of law maintain that it requires compliance only with certain procedural and institutional norms: for example, that laws be general, public, prospective and enforceable by an independent judiciary. Proponents of 'thick' or 'substantive'

---

[22] E.g., A. Hutchinson and P. Monahan, 'Democracy and the Rule of Law', in A. Hutchinson and P. Monahan (eds.), *The Rule of Law: Ideal or Ideology?* (Toronto: Carswell, 1987).

[23] H.W. Arthurs, 'Rethinking Administrative Law: A Slightly Dicey Business' *Osgoode Hall Law Journal* 17 (1979) 1 at 3.

[24] A. Palmer and C. Sampford, 'Retrospective Legislation in Australia: Looking Back at the 1980s' *Federal Law Review* 22 (1994) 213 at 227.

[25] This is true, at least, if the law is conceived of in legal positivist terms. A natural lawyer, who conceives of the law as including transcendent and overriding moral principles, might think that the rule of law requires no more than the rule of the law, which is, ultimately, the rule of those principles.

conceptions maintain that it also includes requirements concerning the substantive content of the law.[26]

Some thick conceptions are criticised for shoe-horning every political virtue into the rule of law, which then amounts to the rule of justice or the rule of good law. These conceptions are too broad: while the rule of law is more than the rule of the law, it must be less than the rule of good law. A conception of the rule of law that incorporated every political virtue, properly weighted and balanced, would be useless for practical purposes. Our question, for example, is whether or not the rule of law requires that legislative power be limited by law. If the answer depended on whether judicial review of legislation is desirable all-things-considered, such as majority rule, minority rights, institutional competence, and so on, then the rule of law would contribute nothing in itself to the enquiry. It would be merely a way of expressing whatever conclusion we reached, without helping us to reach it.

On the other hand, there do seem to be good reasons to go beyond a purely formal conception. Arguably, the rule of law is mainly concerned with limiting or controlling what would otherwise be arbitrary power, whether it be exercised by public officials or private citizens. For example, chronic lawless violence inflicted by some citizens on others would surely be as antithetical to the rule of law as the lawless tyranny of a king or emperor.[27] The same goes for some kinds of lawful violence. If it would be contrary to the rule of law for a king to possess a legally uncontrolled power of life or death over his subjects, then surely it would equally be contrary to the rule of law for a husband or father to possess the same power over his wife or children. But if so, then every kind of power that one person, group or organisation can exercise over others – such as the power of employers over their employees – would be open to question on rule of law grounds. The rule of law would be concerned with the distribution and extent of all forms of power throughout society, and would be difficult to distinguish from the rule of good law.

Perhaps this would so inflate the rule of law that it would no longer serve a useful function. Fortunately, we are concerned with the exercise of legislative power, not private power. We can therefore bypass the question of the extent to which the rule of law is concerned with the exercise of private as well as public power. For the sake of argument, we will proceed

---

[26] See P. Craig, 'Formal and Substantive Conceptions of the Rule of Law: An Analytical Framework' *Public Law* (1997) 467.

[27] Walker, *The Rule of Law*, pp. 2–3.

on the basis that in political and legal theory, it requires only 'that the government should be ruled by law and subject to it'.[28]

IV 'Thin' conceptions of the rule of law

Thin conceptions of the rule of law have become so popular that a consensus about its content may finally have been reached.[29] Joseph Raz's influential analysis exemplifies these conceptions.[30] He denies that the rule of law means the rule of good law: it must be distinguished from other political ideals such as democracy, justice, equality, and human rights of any kind.[31] The basic goal of the rule of law is to ensure that the law is capable of guiding the behaviour of its subjects.[32] This requires that all laws be prospective, adequately publicised, clear and relatively stable; that the making of particular legal orders or directives be governed by general laws that satisfy the criteria just listed, and by the principles of natural justice; and that the implementation of all these requirements be subject to review by a readily accessible and independent judiciary.[33]

Raz insists that full compliance with these requirements is neither a necessary nor a sufficient condition for the achievement of justice. It is not a necessary condition because compliance is a matter of degree, and 'maximal possible conformity is on the whole undesirable (some controlled administrative discretion is better than none)'.[34] Since the rule of law is only one of many political ideals, it can occasionally be outweighed by others.[35] It is not a sufficient condition because '[t]he rule of law ... is compatible with gross violation of human rights';[36] '[m]any forms of arbitrary rule are compatible with the rule of law. A ruler can promote general rules based on whim or self-interest, etc., without offending against the rule of law.'[37]

It is clear that such a thin conception of the rule of law does not require legislative power to be limited by a bill of rights. It is not aimed at eliminating all kinds of arbitrary governmental powers, but only those whose

---

[28] J. Raz, 'The Rule of Law and Its Virtue', in *The Authority of Law* (Oxford: Clarendon Press, 1981) 210 at p. 212.

[29] T. Endicott suggests that it has, in 'The Impossibility of the Rule of Law' *Oxford Journal of Legal Studies* 19 (1999) 1 at 1–2.

[30] Raz, 'The Rule of Law and Its Virtue'. Other examples are J. Waldron, 'The Rule of Law in Contemporary Liberal Theory' *Ratio Juris* 2 (1989) 79; R.S. Summers, 'The Principles of the Rule of Law' *Notre Dame Law Review* 74 (1999) 1691.

[31] Raz, 'The Rule of Law and Its Virtue', p. 211.

[32] *Ibid.*, p. 214.   [33] *Ibid.*, pp. 214–17.   [34] *Ibid.*, p. 222.

[35] *Ibid.*, pp. 219 and 228–9.   [36] *Ibid.*, pp. 220–1.   [37] *Ibid.*, p. 219.

exercise can unfairly upset citizens' expectations about their legal obligations and rights. Extremely unjust or tyrannical laws that are well known
to citizens, because they are prospective, adequately publicised, clear and
relatively stable, are not objectionable on rule of law grounds.

It does not follow that on this conception, legislative power can be completely uncontrolled. Raz suggests that judicial review of parliamentary
legislation is needed to ensure conformity with the formal requirements
of the rule of law, although he adds that this is 'very limited review'.[38] He
does not elaborate, but presumably means that the judiciary should be
able to invalidate legislation that violates the requirements that legislation
be prospective, adequately publicised, clear, relatively stable, and not confer excessive discretion on administrators.[39]

But judicial review of legislation on these grounds would be highly
impractical. Consider the last four of them. None can possibly be absolute. Legislators cannot be required to ensure that every detail of every
new law is brought to the attention of every citizen, that no law include
any vague terms, that the law never be changed, or that no administrator ever be granted any discretionary power. Such requirements would
be highly undesirable from the point of view of the rule of law itself. For
example, the rule of law would suffer if citizens were immune from any
law not specifically brought to their attention. In addition, some vagueness in the law is often necessary if the law is not to be irrational and
arbitrary.[40] The same is true of legal change, and the granting of discretionary powers to administrators.[41] These requirements raise questions
of degree – of more or less – that can be settled only by value judgments.
What methods of publicising new laws give citizens adequate notice of
them? When does vagueness in the law, legal change and administrative
discretion cease to be desirable and become excessive? These questions
require legislators to balance the competing values at stake, and there is
no good reason to think that judges would be better at doing this.

The requirement that seems most conducive to judicial enforcement
is that of prospectivity. But not even this should be made absolute.
Legislation that changes the law retrospectively can often be justified,

---

[38] *Ibid.*, p. 217.
[39] If Raz meant merely that judicial review of 'manner and form' requirements is required,
       that would not ensure that legislation conformed to the requirements of the rule of law
       that he lists.
[40] See Endicott, 'The Impossibility of the Rule of Law', 4–8.
[41] *Ibid.*, pp. 8–9, on legal change; Raz, 'The Rule of Law and Its Virtue', p. 222, on adminis-
       trative discretion.

sometimes by the rule of law itself. In rare cases even retrospective changes to criminal laws can be justified. The strongest argument against retrospectivity is that it is unfair to upset expectations reasonably based on the state of the law at a particular time. But if expectations are based on mistaken but reasonable beliefs about the state of the law, retrospective legislation may be justified to prevent them from being upset. In addition, some expectations, such as an expectation of legal immunity for grossly immoral conduct, are unworthy of respect, and the threat of subsequent retrospective legislation might help deter such conduct.[42] In other words, it might help to deter the exercise of lawless, arbitrary power. That is why '[t]he trial of the German leaders at Nuremberg by a law made *ex parte*, *ex post facto*, and *ad hoc* has been hailed as a vindication of the rule of law'.[43] Recent legislation retrospectively made it an offence against Australian law for persons in Europe during the Second World War, who may have had no connection with Australia at the time, to have committed 'war crimes'.[44] The legislation was justified, notwithstanding its retrospective operation. Moreover, even legitimate expectations can be outweighed by considerations of justice. It has been persuasively argued that the British Parliament in 1965 was entirely justified, by considerations of justice and equality, in enacting legislation that not only retrospectively abolished a legal right to compensation, but reversed a recent judicial decision awarding compensation to a particular party.[45] For similar reasons, judicial decisions altering the common law may justifiably have retrospective effects, even in criminal cases, which can no longer be concealed by resort to the old 'fairy tale' that judges only declare what the law has always been, and do not really change it.[46] German courts dealing with the prosecution of former East German border guards for shooting people attempting to enter West Berlin have felt justified in adopting novel interpretations of relevant East German

[42] For an excellent and thorough discussion of all these themes, see Palmer and Sampford, 'Retrospective Legislation'.

[43] F. Wormuth, 'Aristotle on Law', in M.R. Konvitz and A.E. Murphy (eds.), *Essays in Political Theory Presented to George H. Sabine* (New York and London: Kennikat Press, 1948) 45 at p. 45.

[44] See *Polyukhovich* v. *Commonwealth* (1991) 172 CLR 501.

[45] A.L. Goodhart, 'The Burmah Oil Case and the War Damage Act 1965' *Law Quarterly Review* 82 (1966) 97, discussing the *War Damage Act* 1965 (UK), which retrospectively deprived the Burmah Oil Company of a right to compensation that had been upheld by the House of Lords in *Burmah Oil Co. Ltd* v. *Lord Advocate* [1965] AC 75.

[46] A recent example is *R* v. *R* [1992] AC 599, in which the House of Lords in effect abolished the common law immunity of a husband against being convicted for the rape of his wife, in the course of a case involving a husband charged with that very offence.

laws that in effect amended them retrospectively.[47] The following conclusion to a thorough examination of retrospective legislation in Australia would no doubt be true of most countries:

> Retrospective law-making is neither particularly rare nor necessarily evil. It plays a more significant part in Australian legislation than most would imagine. Much of it can be justified. Some of it is very contentious and the justification should be subject to intensive and, hopefully, rigorous debate … However, the fact that the proposed statute is 'retrospective' should merely be the starting-point of that debate, not its conclusion.[48]

The same goes for another requirement often regarded as central to the rule of law, although not discussed by Raz. This is that legislation should be general in scope rather than aimed at particular persons. Even today, legislation that changes the legal rights or duties of particular legal persons is often regarded as justified, for example, to enable major public works, or unique enterprises such as the staging of an Olympic Games, to proceed expeditiously, by conferring special legal powers and rights on their organisers. Sometimes Acts of indemnity or amnesty, which relieve individuals or groups of liability for breaches of the law, are justified. Usually such breaches have been inadvertent. But as Dicey pointed out, in extraordinary situations of internal disorder or war, the executive might have to break the law deliberately 'for the sake of legality itself' – to uphold the rule of law – and then seek an Act of Indemnity.[49]

  To sum up, thin conceptions of the rule of law do not require that legislative power be limited by a bill of rights. Moreover, there are powerful reasons for denying that even the specific requirements they do impose should be constitutionally guaranteed and made judicially enforceable. They are too vague, and defeasible.[50]

V   'Thicker' conceptions of the rule of law

To argue that the rule of law requires something like a bill of rights, one must first defend a thicker conception of the principle. Rather than attempt that task myself, I will leave it to those who seek to make such

---

[47] See J. Rivers, 'The Interpretation and Invalidity of Unjust Laws', in D. Dyzenhaus (ed.), *Recrafting the Rule of Law: The Limits of Legal Order* (Oxford: Hart Publishing, 1999) p. 40.

[48] Palmer and Sampford, 'Retrospective Legislation', p. 277.

[49] Dicey, *An Introduction*, pp. 411–13.

[50] There may be one or two narrow exceptions – such as a prohibition on Acts of Attainder – but this does not undermine the general conclusion.

an argument. I will consider whether the argument is plausible even if a thicker conception is acceptable.

It is pertinent to observe that proponents of thicker conceptions do not always maintain that legislative power should be limited by judicially enforceable rights. The International Congress of Jurists that met in New Delhi in 1959 endorsed a thick conception of the rule of law, which Raz criticises for mentioning 'just about every political ideal which has found support in any part of the globe during the post-war years'.[51] Yet the Congress did not insist that judicial review of legislation was an inherent requirement of the rule of law. Instead, the 'Declaration of Delhi' stated that:

> In many societies, particularly those which have not yet fully established traditions of democratic legislative behaviour, it is essential that certain limitations on legislative power ... should be incorporated in a written constitution, and that the safeguards therein contained should be protected by an independent judicial tribunal; in other societies, established standards of legislative behaviour may serve to ensure that the same limitations are observed ... notwithstanding that their sanction may be of a political nature.[52]

No doubt the desire to achieve consensus among the representatives of many different legal systems, some of which included doctrines of legislative sovereignty, was one reason for this conclusion. But there are sound reasons of principle for doubting that the rule of law, even when broadly conceived of, requires that legislative power be subject to judicially enforceable limits.

It has frequently been pointed out that the rule of law should not be taken to such extravagant lengths as to condemn all discretionary power. 'No government has ever been a government of laws and not of men in the sense of eliminating all discretionary power. Every government has always been *a government of laws and of men*.'[53] Rules and discretionary power are both essential, and the problem is to find the best combination, given the nature of the task in question and the social and political context in which it must be performed. Among the many powers of government that are necessarily discretionary – which include many judicial as well as other powers – is the legislative power. For practical reasons,

---

[51] Raz, 'The Rule of Law and Its Virtue', p. 211.
[52] 'The Declaration of Delhi', International Congress of Jurists, New Delhi, India, 5–10 January, *Journal of the International Committee of Jurists* 2 (1959) 7 at 8.
[53] K.C. Davis, *Administrative Law: Cases-Text-Problems* (6th edn) (St Paul, Minnesota: West Publishing Co., 1977), p. 26.

it is necessarily the most discretionary of all governmental powers; in addition, unlike all others, it is discretionary by definition. Since it is by definition the power to make new laws and repeal old ones, it cannot be completely controlled by pre-existing laws.

Of course, it does not follow that a legislature's powers cannot be limited by special pre-existing laws that it cannot itself amend or repeal. But as to whether doing so would necessarily enhance the rule of law, two possible problems spring to mind.

The first possible problem is that limiting a legislature's powers in this way may achieve little more than to shift the objectionable phenomenon – legally unlimited legislative power – to a higher level. For how could the law-making power of whoever imposed those limits be itself limited? There cannot be an infinite regress of law-makers able to impose limits on the authority of each one in turn.

One possible solution would be to rely on limits to law-making power that have not been imposed by any human law-maker, such as natural law. But on closer inspection, this would not help. According to natural law theories, the most fundamental legal standards are moral standards prescribed by God or built into nature. But as Jeremy Waldron has persuasively argued, even if such a theory could satisfy our worries about the objectivity of moral standards, none has yet been able to provide a methodology that makes moral disagreements any easier to settle.[54] The identity and content of moral standards is often highly controversial and interminably debatable. If they are to perform the legal function envisaged, some official or institution must be accepted as having ultimate authority to decide which of the competing views will have legal force. A decision of that kind is best described as a legislative decision. But that takes us back to our starting point: that the decision-maker could not be controlled by any standards other than those it decides it ought to be controlled by.

A related difficulty, or perhaps the same one differently described, is this. One of the core requirements of the rule of law is that decision-making be governed by legal norms whose identity and content can be ascertained without excessive difficulty. They must be relatively clear, adequately publicised, and so on. It would seem difficult for moral standards, whose identity and content are often elusive and controversial, to play that role. If so, decisions that are controlled only by moral standards

---

[54] J. Waldron, 'The Irrelevance of Moral Objectivity', in R. George (ed.), *Natural Law Theory: Contemporary Essays* (Oxford: Clarendon Press and New York: Oxford University Press, 1992) and in J. Waldron, *Law and Disagreement* (Oxford: Clarendon Press and New York: Oxford University Press, 1999).

are not subject to the rule of law – which is no doubt obvious, since that is the complaint about legislative sovereignty that we started with. If legislatures governed by nothing more determinate than moral principles are not subject to the rule of law, why should judges be regarded any differently?

An alternative solution would be to rely on 'reason', as opposed to 'will'. Aristotle's conception of government by law rather than by men is said to have amounted to government by reason.[55] But the bare concept of reason, like Kant's categorical imperative, lacks substantive content – which it needs if it is to perform the function required of it. And the moment we try to give it content, we run into the same problem that plagues moral argument: the requisite content is inherently controversial and debatable. In practice, pure reason is unavailable to us: we only have access to the variable, fallible and disputable reason of particular human beings. To say that the rule of law is the rule of reason rather than of will is to beg the question of *whose* reason should rule, and whose should be overridden or discounted on the ground that it is mere 'will'. Should law be based ultimately on the reason of elected legislators, or the reason of judges? It is difficult to see why the rule of law would favour judges rather than legislators.

Another alternative would be to rely on long-standing and immutable customs, rather than deliberately made laws, to limit legislative power. That would be the situation in Britain if the thesis that it has a 'common law constitution', which controls even Parliament, were correct – and if the common law consisted of customs that are 'found but not made' by the judges. But among many difficulties with this idea, it is far too conservative and would cripple the power of elected legislatures. In the modern world of rapid change, legislatures cannot be prohibited from reforming or abolishing customary practices, especially ones that have come to seem oppressive and unjust. Imagine women being told, in the 1970s, that elected legislatures could not validly enact legislation inconsistent with the customary practices that defined their traditional role as wives and mothers! A judicially enforceable 'customary constitution' would be workable only if the judges were able and willing to allow some customs, but not others, to be reformed or abolished. But on what grounds could they do so? Custom itself could not provide them. The judges would have to exercise moral judgment, of exactly the same

---

[55] J. Sklar, 'Political Theory and the Rule of Law', in Hutchinson and Monahan (eds.), *Ideal or Ideology*, 1 at pp. 1–3.

kind that legislatures currently exercise in deciding when to override established customs.

It seems, then, that at the foundation of any modern legal system there must be a human law-maker able to make the requisite moral judgments and override even long-standing customs. But this returns us to the problem of how to subject the power of that law-maker to the rule of law. F.A. Hayek believed that the rule of law would be properly safeguarded only if the power to enact ordinary legislation were limited. But he also believed that the only effective way of doing so was for a superior law-maker to enact a binding constitution, and that its power to alter that constitution could not itself be limited. Ultimately, therefore, the rule of law could not be 'a rule of the law, but [only] a meta-legal doctrine or a political ideal ... [that] will be effective only in so far as the legislator feels bound by it. In a democracy this means that it will not prevail unless it forms part of the moral tradition of the community.'[56] On this view, Hobbes was essentially right to claim that at the foundation of any legal system there must be an unlimited and arbitrary power, which cannot itself be bound by law. It is merely a question of whether that power should belong to a monarch, a legislature, a court, 'the people', or some combination of them. Ultimately there cannot be a government of laws rather than a government of men, or people (as we should now say). And if there must be a government of people at the foundation of any legal system, there are obvious reasons to prefer a government of 'the people', or their elected representatives, to a government of judges.

But this kind of Hobbesian thinking is now discredited.[57] There is no logical reason that prevents constitutions from including provisions that are unalterable, even by the process of constitutional amendment they themselves prescribe, and some constitutions do so. A prohibition on amendment, like any other element of a rule of recognition, can be effective provided that it is generally accepted as binding.[58] Of course, a constitution prohibiting the amendment of some part of it could be overturned by revolution, but the same is true of any constitution.

On the other hand, although constitutional provisions can be made legally unchangeable, it might be unwise to do so, because it is impossible accurately to foresee what changes may be justified in response to unpredictable future events. Each generation should be equally free to reform

---

[56] Hayek, *Constitution of Liberty*, p. 206.

[57] See Goldsworthy, *The Sovereignty of Parliament*, pp. 236–8.

[58] See H.L.A. Hart, *The Concept of Law* (Oxford: Clarendon Press, 1961), ch. 4.

its laws – including its constitution – as it deems appropriate. Only very abstract moral principles, such as democracy, justice and the rule of law, should be regarded as immutable. But they can be embodied in a variety of constitutional arrangements. For example, the rule of law may require that legal disputes be decided by independent judges, but not that any particular judicial structure be preserved for all time. On this view, for practical rather than logical reasons, nothing in a constitution should be made unamendable. If so, we return once again to the problem we started with: the existence of a law-making power that is unlimited by law.

However, this may be less of a problem at the level of constitutional amendment than at the level of ordinary legislation. It can plausibly be argued that the rule of law would be enhanced by the imposition of constitutional limits on ordinary legislative power, even if the extra-ordinary power of constitutional amendment cannot be limited, and can be used to release the ordinary legislative power from those limits. This is so provided that the amending power is more difficult to use than the ordinary legislative power, and is therefore less likely to be used (or abused). So the first possible problem with the idea of limiting legislative power by superior laws is not insurmountable.

The second possible problem is less tractable. It is difficult to think of any limits even to ordinary legislative power that should be made absolute, in the sense of being indefeasible come what may. All human rights can justifiably be outweighed or overridden by ordinary legislation in some circumstances. All the rights that are central to modern bills of rights are sometimes outweighed by other important rights and interests. For example, legislatures enact, and courts uphold, laws restricting free speech in order to protect public safety, public decency, national security, confidential information, privacy, reputation, and so on. Even the right to life itself can be outweighed in unusual situations, such as where self-defence is involved. There is no subject-matter over which legislatures should be denied power altogether. All that should be denied them is the unjustified exercise of their power. That is why, in the enforcement of a bill of rights, the crucial question is never simply whether a law intrudes on some protected subject-matter such as 'speech', but whether it does so unjustifiably.[59]

---

[59] In the Canadian Charter of Rights this necessary value judgment is made explicit: s. 1 provides that the Charter 'guarantees the right and freedoms set out in it subject only to such reasonable limits prescribed by law as can be demonstrably justified in a free and democratic society'.

This has been known for centuries. It has frequently been pointed out that if rigid limits are imposed on legislative power, and judges appointed to enforce them, the legislature may be disabled from doing good as well as from doing evil, and the disadvantages of the former disability may outweigh the advantages of the latter. The need for some power to alter or override any law whatsoever, if only in an emergency, is a theme that runs through centuries of disquisitions on sovereignty.[60] The seventeenth-century lawyer, Bulstrode Whitelocke, argued that no subject-matter could safely be excluded from the reach of legislative power, because what might be required in order to promote peace and good government could not be predicted in advance.

> If it be demanded, what is the subject matter of that good and peace? It will be said: every thing, according as accidents and emergencies, may make application of them, in the wisdom, and judgment, of a public council. And consequently, all matters whatsoever may be accounted legislative affairs, within the authority of parliament.[61]

Constitutional limits to legislative power should therefore not be rigid and absolute. They should allow scope for justifiable qualifications and exceptions. But to decide whether and to what extent a qualification or exception is justified requires judges to make judgments of political morality. They must assess and compare the variable, context-dependent moral weights of all the competing rights or interests that may be affected. The problem with regarding this as a necessary requirement of the rule of law is similar to the problem, mentioned previously, with relying on moral principles as limits to legislative power. The contents of a judicially enforceable bill of rights are principles of political morality whose 'interpretation' is indistinguishable from moral and political philosophy. The fact that they are written is irrelevant. Whether elected legislators, or judges, have ultimate authority to weigh up competing moral principles, and decide which of them ought to prevail, their decisions necessarily depend on controversial judgments of political morality. But why should judges, charged with weighing up and balancing moral principles in concrete cases, be regarded as bound by the rule of law if an elected legislature, responsible for translating the same moral principles into legislation, is not? The judges may or may not be better at making moral

---

[60] See Goldsworthy, *The Sovereignty of Parliament*, 'Index of Subjects', p. 319 ('necessity of power to override law in emergencies').

[61] B. Whitelocke, *Whitelocke's Notes upon the Kings Writt for Choosing Members of Parliament [etc]* (London: C. Morton, 1766), vol. 2, p. 335; see also *ibid.*, p. 185.

judgments affecting rights, but that is beside the present point. The rule of judges may be preferable to the rule of legislatures, but we are concerned with the rule of law. If in both cases decisions involve weighing up competing abstract moral principles, why should the judges, but not the legislature, be regarded as 'ruled by law'? The identity of the decision-maker may be different, but the character of the decision itself remains the same. As J.A.G. Griffith put the point:

> For centuries political philosophers have sought that society in which government is by laws and not by men. It is an unattainable ideal. Written constitutions do not achieve it. Nor do bills of rights. They merely pass political decisions out of the hands of politicians and into the hands of judges or other persons. To require a supreme court to make certain kinds of political decisions does not make those decisions any less political.[62]

This point can be taken further. It can be argued, counter-intuitively, that judicially enforceable bills of rights might not only fail to enhance the rule of law, but actually diminish it. Whether or not bills of rights enhance the rule of law must depend on how they affect the exercise of judicial power as well as legislative power. When bills of rights transfer the ultimate review of legislation from legislatures to judges, they make the law that is likely to be applied by the judges less predictable. Instead of being bound to apply legislation, the judges are authorised to reject it for what are essentially reasons of political morality. Judgments of political morality are generally less predictable than judgments about the proper meaning and interpretation of legislation, which depend on the meanings of words and the probable intentions of legislators in enacting them.[63] As Atiyah and Summers argue, content-oriented standards, such as moral principles, generate more uncertainty in the law than do source-oriented (pedigree) standards.[64] In general, legislation that is alleged to violate constitutional rights does not obviously do so. It is usually possible to make reasonable arguments on both sides, and courts then decide such cases in the same way that legislatures do: by making finely balanced and controversial judgments of political morality, and settling outstanding disagreements by majority vote.

---

[62] J.A.G. Griffith, 'The Political Constitution' *Modern Law Review* 42 (1979) 1 at 16.

[63] Of course, they are not always less predictable. Some issues of political morality are obvious and uncontroversial (such as the immorality of torturing children), and some issues of statutory interpretation are not (words and legislative intentions can both be obscure).

[64] See P.S. Atiyah and R.S. Summers, *Form and Substance in Anglo-American Law* (Oxford: Clarendon Press, 1987), p. 53.

Whether legislation will be subject to constitutional challenge, and whether a challenge is likely to be successful, are often difficult to predict. Legislation that has been widely relied on for some time may unexpectedly be challenged and held invalid, possibly as a result of a perceived or predicted change in judicial philosophy.

All this necessarily produces greater uncertainty about what laws are binding, which should be of some concern to proponents of the rule of law. Indeed, the rule of law has traditionally been concerned much more with the exercise of judicial and executive powers than that of legislative power. As previously observed, legislative power is by definition difficult to limit by pre-existing laws. By contrast, judicial power is by definition ideally suited to it, because in large part it is precisely the power dutifully to apply pre-existing laws. Chief Justice John Marshall expressed this idea in exaggerated terms when he said: 'Judicial power, as contra-distinguished from the power of laws, has no existence. Courts are the mere instruments of the law, and can will nothing.'[65] This is exaggerated because judges necessarily exercise powers other than that of applying pre-existing laws. For example, they must sometimes supplement the law, when it is insufficiently determinate to resolve a dispute, or stray from the strict terms of a law in order to do 'equity' in particular cases. Nevertheless, their ability to stray beyond pre-existing law in exercising such powers is supposed to be strictly confined. In his list of the principles of the rule of law, Robert Summers includes this requirement:

> [A]ny exceptional power of courts or other tribunals to modify or depart from antecedent law at point of application [should] be a power that, so far as feasible, is itself explicitly specified and duly circumscribed in rules, so that this is a power the exercise of which is itself law-governed.[66]

Of course, Summers is not concerned here with judicial power to invalidate legislation inconsistent with a bill of rights. But his requirement reflects the traditional conception of the judicial function, which does not sit altogether comfortably with the enforcement of bills of rights. In effect, they confer on judges a power to veto legislation retrospectively, on the basis of judgments of political morality.[67] It is a power similar to

---

[65] *Osborn v. Bank of the United States* (1824) 22 US 738 at 866.

[66] Summers, 'The Principles', 1694.

[67] Of course, in theory the power is not one of changing the law at all, but merely of declaring what the law has always been. But insofar as its exercise is based on unpredictable judgments of political morality, its effect can be indistinguishable from that of retrospective repeal.

that exercised by upper houses of review, except that it is exercised after legislation has been enacted.[68] This involves adding to the judicial function a kind of power traditionally associated with the legislative function, except that the unpredictability inherent in its exercise is exacerbated by its retrospective effects. That is why, on balance, it may diminish rather than enhance the rule of law.

This problem cannot be evaded by definition. If 'law' is defined to mean any norm that is enforceable by the courts, then it might seem that to subject legislation to review according to judicially enforceable principles is *by definition* to increase the rule of law. That definition is the subject of debate between so-called 'exclusive' and 'inclusive' legal positivists. The former assert that constitutionally protected rights are principles of political morality, which judges are legally required to enforce, and not principles of law.[69] But even if the inclusive legal positivists are right to argue that such rights are both principles of political morality *and* principles of law, that would not settle the question of the effect of bills of rights on the rule of law. This is because, as previously noted, the rule of law is not the same as the rule of the law. The issue is one of substance, not terminology: it concerns the extent to which governmental acts overall are subject to the rule of the right kinds of laws, such as those that enhance predictability. The rule of other kinds of laws can diminish, rather than enhance, the rule of law. Requiring judges to enforce abstract, vague and defeasible principles of political morality arguably have precisely that effect.

The point is not that bills of rights are therefore unjustified. It is merely that they may diminish rather than enhance the rule of law. The point holds even if they do so only to a small extent. But other political principles, such as justice, must also be taken into account. The rule of law is not the rule of justice. It can be argued that judicial enforcement of a bill of rights is likely to enhance substantive justice, to such an extent that

---

[68] It is no accident that judicial review of legislation emerged in the United States as an alternative to non-judicial mechanisms for ensuring legislative compliance with constitutional laws. For example, New York State created a Council of Revision, which included the Governor, Chancellor, and Supreme Court Justices, armed with a limited but not final veto over legislation deemed inconsistent 'with the spirit of [the] constitution'. Similar institutions, regarded as political rather than judicial, were proposed in other states. At the Philadelphia Convention, which proposed the new federal Constitution for ratification by the states, James Wilson and James Madison supported judicial review only after a majority rejected their proposal for a Council of Revision. See Goldsworthy, *The Sovereignty of Parliament*, pp. 212–13.

[69] See W. Waluchow, *Inclusive Legal Positivism* (Oxford: Clarendon Press, 1994).

substantive justice outweighs the rule of law. Whether or not that is so is beyond the scope of this essay. Either way, it is substantive justice, not the rule of law, which best explains the attractions of bills of rights.

In reply, it might be argued that judicial enforcement of a bill of rights is no more unpredictable in its effects than the exercise of some other judicial powers, such as that of overruling earlier decisions at common law, or applying moral principles enshrined in legislation or case-law. But perhaps that merely shows that other judicial powers also tend to diminish rather than enhance the rule of law, whatever their overall merits may be.

It might also be pointed out that judges exercise their powers according to strict procedures that guarantee natural justice: they must reach a decision only after all interested parties have had an opportunity to be heard, they must give reasons for their decisions, and so on. It might then be argued that even if the substance of their power is little different from that of a legislative house of review, their procedures ensure that it is less likely to be exercised in an arbitrary fashion. But it should not be forgotten that legislatures also exercise their power in accordance with mandatory procedures. Legislation in modern democracies does not issue from the mouth of an omnipotent individual. It emerges from the deliberations of a complex, artificial body whose composition, procedures and forms of legislation are defined and structured by laws and standing orders.[70] The laws that govern these matters of composition, procedure and form include the entire legal apparatus of representative democracy. Standing orders may be self-imposed and not legally binding, but many judicial procedures are also self-imposed, including the duty of courts to give reasons for their decisions.

This question of procedures is important. It is often too readily assumed that any legislature whose power is not subject to substantive legal limits has 'arbitrary' power that is uncontrolled by law. But laws governing the composition of legislatures, and the procedures and forms by which they must legislate, in themselves exert a powerful kind of legal control.[71] Historically, the requirement that legislation desired by a monarch could not be enacted without the assent of representatives of the community was a major advance for the rule of law, even though this did not involve the imposition of substantive limits on the power to legislate. The same goes for the other constitutional reforms

---

[70] Dicey relied partly on this: *An Introduction*, 402 and 405.
[71] See A.L. Goodhart, 'The Rule of Law and Absolute Sovereignty' *University of Pennsylvania Law Review* 106 (1958) 943 at 950–2.

that gave birth to modern representative democracy: the development of bi-cameralism, electoral reform, the extension of the franchise, and so on. Indeed, British constitutionalism has always relied on representation, together with 'checks and balances' internal to the legislative process, rather than substantive limits to legislative power enforced by an external agency.[72] These methods of controlling legislative power exemplify what Kenneth Culp Davis famously called 'structuring', as opposed to 'confining' and 'checking', the exercise of discretionary power.[73] All three methods of controlling by law the exercise of what would otherwise be arbitrary power can legitimately be regarded as contributing to the rule of law.

The extent to which laws governing these matters of composition, procedure and form succeed in preventing the arbitrary or tyrannical exercise of legislative power no doubt varies from one country to another. In Britain, deficiencies in the method by which members of the lower house are elected, the length of time between elections, the domination of the lower house by the executive government, and the lack of an adequate upper house of review, may explain most of the widespread contemporary disenchantment with parliamentary democracy. These alleged deficiencies of the British system of parliamentary democracy as it currently operates should not be mistaken for deficiencies of representative democracy as such. It follows that the best remedy may not be the enactment of a judicially enforceable bill of rights, but reform of the laws that govern the electoral process, the composition of the legislature, and the procedures and forms by which it must legislate. In other words, if the problem is that the electoral process, and checks and balances internal to the legislature, are now ineffective or non-existent, the best remedy may be to reconstitute or reinvigorate them. It is often argued that such reforms would be preferable to an American-style bill of rights on democratic grounds. Why not improve the system of representative democracy rather than diminish it even further? But less obviously, it can also be argued that such reforms would be preferable on rule of law grounds. They could make more effective review or veto of legislation part of the legislative process itself, taking place before legislation is enacted and relied on as law by the community. The alternative of a bill of rights inserts a power of legislative review and veto into subsequent judicial processes, where its exercise on grounds of

---

[72] See Goldsworthy, *The Sovereignty of Parliament*, pp. 7–8, 75, 105–6, 200–1 and 234.
[73] K.C. Davis, *Discretionary Justice, A Preliminary Inquiry* (Baton Rouge: Louisiana State University Press, 1969), chs. 3–5.

political morality can have unpredictable, retrospective effects on legislation that has already been enacted, and may have been relied on as law.

VI Conclusion

My objective has not been to completely discredit the idea of subjecting legislative power to judicially enforceable bills of rights. It has merely been to challenge one increasingly popular argument in favour of doing so: namely, that it is required by the rule of law. I have made the counter-intuitive argument that such a reform might actually detract from the rule of law. I do not claim that this argument is sufficiently powerful to be deployed as a positive argument against bills of rights. But it is useful in a defensive role, to refute the argument that bills of rights are required by the rule of law. Even if they do not detract from the rule of law, they are clearly not required by it. They are certainly not required by 'thin' conceptions of the rule of law, and even if a 'thick' conception is preferable, there are other ways of subjecting the exercise of legislative power to appropriate legal control. Perhaps, in the end, all I have succeeded in doing is to show that the issue is relatively unimportant, both because the rule of law is too indeterminate to provide useful guidance, and because in this context other political principles, such as democracy and justice, are much more important. If so, I will be satisfied.

4

Homogenising constitutions

I Introduction

From the late eighteenth century until recently, the common law world included just two alternative constitutional models for the protection of individual rights. The first, developed in Britain, is the model of parliamentary sovereignty, which reposes primary responsibility for protecting rights in parliaments. The second, developed in the United States, is the model of judicial review, which reposes that responsibility in courts of law. In countries founded by Britain, the first model was established; even when federations were formed, in Australia and Canada, judicial review was adopted only as a means of policing the federal distribution of powers, and not (generally speaking) as a means of protecting rights. Some former British dominions adopted the American model upon or after achieving independence, such as Ireland, India and (more recently) South Africa. But otherwise, the British model predominated throughout the common law world.

Recently, Canada, New Zealand and Britain have adopted 'hybrid' models, which allocate much greater responsibility for protecting rights to courts, without altogether abandoning the principle of parliamentary sovereignty. In Canada, judicial enforcement of the Charter of Rights 1982 is for the most part subject to s. 33, which permits legislatures by express provision to override most of the rights protected by the Charter. To that extent, the principle of parliamentary sovereignty has been retained, although in practice the power of override is seldom used.[1] In Britain, the Human Rights Act 1998 requires courts to 'interpret' (which in practice might mean to some extent 're-write') legislation, wherever possible, to ensure that it is compatible with protected rights. But where that is not possible, the courts cannot declare the legislation invalid; they can only issue a declaration of

---

[1] Discussed in Chapter 8, below.

incompatibility, which may or may not persuade Parliament to make an amendment.

The creation of these hybrid models is clearly a very important development.[2] This is because both the traditional models, of parliamentary sovereignty and of judicial review, are subject to well known objections: the former, for endangering individual rights, and the latter, for undermining democracy. Parliamentary sovereignty has always had domestic critics, who have advocated adoption of the rival model of judicial review. But the grass may not be greener on the other side: an increasing number of Americans now question their own model, and advocate a greater role for legislative supremacy.[3] The apparent need to choose between the traditional models required a judgment as to which of their alleged dangers – to individual rights, or to democracy – was more to be feared. But the hybrid models now offer the possibility of a compromise that combines the best features of both the traditional models, by conferring on courts constitutional responsibility to review the consistency of legislation with protected rights, while preserving the authority of legislatures to have the last word.

In view of the apparent possibility of choice among a variety of constitutional models, it is somewhat surprising to encounter an argument that in reality there is only one basic model for protecting rights common to all Western liberal democracies. In his latest book, Trevor Allan argues that all such democracies are committed to the rule of law, which entails an independent judiciary with authority to invalidate legislation that it regards as inconsistent with various rights, including due process, equality and free speech.[4] This is essentially the American model, but according to Allan, it is implicit in a commitment to the rule of law, and to a concomitant concept of law, that is independent of any written constitution. On his view, rights-protecting judicial review is to a large extent intrinsic to the concept of law in liberal democracies, written constitutions are to that extent superfluous, and alternative models (especially unqualified parliamentary sovereignty) are ruled out by the meaning of 'law'. Every genuine liberal democracy has an unwritten bill

---

[2] See, e.g., S. Gardbaum, 'The New Commonwealth Model of Constitutionalism' *American Journal of Comparative Law* 49 (2001) 707; M. Perry, 'Protecting Rights in a Democracy: What Role For the Courts?' *Wake Forest Law Review* 38 (2003).

[3] M. Tushnet, *Taking the Constitution Away From the Courts* (Princeton: Princeton University Press, 2000); D. Lazar, *The Frozen Republic: How the Constitution is Paralyzing Democracy* (New York: Harcourt Brace, 1996).

[4] T.R.S. Allan, *Constitutional Justice, A Liberal Theory of the Rule of Law* (Oxford: Oxford University Press, 2001).

of rights that is judicially enforceable, whether or not it also has a written bill of rights.

I should declare at the outset that this chapter is the latest round of an ongoing debate between Allan and myself. In an earlier book, Allan attempted to show that the doctrine of parliamentary sovereignty was incompatible with the true foundations of the British constitution, which he purported to clarify through Dworkinian 'interpretation'.[5] I subsequently criticised that attempt, and defended the doctrine's legal and philosophical credentials as a fundamental element of the British constitution.[6] I did so both on legal positivist grounds and, in the alternative, on 'interpretive' grounds that include evaluative as well as descriptive criteria.[7] In his latest book, Allan responds at some length to my criticisms.

But Allan now canvasses broader issues than the doctrine of parliamentary sovereignty in Britain. He is concerned with the nature of constitutionalism in all Western liberal democracies. His critique of parliamentary sovereignty, and advocacy of rights-protecting judicial review, now rests not just on an interpretation of the British constitution in particular, but on a philosophical account of the concept of law to which he believes all liberal democracies subscribe. That account has enormous implications for all those countries. For example, it follows that their courts have authority to protect due process, equality or free speech – if necessary, by invalidating legislation – even if their written constitutions are completely silent on those subjects. This is hardly surprising. If judicial authority to protect these principles can exist in the complete absence of a written constitution, as in Britain, it can also exist in the absence of express provisions in a written constitution. On this view, written constitutions are only part – and arguably, the lesser part – of the full constitutions that courts in liberal democracies are legally bound to enforce. Allan's thesis therefore offers comfort to those who have argued that the United States Supreme Court has authority to enforce 'unenumerated rights', and that the Supreme Court of Canada has authority to enforce unwritten 'constitutional principles'.[8] Furthermore, Allan goes so far as to deny that the written constitution of a liberal democracy can validly be

---

[5] T.R.S. Allan, *Law, Liberty, and Justice, The Legal Foundations of British Constitutionalism* (Oxford: Oxford University Press, 1993).

[6] J. Goldsworthy, *The Sovereignty of Parliament, History and Philosophy* (Oxford: Clarendon Press, 1999), esp. ch. 10.

[7] *Ibid.*, esp. pp. 254 and 271–2.

[8] On the United States literature, see T.B. McAffee, 'Inalienable Rights, Legal Enforceability, and American Constitutions: the Fourteenth Amendment and the Concept of Unenumerated Rights' *Wake Forest Law Review* 36 (2001) 747. On recent Canadian

amended in ways that are incompatible with the rule of law and the fundamental rights it embodies. Here, too, his arguments could be invoked to support a position that has occasionally been defended in the United States.[9]

Before resuming my debate with Allan, I should say at the outset that his book is unquestionably an important contribution to legal theory and comparative public law. It is brimming with insights distilled from many years of reflection on the basic principles of public law in liberal democracies. In analysing those principles and their implications, Allan draws on the case law of many countries throughout the common law world, including Australia, Britain, Canada, India, New Zealand and the United States. He ranges over the whole of public law, administrative as well as constitutional, insofar as civil liberties are concerned, including aspects of criminal procedure and evidence that implicate the relationship between the state and the citizen. He discusses such diverse issues as free speech, due process, equality and discrimination, retrospectivity, ad hominem legislation, civil disobedience and conscientious objection, the right to silence, police trickery, rule-governed versus case-sensitive modes of decision-making, justiciability and 'political questions', constitutional conventions, and locus standi. In developing the concrete implications of his abstract conception of the rule of law, his arguments are always illuminating and often persuasive.

That said, I will concentrate in what follows on the jurisprudential and constitutional arguments that underpin his discussion of substantive issues. I will argue that the former are less persuasive than the latter.

II   The rule of law in liberal democracies

Allan describes his book as 'an essay in general constitutional theory', which attempts 'to identify and illustrate the basic principles of liberal constitutionalism, broadly applicable to every liberal democracy of the familiar Western type'.[10] The most fundamental of these shared principles

jurisprudence, see M. Walters, 'The Common Law Constitution in Canada: Return of *Lex Non Scripta* as Fundamental Law' *University of Toronto Law Journal* 51 (2001) 91.

[9]   On implicit limits to constitutional change, see e.g. the essays by Walter F. Murphy, John R. Vile and Mark E. Brandon, in S. Levinson (ed.), *Responding to Imperfection; The Theory and Practice of Constitutional Amendment* (Princeton: Princeton University Press, 1995).

[10]   Allan, *Constitutional Justice*, p. vii ('Preface'). See also p. 1. Sometimes, though, Allan suggests that he is providing an account of 'all forms of legitimate government': *ibid.*, p. 245.

constitute what is known as the rule of law, which is 'the core of the doctrine or theory of constitutionalism, and hence a necessary component of any genuine liberal or constitutional democratic polity'.[11] In explicating the rule of law, he relies mainly on the work of Fuller, but also on that of Hayek and Dworkin. Each of them, he says, 'illuminates different aspects of an integrated vision of constitutional justice', 'whose requirements any acceptable version of liberal democracy should be expected to satisfy'.[12]

He defends Fuller's claim that compliance with the eight well-known 'principles of legality' is of inherent moral value, but rejects Fuller's argument that this is because it facilitates the governance of human conduct by rules. Allan denies that such a purpose is of inherent moral value.[13] He argues, instead, that compliance with the principles is of inherent moral value because it enhances the autonomy and dignity of citizens. It does this first, by giving them fair warning of the exercise of state power, so they can organize their affairs accordingly,[14] and second, by helping them to evaluate and criticise government coercion, as a result of officials having to act consistently with publicised rules rather than through the secret exercise of unfettered discretion.[15]

Allan concludes that the equal dignity of citizens is 'the basic premise of liberal constitutionalism and ... the ultimate meaning of the rule of law'.[16] 'The citizen of a constitutional democracy is to be honoured as an equal, autonomous, moral agent, who takes responsibility for his own actions.'[17] Indeed, 'the role of the individual moral conscience' is '[a]t the heart of the rule of law'.[18] Ultimately, 'the rule of law is most persuasively understood as an ideal of consent to just laws, freely given by all those to whom they apply'.[19] A legal system committed to the rule of law therefore aspires to every citizen's consent: it seeks the citizen's acceptance that its demands ought morally to be obeyed.[20] Indeed, as we will see, Allan claims that the implicit appeal to the rational consent of the citizen is built into the very concept of law in a liberal democracy.[21]

The two most fundamental principles of the rule of law – due process (or procedural fairness) and equality – are designed to implement this aspiration to popular assent.[22] Compliance with these principles helps to ensure that all government acts can be given a reasonable justification – shown

---

[11] *Ibid.*, p. 1.
[12] *Ibid.*, pp. 25 and 29. Allan also relies on A.V. Dicey's influential examination of the rule of law, pp. 13–21.
[13] *Ibid.*, p. 61. [14] *Ibid.*, p. 62. [15] *Ibid.*, p. 75. [16] *Ibid.*, p. 2. [17] *Ibid.*, p. 6.
[18] *Ibid.*, p. 89. [19] *Ibid.*, p. 90. [20] *Ibid.*, pp. 6, 24–5 and 64–5.
[21] *Ibid.*, pp. 65–7, discussed in section IV, below. [22] *Ibid.*, pp. 16–17.

to serve a defensible view of the common good, in which all citizens are accorded equal respect and dignity.[23] For example, due process requires that citizens be provided with an initial right to be heard, so that their interests and point of view must be taken into account, and a subsequent right to require that government actions be justified both legally and (therefore) morally before an independent judge.[24] The principle of equality requires that 'all forms of government discrimination between persons should be adequately justified … [and] reasonably related to legitimate public purposes, reflecting an intelligible view of the common good, consistently maintained, and compatible with the basic principles of the legal and constitutional order'.[25] Those basic principles include a number of 'fundamental freedoms', of thought, speech, conscience and association, which are necessary pre-requisites for the moral autonomy of citizens, including their ability to evaluate whether their putative legal obligations are truly obligatory.[26]

Allan anticipates the criticism that this account of the rule of law is so substantive that it amounts to a complete theory of justice. He describes the rule of law as 'a modest theory of *constitutional* justice', which does not guarantee a perfectly just society, and may even form part of a political culture that is hostile to liberty and careless of human dignity.[27] But it is hard to understand how this could be, given that the rule of law is based on the principle of the equal dignity of all citizens, and the principle of equality requires that all forms of discrimination must be justified to independent courts and, indeed, to every individual citizen affected by them. It is not easy to reconcile his claim that the rule of law is only one political virtue among many, and does not guarantee a just society, with his other claim that at the heart of the rule of law is the ideal of consent on the part of every citizen to just laws.[28] These claims pull in different directions. I suspect that Allan's theory would also not seem particularly modest if a list were made of all the procedural and substantive rights that he maintains are protected from legislative interference.

III   Institutional authority

According to Allan, the rule of law has institutional implications. It 'assumes a division of governmental powers or functions that inhibits the

---

[23] *Ibid.*, p. 2.   [24] *Ibid.*, pp. 8–9 and 79.

[25] *Ibid.*, p. 22. The requirement of consistency is essentially what Dworkin has called 'integrity', p. 40.

[26] *Ibid.*, pp. 3, 23 and 90–5.   [27] *Ibid.*, pp. 29 and 23; see also pp. 202 and 218.

[28] See n. 19, above.

exercise of arbitrary state power'.[29] It requires that the legislature enact general laws, 'formulated in ignorance of the consequences of their subsequent application to particular (identifiable) cases'.[30] An elected legislature broadly representative of the community is particularly well suited to this task.[31] It must be separate from the executive, which is responsible for applying those laws 'impartially to each case without fear or favour'.[32] 'The division of power ensures that public officials cannot create new rules and enforce them at the same time, making people subject to their will as it evolves from case to case.'[33] The rule of law also 'assumes the existence of' independent courts, which act as servants of the constitutional order as a whole rather than of the other branches of government. It is the duty of the courts to ensure that the legislature and the executive comply with the principles of the rule of law, and to invalidate their acts if they do not.[34]

Allan describes the rule of law as a 'rule of reason', because it requires all government actions affecting individuals to be justified, by being shown to serve a defensible view of the common good.[35] The question naturally arises: justified, and defensible, to whom? His theory might be seen as representing a jurisprudential tradition maintaining that law must ultimately be founded on 'reason' rather than 'will'. But that tradition must grapple with a dilemma. It is all very well to assert that judges must ultimately be bound by 'reason', rather than the arbitrary 'will' of a legislature, and that therefore they can invalidate legislation that they deem unreasonable. But what about their own decisions? There are two alternatives. On the one hand, consistency would seem to require that no-one else can be bound by the judges' arbitrary 'will', and therefore that other officials and citizens can invalidate judicial decisions that they deem unreasonable. But as the same reasoning would apply to the decisions of every legal official, and ultimately of every citizen, that risks the complete unravelling of legal authority, and the collapse of law into anarchy.[36] On the other hand, if judicial decisions are legally authoritative, and binding on other officials and citizens even if they deem those decisions unreasonable, the initial denial that legislation can enjoy the same authority seems dubious. Why should courts, but not legislatures, have authority to make decisions that legally bind other officials and citizens regardless of their own views of the merits?

Allan prefers to grasp the first horn of this dilemma, although this is sometimes obscured by his descriptions of judicial authority as 'ultimate'

---

[29] Allan, *Constitutional Justice*, p. 32.   [30] *Ibid.*, pp. 31, 38 and 48.   [31] *Ibid.*, p. 50.
[32] *Ibid.*, p. 39.   [33] *Ibid.*, p. 48.   [34] *Ibid.*, pp. 2, 3, 12–13, 31 and 41.   [35] *Ibid.*, p. 2.
[36] See Goldsworthy, *The Sovereignty of Parliament*, pp. 255–71 and 274–5.

or 'final'. For example, not only is it the 'ordinary constitutional function' of a court to be 'necessarily concerned with the legality, and hence validity, of legislation or an executive order or decision'.[37] 'It is ultimately for the courts to determine the validity of statutes in accordance with the principle of equality and with due regard for the other essential constituents of the rule of law.'[38] He refers to 'the legal sovereignty of the courts, as the final arbiters of the law in particular cases'.[39] 'The authority of the court's decision' – 'its claim to be a uniquely valid resolution of the matter in dispute' – rests on 'its character as a fully reasoned response to specific, and opposing, arguments' concerning 'questions of legal principle'.[40]

I understand these statements to refer only to the relationship between courts and the other branches of government. In other words, judicial decisions are 'ultimate' or 'final' from their point of view. But they are not ultimate or final from the point of view of ordinary citizens. One of Allan's most distinctive and frequently repeated claims is that 'the rule of law attributes responsibility for the identification of "valid" law, in the last analysis, to the conscience of the individual citizen, acting on his own understanding of the needs of the common good'. It follows that 'purported "laws" or policies that are gravely unjust (in the citizen's view) lack both legal and moral authority'.[41] '[T]he rule of law is ultimately premised … on the "sovereign autonomy" of the individual citizen.'[42] He says that 'it is right to treat the judge's duty as analogous to that of the ordinary citizen: each is equally entitled, and bound, to act on the basis of what he believes to be the correct interpretation of the law.'[43] Individuals who repudiate oppressive laws play 'a role analogous to that of a constitutional court, or its common law equivalent'.[44] On this view, legal judgment, being a species of moral judgment, partakes of the same inescapable autonomy as moral judgment. Every individual is ultimately responsible for deciding how he or she morally, and therefore legally, ought to act.[45]

This is a striking claim, which directly challenges legal positivist understandings of authority, law and the rule of law. Before examining that challenge in the next section, it is worth noting that some lingering uncertainties are left by Allan's different descriptions of judicial authority

---

[37] Allan, *Constitutional Justice*, p. 162.   [38] *Ibid.*, p. 3.
[39] *Ibid.* See also p. 202: 'judicial sovereignty as regards the application of law to particular cases'.
[40] *Ibid.*, p. 190.   [41] Both quotes p. 7. See also pp. 220–1.   [42] *Ibid.*, p. 281.
[43] *Ibid.*, p. 217.   [44] *Ibid.*, p. 312.   [45] *Ibid.*, p. 89.

to invalidate legislation that violates the rule of law. First, legal officials are also individual citizens, and so if judicial decisions are not ultimately or finally authoritative for individual citizens, it is not entirely clear how they can be for officials of the other branches of government. They are presumably just as entitled as ordinary citizens to act on the basis of their own sovereign autonomy. Secondly, if judges possess only the same authority as ordinary citizens, then it is arguably confined to very unusual circumstances of quite extreme legislative injustice. This seems to be confirmed by Allan's choice of horrific Nazi laws as examples of the kind of legislation that judges would be justified in holding invalid.[46] If, on the other hand, it is part of the judges' 'ordinary constitutional function' to invalidate legislation inconsistent with the rule of law, then arguably it is properly exercisable much more frequently – even routinely – with a much lower threshold of deference owed to legislative judgment.

IV The concept of law

Allan urges us to 'reject an ethically neutral, "positivist" definition of law, in favour of the "liberal" conception implicit in the constitutional ideal of the rule of law'.[47] He relies heavily on a Fullerian account of the concept of law, while also invoking Dworkin in support.[48] 'Fuller's basic (if partly disguised) jurisprudential endeavour', he claims, was 'to illuminate the value-laden character of the concept of law on which liberal democracy is founded'.[49] On this view, 'the basic values of human dignity and individual autonomy are taken to be instrinsic features of law.'[50] He takes Fuller to have demonstrated 'that there are modest, but significant, constraints on the nature and content of law': most importantly, 'the principles of procedural due process and equality impose constitutional limits on the kinds of enactment that can qualify as "law".'[51]

Allan has to show first, that certain principles constitute the 'rule of law', and secondly, that they are not only political ideals within Western liberal democracies, but also internal to the concept of law itself. That is essential to his claim that putative legislation inconsistent with the rule of law is not valid law. He says that '[a]t the heart of the analysis of the rule of law, as an ideal of constitutionalism, lies [a] distinctive concept of

---

[46] *Ibid.*, pp. 69–72. [47] *Ibid.*, p. 75.
[48] The emphasis is on Fuller at, e.g., p. 202. At p. 72, Dworkin's theory of law is said to be 'squarely built on these Fullerian foundations'.
[49] *Ibid.*, pp. 62 and 66–7. See also p. 6. [50] *Ibid.*, p. 6. [51] *Ibid.*, p. 202.

"law".[52] But argument is required to demonstrate that the concept 'law' in the phrase 'the rule of law' is necessarily the same as the concept in professional legal usage. It is far from obvious that it is. Although the content of 'the rule of law' is contested, it is generally agreed to be a morally laden principle or ideal. Many legal positivists, who maintain that the concept 'law' in professional legal usage is morally neutral, therefore deny that 'the rule of law' is identical to 'the rule of *the* law' in that professional sense (and vice versa).[53] They insist that 'the rule of law' is a distinctive concept, which includes moral criteria that are inapplicable to the concept of 'law' per se. They might therefore agree with much of Allan's analysis of 'the rule of law', and acknowledge that it is an ideal to which (for the most part) liberal democracies aspire, but reject his claim that it also informs the meaning of 'law' per se and therefore the validity of legislation.

Allan maintains that we currently have more than one concept of law. One is broader, morally neutral, and descriptive, and the other is narrower, morally loaded, and evaluative. He argues that whatever the utility of the former in the general descriptive jurisprudence pursued by legal positivists, the latter is essential to practical reasoning about authority and obligation (legal and moral) within the context of a liberal democracy, including the reasoning of judges.[54] But there is some tension in Allan's account between, on the one hand, statements suggesting that he is merely analyzing a concept of law that we already accept – at least implicitly – and on the other hand, statements suggesting that he is recommending a revised concept of law, on the ground that it would advance our moral aspirations and practical deliberations.[55]

He insists that the ideal of the rule of law, and the concomitant concept of legal obligation, 'forge the link between law and justice'.[56] A government committed to the rule of law is committed to respecting the dignity and autonomy of its citizens, and therefore to seeking its citizens' assent to the legal obligations it purports to impose on them. Allan infers from this that those purported obligations are genuine obligations only if the citizens ought to assent to them, and therefore that legal obligations are a species of moral obligation. 'If the law should be understood as demanding the citizen's assent, the existence of legal obligations (as

---

[52] *Ibid.*, p. 6. See also p. 1.
[53] For general discussion, see Chapter 3, above.
[54] Allan, *Constitutional Justice*, pp. 6 and 71–2.
[55] The word 'implicit' is frequently used: see, e.g., pp. 64–6. For examples of statements suggesting a revisionary purpose, see *ibid.*, pp. 62, 64, 66 and 72.
[56] *Ibid.*, pp. 61 and 67.

opposed to illegitimate demands) must be in every case a matter of moral judgment.'[57] I am not sure that I understand exactly how this argument proceeds. At one point, he observes that the law claims to be authoritative, and to impose obligations, and argues that such claims 'differ from mere assertions of will or power in seeking the co-operation of the citizen as a rational, responsible and autonomous agent'.[58] But that argument seems independent of the liberal democratic concept of the rule of law, because as Raz has insisted, it is true of law everywhere that it claims to be authoritative and to impose obligations.[59]

But however the argument proceeds, its conclusion does not follow from its premise. A government might be committed to seeking its citizens' assent to the legal obligations it imposes on them – and might even sincerely believe that they ought to assent to them – without their having to be conceived of as moral obligations. Legal obligations could be conceived of as the government's posited declarations of what its citizens morally ought to do. It does not follow from the fact that the government seeks the citizens' agreement with its posited declarations, that if a citizen rightly disagrees with one of them, it is not a genuine legal obligation. All that follows, at most, is that the citizen has no moral obligation to obey that legal obligation – which is, of course, just how a legal positivist would describe the situation. Allan needs an additional premise to establish that in liberal democracies, legal obligations are conceived of as moral obligations rather than as posited declarations of moral obligations.

Allan does advance a further argument to support his conclusion. This is that legal positivist conceptions of law and legal obligation offer no guidance to those faced with difficult practical questions concerning authority, obligation and law enforcement. Whatever analytical clarity legal positivism may achieve, it offers 'empty counsel in the face of pressing moral dilemmas, which demand legal solution'.[60] This may be so – but then, legal positivism does not purport to offer solutions to moral dilemmas. Allan quotes Fuller's complaint that the positivist severance of law from morality removes any way of weighing the obligation to obey the law against other, competing moral obligations.[61] But this is not so.

---

[57] *Ibid.*, p. 67, see also p. 218.   [58] *Ibid.*, p. 65, see also p. 202.

[59] J. Raz, *Ethics in the Public Domain, Essays in the Morality of Law and Politics* (Oxford: Clarendon Press, 1994), pp. 215–26.

[60] Allan, *Constitutional Justice*, pp. 68–9.

[61] *Ibid.*, p. 68. Later Allan objects that positivists cannot account for the citizen's moral obligation to obey the law, p. 218. But legal positivists can account for such an obligation, provided that it is understood to be a contingent rather than a necessary and universal obligation.

Legal positivists would concede that legal obligations and moral obligations are, in themselves, incommensurate. This is because legal obligations, unlike moral obligations, are matters of fact, which by themselves have no practical, action-guiding force. But positivists would argue that legal obligations are usually (although not necessarily) accompanied by moral obligations to obey the law, and it is always possible to weigh those moral obligations against competing ones. There is no practical difficulty here at all.

Allan also appeals to practical dilemmas confronting West German courts after the Second World War. By adopting a non-positivist conception of law similar to Fuller's, those courts were able to declare egregious Nazi statutes legally void, and therefore ineffective to deprive Jewish citizens of basic rights or to provide Nazi spies and informers with a defence of legality.[62] But as H.L.A. Hart argued in response to Fuller, there is more than one way to achieve the same results. He argued that openly retrospective legislation would be a more frank and clear-headed way of dealing with the problem. It is worth noting that Allan's preferred Fullerian solution also involves an element of retrospectivity: it involves culling the Nazi statute book to accord with a concept of law that Allan claims is distinctive to liberal democracies, and which therefore was presumably alien to Nazism itself. As Hart observed, a 'case of retrospective punishment should not be made to look like an ordinary case of punishment for an act illegal at the time'.[63] In addition, the maxim 'hard cases make bad laws' might be invoked here – rephrased as 'hard cases make bad concepts of law'. It is arguably unwise to advocate a particular concept of law for all liberal democracies on the ground that it has proved useful in dealing with a very unusual situation that existed only at the birth of one or two of them, and not thereafter, especially when that situation can be dealt with in other ways. Even if that concept was practically useful in that unusual situation, it might prove to be counter-productive in other situations that are much more likely to arise in a majority of liberal democracies.[64]

Allan summarises his position thus: 'it serve[s] no useful purpose, relevant to any question of practical governance, to attribute legal validity to a measure that wholly lack[s] moral legitimacy and ought, so far as

---

[62] Ibid., p. 69.

[63] H.L.A. Hart, The Concept of Law (2nd edn) (Oxford: Clarendon Press, 1994), pp. 211–12.

[64] See Goldsworthy, The Sovereignty of Parliament, pp. 267–9, for general discussion of this issue.

possible, to be resolutely resisted'.[65] But at least four arguments can be made to the contrary.

The first argument, which forms an influential strand in the legal positivist tradition, is that making legal validity partly dependent on moral criteria would create an undesirable risk of legitimating unjust laws and regimes. The argument has recently been developed at length by Liam Murphy, who concludes that:

> So long as a moral test is thought to play a role in the determination of what the law already is, there will be the danger that apparent laws will be given the benefit of the doubt, assumed to be true law, and thus assumed to have satisfied the moral test. And there is the second danger too, that when official directives are regarded as unjust, this will be characterized as a kind of internal malfunction on the part of the legal regime, not in itself cause for great alarm, certainly not cause to subject the legal system as a whole to searching criticism.[66]

It could possibly be argued by those sympathetic to Allan's normative commitments that his project risks just this kind of complacency. He is arguing, in effect, that constitutions such as those in Britain and Australia do not need fundamental reforms to ensure adequate protection of rights, because such protection is already enabled by their abstract commitment to the rule of law. On his view, the courts already possess all the powers they need, and if they are not exercising them properly, criticism should be directed at the judges rather than at the constitution.

The second argument emphasises the need for precision and predictability in legal reasoning. The argument is made by Finnis, although he is not a legal positivist.[67] He distinguishes between the moral senses of words such as authority, obligation and validity, when they are used in unfettered practical reasoning that is ultimately governed by moral norms, and the purely legal senses of the same words when they are used by lawyers for professional purposes.[68] He argues that these distinctions are motivated by sound, practical reasons for insulating legal reasoning from the general flow of practical reasoning.[69] One such reason concerns predictability. An important objective of law is to bring 'definition, specificity,

---

[65] Allan, *Constitutional Justice*, p. 72.
[66] L. Murphy, 'The Political Question of the Concept of Law', in J. Coleman (ed.), *Hart's Postscript, Essays on the Postscript to the Concept of Law* (Oxford: Oxford University Press, 2001), p. 371.
[67] Allan notes and responds to Finnis's argument in *Constitutional Justice*, p. 76.
[68] J. Finnis, *Natural Law and Natural Rights* (Oxford: Clarendon Press, 1980), pp. 27, 234–7, 276–280, 282–3, 309–12, 316–321 and 354.
[69] *Ibid.*, pp. 277–80, 309–12, 316–20, 354–7 and 363–6.

clarity, and thus predictability' to human affairs, by way of rule-governed institutions charged with establishing a stable framework for social inter-action.[70] Evaluation of authority, obligation and validity, in their moral senses, often leads to conclusions of degree – of 'more or less' – that are too imprecise for lawyers' purposes. Such concepts have, in legal usage, an invariant, 'black and white' quality because the law seeks to be 'relatively impervious to discretionary assessments of competing values'.[71]

The third argument, an extension of the second, applies this concern for clarity to the legal rules that allocate decision-making authority among legal institutions. It alleges that this allocation of authority might be eroded or confused if it also depended on unwritten, abstract and impre-cise moral criteria. The argument is most powerful where the authority of democratically elected legislatures is concerned. In developing his theory of 'ethical positivism', for example, Tom Campbell places considerable weight on the dangers to democracy of unelected judges claiming author-ity to invalidate laws enacted by elected legislatures, on the basis of vague moral criteria of authority and validity.[72]

Finnis, too, emphasises the importance of basic legal norms that confer law-making authority on some institutions rather than others, and limit when and how they may exercise it.[73] When judges swear to do justice 'according to law', they accept these basic norms, which constitute the framework for legal reasoning 'for intra-systemic purposes (rather than for private moral reasoning about the law)'.[74] Finnis accepts that judges, no less than citizens, are entitled to evaluate laws from the broader perspec-tive of practical reason. They might be justified in condemning an egre-giously unjust law as lacking authority and validity, in the unrestricted, moral senses of those terms, and in an extreme case, as undeserving of obedience. But there are sound practical reasons for insulating questions of legal validity and authority from such moral evaluations.

These reasons can perhaps be illuminated by considering Allan's claims that legal and moral authority and validity are ultimately indis-tinguishable, and that legal authority and validity are ultimately matters for determination by individual citizens.[75] Legal positivists would argue that although individual citizens must ultimately decide whether or not

---

[70] *Ibid.*, p. 268.   [71] *Ibid.*, pp. 312 and 319–20.
[72] T. Campbell, 'Democratic Aspects of Ethical Positivism', in T. Campbell and J. Goldsworthy (eds.), *Judicial Power, Democracy and Legal Positivism* (Aldershot: Ashgate/Dartmouth, 2000), p. 3.
[73] Finnis, *Natural Law*, pp. 312 and 317.   [74] *Ibid.*, pp. 317–18.
[75] See text to nn. 41–45, above.

they ought morally to obey legally valid legislation, the obliteration of any distinction between moral and legal validity would tend to obscure the likely costs and benefits of such decisions. As Allan acknowledges, there are powerful reasons, concerning the maintenance of legal authority, why individuals often ought morally to obey legislation that they regard as morally wrong.[76] These reasons are likely to be obscured if legislation that is deemed morally wrong is for that reason also deemed legally invalid. This is because disobeying legally invalid legislation does not directly challenge legal authority, and therefore does not obviously threaten its maintenance. The threat is more plainly apparent if the legislation in question is regarded as legally valid. To put this another way: while it is clear that there can be good reasons for obeying legislation that is immoral but legally valid, it is not so clear that there can be good reasons for obeying legislation that is both immoral and legally invalid.

Much the same point bears on how we should think about judicial obedience to Parliament. Allan and I agree that judges should disobey egregiously immoral legislation.[77] I suspect that we also agree that outright disobedience is an extra-ordinary response – a remedy of last resort – that should be reserved for quite exceptional circumstances. We agree, in other words, that the judges' normal stance should be one of obedience, albeit tempered by strict interpretation of legislation impinging on common law rights. But whereas I conceive of disobedience as an exercise of moral authority, which overrides the judges' legal duty, Allan conceives of it as an exercise of both moral and legal authority. I regard the distinction between legal and moral authority as a conceptual device that helps prevent the extra-ordinary response of disobedience being resorted to excessively, thereby eroding the normal judicial stance of obedience, and undermining democracy. I previously showed that precisely this concern contributed to the historical development of the doctrine of parliamentary sovereignty.[78] Allan, on the other hand, is motivated by the opposite concern, that adherence to the distinction might deter judges from departing from their normal stance of obedience when necessary, leading to craven judicial acquiescence in egregious injustice. That is also a legitimate concern, but not necessarily the paramount one:

> The price that must be paid for giving judges authority to invalidate a
> few laws that are clearly unjust or undemocratic is that they must also be

---

[76] Allan, *Constitutional Justice*, pp. 76 and 221.
[77] Goldsworthy, *The Sovereignty of Parliament*, pp. 261–70.
[78] *Ibid.*, pp. 178–82, 196 and 267–9.

> given authority to overrule the democratic process in a much larger num-
> ber of cases where the requirements of justice or democracy are debatable.
> The danger of excessive judicial interference with democratic decision-
> making might be worse than that of parliamentary tyranny, given the
> relative probabilities of their actually occurring.[79]

This leads to the fourth argument. For the reason just given, the desirability of judicial authority to invalidate legislation is a question of institutional design that cannot have any straight-forward and universally
applicable answer. Much depends on the culture, social structure and
political organization in which each legal system operates.[80] No single
answer will fit all cases. For example, it now seems that hybrid constitutional models might strike an attractive compromise between the
competing traditional models. The point is that legal positivism is neutral between all the options: it is compatible with parliamentary sovereignty, full judicial protection of constitutional rights, and the various
hybrid models. But Allan's non-positivist theory is not neutral: it builds
moral criteria into the concept of law in such a way that judicial review of
fundamental rights is required by definition. Excluding alternative constitutional models by definitional fiat would severely hamper practical
institutional design. That is a further reason for legal positivists to argue
that their concept of law is superior for practical purposes.

These four arguments are not, of course, necessarily conclusive. But
they demonstrate that the question of which concept of law is superior
for practical purposes is far from easy. Allan needs to provide much more
argumentation to rebut them.

Worse still for Allan, it is not obvious that the answer he gives greatly
assists his main thesis. That thesis concerns what concept of law does
in fact prevail in liberal democracies such as Britain, not what concept
of law ought to prevail for reasons of practical utility. Showing that one
concept of law would be superior to an alternative, in terms of practical
utility, does not show that it already prevails. Allan's own text sometimes
suggests that he is recommending a revised concept of law, rather than
analysing a concept already in use.[81] He would no doubt reply that he is
engaged in Dworkinian interpretation, a partly evaluative exercise, rather
than purely empirical description. But interpretation is not purely evaluative either: any plausible interpretation must satisfy a 'dimension of fit'

---

[79] *Ibid.*, p. 269.
[80] *Ibid.*, p. 279. See also W. Sadurski, 'Judicial Review and the Protection of Constitutional
Rights' *Oxford Journal of Legal Studies* 22 (2002) 275.
[81] See n. 55, above.

as well as a 'dimension of morality'.[82] Opponents of legal positivism deny that 'what the law is' can be cleanly separated from 'what the law ought to be'.[83] But even they accept that there is a distinction: no-one argues that the law is whatever it ought to be. The same goes for concepts of law.

Since liberal democracies have in fact adopted very different constitutional models, they surely cannot accept the uniform concept of law that Allan recommends. Otherwise, those democracies that have not adopted his preferred model would be guilty of misunderstanding and systematically misusing their own concept of law, which is implausible. Allan comes close to claiming that they are guilty of this, when he asserts that 'the doctrine of absolute or unqualified parliamentary sovereignty, though generally treated as a characteristic feature of English law, is none the less seriously confused as a matter of constitutional theory'.[84] But there must be some basis within local practice for this assertion: some evidence that despite what senior legal officials usually say, they do not really accept that Parliament is sovereign. That is the crucial issue, to which I now turn.

V The rule of law as law

Allan acknowledges that his project requires him to show that his conclusions are sound not only as a matter of abstract political theory, but also as a matter of substantive law.[85] In other words, it is one thing to construct a normative theory of the rule of law, by fitting together the contributions of philosophers such as Fuller, Hayek and Dworkin. It is another thing to show that the theory accurately describes, or (for Dworkinians) interprets, the constitutions of the liberal democracies he is concerned with.

Britain poses the toughest test for Allan where, he concedes, 'important individual liberties and safeguards are widely thought to be wholly at the mercy of an omnipotent legislature'.[86] Indeed, he acknowledges that A.V. Dicey's insistence on the unqualified nature of parliamentary sovereignty 'has become established as current orthodoxy'.[87] Given the long history of the doctrine of parliamentary sovereignty, and the frequency with which it has been affirmed by judges throughout the twentieth

---

[82] See n. 7, above.   [83] Allan, *Constitutional Justice*, p. 71.
[84] *Ibid.*, p. 201.   [85] *Ibid.*, p. 4.   [86] *Ibid.*, p. 5.
[87] *Ibid.*, p. 13. See also p. 201: it is 'generally treated as a characteristic feature of English law'.

century, Allan must attempt to show that it is an 'error' attributable to a 'failure to understand the full implications of the rule of law'.[88]

He maintains that there is '[a] general commitment to certain foundational values that underlie and inform the purpose and character of constitutional government, at least as it has been understood in the Western democracies'.[89] For example, 'it is a basic premise of a liberal, democratic constitutional order that the legislature is bound by fundamental principles of equality and procedural due process'.[90] A critic might agree that this is true of Britain, but only if 'bound by' does not entail judicial enforceability. Senior legal officials in Britain have long regarded Parliament as bound by such principles as a matter of political morality and constitutional convention, rather than judicially enforceable law.

Allan, of course, regards this as insufficient protection of the rule of law. But where, in addition to constitutional conventions, might we find a commitment to these foundational values in the British constitution? He refers to the 'constitutional role' of the common law 'in reflecting and preserving the rule of law'.[91] Indeed, he describes the common law as the ultimate foundation of the British constitution, and claims that the authority of Parliament is itself conferred by the common law.[92] This is a claim that I previously disputed. I argued that the fundamental norms of the British constitution could not be regarded as creatures of common law in the modern sense of judge-made law.[93] Allan now concedes my principal contention. 'Goldsworthy rightly reminds us', he says, that a rule of recognition 'does not rest on the practices and convictions of the judiciary alone'.[94] '[I]t is undoubtedly true ... that the power of judges to settle constitutional questions depends in the last resort on the acquiescence of other senior officials.'[95] Fundamental secondary rules such as rules of recognition are constituted by a consensus among the most senior legal officials of a legal system, from all branches of government. The common law can be described as the ultimate foundation of the British constitution only in an older sense of 'common law', meaning a body of custom (in this case, custom among senior legal officials) that the courts have recognised, but did not unilaterally create.[96] Allan must show that there is a general

---

[88] *Ibid.*, pp. 5 and 13. See also p. 201: it is 'seriously confused as a matter of constitutional theory' and 'mistaken'.

[89] *Ibid.*, p. 4.   [90] *Ibid.*, p. 232.   [91] *Ibid.*, p. 240.

[92] *Ibid.*, pp. 139, 225, 229, 243 and 271.

[93] See Chapter 2, above, and Goldsworthy, *The Sovereignty of Parliament*, pp. 238–43.

[94] Allan, *Constitutional Justice*, p. 219.   [95] *Ibid.*, pp. 223–4.

[96] Chapter 2, above, and Goldsworthy, *The Sovereignty of Parliament*, p. 243.

commitment to the rule of law, as he understands it, not just in ordinary doctrines of judge-made common law, but implicit in the official consensus that constitutes Britain's constitutional foundation. He says that:

> … legal validity ultimately depends on compliance with basic constitutional values or assumptions: for it is these values, reflecting considerations of justice and propriety (however conceived), that account for the consensus, at least among officials, on which the survival of any system of government depends.[97]

But since Allan agrees that the issue turns on the consensus among senior legal officials that underpins the legal system, one might expect him to carefully examine the evidence of what that consensus actually is. An example of relevant evidence is the government's White Paper that accompanied the Human Rights Bill when it was introduced into the House of Lords in 1997. It reaffirmed the doctrine of parliamentary sovereignty, and asserted that a power to invalidate Acts of Parliament is something 'which under our present constitutional arrangements they [the judges] do not possess, and would be likely on occasions to draw the judiciary into serious conflict with Parliament. There is no evidence to suggest that they desire this power, nor that the public wish them to have it.'[98] A second example is a lengthy discussion that took place in the House of Lords in 1996, concerning the relationship between the three branches of government. The present (then Shadow) Lord Chancellor, Lord Irvine of Lairg, criticised statements by senior judges challenging the doctrine of parliamentary sovereignty as 'unwise', and disparaged the alternative they advocated as 'obsolete'.[99] Two of those judges, Lords Woolf and Cooke, were present, and neither mounted a defence of the opinions that Lord Irvine criticised. Lord Woolf expressed confidence that the judges would faithfully obey every statute that he could contemplate Parliament enacting.[100] The then Lord Chancellor, Lord Mackay, and Lord Wilberforce, strongly affirmed Parliament's sovereignty.[101]

These are just two examples of a mountain of evidence that could be assembled to demonstrate that the doctrine of parliamentary sovereignty is, as Allan actually concedes, the 'current orthodoxy'. Statements to that effect, by judges as well politicians, are both numerous and explicit. The

---

[97] Allan, *Constitutional Justice*, p. 219.
[98] *Rights Brought Home: The Human Rights Bill, Presented to Parliament by the Secretary of State for the Home Department* (October 1997), 2.13.
[99] *Parliamentary Debates, Fifth Series*, House of Lords, vol. 572, 5 June 1996, 1254–1313.
[100] *Ibid.*, 1273.   [101] *Ibid.*, 1310 and 1268 respectively.

counter-evidence that Allan presents is, by comparison, either sparse, or inexplicit and inconclusive.

His main strategy is to rely on cases in which courts interpret legislation narrowly and sometimes non-literally, to give effect to the presumption that traditional common law rights and liberties should not be infringed.[102] He says that 'it is when we turn to the interpretative power of the courts ... that we discover the dual nature of sovereignty in the British constitution' (whereby the courts possess 'legal sovereignty' as the final arbiters of individual cases).[103] He offers two different justifications for this interpretive practice, but seems reluctant to choose between them. The first is fully consistent with parliamentary sovereignty. For example, after explaining why general rules are necessarily insensitive to morally relevant circumstances in some individual cases, he comments that in applying legislative rules the courts

> ... should seek to limit adverse consequences, incidental to the statutory purpose. Quite apart from overriding constitutional limitations, it is usually reasonable to assume that a general rule was not intended to cause serious harm to individuals without any (or sufficient) countervailing benefit to the public good. The discovery of such *implicit* qualifications ... is none the less entailed by an intelligent construction of the 'statutory meaning': such assumptions show proper respect for the legislators' general good faith and moral integrity.[104]
>
> It is unlikely, in practice, that members of the legislature will have specifically addressed the precise question of interpretation that the court must now decide; and it is rarely, if ever, safe to assume that a majority of members necessarily agreed (or would have agreed) on any particular answer ... It is precisely because there is no legislative intention with regard to the particular case, as opposed to the general objective to be attained, that judicial interpretation faithful to basic constitutional values is consistent with parliamentary sovereignty, properly understood.[105]

This is the orthodox justification of this interpretive practice, which I happily accept (although Allan seems to think otherwise).[106] We part company only when he offers a second, very different, justification: for example, when he refers to 'the controlling influence of transcendent constitutional

---

[102] Allan, *Constitutional Justice*, pp. 13–14,
[103] *Ibid.*, pp. 13–14; and see also pp. 3 and 201–2.
[104] *Ibid.*, pp. 127–8, emphasis in original.
[105] *Ibid.*, p. 206. See also pp. 45, 210 and 211–12.
[106] See Chapter 9, Section II, Part A below, and Goldsworthy, *The Sovereignty of Parliament*, pp. 250–2.

values', and suggests that Parliament would be unable to override them even by express provision.[107] This is inconsistent with parliamentary sovereignty and, if sound, renders the first justification otiose and disingenuous. It would justify judicial 'interpretations' of statutes that are plainly contrary both to clear statutory language and Parliament's general objective, when the individual case falls squarely within that objective and cannot plausibly be regarded as implicitly excepted from it.[108] This could not plausibly be justified by presumptions of legislative intent. As Allan acknowledges, '[t]here are limits to the extent to which language can be read inconsistently with its "natural" or "ordinary" meaning, even when the wider context is fully taken into account. When enactments are deprived of all practical authority to change existing law, interpretation has indisputably given way to judicial disobedience.'[109]

Allan at one point suggests that the power to determine the meaning of statutes in particular cases may be all that is needed to maintain the rule of law: '[e]ven the most egregious violation of fundamental rights ... may properly be averted' by the presumption that Parliament intends the rule of law to be preserved.[110] He even says that 'legislative supremacy may be accepted with equanimity on the understanding that statutes must always be interpreted in accordance with the rule of law' (i.e., even when that was clearly not Parliament's intention).[111] But elsewhere he acknowledges that:

> [w]hen the courts are confronted by the starkest violations of equality and due process, an interpretive approach may be too weak (or implausible) to provide adequate protection against arbitrary power. It may therefore be necessary ... to repudiate the offending legislative provision altogether.[112]

It is his claim that British courts possess legal authority to do so that is inconsistent with constitutional orthodoxy, and which he fails to substantiate.

Allan does not provide any example of a British court purporting to invalidate a statute. It is true that decisions can be found – especially in the field of administrative law – which raise at least a strong suspicion that the judges defied Parliament, and covertly overrode a statutory provision

---

[107] Allan, *Constitutional Justice*, pp. 202–3 and 205.
[108] See *ibid.*, p. 145.   [109] *Ibid.*, pp. 229–30.
[110] *Ibid.*, p. 207; see also p. 202. At p. 210, the lesser claim is made that the power of interpretation will 'almost always' be sufficient to preserve the rule of law.
[111] *Ibid.*, p. 214; see also p. 210.   [112] *Ibid.*, p. 233.

while pretending to interpret it.[113] But the occasional judicial 'noble lie' does not demonstrate that the legal system as a whole is committed to judges having constitutional authority to do this. As Allan concedes, a rule of recognition 'does not rest on the practices and convictions of the judiciary alone'.[114] Moreover, as I argued previously, 'the fact that the lie is felt to be required indicates that the judges themselves realize that their disobedience is, legally speaking, illicit'.[115]

Another of Allan's strategies is to rely on judicial decisions that protect basic rights indirectly without claiming constitutional authority to do so directly. An example is a decision of the Australian High Court to invalidate a statute that required a state Supreme Court to decide whether a particular, named individual should be imprisoned in the interest of public safety.[116] The High Court managed to do this by manipulating the doctrine of the separation of federal judicial power, which had never before been applied to state courts, rather than by objecting directly to the *ad hominem* nature of the law or its authorisation of preventive detention. Allan says that 'judges have often reached correct legal conclusions – those indicated by a persuasive conception of the rule of law – which are none the less poorly supported by the reasons offered in their defence. A bolder, if less conventional, analysis, that frankly acknowledged the constraints on governmental decision-making inherent in the rule of law, would have strengthened these judicial opinions.'[117] But of course, what is really happening in such cases is that although the judges would prefer to be able to protect certain rights directly, they know that they lack the constitutional authority to do so. They reach the result they desire by bending or stretching other legal doctrines, or inventing new ones, that are less controversial than a naked assertion of the constitutional authority they lack. Allan would prefer them to declare their objective more openly, even though this would be 'less conventional'. But the very fact that they do not openly claim constitutional authority to invalidate legislation in order to protect the rights in question, surely indicates that their legal systems do not recognise that they possess it. That is why they proceed indirectly.

---

[113] Although Allan does not seem to suggest that this was true in the celebrated *Anisminic* case, which is usually cited in this regard: *ibid.*, pp. 211–12.

[114] *Ibid.*, p. 219.

[115] Goldsworthy, *The Sovereignty of Parliament*, p. 252.

[116] *Kable* v. *Director of Public Prosecutions (NSW)* (1996) 138 ALR 577, discussed in Allan, *Constitutional Justice*, pp. 5, 234–40 and 245–6.

[117] Allan, *Constitutional Justice*, p. 5.

Allan claims that any interpretation of the British constitution is likely to be controversial, and that 'in the absence of conclusive "evidence" to resolve such questions of interpretation, the outcome is likely to depend on the strength of a theory's appeal on grounds of political morality'.[118] I submit that the evidence *is* conclusive, and only wishful thinking, not 'interpretation', can evade the conclusion that the doctrine of parliamentary sovereignty is fundamental to the British constitution. Even Dworkinian interpretation must be generally consistent with the thought and practice of participants in the institution being interpreted.[119]

I will next argue that Allan also fails to provide an accurate account of the constitutional law of some other liberal democracies that have written constitutions.

VI   The interpretation of written constitutions

Allan argues that all Western liberal democracies, by virtue of their commitment to the rule of law, are based on similar unwritten, but nevertheless justiciable, constitutional principles. Because these democracies evince 'a general commitment to certain foundational values', they 'should, to that extent, be understood to *share* a common law constitution ... These shared features are ... ultimately more important than such differences as the presence or absence of a "written" constitution, with formally entrenched provisions, whose practical significance may easily be overestimated.'[120] Whether or not they also have written constitutions expressly protecting those principles is therefore less significant than might be thought. Although Britain lacks a written constitution, its courts possess authority to protect those principles, by interpretation or, if necessary, invalidation of legislation. The same goes for Australia, whose written constitution does not expressly protect equality, due process, or freedoms of speech and association.

The Australian High Court in 1992 purported to find some of these principles to be implied by the written constitution, and its more activist members urged it to go even further in that regard. For example, it found that by implication, the constitution guarantees freedom of political speech, and some of the judges have also accepted the existence of an

---

[118] *Ibid.*
[119] Goldsworthy, *The Sovereignty of Parliament*, pp. 253–4 and 271–2.
[120] Allan, *Constitutional Justice*, pp. 4–5. See also *ibid.*, p. 243.

implied right to equality.[121] Allan argues that the reasoning in such cases would often be more plausible if the judges frankly admitted that the true source of these implied rights is not the constitutional text, but deeper, unwritten principles:

> The absence of explicit guarantees of due process and the equal protection of the laws in the Commonwealth constitution, though frequently noted by the High Court's critics, is immaterial if, as I have argued, these principles are inherent in a constitution founded on the rule of law.[122]
>
> [T]he written document is, in effect, subordinated to 'higher principles' of 'natural' or 'fundamental law' – the principles that together embody a coherent theory of liberal constitutionalism.[123]

He rejects counter-arguments based on the undisputed fact that the founders of the Constitution deliberately chose not to include such protections within it:

> It was not open to the framers to choose only partial implementation of the rule of law, or to leave its enforcement to other organs of government, or to rely on the tolerant goodwill of the community at large: such a choice would only have betrayed confusion about the nature of law in a constitutional democracy. Admittedly, the framers may have entertained a narrower conception of the rule of law than that defended in this book, one that accorded a more closely circumscribed role for courts ... We cannot, however, now ignore our own conclusions about the proper reconciliation of these basic legal doctrines [parliamentary sovereignty, and the rule of law]: our present understanding inevitably, and rightly, colours our attempt to make sense of the constitutional scheme. It is only by engaging in the philosophical debate that constitutional interpretation entails that the original text can be made to serve the needs of the polity today. Every generation must read the text in the light of its own understanding of the essentials of legitimate government, as informed by study and experience.[124]

These are remarkable claims. Those who frame a written constitution usually deliberate very carefully about what institutions it should establish, what authority it should confer on them, what rights it should guarantee and protect through judicial review, and so on. But according to Allan, if they make 'mistakes', by not giving courts sufficient authority to protect

---

[121] Discussed in L. Zines, *The High Court and the Constitution* (4th edn) (Sydney: Butterworths, 1997), pp. 202–12, 377–99 and 415–23. There is a much stronger case for implied protection of due process than of free speech or equality.

[122] Allan, *Constitutional Justice*, p. 250.   [123] *Ibid.*, p. 263.

[124] *Ibid.*, p. 264. See also p. 259.

the rule of law, their mistakes should be overridden – by judicial fiat, rather than subsequent constitutional amendment. Neither the framers, nor subsequent majorities who approve of their 'mistakes' (and oppose a constitutional amendment), should be permitted to opt for institutional arrangements that (in Allan's opinion) offer insufficient protection of the rule of law. Indeed, Allan goes so far as to deny that the constitution of a liberal democracy could be validly amended so as to remove judicial protection of fundamental rights essential to the rule of law:

> There are certain freedoms so elementary … that it was unnecessary to mention them in the constitution, and which cannot be destroyed … Popular sovereignty should no more be identified with power to repudiate such values, by resort to constitutional amendment, than equated with ordinary majoritarianism. In the same way that Parliament enacts laws for a constitutional democracy, whose essentials therefore limit the scope of legislative power, a constitutional 'amendment' (if properly so described) must truly serve the polity – the legally constituted political community – for whose governance the constitution provides.[125]

It surely follows from this that s. 33 of the Canadian Charter of Rights should be nullified, at least in part, by Canadian courts. Section 33 expressly authorises Canadian legislatures to override most Charter rights, including rights to equality, free speech and due process, by enacting a 'notwithstanding clause'. Allan would have to say that this contradicts the rule of law as he has defined it. It would then seem to follow that 'it was not open to the framers [of the Charter] to choose only partial implementation of the rule of law', and that Canadian courts should ignore any notwithstanding clause that overrides a right that is essential to the rule of law, thereby treating s. 33 as, in effect, partly invalid.

Allan's assessment of Britain's Human Rights Act 1998 is of interest for similar reasons.[126] The Act authorises courts to declare legislation incompatible with protected rights, if they cannot achieve compatibility through 'interpretation', but it does not mention any power of invalidation. It is undeniably based on an assumption that the courts do not possess such a power, and on a decision not to give it to them.[127] This is problematic for Allan, because he holds that such a power does pre-exist the Act. I would expect him to argue that the Act does not remove that power. He could do so on the ground that the assumption underlying the Act should be ignored, because it is both erroneous, and extrinsic to the Act. On this view, since British courts already possess power to invalidate

---

[125] *Ibid.*, p. 263.   [126] Human Rights Act 1998 (UK).   [127] See text to n. 98, above.

legislation in order to protect rights essential to the rule of law, the Act does not affect that power, but merely grants the courts a supplementary power to declare legislation incompatible with other rights that are not essential to the rule of law. It might be argued, to the contrary, that the assumption and decision underlying the Act justify its being interpreted as impliedly revoking any power to invalidate legislation that the judges may previously have possessed. But Allan would surely reply that this would be invalid, because (like s. 33 in Canada) it would contravene the rule of law. 'It was not open to the framers [of the Act] to choose only partial implementation of the rule of law, or to leave its enforcement to other organs of government.'[128] Surprisingly, however, Allan does not explicitly draw these conclusions, although he does say that 'the new arrangements serve to emphasise the dual sovereignty that previously existed'.[129]

VII   Conclusions

Allan's conception of the rule of law, encompassing rights to due process, equality, free speech and association, and strong judicial review to protect them, is powerful and attractive from a normative point of view. But his claim that it lies at the heart of the constitution of every liberal democracy is implausible. It is no doubt true that all liberal democracies are committed to the rule of law, in some sense of the term, as an ideal. But Allan relies too heavily on claims about what he supposes to be 'implicit' in this ideal.[130] The rule of law is an abstract, vague and contestable ideal, which is compatible with a variety of understandings and institutional arrangements. That is why there is such a variety among the constitutions of liberal democracies. The most fundamental principles to which they are committed may be homogeneous, but the means by which they attempt to implement them are not. Allan could have argued that some of those means are inadequate or misguided, and should be reformed or replaced. Instead, he suggests, in effect, that reforms are unnecessary, because all liberal democracies are committed to protecting the rule of law in much the same way. This homogenisation of constitutions ignores crucial differences that currently exist, and if accepted, could stultify or frustrate creative reforms that do not fit his preferred model.

As previously noted, the two traditional constitutional models are both subject to well known criticisms: that of parliamentary sovereignty, for

---

[128] See text to n. 124, above.   [129] Allan, *Constitutional Justice*, pp. 225–8.
[130] See, e.g., *ibid.*, pp. 64–5.

endangering individual rights, and that of judicial review, for endangering democracy. The constitutional traditions of different countries reflect different views as to which of those dangers is more to be feared, a question that continues to engage legal and political theorists. It is surely possible that the answer varies from one country to another, depending on their different political, social and cultural circumstances.[131] Yet Allan assumes that there is a single answer to the question, which applies to all liberal democracies: namely, that the danger to individual rights posed by legislative sovereignty is more to be feared than the danger to democracy posed by judicial review. Moreover, his approach makes it impossible to achieve the kind of compromise sought by the 'hybrid' models recently adopted in Canada, New Zealand and Britain, which aim to combine the more attractive features, while minimising the dangers, of the traditional models. According to Allan, the rule of law requires that basic rights be protected by an independent judiciary with authority to invalidate legislation if necessary. There can be no compromise.

Allan acknowledges that whether or not legislation is just, or violates rights, is frequently a subject of reasonable disagreement, and that courts should then defer to the outcome of the democratic process.[132] But he fails to acknowledge that much the same is true of constitutions. He is inclined to reject institutional arrangements he disapproves of as erroneous. But whether or not judges should have authority to invalidate legislation is in many communities itself a subject of reasonable disagreement. When a constitution is based on the reasonable opinion that judges should not have it, they should defer to that opinion, at least if the constitution was originally adopted, and is open to amendment, by democratic processes.

---

[131] See n. 80, above. [132] See, e.g., Allan, *Constitutional Justice*, pp. 22 and 163.

5

Abdicating and limiting Parliament's sovereignty

I Introduction

The doctrine that Parliament possesses sovereign – legally unlimited – legislative authority has long been part of the foundation, if it is not indeed the foundation, of Britain's largely unwritten constitution.[1] But the doctrine gives rise to a well-known conundrum: can Parliament's authority be used to limit itself? If it cannot, then it is already limited in this one respect; on the other hand, if it can, then while it is unlimited today it might not be tomorrow. According to the former view, Parliament's unlimited, sovereign authority is 'continuing'; on the latter view, it is 'self-embracing'.[2] On the former view, parliamentary sovereignty is a potential obstacle to effective constitutional reform: any statute purporting to limit Parliament's authority can supposedly be repealed, even by implication, which means that it can be simply ignored. In the past, this view made it difficult for constitutional lawyers to conceive of how Britain's dominions could ever achieve full constitutional independence by lawful, rather than revolutionary, means. Even today, some lawyers have difficulty conceiving of how Parliament could effectively subordinate its authority to a constitutionally entrenched Bill of Rights, to a federal constitution transferring part of its authority to other legislatures within Great Britain, or to a new constitution for the European Union.

In an important new book, Peter Oliver deals with the question of colonial independence, although he hopes that his theoretical insights will shed light on other types of constitutional reform.[3] He offers an

---

[1] J. Goldsworthy, *The Sovereignty of Parliament, History and Philosophy* (Oxford: Clarendon Press, 1999).

[2] H.L.A. Hart, *The Concept of Law* (2nd edn) (Oxford: Clarendon Press, 1994), ch. 7, s. 4. But see the penultimate paragraph in Section II, below, on the ambiguity of the label 'continuing'.

[3] P. Oliver, *The Constitution of Independence, The Development of Constitutional Theory in Australia, Canada and New Zealand* (Oxford: Oxford University Press, 2005). This book will be cited henceforth as '*Independence*'.

explanation of how the 'well-behaved' British dominions[4] – Australia, Canada, and New Zealand – achieved genuine constitutional independence by means that were fully lawful rather than revolutionary. It cannot be disputed that they have achieved genuine independence. The question is how they did so, and whether the means used were fully lawful. Arguably, they could not have been fully lawful if Parliament's authority is continuing. On that view, the argument goes, Britain's dominions must either remain permanently subject to Parliament's continuing sovereignty, regardless of any purported abdication of its authority over them, or achieve independence by revolution – although this could be an amicable 'legal' revolution, consisting of a consensual change in the most fundamental norms of the legal system, and in particular, a repudiation by local officials of the doctrine of continuing sovereignty. Oliver rejects that argument, and proffers a theoretical explanation of the lawful acquisition of genuine independence, based partly on the self-embracing theory of parliamentary sovereignty.

Oliver confronts apparent difficulties with the self-embracing theory. He asks how Parliament could abdicate its authority to change a dominion's law without undermining the validity of that law, which had previously derived from its authority.[5] Borrowing Philip Joseph's analogy, the question is how an axeman sitting on a tree branch can sever the tree's trunk without everything toppling down, himself included.[6] What can replace the authority of Parliament, if it is withdrawn, in supporting the validity of the newly independent legal system? This is not a problem on the 'legal revolution' theory, which postulates a change in the underlying rule of recognition, involving the substitution of a local legal foundation for the previous Imperial foundation. That theory has the additional merit that a newly independent constitution can be regarded as deriving its authority or legitimacy from popular acceptance – 'the sovereignty of the people' – rather than from the grace of the former Imperial Parliament. But according to the self-embracing theory, independence is owed to a final exercise of Imperial authority – an authority that is supposedly necessary for this purpose, but expires the moment after it is exercised. If it is genuinely necessary at one moment, how can it cease to be necessary the next? Oliver argues in response that it is possible for us 'to have the constitutional cake and eat it too: to respect the rule of law and thereby maintain constitutional continuity [i.e., to eschew "legal revolution"]

---

[4] Oliver, *Independence*, p. 1.   [5] *Ibid.*, pp. 284 and 297.   [6] *Ibid.*, p. 263.

while achieving constitutional independence, a new beginning and a foundation based on popular acceptance'.[7]

Someone might object that this long book makes a big fuss about very little: why does it matter if undisputed independence was achieved in a lawful rather than revolutionary manner, if the revolutions were technical, 'legal' ones achieved in a wholly amicable fashion? Oliver tackles this 'so what?' objection head-on, and offers various reasons for the importance of his analysis.[8]

One of his major concerns is that even an amicable 'legal' revolution is inconsistent with the Rule of Law, and since officials and citizens of the 'well-behaved dominions' value that ideal, they may benefit from reassurance that their acquisition of independence did not violate it. Unfortunately, Oliver does not attempt to explain why such a revolution should be thought inconsistent with the substantive values protected by the Rule of Law, such as freedom from the arbitrary and unpredictable imposition of punishments or legal disabilities on people who have no opportunity to anticipate and take steps to avoid them. Nothing in the history of the 'well-behaved dominions' suggests that the process by which they acquired independence jeopardised any of these values. If a 'legal' revolution is such only in a formal, technical sense, perhaps any breach of the Rule of Law is purely formal and technical as well, and therefore, of no real concern. In this regard, Oliver may be proposing a complex, and possibly artificial, solution to a non-existent problem.

But there are other, more theoretical, concerns that motivate Oliver's project. He argues that the orderly creation of two separate legal systems out of one can reveal much of theoretical interest about the nature of legal systems and of sovereignty. He hopes that these revelations will illuminate other processes of constitutional change, such as the reverse process by which separate legal systems merge into a single system (as might happen in the case of the European Union).[9] When a legal system, like Britain's, rests ultimately on unwritten, customary norms, and lacks a clear, generally accepted procedure for changing them, illumination is certainly needed.

Oliver's book is thoroughly researched, carefully argued and well written, and his analysis is a thought-provoking contribution to our understanding of the issues. Nevertheless, I have reservations about it, which I will attempt to explain. His analysis is complex, and to explain my reservations I need to introduce even more complexity – hopefully, without

---

[7] *Ibid.*, pp. 7, 11 and 107.   [8] *Ibid.*, pp. 15–18.   [9] *Ibid.*, pp. 4–6.

vindicating his warning that '[i]f we are not careful, theoretical explanations can cause yet further confusion'.[10] I realise, however, that further confusion may be unavoidable.

II   Some clarifications

One matter that needs to be clarified at the outset is the nature of the legislative authority, with respect to its former dominions, which the 'continuing' theory denies that Parliament can lawfully limit or abdicate, but which it has plainly lost. It is not authority to enact valid legislation with respect to persons or activities within these countries' borders. That is authority to legislate with extra-territorial effect, which Parliament continues to possess with respect to the entire world, enabling it to prohibit people (even the French) from smoking cigarettes in Paris. Even today, Parliament can make it an offence to smoke cigarettes in Sydney, Toronto or Auckland. The point is that in passing such laws, it would be changing British law, but not the law of France, Australia, Canada or New Zealand. By contrast, the authority it has plainly lost with respect to the former dominions is precisely authority to change *their* law. This is a distinction that Oliver appears to overlook, for example, when he says that according to the 'standard' (continuing) theory, Parliament's authority to legislate 'for Australia, Canada and New Zealand' cannot have been terminated, because '[a]s a matter of United Kingdom law ... the Westminster Parliament can legislate for [these countries] just as easily as it can legislate for Mexico and France'.[11] This misses the point, because what has been terminated is authority to change the law of Australia, Canada and New Zealand, and an equivalent authority with respect to Mexico and France has never been claimed. The effect of the termination is to put Australia, Canada and New Zealand in the same position as Mexico and France, and all other countries in the world whose legal systems are independent of Britain's.[12]

Oliver discusses a bewildering variety of theories of parliamentary sovereignty and dominion independence. In analysing them, he frequently invokes Kelsen's concept of the *grundnorm*, and Hart's concept

[10] *Ibid.*, p. 350.   [11] *Ibid.*, pp. 286–7; see also p. 289.
[12] It is also worth noting that the Australian and New Zealand Parliaments both possess the same unlimited extra-territorial authority as the British Parliament, and can legislate with respect to persons and activities in Mexico, France, and anywhere else outside their countries' borders. But they do not foolishly claim authority to change the law of any other country.

of the rule of recognition. I will refer only to the latter. For readers who need a reminder, according to Hart, rules of recognition are among the most fundamental norms of a legal system, and govern what other norms should be recognised as members of their system, or, in other words, as valid laws. For example, a rule of recognition might recognise a written constitution as valid law, as well as any statutes enacted by legislatures, and any rules and principles adopted by courts, in accordance with that constitution.[13] Whether there is a single, complex, rule of recognition in every legal system, or a number of such rules, is unimportant for present purposes. Rules of recognition are intimately related to another kind of fundamental norm – which Hart called rules of change – that author-ise particular officials or institutions to change the law through specified procedures. If a rule of change authorises some institution to make new laws, then consistency demands that the (or a) rule of recognition recog-nise as valid the laws made by that institution. The existence of funda-mental norms of change and recognition depends, in large part, on their being accepted as binding by the most senior officials of all branches of government. They do not owe their existence to acceptance by the judi-ciary alone.[14] Hart himself regarded the doctrine of parliamentary sover-eignty as a fundamental component of the rule of recognition in Britain, and it is also a rule of change.[15] The crucial question concerns the content of this doctrine, and how it can itself be changed.

Oliver uses the terms 'constituent power' or 'constituent process' to denote the power or process by which the most fundamental norms – which is to say, the constitution – of a legal system can be changed. In a legal system such as that of the United States, one of the most basic com-ponents of the rule of recognition is recognition as valid law of the written constitution, and of any amendments made by the procedure prescribed by the constitution for its own amendment. Whatever the original con-stituent power that enacted or created the constitution – and often it would have been an extra-legal, perhaps revolutionary, power – while that con-stitution persists, the only constituent power by which it may be lawfully changed is the amendment procedure that it itself prescribes. Crucial to

---

[13] I use the term 'rule of recognition' to refer only to the most fundamental components of the law governing recognition within a legal system. For an attempt to spell out the rule of recognition in the United States, see K. Greenawalt, 'The Rule of Recognition and the Constitution' (1987) 85 *Michigan Law Review* 621, esp. at 659–60.

[14] For elaboration, see Goldsworthy, *The Sovereignty of Parliament*, pp. 236–43.

[15] Hart, *The Concept of Law*, pp. 144–8.

recognition of the constitution itself as valid law, is the consensus among senior officials that Hart describes, yet it is part of that very consensus that the constitution can only be altered by its own amendment procedure. In other words, the amending procedure is the only legally recognised constituent power, which officials have agreed to be bound by. If the consensus among officials were to change, such that the constitution were replaced or substantially changed without that procedure being followed, the process of change would have to be regarded as extra-legal, and perhaps even revolutionary.[16]

Provisions of written constitutions are often vague and ambiguous, but the content of an unwritten constitution, such as that of the United Kingdom (and that of its former Empire), can be even more obscure. The most fundamental rules of change and of recognition are constituted by a consensus among senior officials, but not having been set down in a written document, their content must often be inferred from orthodox official practice and authoritative interpretations of it. On some important points there may simply be no consensus, and therefore – according to a legal positivist like Hart, at least – no law. The doctrine of parliamentary sovereignty is a case in point. Parliament can be said to have constituent power to change every part of the unwritten constitution except, arguably, that which grants its own law-making authority. Whether Parliament has constituent power to limit or abdicate parts of its own sovereignty is just another way of asking whether its sovereignty is continuing or self-embracing. If Parliament does not have that power, then either its sovereignty is the one element of the unwritten constitution that is legally immutable – like provisions of a written constitution that can never be amended – or it must be subject to some other method of constitutional change. The most likely alternative method is change in the consensus among senior officials that constitutes the fundamental rules of the system. In countries such as the United States, as we have seen, if the consensus among officials changes, so as to replace or change the written constitution without the prescribed amendment procedure being followed, the process of change must be deemed extra-legal, even revolutionary. In Britain, as we will see, it is far less clear that constitutional

---

[16] This proposition is not uncontroversial, as some theorists argue that the United States Constitution can be lawfully changed by other means. See the discussion in D. Dow, 'The Plain Meaning of Article V', in S. Levinson (ed.), *Responding to Imperfection, The Theory and Practice of Constitutional Amendment* (Princeton: Princeton University Press, 1995), p. 117.

changes resulting from changes in official consensus should be characterised in that way.[17] This is partly because it is less clear that officials
have agreed either that some aspects of the unwritten constitution are
immutable, or that they can be changed only by some other, specific procedure (such as statute).

The thesis that Parliament's sovereignty is continuing is ambiguous in
this respect. It might mean merely that Parliament cannot limit or abdicate its own authority, or it might mean that there is no method at all by
which its authority can be lawfully limited or abdicated. I will refer to
the first interpretation as the 'weak' version of the thesis of continuing
sovereignty, and to the second interpretation as the 'strong' version. The
weak version is consistent with Parliament's authority being limited by a
change in the official consensus that constitutes the rule of recognition.
Oliver seems to assume that we must choose between continuing and self-
embracing sovereignty: he does not acknowledge any lawful method of
changing the constitution except by statute. 'Either Parliament as presently constituted ... is frozen for all time as a legally untouchable and
prior rule as in Dicey's version of continuing sovereignty; or Parliament
itself has self-embracing power ...'[18] It follows that he has in mind only the
strong version of continuing sovereignty: if Parliament's sovereignty cannot be limited by statute, then for legal purposes it can never be limited,
alienated or extinguished. Indeed, he asserts that 'the dominant approach
in the United Kingdom was to assume that Parliament's sovereignty was
continuing *and that it must forever be so*'.[19]

I doubt that there is much evidence in favour of the strong version of
continuing sovereignty. In any event, it seems bizarre, because it is naïve
and futile to purport to forbid constitutional change of this kind in per-
petuity. If the rule of continuing sovereignty is constituted by official consensus, then according to the strong version, officials share a consensus
that their consensus must never change: that they and their successors
must *forever* accept that Parliament is sovereign. But obviously they cannot effectively prevent themselves from changing their own minds, let
alone prevent officials in the future from doing so. It might be argued that
even if such a change cannot be effectively prevented, it can be deterred,

---

[17] See Section III, C(2) and (3), below.

[18] Oliver, *Independence*, p. 87; see also p. 297.

[19] *Ibid.*, p. 9, emphasis added. See also p. 312: 'the United Kingdom Parliament can be seen
either (on the continuing version) to remain *perpetually* at the apex of the Australian,
Canadian and New Zealand legal systems, or (on the self-embracing version) to provide
for its own replacement as the supreme amending procedure' (emphasis added).

by condemning it in advance as illegal and revolutionary. But would it not be foolish as well as arrogant to condemn in advance possible changes that, in the unforeseeable circumstances of the future, might be eminently desirable or even necessary? The strong version of continuing sovereignty should be rejected. But the weak version remains plausible: we will soon see that there are good reasons why Parliament should not be able to limit – at least substantively – its own law-making authority.[20]

III   Competing theories

We can now turn to the main alternative theories of how Parliament's authority can be limited, alienated or extinguished. For ease of subsequent reference, I will give each one a label.

A   Limitations imposed by the judiciary: common law constitutionalism

The first alternative is that this can be achieved by the courts changing the so-called 'common law constitution'. According to a theory that has become increasingly popular in recent years, the doctrine of parliamentary sovereignty (and, at least to that extent, the rule of recognition) is a matter of judge-made common law.[21] The judges can therefore modify or repudiate the doctrine, so as to limit or extinguish Parliament's authority. This theory could be deployed to argue that even if prior to independence, the common law of the British Empire held that Parliament possessed continuing sovereignty, judges in former dominions are able to change the common law of their newly independent legal systems so that it deems Parliament's sovereignty to have been permanently terminated.

Oliver mentions this theory, and rightly dismisses it, although without adequate discussion.[22] It is worth reflecting on why it is wrong. If Hart is right about the nature of fundamental rules of recognition, the doctrine of parliamentary sovereignty is constituted by a consensus among the senior officials of all branches of government. It was not (as history confirms) made by the judges alone. Its content is fixed by official consensus, and it is unclear insofar as there is no consensus. It cannot be changed unilaterally by any one branch of government, unless it is part of the consensus that

---

[20]   See final paragraph of Section III, Part B(2), below.
[21]   The latest expression of this theory is in the judgment of Lord Steyn in *Jackson v. Her Majesty's Attorney-General* [2005] UKHL 56 at para. 102.
[22]   Oliver, *Independence*, pp. 10, 80, 300 and 304 n. 71.

it can be so changed, and there is little evidence that there is. Of course, any change to a rule of recognition must start somewhere: someone has to initiate the requisite change in consensus. The courts can attempt to initiate change, but they can succeed only if other branches of government are willing to accept it.[23]

B   Limitations imposed by Parliament

The second alternative is that Parliament can limit or abdicate its own authority. There are at least four versions of this alternative:

(1)   The procedurally self-embracing theory

According to the so-called 'new' theory of parliamentary sovereignty, originating in the work of Ivor Jennings, Parliament can subject itself to manner and form requirements but not substantive limits.[24] On this view, Parliament's authority is procedurally self-embracing but substantively continuing.[25] Oliver argues that the new theory collapses into a full self-embracing theory, because no stable distinction can be drawn between procedural requirements and substantive limits.[26] I disagree, on the ground that courts are capable of sensibly drawing such a distinction, notwithstanding the possibility of difficult borderline cases raising questions of degree.[27] A procedurally self-embracing theory is explained and defended in Chapter 7, below. But in any event, the 'new' theory is irrelevant for Oliver's purposes, because genuine dominion independence involves the termination of Parliament's substantive authority, which cannot be achieved by manner and form requirements. But the new theory remains highly relevant to constitutional reform within the

---

[23] For more detailed discussion, see Chapter 2, Section III above.

[24] Oliver, *Independence*, pp. 80–1.

[25] G. Winterton, 'The British Grundnorm: Parliamentary Sovereignty Re-examined' *Law Quarterly Review* 92 (1976) 591 at 604.

[26] Oliver, *Independence*, pp. 77–9. Winterton expresses the view that it is logically incoherent to maintain that sovereignty can be procedurally self-embracing but substantively continuing, but nevertheless advocates the manner and form theory for pragmatic reasons: Winterton, 'The British Grundnorm', 604–5.

[27] I advocated that the new theory be adopted in Goldsworthy, *The Sovereignty of Parliament*, at pp. 14–15 and 244–5. However, the failure of British courts to accept the theory means that it cannot yet be regarded as an established part of the rule of recognition in Britain. For my views on drawing the necessary distinction, see J. Goldsworthy, 'Manner and Form in the Australian States' *Melbourne University Law Review* 16 (1987) 403 at 417–25 and Chapter 7, below.

United Kingdom.[28] It is worth noting, in this regard, that the new theory is inconsistent with the popular notion that the doctrine of implied repeal is somehow essential to parliamentary sovereignty. As I will later argue in more detail, it is difficult to find any good reason for that notion.[29]

(2)   The full self-embracing theory

Oliver discusses in more depth the theory that 'Parliament had unused (and therefore hidden) powers' (that is, not widely recognised) to limit, procedurally or substantively, or even to abdicate, its own authority.[30] He calls this the 'revised' theory of parliamentary sovereignty, and credits R.T.E. Latham with its first scholarly exposition.[31] It is an extension of the 'new' theory. In my opinion, the main objection to the 'revised', or full self-embracing, theory is essentially the same as the objection to common law constitutionalism. Indeed, the two theories may have originated in the same error. Ivor Jennings seems to have been among the first theorists to mistakenly claim that the doctrine of parliamentary sovereignty was a creature of common law,[32] and then to infer that, since Parliament can change the common law, it can change the law concerning its own authority. The problem is that the doctrine is quite unlike ordinary common law rules and principles, because it was not made by the judges and cannot be unilaterally revised by them. By the same token, it was not made by Parliament: it was not, and could not have been, prescribed by statute, since any such statute would beg the question of Parliament's authority to enact it. It is deeper and more enduring than both statute law and ordinary common law. Since it is the source of Parliament's authority, it is prima facie superior to Parliament, and the notion that Parliament can alter it at will is therefore implausible. It is a creature of consensus among the senior legal officials of all branches of government. It can be altered by Parliament unilaterally only if there is a consensus to that effect among senior officials, and there is little evidence that there is. Indeed, Oliver concedes that the continuing theory has traditionally enjoyed much more support among officials, as well as theorists, than the self-embracing theory.[33] A rule of recognition can be changed only if the consensus that constitutes it changes. Parliament can

---

[28] See the Conclusion to this chapter.
[29] See Chapter 7, Section III, below.
[30] Oliver, *Independence*, p. 9.   [31] *Ibid.*, pp. 85–6.   [32] *Ibid.*, p. 82.
[33] *Ibid.*, pp. 77 and 294. The decision in *Factortame* v. *Secretary of State for Transport (No. 2)* [1991] AC 603 (HL) is arguably consistent with the continuing theory, as Oliver concedes at *ibid.*, p. 10. For discussion of the case, see Chapter 10, Section III, Part C, below.

attempt to initiate such a change, by enacting legislation that purports to limit or abdicate part of its authority, but it will succeed only if the courts are willing to accept it.[34]

It is worth noting that there are reasons of political morality, as well as of jurisprudential analysis, to prefer that the doctrine of parliamentary sovereignty be changed – and Parliament's authority limited – only through a change in the consensus among senior legal officials in general, rather than by either the courts, or Parliament, unilaterally. In other words, there are reasons to prefer the weak version of the theory of continuing sovereignty, together with a theory of change in official consensus, to either common law constitutionalism or the theory of full self-embracing sovereignty. These are reasons of democratic principle. If the courts had authority unilaterally to change the doctrine, they could impose all kinds of limits on Parliament's authority without any democratic input. This would amount to a profoundly undemocratic process of constitutional change. And if Parliament had such authority, a political party with temporary control of both Houses could protect its partisan policies, enacted into law, from amendment or repeal by majorities in future Parliaments, which would also be undemocratic. Full self-embracing sovereignty is undiscriminating: it seems to maintain that Parliament has authority 'to bind itself by any and all means' so long as these means are very explicit.[35] This entails that Parliament can bind itself not only in ways that would generally be regarded as desirable, but also in ways that would generally be regarded as profoundly undemocratic. Requiring a change in the consensus of senior legal officials in general, builds some checks and balances into the process of constitutional change.[36]

(3)   The constituent power theory

Another version of the second alternative is that, although the rule of recognition included the rule that Parliamentary sovereignty was continuing, Parliament possessed constituent (constitution-amending) authority to alter the rule of recognition, in order to give itself

---

[34] See text to n. 23 above.

[35] Oliver, *Independence*, p. 308.

[36] Elsewhere, Oliver has remarked that '[i]ronically, if Parliament's ... self-limiting ambitions are to be checked in the future, Goldsworthy and others may find themselves arguing that it is up to the courts to intervene': P. Oliver, 'Sovereignty in the Twenty-First Century' *KCL* 14 (2003) 137 at 169. In a case such as that mentioned in the previous sentence, I would indeed urge them to do so. See also the second paragraph of the Conclusion, below.

self-embracing legislative authority, and it was then able to abdicate its authority over the dominions.

Oliver attributes this view to Neil MacCormick (whether correctly or not), and without advocating it himself, apparently regards it as arguable.[37] But to me it seems bizarre. Why would the rule of recognition maintain that Parliament has no authority to limit its own authority, but does have authority to give itself authority to limit its own authority, by changing the rule of recognition? What would be the point of an official consensus to that effect? Moreover, how in practice would Parliament alter the rule of recognition, other than by simply ignoring its supposed inability to limit its own authority, enacting a statute that imposes such a limit, and thereby altering the rule of recognition by implication? Surely it would not have to enact two statutes in sequential order: first, one that expressly changes the rule of recognition, by declaring that henceforth it can limit its own authority, and only then, one that imposes such a limit? According to Oliver, MacCormick's view was based partly on the *Factortame* case, which 'confirmed that the power of change was available even to modify the supreme criterion of the rule of recognition'.[38] But, as Oliver acknowledges, if the European Communities Act 1972 managed to impose limits on Parliament's authority by changing the rule of recognition, it did so in one fell swoop, rather than by a two-step process.[39] In other words, on this view, Parliament limited its authority by simply ignoring the supposed rule that it could not do so. What, then, could the practical point of that rule have been? Even if Parliament did have to use a two-step process, it would be so easy to do so that the point of initially denying that it could bind itself would be obscure. Perhaps that is why Oliver at one point describes MacCormick's position as 'an outright endorsement of the "revised" or "self-embracing" view of parliamentary sovereignty'.[40] If it is, then B(3) collapses into B(2).

In any event, the view attributed to MacCormick is incompatible with Oliver's acknowledgement that 'Parliament cannot literally amend or change the rule of recognition'. All it can do is 'propose' new criteria for potential recognition, which are 'confirmed' only if and when the courts accept them. Oliver emphasises that neither Parliament nor the courts have exclusive authority in such matters. 'A true account [lies] somewhere

---

[37] Oliver, *Independence*, pp. 307–8, summarising pp. 303–6. MacCormick's theory is also discussed in A. Young, *Parliamentary Sovereignty and the Human Rights Act* (Oxford: Hart Publishing, 2009), pp. 89–90.

[38] Oliver, *Independence*, p. 305.

[39] *Ibid.*, p. 309.   [40] *Ibid.*, p. 304.

in between, in the relationship between [Parliament's] power and [the courts'] recognition.[41] The consensus that constitutes the rule of recognition can only be changed by Parliament and the courts coming to agree on such a change. But this sounds like my own theory (C(3)), which is explained below.

(4)   The abdication theory

A.V. Dicey's view was that, although Parliament cannot limit its authority, it can abdicate it. On this view its authority is for the most part continuing, but self-embracing in the case of abdication. Oliver, following H.W.R. Wade, doubts the coherence of this view and does not take it seriously.[42]

I agree that Dicey's view is erroneous, but not that it is incoherent. Indeed, it is superficially quite plausible. There are at least three important differences between an abdication of Parliament's authority, at least with respect to some external territory, and an attempt to limit its authority within (say) England itself: (a) a difference in political principle; (b) a difference in the likelihood of a subsequent attempt to reverse the abdication or limitation; and (c) a difference in the likelihood that an attempted reversal would succeed.[43]

The first difference is that the principle of democracy will often disfavour a limitation, but favour an abdication. As Oliver points out, from the perspective of democracy, continuing sovereignty may seem desirable if it disables a bare parliamentary majority from preventing its enacted policies being amended or repealed by a future majority of a different political persuasion, but is plainly undesirable if it prevents a majority of Canadians from governing their own affairs free of external interference.[44]

The second difference is straight-forward: the historical record shows that once Parliament abdicates its authority to change the law of a dominion, it is very unlikely that any future Parliament will seek to resume that authority. This is partly because it is almost always regarded as irreversible, for practical if not legal reasons. The same is not true of attempts to limit

---

[41]   *Ibid.*, p. 303–4, n. 71.

[42]   *Ibid.*, pp. 289 n. 15, 59–60 and 315 n. 1. See also Winterton, 'The British Grundnorm', 602.

[43]   I acknowledge that Dicey may have had in mind only a complete abdication of the entirety of Parliament's authority, and not a partial abdication of its authority with respect to some external dominion: see Oliver, *Independence*, pp. 60 and 289, n. 15. But any reasons for conceding the possibility of a complete abdication apply equally to such a partial abdication.

[44]   Oliver, *Independence*, p. 324.

Parliament's authority to legislate within territory over which it other-wise retains legislative authority. In many conceivable cases – admittedly not all – future parliaments are quite likely to want to repeal or even just ignore those limits.

The third difference is equally straight-forward. If Parliament purports permanently to abdicate its authority with respect to a dominion, whose officials (including judges) consequently regard their legal system as inde-pendent, it becomes impossible for Parliament unilaterally to reimpose its authority to change the law of their system. Its authority can be reimposed only with their acquiescence or by conquest. This was well understood by Sir William Anson in 1886:

> Suppose that legislative independence were to be conceded to the col-ony of Victoria ... Would it be maintained that our Parliament could still legislate for Victoria, or that the Victorian Courts need regard such laws as anything but specimens of legislation, instructive perhaps, but cer-tainly inoperative? I should be disposed to contend that Parliament could only regain its power in one of two ways. Acts passed by the Parliament of Victoria and the Parliament at Westminster might provide for a legislative re-union of the two countries ... Or war and the suspension for a while of all legal relations might leave Victoria in the position of a conquered terri-tory with which the Imperial Parliament could deal as it pleased.[45]

British judges could, of course, pretend that Parliament retained author-ity to change the former dominion's law – rather than merely to change British law concerning persons or activities within its territory[46] – but that would be transparent make-believe. Even they would know that it was pure fiction. On the other hand, if Parliament purports to limit its authority within territory (such as England) over which it otherwise retains general legislative authority, it is much less likely to be impos-sible for it subsequently to repeal the limit. Given the number of times British judges have endorsed the theory of continuing sovereignty, it seems very likely that, in many cases, they would uphold the validity of such a repeal.

The difference between abdicating and limiting legislative sovereignty is like the difference between a chocoholic giving his chocolate to some-one else to eat, and keeping it while promising not to eat it. Once he has given the chocolate away, it may be practically impossible for him to get it back – and definitely will be, once it has been eaten; whereas his promise

---

[45] 'The Government of Ireland Bill and the Sovereignty of Parliament', *Law Quarterly Review* 2 (1886) 427 at 440.

[46] See the explanation of this distinction at the start of Section II, above.

not to eat chocolate remaining in his possession is unlikely to be effective once his craving for it revives.

This third difference is the most significant for legal purposes. Advocates of parliamentary sovereignty have always acknowledged that Parliament cannot do what is naturally impossible, such as to change a man into a woman. If it is practically impossible for Parliament unilaterally to reimpose its authority to change the law of an independent former dominion, why should the doctrine of parliamentary sovereignty not acknowledge that fact? On the other hand, someone once said that Parliament could require that a man be treated as if he were a woman. Perhaps, then, Parliament could require British judges to treat the law of Canada or Australia – for purposes of private international law, for example – as if it were something it is plainly not. But what would be the point? After all, Parliament could also enact a law purporting to change the law of France, Mexico or any other country, and require British judges to pretend that it had succeeded. When pushed this far, the theory of continuing sovereignty starts to look silly.

Another way of trying to tease out this third difference is as follows. The orthodox theory of continuing sovereignty does not assert that it is positively unlawful (whatever that might mean in this context) for Parliament to pass a statute including a provision purporting to restrict its authority to amend or repeal the statute. What that theory asserts is, instead, that any such provision is doomed to be ineffective, because it can at any time be repealed by a later statute, impliedly as well as expressly – which means that it can be ignored. According to Wade, such a provision is perfectly valid, but subject to the same infirmity that 'is shared by all the Acts that are ever passed, viz., the possibility of being repealed'.[47] This has been disputed: it has been argued that such a provision is therefore void *ab initio*, because it is in effect a nullity. As Michael Detmold puts it, 'nothing can be law which does not bind the only body it purports to bind'.[48] But now consider an Act granting independence to a dominion, which includes a provision that purports to terminate Parliament's authority to repeal the Act. If Wade is right, then if a later statute purporting to repeal that Act is ineffective, does it not follow that the provision, valid when passed, remains valid and effective? And even if Detmold is right, if the later

---

[47] See H.W.R. Wade, 'The Basis of Legal Sovereignty' *Cambridge Law Journal* (1955) 177 at 186.

[48] See M.J. Detmold, *The Australian Commonwealth, A Fundamental Analysis of Its Constitution* (Sydney: Law Book Co., 1985), p. 212.

statute is ineffective, is it not void in the independent former dominion, because there, it does not bind the only bodies that it purports to bind – namely, the officials including judges who administer the local law? To put this another way, if the original Act granting independence cannot *effectively* be repealed, then in practical terms, Parliament has succeeded in binding itself, even if British courts choose to pretend otherwise.

The most likely response to this argument is that it rests on practical rather than legal (normative) efficacy, and is a fig leaf for successful revolution and real-politic. Both Wade and Detmold rely on considerations of efficacy. Wade maintains that a provision that prohibits its own repeal is doomed to be ineffective – even though it is legally valid – because it can be repealed at any time. If it is, in fact, legally valid, then its repeal must be legally invalid, in which case Wade is relying on practical rather than legal efficacy. Perhaps this shows that Detmold is right – the original provision prohibiting its own repeal must have been void all along – and that Detmold is speaking here of legal rather than practical efficacy. But I will drop the analysis at this point: it is, perhaps, becoming unprofitably convoluted.

Whatever the merits of the preceding argument, Dicey's opinion that Parliament cannot limit, but can abdicate, its authority is flawed. Even when Parliament appears to have successfully abdicated its authority, independence is not the consequence of the abdication by itself, but of the abdication together with its acceptance by officialdom within the newly independent legal system. In other words, it is the consequence of a change in the official consensus that constitutes the rule of recognition of that legal system. An attempted abdication might not always contribute to such a change. Imagine a situation, for example, in which Parliament purports irrevocably to abdicate its authority with respect to a colony whose population and officials do not want independence. If a subsequent Parliament, at the request of the former colonials, were to pass a statute repealing the abdication and reasserting British sovereignty over them, that statute would no doubt be accepted as valid and binding by their courts as well as British ones. (Indeed, the original abdicating statute might simply be ignored – and repealed by implication – by Parliament passing ordinary legislation changing the law of the former colony.) Furthermore, it is possible – as we will see – for the rule of recognition within Britain itself to change, so that Parliament's authority might be limited at home. Dicey was wrong to say that Parliament can abdicate, but not limit, its authority. It cannot achieve either result unilaterally: such changes require a change in the broader official consensus that constitutes the relevant rule of recognition. The truth in Dicey's distinction is that a purported abdication is much more likely to contribute to the requisite change in that consensus, and therefore to prove enduring, than a purported limitation.

C   Limitations imposed by a change in official consensus

The third alternative is that, as explained previously, the rule of recognition is constituted by a consensus among all branches of government, and therefore can be changed neither by the courts, nor by Parliament, unilaterally, but only by a change in the consensus that they share. There are three versions of this alternative:

(1)   The hard cases theory

Oliver's own theory is that prior to dominion independence, it was unclear whether parliamentary sovereignty was continuing or self-embracing. Both theories were equally plausible from the points of view of logic and precedent.[49] The apparent dominance of the continuing theory within Britain itself was based more on dogma than judicial authority, because Parliament had not yet made an unambiguous attempt to limit or abdicate its authority, and there had been no firm judicial determination of the question. (Oliver shows that the trio of early twentieth-century cases most often cited in support of the continuing theory are, in fact, equivocal on the point.[50]) When Parliament unambiguously purported to confer independence on its dominions, its actions raised a question not settled by determinate law. If judges are ever required to resolve that question, it will be a 'hard case' that requires them to make a choice guided by principles of political morality.[51] Judges in the former dominions could and should choose to interpret Parliament's sovereignty as self-embracing,

---

[49] If the law concerning Parliament's power to limit itself really is indeterminate, then is it arguable that Parliament is not legally barred from conferring independence on a dominion or limiting its powers in some other way – and therefore, that it has legal liberty to do so? In other words, is there a kind of default position, similar to the way in which common law liberty is usually conceived of: whatever is not positively prohibited, is permitted? The problem with this is that it is self-contradictory: the conclusion that Parliament is at liberty to limit its own power, because it is not positively prohibited from doing so, contradicts the premise that the law is indeterminate. If Parliament is at liberty to limit its own power, then a self-embracing theory (B(1) or (2)) should be preferred. In effect, on this view, a self-embracing theory is the default position if the continuing theory is not firmly established as law.

[50] Oliver, *Independence*, pp. 9, 70–2 and 306–8.   [51] *Ibid.*, pp. 54 and 341.

even if their British counterparts were to interpret it as continuing.[52] (At this point, Oliver invokes a theory of legal systems to show that there is no good reason why judges in separate legal systems should not adopt different, even contradictory, interpretations of legal norms, even those they once held in common: 'Australia, Canada and New Zealand are entitled to adopt distinct interpretations of the Westminster Parliament's powers in so far as that institution affects their own legal systems, just as they may adopt distinct interpretations of what was originally a common law of contract and tort.'[53]) This is because the former should choose the solution that is 'most fitting according to an amalgam of cultural, social, political and historical factors, including the issues of popular sovereignty, international acceptance and inter-societal acceptance and legitimation'.[54] Note that on this view, when the judges hold that Parliament has self-embracing sovereignty, they (together with Parliament) are changing the rule of recognition only by adding something to it in order to resolve an indeterminacy – they are not changing something that was previously well settled.

As previously mentioned, I also have reservations about this theory, which I will attempt to explain after summarising the other alternatives.

(2)   The legal revolution theory

On one view, any change in the consensus that constitutes a rule of recognition, and therefore in the rule itself, amounts to a revolution, even if it is an amicable, 'legal' revolution. According to the original rule of recognition, Parliament's authority was continuing – in the strong sense of the term – not self-embracing.[55] Modern developments, including the acquisition of independence by former dominions, and the disapplication of statutes pursuant to the European Communities Act 1972, are incompatible with that rule. The rule has therefore been changed by a legal revolution. This is the theory of H.W.R. Wade, whom Oliver describes as Dicey's most eloquent apologist.[56]

There is much of merit in Wade's theory. He is right to deny that Parliament can unilaterally limit or abdicate its own sovereignty. What is required is a change in the official consensus that underpins Parliament's authority. But why describe a wholly consensual change in that consensus as extra-legal and revolutionary? There are two possible reasons. One

---

[52] *Ibid.*, pp. 10–1 and 341.   [53] *Ibid.*, p. 311.   [54] *Ibid.*, pp. 341–2; see also pp. 318 and 24.
[55] See last two paragraphs in Section II, above.
[56] Oliver, *Independence*, pp. 8–9 and 20.

is that the current official consensus positively forbids such a change in relation to parliamentary sovereignty: this is the strong version of the theory of continuing sovereignty. I have already argued that this should be rejected, because it would be foolish and arrogant to purport to forbid the consensus from evolving to satisfy unforeseeable future needs.[57] The second possible reason is that the rule of recognition does not self-consciously recognise the process by which it was itself created, and can be changed, as authorised by a legal 'rule of change'. Because the rule of recognition is itself the foundation of the legal system, its own foundation – the circumstances that explain its own existence and content, and the process by which those circumstances change – are necessarily 'extra-legal', lying beneath or outside the law.

But surely it can be argued, to the contrary, that in an unwritten constitution such as Britain's, the most fundamental secondary rules including the rule of recognition are a kind of customary law, comprised of customary norms of legal officialdom that are acknowledged to be justiciable.[58] Customary law is not static: it evolves along with the consensus that constitutes it. Elsewhere, I have argued that '[t]here are important differences between abrupt changes to fundamental legal rules, imposed on many senior officials through their coercion or removal from office, and gradual changes resulting from a voluntary change of mind on their part in response to broader social developments. In the latter case, it may be appropriate to say that the rules have evolved legally.'[59] Hart himself had reservations about Wade's use of the term 'revolution' in this context, and called for criteria to distinguish non-revolutionary changes in *grundnorms* from genuine revolutions.[60] As John Allison observes, Hart's account of the rule of recognition as a kind of official customary rule, which changes by implication as custom changes, 'is less vulnerable to sociological criticism than is Wade's analysis of a fundamental rule changed only by judicial revolution'.[61]

This leads to the third version of this alternative:

---

[57] See the final paragraph of Section II, above.
[58] Other, non-justiciable, customary norms of legal officialdom are called constitutional conventions rather than constitutional laws.
[59] Goldsworthy, *The Sovereignty of Parliament*, p. 245.
[60] J. Allison, 'Parliamentary Sovereignty, Europe and the Economy of the Common Law', in M. Andenas (ed.), *Judicial Review in International Perspective: Liber Amicorum in Honour of Lord Slynn of Hadley* (Kluwer, 2000), 177 at p. 185, quoting unpublished correspondence between Hart and Wade.
[61] J.F. Allison, *The English Historical Constitution* (Cambridge: Cambridge University Press, 2007), p. 119, the conclusion of an illuminating discussion at pp. 110–19.

(3)   The consensual change theory

A wholly peaceful, consensual change in a customary rule of recognition should be regarded as lawful, not revolutionary, and therefore dominion independence was acquired lawfully. This is my own theory, adapted from Hart,[62] although Oliver's description of my book as endorsing 'the traditional, absolutist, orthodox or Diceyan account' suggests otherwise.[63]

It is also a theory recently defended at length by Alison Young.[64] She argues that the theory is perfectly consistent with the doctrine of continuing parliamentary sovereignty, because both the theory and the doctrine deny that Parliament has authority to bind itself.[65] Therefore, she concludes, if Parliament were to be bound (for example, by a requirement that some future law can only be passed with the approval of a majority of voters in a referendum) as a result of a change in the rule of recognition, rather than just by Parliament itself, the doctrine of continuing parliamentary sovereignty would not be 'breached' or 'violated'.[66] This is true in one sense; but of course, if parliament were to be bound in that way, it would no longer possess sovereignty of any kind – continuing or self-embracing – and so the doctrine of continuing parliamentary sovereignty would be breached or violated in another sense. Perhaps all that Young has in mind in her discussion of a change in the rule of recognition is the imposition of 'manner and form' requirements that do not diminish Parliament's sovereignty because they leave intact its substantive power to change the law.[67] But if so, the main reason for Parliament continuing to possess sovereignty would be that such requirements pose no threat to it, regardless of how they are imposed. It would not matter very much

---

[62] See text to n. 59, above.

[63] Oliver, *Independence*, p. 76. It is not clear what this orthodox, Diceyan account is: of the alternatives listed above, is it B(4) – Dicey's own view – or C(2) – Wade's view? Oliver suggests that the Diceyan account is incompatible with twentieth century developments, such as dominion independence and European legal order: loc. cit. Yet neither B(4) nor C(2) are incompatible with both of those developments, although C(2) is incompatible with their being 'lawful'. Neither is my own theory, according to which the customary rule of recognition can evolve lawfully. Oliver's suggestions are therefore puzzling. Furthermore, in my book I explicitly adopt what Oliver calls the 'new view', which accepts the validity of 'manner and form' requirements: see n. 27, above.

[64] Young, *Parliamentary Sovereignty and the Human Rights Act*, ch. 3.

[65] *Ibid.*, pp. 15, 66, 73–4, 82–5, 90 and 168.

[66] *Ibid.*, pp. 15, 23–4, 65, 68, 75, 77, 83, 85, 86 and 93.

[67] This is suggested by statements at *ibid.*, pp. 28 ('It is possible for rights to be entrenched and for Parliament to retain continuing sovereignty'), 83 ('the sovereignty of Parliament is preserved, as courts only recognise as valid those legislative measures passed by the sovereign law-making institution in the prescribed manner') and 161.

whether we were to explain their imposition in terms of a change in the rule of recognition, or in terms of the procedurally self-embracing theory (theory B(1) above).

My own theory requires some elaboration. If, contrary to a firmly established rule that a constitution or some part of it is either immutable, or can be changed only by a particular process, all the senior officials agree to change it – or perhaps even to adopt an entirely new constitution – without following that process, their behaviour could fairly be described as revolutionary even if it is wholly consensual. I am assuming that Britain's unwritten, customary constitution does not include any such established rule that either forbids fundamental constitutional change, or mandates a specific procedure for bringing it about.[68] As John Allison has shown, it is the nature of such a constitution that it undergoes 'minimal and gradual revision'.[69] Even so, a radical change from one system of government to another – say, from parliamentary democracy to fascist dictatorship – might aptly be described as revolutionary even if it were brought about by a peaceful change in the consensus among senior officials. The distinction between revolutionary and non-revolutionary change in an unwritten, customary constitution probably depends partly on the extent to which change is incremental rather than radical (however that is measured). It seems to me that the concept of revolution is incurably vague in this respect.

IV   Oliver's theory scrutinised

If we reject Wade's talk of revolution, along with the other theories that I have previously criticised, the remaining contenders are Oliver's theory and my own. It is now time to explain my reservations about his theory.

1. Oliver often refers to the rule of recognition – which includes the doctrine of parliamentary sovereignty – as something that changes or evolves. He accepts that it is a kind of customary law.[70] In an important passage that is unfortunately relegated to a footnote, he acknowledges that it cannot be changed either by the courts or by Parliament unilaterally. Parliament cannot make changes by itself: it can only propose changes, which must then be accepted, or 'recognised' as law, by the courts. The courts also cannot change the rule of recognition on their own initiative

---

[68] See text to n. 47, and the final paragraph of Section II, above.
[69] Allison, *The English Historical Constitution*, p. 127.
[70] Oliver, *Independence*, pp. 19, 24, 82, nn. 41 and 313.

and by their own authority. Their role is limited to deciding whether or not to recognise changes to the rule proposed by Parliament when it enacts constitutionally novel legislation. Change to the rule of recognition is therefore the product of agreement between Parliament and the judiciary.[71]

The argument in this footnote does not fit altogether comfortably with Oliver's recommendation that dominion courts adopt the self-embracing theory of Parliament's sovereignty. The self-embracing theory holds that Parliament has authority to change the rule of recognition by limiting its own authority, whereas the footnote maintains that Parliament can only propose such a change. If Parliament has authority to make changes, then the courts must recognise them; but if Parliament is only able to propose changes, then the courts must choose (on grounds of political morality) whether or not to accept and recognise them. I take it that Oliver reconciles these positions in the following way: (a) before the courts adopt the self-embracing theory, Parliament does not have authority to change the rule of recognition by limiting its own authority, because the question is legally indeterminate; (b) when the courts accept Parliament's first attempt to do this, it acquires self-embracing authority, and can then change the rule of recognition in relevant respects by imposing new limits to its authority. In other words, the self-embracing theory becomes law prospectively, through the courts' acceptance of Parliament's innovation. I will return to this point.

2. The position Oliver adopts in this footnote sounds much like Hart's theory, which I have adopted, of how a customary rule of recognition can change.[72] Are there any significant differences between us? One difference is that Oliver apparently regards change in a customary rule of recognition as lawful rather than revolutionary only if it amounts to the resolution of indeterminacy in the rule, by way of clarification of some question that was previously unclear. He agrees with Wade that any change to a determinate, settled aspect of the rule – even if the change is consensual – must be classified as revolutionary.[73]

---

[71] *Ibid.*, pp. 303–4 n. 71.

[72] So much so that I am puzzled as to why Oliver alleges that I pay little attention to the possibility of change initiated by Parliament (p. 300), claims that MacCormick has addressed precisely that issue (*ibid.*), but then while expounding MacCormick's views, adopts in a footnote a position much closer to mine than to MacCormick's (pp. 303–4 n. 71). See Goldsworthy, *The Sovereignty of Parliament*, pp. 244–5.

[73] See Oliver, *Independence*, p. 314: Parliament's relinquishing of its powers 'is a "disguised revolution" if that Parliament's powers are irrevocably continuing in nature'.

This position is vulnerable to two objections. The first is that the putative distinction between lawful judicial resolution of an indeterminate aspect of the rule of recognition, and revolutionary consensual change of a determinate aspect of it, is dubious. It seems to assume that, just as courts have acknowledged authority to resolve uncertainties in ordinary laws, or in written constitutions, they must also have authority to resolve uncertainties in unwritten, customary rules of recognition.[74] Hart denied this:

> The truth may be that, when courts settle previously unenvisaged questions concerning the most fundamental constitutional rules, they get their authority to decide them accepted after the questions have arisen and the decision has been given. Here all that succeeds is success ... Where this is so, it will often in *retrospect* be said, and may genuinely appear, that there always was an 'inherent' power in the courts to do what they have done. Yet this may be a pious fiction, if the only evidence for it is the success of what has been done.[75]

If Hart was right, then *any* substantial change to a customary rule of recognition – even the settlement of some previously unsettled question – requires a change in the consensus of senior officials that constitutes the rule. The courts should not be assumed to possess inherent legal authority to bring about any change of that kind. Oliver appears to agree. But if in some cases such a change is revolutionary, because it is brought about without lawful authority, why is it not revolutionary in all cases – in other words, whether or not the rule of recognition was previously indeterminate? My theory draws a different, arguably more plausible, distinction between lawful and revolutionary change.

The second objection is that, if the continuing theory of parliamentary sovereignty was, as a matter of law, firmly established immediately prior to dominion independence, then even Oliver would have to agree with Wade that independence was achieved through legal revolution. His theory is therefore hostage to proof that the continuing theory was indeed firmly established at that time. If it could be shown that Hart was right to assert, in 1961, that 'it is clear that the presently accepted rule is one of continuing sovereignty', then Oliver's theory would be refuted.[76] His own acknowledgements that, in the early part of the twentieth century, the continuing theory was almost universally accepted by lawyers in the dominions as well as the United Kingdom,[77] count against him. He has

---

[74] See Oliver, *Independence*, p. 94.   [75] Hart, *The Concept of Law*, p. 149.   [76] *Ibid.*, p. 146.
[77] E.g., Oliver, *Independence*, pp. 5, 8, 9, 21 and 294.

two counter-arguments. One is that those lawyers were deceived by faulty logic and an erroneous reading of the case-law.[78] But it could be urged in response that a rule of recognition simply is whatever rule officials in fact accept, regardless of how erroneous their underlying reasoning might be. His second counter-argument is that the law on such a matter cannot be regarded as settled until it has been authoritatively determined by a court.[79] But this may be to confuse rules of recognition with ordinary common law rules. If it were sound, then arguably the doctrine of parliamentary sovereignty as a whole – and not just the side-issue concerning whether Parliament can limit itself – would be 'penumbral' and legally uncertain.[80] According to Hart, rules of recognition are often not explicitly formulated, but must be inferred from the practices of officials in general.[81] If so, then their existence does not depend on their being, like common law *rationes decidendi*, laid down by an authoritative judicial decision.[82]

My theory has the advantage that it does not depend on the rule of recognition being, in this respect, unsettled before dominion independence was achieved. Even if the rule did clearly maintain that Parliament's authority was continuing, I would describe the termination of Parliament's authority as lawful. My theory does not formally contradict the thesis that Parliament's power was continuing, if that is the sensible, weak version of the thesis, meaning merely that Parliament cannot bind itself.[83] My theory maintains not that Parliament can bind itself, but that Parliament can become lawfully bound as a result of consensual change in the customary rule of recognition. On the other hand, as previously noted, Oliver does not countenance this possibility.[84] He appears to assume that there are only two alternatives: either Parliament's authority is continuing, in the strong sense that rules out the imposition of any substantive limit on Parliament's authority, or its authority is self-embracing.[85] He ignores the

---

[78] *Ibid.*, pp. 9 and 306.
[79] *Ibid.*, pp. 10, 307 and 319.
[80] Oliver implies as much at *ibid.*, p. 10, where he says that 'one sort of penumbral issue' is whether 'certain imaginary and as yet unenacted legislation by Parliament is beyond the pale'. But this seems inconsistent with his usual stance of accepting that the 'core' of the doctrine of parliamentary sovereignty is firmly established.
[81] Hart, *The Concept of Law*, p. 98.
[82] See Goldsworthy, *The Sovereignty of Parliament*, pp. 6 and 238–43.
[83] See the final paragraph in Section II, above.
[84] See text to nn. 18 and 19 above.
[85] For examples of his expression of this assumption, see Oliver, *Independence*, pp. 87 and 297.

possible third alternative: that Parliament's authority is continuing, in the sense that Parliament cannot unilaterally limit it, but can be lawfully limited through a change in the official consensus from which it derives.

3. Since Oliver's argument depends on the law on this point not being settled one way or the other – in other words, on the question being a 'hard case' – he can fairly be asked to choose between a Dworkinian and a positivist account of hard cases. He expresses a preference for a positivist account, but claims that both would reach the same conclusion on the question of dominion independence.[86]

I suspect that a Dworkinian account would be problematic for Oliver. For one thing, Dworkin does not accept the existence of rules of recognition that provide the foundation or source of legal authority. In addition, Dworkin assumes that there is always a 'right answer' to legal disputes. If so, the law must have granted either full self-embracing, partial self-embracing (abdicating), or continuing authority to Parliament, even though its content was so unclear that it may be impossible to conclusively establish except by a superhuman, omniscient judge (Dworkin's imaginary Judge Hercules). Courts are not free to adopt whatever answer seems most convenient, or most politic. They are duty bound to seek the right answer, which is the answer that makes the law as a whole 'the best it can be'. This means that it is the morally best answer of all those that 'fit' the institutional history of the legal system in question.

One obstacle to Oliver accepting such an approach is that it threatens his theory (C(1)) with collapse into the full self-embracing theory (B(2)) (or perhaps the abdication theory (B(4)). If the right legal answer, notwithstanding its obscurity, is that Parliament did possess some kind of self-embracing sovereignty, then either the full self-embracing theory, or the abdication theory, would seem to be vindicated. Parliament had self-embracing powers all along – either full or partial – even though they were 'hidden'.[87]

Oliver might reply that there is no single right answer, but many of them, because rightness varies from one legal system to another. It is possible that the right answer in a newly independent dominion might

---

[86] Oliver, *Independence*, p. 318, n. 10. Sometimes, though, Oliver writes as if he accepted a Dworkinian account. For example, he says that when courts resolve a hard case concerning whether or not Parliament possessed self-embracing authority, they settle the 'true' nature of its sovereignty – as if there were a 'right answer' waiting to be authoritatively identified: p. 319. But perhaps he means merely that a judicial determination creates legal truth prospectively, rather than discovers what the truth was all along.

[87] Oliver, *Independence*, p. 9.

be different from the right answer in Britain, because they have different bodies of law, and the answer that makes each of them 'the best it can be' might therefore be different. He sees no difficulty here, no reason why independent legal systems should not adopt distinct, even conflicting, interpretations of laws or legal processes they once held in common (in this case, the law governing parliamentary sovereignty).[88] Such 'local interpretations of the same Westminster processes are clearly incompatible, but as separately functioning internal perspectives this incompatibility is of no consequence'.[89]

At the risk of over-complicating matters, and then leaving them unresolved, I will simply pose some questions about this possible reply. One is whether Oliver would be begging the central question. The central question is whether or not the independence of the former dominions was acquired lawfully. Oliver relies on theories of legal systems to demonstrate that they are independent, and then argues that consequently, their courts are entitled to adopt distinct interpretations of the process by which they acquired independence.[90] But if the theories of legal systems that he relies on merely establish de facto independence, how can they assist in vindicating de jure independence? If, as a matter of law, their independence was acquired unlawfully, how can the mere say-so of de facto independent courts override that fact?[91] And if a court's legal system is not de jure independent, is it entitled to infer a distinct 'right answer' from a separate, selective institutional history?

My second, related question concerns Dworkin's thesis that the right answer must be derived from the principles of political morality that provide the best justification of the institutional history of the legal system in question. If a hard case concerns the nature of a power or right exercised by a person or institution at some past time, does the Dworkinian judge seek the best justification of the institutional history as it stood *at that time*, or of the institutional history right up to the time when the judge must decide the hard case? If the former, then there can be only one right answer to a question about the nature of the power possessed by the Westminster Parliament at a particular time. If the latter, then there could in principle be many right answers, because truth would be relative

---

[88] *Ibid.*, pp. 11 and 17.
[89] *Ibid.*, p. 23; see also pp. 16 and 311.   [90] *Ibid.*, pp. 291–300.
[91] If the Westminster Parliament enacted legislation not only reasserting its legislative authority over a former dominion, but also reintroducing a right of appeal from that country's highest court to the Privy Council, then arguably that court would no longer enjoy de jure independence.

to the time and place at which the question is answered. Different answers given by courts in different legal systems at different times – even to a question concerning the same legal power that existed when all were part of a single legal system – might all be correct.

My third question, which arises whenever and from whatever perspective the central question is asked, is whether the morally best answer could possibly be that an obviously independent former dominion, with its own flourishing democratic institutions, is not lawfully independent? The moral case in favour of even British courts acknowledging the legality of independence might be overwhelming. But if so, then if they adopted a Dworkinian approach, they should accept something like the self-embracing theory, or at the very least the abdication theory, as the right answer.

We can perhaps bypass these questions, because Oliver prefers a legal positivist account of hard cases.[92] This assumes that there is no right answer as a matter of law: the law was indeterminate, and neither affirmed nor denied that Parliament possessed either full or partial self-embracing authority. Faced with such a question, courts are at liberty to exercise discretion on grounds of political morality. Oliver argues that courts in former dominions might legitimately choose one answer, and courts in Britain another, given that somewhat different considerations of political morality might bear on their choices. Considerations such as de facto independence, popular sovereignty and democracy should persuade courts in the former dominions to accept that their legal system has lawfully achieved independence, whereas considerations of democracy might persuade British courts to comply with a statute enacted by their Parliament, attempting to reassert its authority to change the law of an independent, former dominion.

A possible problem here concerns intellectual honesty. Oliver says that adopting a self-embracing interpretation of Parliament's powers would 'fulfil the function' of vindicating the constitutional independence of these dominions.[93] But if the law were truly indeterminate – if, as a matter of law, it were not true either that Parliament possessed self-embracing authority, or that it did not – then would it not be intellectually dishonest for courts to hold that as a matter of law it did possess such authority? It would amount to them adopting the self-embracing theory (B(2)) that Oliver himself rejects. It would also be a pious fiction. Its fictional nature would be accentuated if, as Oliver suggests, British judges were to adopt the opposite, but supposedly equally valid, answer to the same question. This might not, as he asserts, cause any practical difficulty. But to hold that both answers would be equally valid because they would express different 'perspectives' just reinforces the conclusion that they would both be pious fictions. The honest answer would be that the law was indeterminate, and therefore that whether or not independence was acquired lawfully is also legally indeterminate.[94] A court in a former dominion, which adhered to a legal positivist philosophy, could say as much, and then explain that since it must decide the question of independence one way or the other, it would hold the former dominion to be legally independent for reasons of political morality. Admittedly, courts do not usually speak so frankly about their exercise of necessary discretion to resolve legal indeterminacies: they usually speak as if they have uncovered the 'right answer' that was latent in the legal material all along. Dworkin cites just that kind of judicial rhetoric to support his theory. But there is no reason for Oliver to shy away from blunt truths.

Oliver might reply that for a court in a former dominion to hold, for reasons of political morality, that it acquired its independence lawfully, the court would have to hold that the British statute that granted independence was valid – and therefore, if only by implication, that the Westminster Parliament had authority to enact it. And that would amount to choosing the self-embracing theory. But this strikes me as fallacious. Why should the court attribute either continuing, or self-embracing, authority to the Westminster Parliament? Imagine that it must decide whether or not to recognise the validity of a British statute purporting to repeal an earlier statute that granted independence to the dominion. Arguably, all it needs to do is choose whether or not to regard its legal system as independent. It does not need to decide whether or not that independence was acquired lawfully, let alone attempt to explain why it was or wasn't. It could simply accept independence as an established fact, which must now be accepted for legal purposes. If it were to address the question of whether independence was acquired lawfully, it should say that no answer could be given because (*ex hypothesi*) the law was indeterminate. It might *deem* it to have been acquired lawfully, for reasons of political morality. Those reasons have to do with the irreversible change in the political allegiance of legal officials (the judges included), other political elites and the general public in the former dominion, together with principles such as popular sovereignty and democracy. My theory frankly acknowledges that these

---

[94] See n. 49, above, to help avoid a false step here.

would be the crucial reasons. But for Oliver, it seems, they are inadequate, because they cannot establish that independence was acquired lawfully. They must therefore be supplemented by a post hoc endorsement of the self-embracing theory, which given the fact of independence, has no remaining practical relevance other than as a fictional legal rationalisation for a decision really reached on other grounds.

Could it be plausibly argued that even if the retrospective adoption of the self-embracing theory would be pious fiction, it should be adopted prospectively?[95] The problem is that a hard case involving the granting of independence to a former dominion is unlike most hard cases that must be decided by courts. Usually, a legal indeterminacy concerning the scope of some right or power must be resolved prospectively, one way or the other, in order to pre-empt other disputes that might arise in the future. But here, no future disputes can arise. A court's acceptance that its legal system is lawfully independent entails that Parliament's authority is of no further relevance to it. Parliament no longer has any authority, continuing or self-embracing, to change its laws. Therefore, no future disputes about the nature of that authority can have any relevance to it.[96] It follows that there is no need for the court of the former dominion to adopt a position one way or the other, as to whether Parliament's authority is continuing or self-embracing. That is a matter that can and should be left to British courts.

To summarise this part of the argument: on a positivist analysis, if the nature of Parliament's authority when it purported to grant independence was, as a matter of law, indeterminate, then (a) a decision that it possessed self-embracing authority at that time would be a pious fiction, and (b) a decision that it should thenceforth be taken to possess full self-embracing authority (theory B(2)) would be irrelevant to the circumstances of independent former dominions, and therefore unnecessary.

4. My theory may have the additional advantage, compared with Oliver's, of enabling more fine-grained, discriminating conclusions to be reached. Mine can explain how the rule of recognition can come to accept the validity of some limits to Parliament's authority, but not others. For example, the rule might come to accept the validity of a Bill of Rights enacted by large majorities in both Houses of Parliament after being approved by a majority of voters in a referendum, which future parliaments

---

[95] See the conclusion of point 1 in this section, above.
[96] Subject to one exception: the nature of Parliament's authority might have some bearing on the nature of the authority that it originally conferred upon the Parliament of the dominion. But any questions of that kind could be decided if and when they arise.

cannot violate without the approval of voters in another referendum, but not the validity of a provision forbidding future parliaments to repeal an ordinary statute passed by a small parliamentary majority from only one political party. On the other hand, the self-embracing theory that Oliver recommends to courts in former dominions seems undiscriminating.[97] It is hard to see how that theory can be subject to qualification. To hold that Parliament has a general authority 'to bind itself by any and all means'[98] is to hold that it can bind itself for either of the purposes just mentioned, or any others.

Even if all of Oliver's premises are well founded, it seems unnecessary, unrealistic and somewhat presumptuous for the court of a former dominion to hold, not only that Parliament was able to abdicate its authority by granting independence to that dominion, but that it possessed full self-embracing sovereignty that could be used for other purposes as well. Oliver insists that the courts of the former dominions should choose the solution that is most fitting to their own circumstances, including 'an amalgam of cultural, social, political and historical factors'.[99] But surely they should also acknowledge that their circumstances are not those of Britain itself, and therefore, that Parliament's sovereignty might not be self-embracing with respect to Britain. Oliver says that dominion courts 'are entitled to adopt distinct interpretations of the Westminster Parliament's powers *in so far as that institution affects their own institutions*'.[100] As previously observed, the principle of democracy would condemn many conceivable attempts to limit parliamentary authority within Britain, while approving most attempts to abdicate authority over stable, self-governing dominions.[101] If so, then instead of adopting the self-embracing interpretation of Parliament's authority, dominion courts should go no further than to adopt the abdication theory (B(4) above), and hold that Parliament was able to abdicate its authority with respect to them, while leaving open the question of whether it could limit its authority in other ways, particularly within Britain itself. Indeed, it may be unrealistic even to assert that Parliament possessed general authority to abdicate its sovereignty. As previously suggested, if Parliament purported to confer independence irrevocably on a dominion that did not want it, and a later Parliament (with that dominion's consent) repealed the independence

---

[97] See text to n. 35, above.
[98] Oliver, *Independence*, p. 308 (so long as those means are very explicit).
[99] *Ibid.*, p. 341.　　[100] *Ibid.*, p. 311, emphasis added.　　[101] See text to n. 44, above.

statute and resumed its authority over the dominion, the dominion's own courts would no doubt accept the repeal as valid, thereby presumably rejecting the theory that the earlier Parliament possessed authority to abdicate its sovereignty.[102] Only my own theory, or Wade's, can accommodate the ad hoc, case-by-case way in which a customary rule of recognition might evolve in response to the wide variety of challenges to parliamentary sovereignty that might arise.

Admittedly, Oliver does at one point suggest that his theory could be applied in a discriminating fashion:

> [I]t is wrong to imply … that having identified the power of change … all manner of constitutional change is possible. Significant constitutional change may indeed be possible where recognition [by the courts] can confidently be predicted, as with the devolution legislation and constitutional independence legislation: however, on more controversial matters, the proposed constitutional change is only confirmed when the courts eventually shed light on the rule of recognition's previously penumbral areas.[103]

This implies that courts might accept that Parliament has only partial self-embracing authority, enabling it to limit its authority in some respects, but not others. This would require a case-by-case determination of whether or not attempts by Parliament to limit its authority should be accepted as valid. The problem for Oliver is that it is hard to see how this can be squared with his usual insistence that the courts must choose between the continuing and the self-embracing theory. A court that accepted the validity of any limit imposed by Parliament on its own authority would have to reject the continuing theory, but if it therefore accepted the self-embracing theory, it would be conceding the validity of any other limit that Parliament might attempt to impose in the future. What general rule, defining Parliament's authority to limit itself, could explain the validity of one limit, without conceding the validity of any others?

My own theory can account for the way in which some attempts by Parliament to limit its own powers have succeeded, and might succeed in the future, while others will probably not. It does so by frankly acknowledging that the difference lies in the evolution of the requisite consensus among senior legal officials whose opinions count for practical purposes. On this view, it cannot accurately be said that Parliament possesses either continuing sovereignty (in the strong sense), or self-embracing

---

[102] See the final paragraph of Section III, B(4), above.

[103] Oliver, *Independence*, p. 304, n. 71.

sovereignty. Both propositions are too general to be serviceable, and it would therefore be misleading for a court to endorse either of them.

5. Finally, I have some doubts as to whether Oliver's theory really does allow the former dominions to have their cake and eat it too: to have their independence established lawfully, and also to have it rooted in local political allegiances or popular sovereignty.[104] For Oliver, the conclusion that independence was established lawfully depends on the former dominions' courts holding that Parliament possessed self-embracing sovereignty, which enabled it to grant independence by abdicating its sovereignty with respect to them. Surely this is to conceive of independence as a gift from the imperial legislature. What Oliver calls 'new beginnings and popular acceptance' are for legal purposes irrelevant. He himself observes that respect for the rule of law can look 'thin and inadequate ... if not accompanied by some measure of real authority and legitimation'.[105] My own theory, which explains independence in terms of the evolution of the rule of recognition accepted by officials in the former dominions, seems more compatible with the desire for local roots.

V Conclusion

In an earlier essay, Oliver expressed hope that '[o]nce the possibility of self-embracing sovereignty is acknowledged ... over the coming decades and centuries, the United Kingdom could cautiously and pragmatically develop an organic constitution'.[106] I see no good reason why such a constitution should not be developed, but I doubt that the best way forward is for the courts to proclaim that Parliament possesses full self-embracing sovereignty. The adoption of such a general rule would allow Parliament to impose whatever limits it should choose – substantive, as well as formal and procedural – on its own authority. That would allow democracy to be subverted. For example, a political party might use a temporary majority in Parliament to prevent future parliaments from altering or repealing statutes implementing its favoured policies. Or it might include in a particular statute a requirement that the assent of an unrepresentative body, such as a private corporation, be obtained in order to amend or repeal parts of the statute. This may seem far-fetched, but a corporation entering into an agreement with the government involving the investment of a

---

[104] See text to n. 7, above.   [105] Oliver, *Independence*, p. 11.
[106] P. Oliver, 'Sovereignty in the Twenty-First Century' *KCLJ* 14 (2003) 137 at 156.

large sum of money for the sake of long-term returns might seek binding guarantees that the agreement will not be unilaterally changed by either the government or Parliament.[107]

It might be thought inconsistent for me, having argued on a previous occasion that it is not unreasonable to trust Parliament with legislative sovereignty, to warn against possible abuses of self-embracing sovereignty. But one of the reasons for entrusting Parliament with ordinary legislative sovereignty is that mistakes and injustices can be corrected by future Parliaments, whereas if full self-embracing authority (theory B(2)) were used to limit their ability to do so, this could become difficult or impossible.

A more discriminating approach seems desirable, which enables the courts to uphold some limits, but not others. It would help if the courts adopted theory B(1) – the theory of procedural self-embracing sovereignty – which holds that Parliament can subject itself to manner or form requirements that do not limit its substantive authority.[108] Such requirements allow Parliament to exercise its substantive authority to legislate, which is 'continuing', but require it to follow some special but relatively undemanding procedure or form in order to do so. Manner or form requirements can be used to protect legislation of special importance from inadvertent or ill-considered amendment or repeal, by encouraging more careful or extensive deliberation than is usually required. For example, 'express repeal' requirements and absolute majority requirements can have this effect. This might be invaluable, provided the courts refuse to enforce substantive limits that are disguised as manner and form requirements.[109] On the other hand, for that very reason, this theory would not be able to accommodate every desirable reform. For example, a referendum requirement, despite being perfectly democratic, cannot logically be classified as a mere requirement as to manner or form. Such a requirement goes much further than just requiring Parliament to follow a particular procedure or adopt a particular form in exercising its substantive authority to enact law: by forbidding Parliament to enact law without the approval of an external body – namely, the electorate – it plainly limits its substantive authority.[110] (The usual way of attempting

---

[107] Two Australian cases in which this was argued to have happened are *Commonwealth Aluminium Corporation Pty Ltd* v. *Attorney-General* (Western Australia) [1976] Qd R 231 and *West Lakes Ltd* v. *South Australia* (1980) 25 SASR 389.

[108] See text to nn. 24–26, above; for further discussion, see Chapter 7, below.

[109] See n. 27, above.

[110] Contra, Winterton, 'The British Grundnorm', 604–6. For this reason, the decision of the High Court in *A.G. (NSW)* v. *Trethowan* (1931) 44 CLR 394 was legally erroneous,

to avoid this conclusion is to argue that a referendum requirement, rather than laying down a requirement as to the manner by which, or the form in which, Parliament must pass laws, changes the composition of Parliament, by making the electorate a part of it for special purposes. This is a patent rationalisation of a desired conclusion. A 'parliament' is a body that at least in part represents the electorate; it is nonsense to say that the electorate can be made part of the parliament that represents it.[111]) Super majority requirements raise particular difficulties, since they give a minority of members the power to veto legislation. They do diminish parliament's substantive power by making it considerably more difficult (and in an extreme case perhaps impossible) for it to legislate.

For the courts to adopt the theory of procedural self-embracing sovereignty – in response to an attempt by Parliament to subject itself to purely procedural or formal requirements – would involve a change in the rule of recognition, since that theory has not so far been authoritatively accepted. To go even further, and allow Parliament to impose constraints on its substantive powers, without running the dangers created by the full self-embracing theory, would require a more radical change in the consensus among senior legal officials that constitutes the rule of recognition. This has two desirable consequences. First, it requires the courts to determine whether the consensus among legislators themselves has truly evolved, as distinct from one political party attempting constitutional change without broader support. For example, there is a widespread consensus even among legislators that legislation inconsistent with European law should be disapplied pursuant to the European Communities Act 1972: the decision in *Factortame* did not provoke angry protests from any political party.[112] On the other hand, an attempt by one political party to use its temporary majority in Parliament to entrench partisan legislation should not prevail over a subsequent attempt to amend or repeal that legislation by the ordinary legislative procedure, partly because the entrenchment would not have been broadly accepted as legitimate even among legislators.

What about an attempt to entrench a Bill of Rights, by requiring that protected rights can be altered only by a future law approved of in a referendum? This might be controversial, and opposed by one side of politics, but if the Bill of Rights were itself first approved in a referendum, there

despite being pragmatically desirable: see Chapter 6, below. British judges, too, might be tempted to take the pragmatic rather than the logical course: see Winterton, 'The British Grundnorm', 605.

[111] See Chapter 7 Section IX, below.

[112] *Factortame* v. *Secretary of State for Transport (No. 2)* [1991] AC 603 (HL).

might be a broad consensus among legislators that the will of the electorate should be respected, and another referendum required in order to amend or repeal the Bill. In other words, by greatly enhancing the political legitimacy of a limit imposed on Parliament's authority, a referendum might also contribute to general official acceptance of that limit. The second consequence of my theory is that in each case, the judges would also have to be guided by their own assessment of constitutional principles, such as democracy and the rule of law, in deciding whether or not they should endorse any attempted entrenchment by Parliament. The danger of Oliver's approach is that the courts might be guided by such principles only in the first hard case that arises, which presents them with the opportunity to adopt the full self-embracing theory. Thereafter, that theory might – as a matter of logic – have to be applied in an undiscriminating fashion. That would make it more difficult for the judges to insist that only important constitutional rules or principles, which enjoy widespread, non-partisan support, may be entrenched, and only in ways that are consistent with democratic principle.[113]

---

[113] For similar reasoning, see Young, *Parliamentary Sovereignty and the Human Rights Act*, pp. 168–75.

6

Trethowan's case

I Introduction

Trethowan's case is among the most important and influential constitutional cases decided in any jurisdiction of the British Commonwealth. It was the first major case to deal with a problem common to many of these jurisdictions, including Britain itself: namely, whether, and to what extent, a Parliament can control or even restrict the future exercise of its own legislative power. The problem includes, for example, whether a Parliament can make the future enactment of legislation conditional on its being passed by super-majorities in Parliament, or by a majority of electors in a referendum. Moreover, the ingenious arguments put forward in the case, and adopted in various judgments, proposed novel solutions to the problem that have greatly influenced constitutional thought, throughout the Commonwealth, ever since. They are generally acknowledged to have inspired new theories of Parliamentary sovereignty, which are more amenable to Parliaments being able to bind themselves in these ways. But, however beneficial its consequences may have been, the decision in the case was almost certainly wrong as a matter of law. It is an example of creative judicial statecraft surmounting legal obstacles in the interests of good government.

II Background

In the early part of the twentieth century, members of Upper Houses in State Parliaments were either elected on a restricted property franchise, or (in New South Wales and Queensland) appointed for life by the Governor. Consequently, they 'were more patrician than democratic in character, their membership reflecting the interests of wealth and privilege'.[1] They

---

[1] D. Clune and G. Griffith, *Decision and Deliberation: The Parliament of New South Wales 1856–2003* (Sydney: Federation Press, 2006), pp. 242–3. Much of the information in this Section was found in this book's thorough account of the political background to the *Trethowan* litigation.

blocked legislation sponsored by Labor governments far more often than that of conservative governments.[2] In New South Wales, Labor quickly committed itself to either abolishing or radically reforming the Legislative Council, on the ground that it was an impediment to the sovereignty of the people who were more accurately represented in the Lower House. Abolition of the Council – to be replaced by popular initiative, referendum and recall, as a check on executive and legislative excess – became part of the party's State platform in 1898 and, from 1911, Labor appointees to the Council were required to 'hereby pledge myself on all occasions to do my utmost to ensure the carrying out of the principles embodied in the Labor Platform, including the abolition of the Legislative Council'.[3] In 1922, the Upper House of the Queensland Parliament was abolished, and in New South Wales, when the radical Labor government of Premier Jack Lang – elected in June 1925 – found itself continually stymied by the Upper House, it determined to follow suit. The brilliant young Labor lawyer H.V. Evatt, then a member of the State Parliament, provided the initial impetus for abolition.[4] By that time, it was widely acknowledged – even by most conservatives – that the Council had to be reformed, if it were to avoid abolition. A nominated Upper House was no longer acceptable.[5]

A Bill to abolish the Council was introduced in January 1926, but abolition had not been an issue at the preceding election, which allowed opponents to object that there was no popular mandate for it. Lang initially tried to ensure its passage by persuading the Governor to appoint to the Council a sufficient number of Labor nominees who were pledged to vote for it. This strategy led to dispute as to whether the Governor was bound by the conventions of responsible government to accede to whatever request for appointments the Premier might make. Twenty-five new members were appointed in December 1925, although the Governor did so 'under protest' after being advised accordingly by the Secretary of State for Dominion Affairs.[6] Nevertheless, when the Council came to vote on its own abolition, enough Labor members either absented themselves or voted against for the Bill to be narrowly defeated (they were subsequently expelled from the Party). When the Governor refused to make

[2] *Ibid.*, p. 313.   [3] *Ibid.*, pp. 243 and 248.
[4] P. Crockett, *Evatt, A Life* (Melbourne: Oxford University Press, 1993), p. 111; K. Buckley, B. Dale and W. Reynolds, *Doc Evatt* (Melbourne: Longman Cheshire, 1994), p. 58.
[5] Clune and Griffith, *Decision and Deliberation*, pp. 278–9.
[6] *Ibid.*, pp. 280–2; A.S. Morrison, 'Dominion Office Correspondence on the New South Wales Constitutional Crisis 1930–32' (1976) 61 *Journal of the Royal Australian Historical Society* 323 at 325.

ten further appointments to secure the Bill's passage, Attorney-General Edward McTiernan travelled to London to request that the Governor be instructed to change his mind. Lord Amery, the Secretary of State for Dominion Affairs, turned him down.[7] (Lang later castigated the 'crusted conservatives and … hidebound protocol specialists of Whitehall' for secretly directing the Governor while pretending not to.[8]) Eminent legal scholars such as Arthur Berriedale Keith and William Harrison Moore disagreed about the propriety of the Governor's conduct, although even H.V. Evatt later acknowledged that neither view could be said to be absolutely right or wrong.[9] Keith argued that it was a 'fundamental principle of democracy that changes of substance in the Constitution should only be carried out after they have been definitely and distinctly made the subject of a general election'[10] – or, he might have added, a referendum.

Lang lost an election in late 1927, and the conservative government of Sir Thomas Bavin came to power. Bavin proposed to reform the Legislative Council by making it an elected chamber, and also to protect it from being abolished or stripped of power except with the approval of a majority of voters in a referendum.[11] 'We are determined', he explained, 'that there should be no repetition of what we saw in the last Parliament, when there was an effort to destroy the Legislative Council and to make a fundamental alteration in the Constitution of the state without consulting the people'.[12] Sir John Peden, a long-standing Professor and Dean of Law at Sydney University, and a member of the Council since 1917, is credited with devising the government's strategy: it has been said that Peden's initial idea was 'for a time regarded as so important that the [University Law] faculty administrative officer used to take visitors to the spot in the library where Sir John was said to have had it'.[13] The idea was not original: he was undoubtedly influenced by the views of Berriedale Keith, then the leading British authority on colonial and Dominion constitutions. Peden drafted

[7] Clune and Griffith, *Decision and Deliberation*, pp. 283–5.

[8] J.T. Lang, *I Remember* (Sydney: Invincible Press, 1956), p. 297 and ch. 56 *passim*.

[9] Clune and Griffith, *Decision and Deliberation*, pp. 285–6 and 281 respectively. See also H.V. Evatt, *The King and His Dominion Governors* (2nd edn) (Melbourne: FW Cheshire, 1967), pp. 134–5.

[10] *Scotsman*, 4 March 1927, quoted in Evatt, *The King and His Dominion*, p. 134 (also referred to by Clune and Griffith, *Decision and Deliberation*, p. 286).

[11] Clune and Griffith, *Decision and Deliberation*, p. 287.

[12] *Parliamentary Debates, New South Wales*, 2nd ser. (*NSWPD*), vol. 117, p. 3621, quoted in C.H. Currey, 'The Legislative Council of New South Wales, 1843–1943' *Journal and Proceedings of the Royal Australian Historical Society* 29 (1943) 337 at 417.

[13] W. L. Morison, 'The Future Scope of Australian Common Law' *Sydney Law Review* 13 335 (1991) at 338.

the Bill to require a referendum with the assistance of Attorney-General
F.S. Boyce KC, another member of the Council who was later appointed
to the Supreme Court, and E.M. Mitchell K.C., a one-time Law School
colleague of Peden's who subsequently helped represent the plaintiffs
in *Trethowan's* case.[14] It might be noted that Bavin was himself a barris-
ter of considerable experience and reputation, and was appointed to the
Supreme Court in 1935.[15]

The Constitution (Legislative Council) Amendment Bill inserted a new
section – s. 7A – into the State's Constitution Act. The crucial provisions
of this section are as follows:

> (1) The Legislative Council shall not be abolished nor … shall its con-
>   stitution or powers be altered except in the manner provided in this
>   section.
> (2) A Bill for any purpose within subsection one of this section shall not
>   be presented to the Governor for His Majesty's assent until the Bill
>   has been approved by the electors in accordance with this section.
> (6) he provisions of this section shall extend to any Bill for the repeal or
>   amendment of this section …

This was described by the Labor Opposition as extraordinarily cun-
ning, largely because of sub-section (6).[16] Crucial to Peden's strategy,
this is an example of what has come to be called a 'self entrenching' or
'double entrenching' provision: it applies the referendum requirement
to its own future repeal or amendment. Without it, the requirements
in sub-sections (1) and (2) would have been ineffective, because a later
Parliament wanting to abolish the Legislative Council without holding
a referendum could simply have repealed s. 7A by ordinary legislation,
and then proceeded to abolish the Council in the same way. The device
of self or double entrenchment appears to have been first proposed by
Berriedale Keith.[17]

---

[14] Clune and Griffith, *Decision and Deliberation*, pp. 288–9; K. Turner, *House of Review?
The New South Wales Legislative Council, 1934–68* (Sydney: Sydney University Press,
1969), pp. 14 and 17.
[15] See T. Blackshield, M. Coper, G. Fricke and T. Simpson, 'Counsel, notable', in
T. Blackshield, M. Coper and G. Williams (eds.), *The Oxford Companion to the High
Court of Australia* (Melbourne: Oxford University Press, 2001), pp. 160 at 163 and 166.
[16] *NSWPD*, vol. 113, 15 May 1928, pp. 572–3 (A.C. Wills) and 597 (W. Brennan).
[17] A.B. Keith, *Imperial Unity and the Dominions* (Oxford: Clarendon Press, 1916),
pp. 389–90, quoted in *Attorney-General (NSW)* v. *Trethowan* (1931) 44 CLR 417 at 424
(Starke J). See also A.B. Keith, *Responsible Government in the Dominions* (2nd edn)
(Oxford: Oxford University Press, 1928), pp. 352–3.

Bavin taunted the Labor Party by asking how, given its long-standing commitment to the referendum as the epitome of democracy, it could possibly oppose s. 7A.[18] In the Council, Labor members pledged to support s. 7A if, as logic and consistency demanded, it were itself submitted to a referendum before being enacted; but their proposed amendment along these lines was defeated by a vote of 34–14.[19]

There seems to have been some confusion as to the intended effect of the section. Even Attorney-General Boyce, on introducing the Bill containing s. 7A in the Assembly, assured members that it could be repealed by a subsequent Parliament, quoting Bacon and Dicey as authorities for the proposition that no Parliament could bind itself. 'All that we can do is to throw obstacles in the way of repeal', he added.[20] When reminded by Sir Joseph Carruthers that the whole point of the section was to bind future Parliaments, he replied: 'It is the best we can do.'[21] According to the historian Charles Currey, who lived through the events, opinion as to the bindingness of s. 7A was sharply divided. The view that it was legally binding 'was scoffed at by men of legal learning', both within the legislature and outside.[22] One said that sub-section (6) was 'an absolute absurdity ... For this Parliament to purport to bind future Parliaments in this way is simply futile and, to that extent, the Bill is not worth the paper it is written on'.[23] Even Peden was reported to have expressed doubt, acknowledging in April 1930 that 'some eminent lawyers believed that the courts would decide that the Act could be repealed in the ordinary way'.[24] Due to various delays, the Bill did not come into force until just before the general election of October 1930 that returned Labor to government.[25] In the meantime, legislation to reform the Upper House had been introduced, debated and amended, but a proposed referendum not proceeded with.[26]

Upon resuming office as Premier, Lang immediately revived his campaign to abolish the Council. This time he could claim a mandate from

---

[18] *NSWPD*, vol. 117, 12 March 1929, pp. 3619–21, 3626 and 3715.
[19] *NSWPD*, vol. 113, 15 May 1928, pp. 598–601.
[20] *NSWPD*, vol. 113, 10 May 1929, p. 502.
[21] *Ibid.*, p. 506; Clune and Griffith, *Decision and Deliberation*, p. 288.
[22] Currey, 'The Legislative Council', 417.
[23] *NSWPD*, vol. 117, 13 March 1929, p. 3704 (Mr McKell).
[24] Sydney Morning Herald, 1 April 1930, p. 10, quoted in Clune and Griffith, *Decision and Deliberation*, p. 294.
[25] Clune and Griffith, *Decision and Deliberation*, p. 289.
[26] *Ibid.*, pp. 289–93.

the people, since his policy speech had plainly spelled out this objective.[27] Even Carruthers, a veteran conservative Councillor, agreed that Lang had a mandate, but insisted that a referendum should nevertheless be held.[28] Governor Sir Philip Game also acknowledged that Lang had a 'popular mandate' to abolish the Council, and that this policy had been 'placed first on the programme he put before the electors in his Policy Speech'.[29] Two Bills – one to repeal s. 7A, and the other to abolish the Council – were introduced in the Council, and quickly passed by both Houses without opposition. Opponents of the Bills apparently decided not to defeat them in the Council, which might have led the Governor to appoint new Labor members at the government's behest, but instead, to seek judicial enforcement of the requirement in s. 7A that a referendum had to be held.[30] In fact, Premier Lang had already sought further appointments, the very day after he was returned to office, and continued to do so while litigation proceeded through the courts, although the Governor, Sir Philip Game, held out until November 1931.[31]

Lang could have submitted the Bills to a referendum, and it has been suggested that 'after his resounding electoral success, the chance of further approval by voters was reasonably good'.[32] He recalled many years later that he was unwilling to do so because 'I had in effect referred it to the people by asking for a mandate that had been given to me'.[33] He was fortified by a legal opinion of the Crown Solicitor, John Tillett, obtained by Attorney-General Andrew Lysacht at the Governor's request, that a referendum was not legally mandatory.[34] The opinion stated that British Parliamentary tradition prevented any Parliament from binding itself in the future.[35]

[27] Turner, *House of Review?*, p. 17.

[28] N.B. Nairn, *The Big Fella: Jack Lang and the Australian Labor Party 1891–1949* (Melbourne: Melbourne University Press, 1995), p. 214.

[29] Letter from Governor to Premier, 2 April 1931, printed by the Legislative Assembly (NSW), State Records Office (NSW), CGS 4545 (2/8206; microfilm copy SR Reels 2784–2785, Folio 650); Premier to Secretary of State for Dominion Affairs, 11 November 1930, DO 35/11156/8–9, quoted in F. Cain, *Jack Lang and the Great Depression* (Melbourne: Australian Scholarly Publishing, 2005), p. 222; see also Currey, 'The Legislative Council', 419.

[30] Clune and Griffith, *Decision and Deliberation*, p. 294.

[31] *Ibid.*, pp. 296–9; Turner, *House of Review?*, p. 17.

[32] Nairn, *The Big Fella*, p. 213.

[33] J.T. Lang, *The Turbulent Years* (Sydney: Alpha Books, 1970), p. 108.

[34] Nairn, *The Big Fella*, p. 213; Currey, 'The Legislative Council', 419; Morrison, 'Dominion Office Correspondence', 326.

[35] Memo, 'Repeal of Constitution (Legislative Council) Amendment Act, 1929', 6 November 1930, papers regarding differences between Governor Game and Premier Lang, CGS

On 10 December 1930, the day the Bills were passed, Lang presented Governor Game with a memorandum, which he was advised to send forthwith by cable to the British government, requesting that Game assent to the Bills immediately. Game sent it, adding to the cable that he could see no reason why he should not accept his Ministers' advice.[36] This cable included further legal advice supplied to the Governor, which described s. 7A as

> an unprecedented attempt to convert a flexible and an uncontrolled Constitution into a rigid and controlled one, not by the will of the Imperial Parliament, but by the mere operation of an ordinary local law passed according to the views of a casual and accidental majority in one Parliament.[37]

But on 11 December, several members of the Council, led by Arthur K. Trethowan, instituted proceedings in the State's Supreme Court, seeking a declaration that presentation of the Bills to the Governor for the royal assent would be unlawful, absent a referendum, and also an injunction to restrain such action. Peden, who had become President of the Council in February 1929, was ironically named as the first defendant, because Standing Orders required him to present Bills originating in the Council to the Governor. (In fact, according to newspaper reports, Lang had considered attempting to dismiss Peden as President, by executive minute – to which Game would have had to consent – for refusing to present the Bills.[38]) The other defendants were Ministers of the Crown. Long Innes J granted an interim injunction until the matter could be dealt with by the Full Court. According to one historian, the Chief Justice, Sir Philip Street, was keen to expedite proceedings, and the Full Court of five judges appointed to sit just a few days later was the first for twenty-five years.[39]

Game's cable to London triggered a flurry of activity, in which the Secretary of State for Dominion Affairs, J.H. Thomas, explored alternative ways of saving the Legislative Council, including the exercise of the King's power of disallowance. It was eventually decided that there was too

---

4545 reels 2784–5, folio 844, State Records Authority of New South Wales, quoted in Cain, *Jack Lang*, p. 222.

[36] Cable, 'Game to Secretary of State for Dominion Affairs', 10 December 1930, DO 35/11156/10, NA, quoted in Cain, *Jack Lang*, p. 224; also referred to by Currey, 'The Legislative Council', 422.

[37] Cable from Governor to Secretary of State, 11 December 1930, DO 35/400 11156/6.

[38] *Morning Post*, 4 December 1930, and *Daily Mail*, 9 December 1930, press clippings, DO 35/400 11156/5.

[39] Crockett, *Evatt, A Life*, p. 112.

great a risk that this might arouse a political 'storm which would sweep away the power itself'.[40]

Argument before the Full Court was heard from 15–18 December, just in time for Evatt to appear for the defendants, since he was appointed to the High Court by the Scullin Labor government on 19 December (McTiernan was appointed to that Court the following day). On 23 December, the Full Court handed down its judgment. The expedited nature of the proceedings should be kept in mind when evaluating the quality of the opinions delivered. The Court held by a majority of 4–1 that the requirements of s. 7A were binding, and granted the relief sought. Street C.J., Ferguson, James and Owen J.J. found for the plaintiffs, and Long Innes J dissented.

An appeal was immediately taken to the High Court. Evatt was precluded from sitting in the case, because of his previous involvement as counsel, but McTiernan sat, even though as Lang's Attorney-General in 1926 he had been intimately involved in the initial attempt to abolish the Council (he had fallen out with Lang, and not contested his seat at the 1927 election). After hearing argument on 20–21 January, the High Court on 16 March 1931 rejected the government's appeal by a majority of 3–2. Rich, Starke and Dixon J.J. made up the majority; McTiernan and Gavan Duffy C.J., an earlier Labor appointee to the Court, dissented. Interviewed by Morrison in 1975, at the age of 98, Lang recalled 'a little story told to me by one of the judges' (allegedly McTiernan):

> On the morning the [*Trethowan*] judgment was given in the High Court the weather was very bad. The Chief Justice, Sir Gavan Duffy, came down the stairs and said … 'A dirty day for a dirty deed'.[41]

But either Lang's memory or Morrison's report is untrustworthy, because in 1970, Lang claimed that Gavan Duffy had made this comment just before judgment was handed down in one of the *Garnishee* cases.[42]

A further appeal, to the Judicial Committee of the Privy Council, was rejected on 31 May 1932. The Attorney-Generals for both England (Sir William Jowitt) and the Commonwealth of Australia (Sir John Latham) intervened at the request of that court. Lang had asked the Dominions

---

[40] Memo from Chancellor of the Exchequer, 19 December 1930, DO 35/400 11156/10.

[41] A.S. Morrison, 'Further Documents and Comment on the New South Wales Constitutional Crisis 1930–1932' *Journal of the Royal Australian Historical Society* 68 (1982) 122 at 129.

[42] Lang, *Turbulent Years*, p. 187; see *New South Wales* v. *Commonwealth (No 1)* (1932) 46 CLR 155 and *(No 2)* (1932) 46 CLR 246.

Office to advise Jowitt to support the State government's case, but was told that this was constitutionally impossible because the Attorney-General acted independently.[43] In fact, the Attorney-General was initially advised by the Dominions Office that it might embarrass the British government if he openly supported either party in the case. But due to concerns about other Dominion constitutions – in particular, those of South Africa and the Irish Free State – he was eventually asked to support, if he found it possible to do so, the judgment of the High Court, so that those constitutions could have some degree of rigidity.[44] Sir Thomas Inskip, who replaced Jowitt as Attorney-General, did find this possible.[45] Latham for the Commonwealth also supported the plaintiffs.[46] The Privy Council's judgment was delivered in the middle of a State election campaign, brought about by Premier Lang having been dismissed, on 12 May, by Governor Game. Labor lost the ensuing election.

Sydney was at this time a small world, as was the Australian legal profession as a whole. Peden had taught both Evatt and McTiernan at Sydney Law School, and was held in high regard by Evatt.[47] Sir Philip Street, the State's Chief Justice, provided legal advice to Governor Game during the crisis leading to Lang's dismissal; by then, Lang regarded Street as the 'leader' of his government's enemies.[48] Lang's government was notoriously unpopular among Sydney's commercial and legal elites.[49] Owen Dixon believed it to be 'dangerous and thoroughly corrupt, and Evatt and McTiernan as forever stigmatised by their former intimate association with it'.[50] Commonwealth Attorney-General Latham was a personal friend of Bavin's, both being members of the 'Waterfall Fly Fishing Club', which Lang denounced as a sinister cabal of politicians, judges and businessmen.[51]

---

[43] Telegram from Game to Secretary of State for Dominion Affairs, 20 March 1931; reply, 26 March 1931, DO 35/400 11156/15.

[44] Minute of meeting between H. Bushe, H. Batterby and W. Jowitt, 24 September 1931, DO 35/400 11156/59 and other documents included there; minutes of a further meeting on 6 April 1932, DO 345/400 11156/85.

[45] *Attorney-General (NSW)* v. *Trethowan* [1932] AC 526 at 532.

[46] 'Case for the Intervenant', Privy Council Appeal Book, University of Sydney Law Library (Call No 342.940238).

[47] Buckley, Dale and Reynolds, *Doc Evatt*, p. 54; K. Tennant, *Evatt, Politics and Justice* (Sydney: Angus & Robertson, 1970), pp. 22 and 32.

[48] Morrison, 'Constitutional Crisis', 128–30.

[49] Cain, *Jack Lang*, p. 230.

[50] P. Ayres, *Owen Dixon* (Melbourne: Miegunyah Press, 2003), pp. 60, 182–3.

[51] See 'Latham, Sir John Greig', *Australian Dictionary of Biography Online Edition*, www.adb.online.anu.edu.au/biogs/A100002b.htm?hilite=latham.

III Parliamentary privilege

The litigation in *Trethowan* was remarkable for several reasons. One was that the Supreme Court was prepared to issue an injunction restraining the presentation of Bills to the Governor for the royal assent. Evatt had objected that this would amount to an interference with Parliamentary privilege.[52] Long Innes J. expressed disquiet concerning this aspect of the case. The object of the suit, he observed, was 'to prevent the two Houses of the Legislature from communicating to the third element thereof, His Majesty, their advice in regard to legislation in the process of making', and therefore 'to interfere with the internal affairs of Parliament'. This would 'in all probability, constitute an infringement of the privileges of Parliament, and may provoke a most undesirable conflict between Parliament and the Judiciary'.[53]

Nevertheless, His Honour agreed that the Court had jurisdiction to issue the injunction, and discussed whether it should exercise its discretion in favour of granting the remedy. He indicated that, if compelled to choose between Parliamentary privilege and the rule of law, he would prefer to uphold the latter.[54] Given the decision of the majority on the question of substance, an injunction should be granted if the defendants might otherwise flout the law. He expressed 'great regret and astonishment' that Lang's Ministers had refused to undertake not to present the Bills to the Governor until the final disposition of the case on appeal. The principal defendant, Sir John Peden, was unable to give such an undertaking because he had chosen not to appear or be represented.[55]

Street C.J. and Owen J. also discussed this issue, while Ferguson and James J.J. simply agreed with the view of the Chief Justice. They did not share Long Innes J.'s qualms about the propriety of intervening, because Parliament had itself specifically provided in s. 7A that Bills of the kind in question 'shall not be presented to the Governor for His Majesty's assent' until approved at a referendum. They described this as a 'statutory inhibition' and 'prohibition', whose violation would constitute an illegal act that the courts might be bound to restrain.[56] Owen J. said that to prevent the President of the Legislative Council from presenting the Bills to the Governor 'in direct contravention of an Act duly passed by Parliament is, in no sense, an interference with the rights, powers and privileges of Parliament'.[57]

---

[52] *Trethowan* v. *Peden* (1930) 31 SR (NSW) 183 at 195.
[53] *Ibid.*, 234.   [54] *Ibid.*, 235.   [55] *Ibid.*, 234–5   [56] *Ibid.*, 205 (Street C.J.); 221 (Owen J.).
[57] *Ibid.*, 221; see also 205 (Street C.J.).

As for the Court's discretion to decline to issue an injunction, Owen J. indicated that, if some other remedy issued post-enactment – such as a declaration of invalidity, or damages – would be adequate, that would be the preferred course. But in his opinion, the injury that the plaintiffs would suffer – the temporary deprivation of their rights and privileges as members of the Council – could not be properly compensated by an award of damages.[58] The majority agreed with Long Innes J., that if the defendants had undertaken not to present the Bills to the Governor, an injunction would not have been appropriate.[59]

The High Court did not discuss this issue, because it limited the grounds of appeal to the abstract question of whether the two Bills, if enacted contrary to s. 7A, would be valid. But in 1954, in *Hughes and Vale* v. *Gair*, Dixon C.J. expressed doubt as to the correctness of the Supreme Court's issue of an injunction in *Trethowan*, notwithstanding the express prohibition in s. 7A. He stated that an application for such an injunction is 'very exceptional. We do not think it should be granted on this occasion or in any case'.[60] It is unclear whether the other members of the Court agreed with him in this regard.

The propriety of judicial intervention in on going legislative proceedings has been raised in a number of subsequent cases, including *Attorney-General (WA)* v. *Marquet*, and is thoroughly canvassed elsewhere.[61]

IV   The validity and bindingness of s. 7A

The substantive issues were well defined from the start, and ingenious arguments were put by counsel on both sides. In explaining their arguments and counter-arguments, and the judges' responses, I will draw upon judgments from all three of the courts that became involved. For simplicity, I will use the term 'plaintiffs' to refer to the Legislative Councillors who first instituted the proceedings before the Supreme Court, and 'defendants' to refer to the government Ministers against whom relief was sought, in relation to proceedings in all three courts. I will use the term 'majority judges' to refer to those in all three courts who decided in favour of the plaintiffs – in other words, all the judges involved, except Long Innes J. in the Supreme Court, and Gavan Duffy C.J. and McTiernan J. in the High Court.

[58] *Ibid.*, 221 (Owen J.).
[59] *Ibid.*, 206 (Street C.J.), 221–2 (Owen J.).
[60] (1954) 90 CLR 203 at 204.
[61] E. Campbell, *Parliamentary Privilege* (Sydney: Federation Press, 2003), ch. 7; A. Twomey, *The Constitution of New South Wales* (Sydney: Federation Press, 2004), pp. 240–5.

The defendants challenged the validity or bindingness only of sub-s (6) of s. 7A.[62] They conceded, perhaps wrongly, that s. 7A was otherwise valid and binding. The legislature could validly require that a referendum be held before legislation of a certain kind could be enacted – except for legislation altering or repealing that requirement itself, which the legislature necessarily retained power to enact in the ordinary way. As Loxton KC put it: 'It was legitimate for the legislature to shut a gate and lock it, but we say, that it has in s. 7A thrown away the key.'[63] This argument appears to concede that such a requirement is binding only in the sense that it cannot be ignored, and repealed by mere implication, in accordance with the principle in *McCawley's* case[64] – in other words, it must be expressly repealed before Parliament can act contrary to it.[65] But Parliament necessarily remains free to change its mind and remove the requirement.[66]

It is not clear why the defendants conceded the validity of s. 7A apart from sub-s (6). It is tempting to construe their argument as follows: Parliament can require that a referendum be held for ordinary legislation because it has constituent power, that is, power to change the constitution itself, including provisions governing law-making. But it can subsequently alter or repeal such a requirement for precisely the same reason: it necessarily retains that same constituent power. In other words, it can exercise its constituent power so as to fetter its ordinary power – its power to enact ordinary legislation – but it cannot fetter the constituent power itself. But this distinction is untenable on the facts, because s. 7A (1) and (2), as well as sub-s (6), purported to fetter Parliament's constituent, rather than its ordinary, legislative power. Bills to abolish the Legislative Council, and to change its constitution or powers, are concerned with constitutional matters. Therefore, s. 7A as a whole purported to fetter the constituent power.

Be that as it may, the defendants argued that sub-s (6) was either invalid or ineffectual because: first, under the State's flexible, uncontrolled constitution, Parliament enjoyed plenary authority of the same sovereign nature as that of the United Kingdom Parliament, and a sovereign Parliament

---

[62] On the distinction between validity and bindingness, see J.D. Goldsworthy, 'Manner and Form in the Australian States' *Melbourne University Law Review* 16 (1987) 403 at 405–6.

[63] Reported in *Sydney Morning Herald*, 21 January 1931, p. 17.

[64] *McCawley* v. *R* [1920] AC 691.

[65] See summary of the defendants' argument at (1930) 31 SR (NSW) 183 at 187–8 and 188–9.

[66] Argument of Loxton KC reported at (1931) 44 CLR 394 at 401–2.

cannot bind itself; and secondly, sub-s (6) was repugnant both to s. 4 of the Imperial Act 18 and 19 Vict c. 54, and to s. 5 of the Colonial Laws Validity Act.[67]

As for the first argument, the plaintiffs replied that general theories concerning Parliamentary sovereignty, and the powers of the Imperial Parliament, were irrelevant. The State Parliament was a subordinate legislature, whose powers were conferred by superior constitutional instruments. Whether s. 7A was valid and binding turned on the meaning of these instruments, and not on false analogies between the State and the Imperial Parliaments, or on philosophical analysis of the abstract concept of sovereignty. This reply arguably overlooked the established principle that the Imperial Parliament had intended to invest colonial legislatures with power of the same plenary nature as its own power, but almost all the judges in all three courts agreed with the submission.[68] They directed their attention to the two Imperial Acts that conferred constituent power on the State Parliament, and therefore, so shall we.

The first Act, commonly called the Constitution Statute, enacted the State's first Constitution Act, an amended version of legislation passed in New South Wales that was included in a schedule to the Statute.[69] Section 4 of the Statute provided that:

> It shall be lawful for the legislature of New South Wales to make laws altering or repealing all or any of the provisions of the said reserved Bill [the Constitution Act], in the same manner as any other laws for the good government of the said Colony, subject, however, to the conditions imposed by the said reserved Bill on the alteration of the provisions thereof in certain particulars, until and unless the said conditions shall be repealed or altered by the authority of the said legislature.

Section 5 of the Colonial Laws Validity Act 1865 (the 'CLVA'), which applied to the New South Wales legislature, provided that:

> [E]very Representative Legislature shall ... have, and be deemed at all Times to have had, full Power to make Laws respecting the Constitution, Powers, and Procedure of such Legislature; provided that such Laws shall

---

[67] (1930) 31 SR (NSW) 183 at 187.

[68] *Trethowan v. Peden* (1930) 31 SR (NSW) 183 at 198–9 (Street C.J.), 208 (Ferguson J.), 213 and 216 (Owen J.), 228–9 (Long Innes J.); *Attorney-General (NSW) v. Trethowan* (1931) 44 CLR 394 at 418 (Rich J.), 422 (Starke J.), 425–7 (Dixon J.), 434–5 (McTiernan J.); *Attorney-General (NSW) v. Trethowan* (1931) 47 CLR 97 at 99 and 104 (PC).

[69] The terms 'Constitution Statute' and 'Constitution Act' were prescribed by the Interpretation Act 1897 (NSW).

have been passed in such Manner and Form as may from Time to Time
be required by any Act of Parliament, Letters Patent, Order in Council, or
Colonial Law for the Time being in force in the said Colony.

With respect to s. 4, the defendants argued that the Imperial Parliament
had expressly declared that the State legislature could alter the
Constitution Act 'in the same manner as any other law', subject only to
conditions imposed in the original Act, which could themselves be – and
had in fact already been – repealed.[70] They also argued that the CLVA had
been intended merely to reaffirm the pre-existing law, and not to affect
the operation of s. 4.[71] The plaintiffs replied that s. 4 applied only to the
original Constitution Act, and therefore was exhausted or 'spent' when
that Act was repealed and replaced by the State's Constitution Act of 1902.
Moreover, of the two Imperial instruments, the CLVA was intended to be
comprehensive and paramount, and being the most recent statement of
the Imperial Parliament's will, it impliedly repealed s. 4 insofar as there
was any discrepancy between them.[72] Most of the judges accepted one or
the other of the plaintiffs' submissions.[73] I will assume that they were right
to do so, and in what follows, confine my analysis to the meaning and
effect of CLVA, s. 5. This does not affect the substance of the defendants'
arguments.

The defendants' objection to sub-s (6) was that it purported to restrict
a constituent power – to make laws with respect to the legislature's own
constitution, powers and procedure – which CLVA, s. 5 conferred on all
representative colonial legislatures, including that of New South Wales.
Section 5 declared that such legislatures 'shall … have, and be deemed
at all times to have had' this 'full power'. The defendants insisted that it
was therefore a 'continuing' power: the legislature could not abdicate,
alienate or restrict a power that the Imperial Parliament had declared it
'shall have', because the legislature could not amend or repeal an Imperial
Act applying to it by paramount force.[74] It could not have been plausibly

---

[70] (1930) 31 SR (NSW) 183 at 188. It was clear from the Despatch from the Secretary of
State for the Colonies to the Governor of NSW, which accompanied the Constitution
Statute, that s. 4 was intended to enable those conditions to be repealed by ordinary legis-
lation: see the judgment of McTiernan J, (1931) 44 CLR 394 at 439.

[71] (1930) 31 SR (NSW) 183 at 188; (1931) 44 CLR 394 at 403.

[72] *Ibid.*, 183 at 191–2.

[73] *Ibid.*, 183 at 200 (Street C.J.), 212 (James J. concurring), 217 (Owen J.); (1931) 44 CLR 394
at 417 (Rich J.), 428–9 (Dixon J.); (1932) 47 CLR 97 at 104 (PC).

[74] Dixon J. placed some emphasis on the phrase 'shall … be deemed at all times to have
had' the power: (1931) 44 CLR 394 at 430. It could be argued to mean that the legislature
must be deemed at all times, *past and future*, to have had the power. But it was probably

supposed that the Imperial Parliament would have countenanced a colonial legislature discarding the power that it had been given. As Dixon J. paraphrased this argument, the power was 'superior and indestructible', because 'the legislature ... continues to retain unaffected and unimpaired by its own laws the power given by this provision'.[75] Or as McTiernan J. put it, s. 5 was 'an overriding charter which keeps the legislature continuously supplied with plenary power to make laws respecting its own constitution, powers and procedure', notwithstanding any attempt to divest itself of the power.[76]

For the defendants, it logically followed that sub-s (6) was invalid, because 'the provision for a referendum takes from Parliament the power to do as it likes and makes its will dependent on the volition of a body it is unable to control', and Parliament 'could not submit its volition to the volition of a third person'.[77] Since Parliament necessarily retained the continuing power conferred on it by CLVA, s. 5, it remained free to alter its own constitution, powers or procedure, and could not be compelled to first seek the approval of a person or group external to it – not even its own electors. Section 5 conferred the power on Parliament alone, and not on Parliament plus the electors. As Long Innes J. put it:

> 'Full power' to make laws necessarily involves equally full power to unmake or repeal them; and sub-section 6 of section 7A purports to shackle or control that full power, because it makes the exercise of that power dependent upon the approval of an outside body which does not form part of the Legislature itself.[78]

The plaintiffs replied that CLVA, s. 5 empowered a representative legislature to convert its Constitution into a rigid or controlled one, even by the insertion of a referendum requirement. It was the intention of the Imperial Parliament to make colonial legislatures their own constitution-makers, and if they wanted to insert a referendum requirement into their constitutions, they should not have to go cap-in-hand and beg the Imperial Parliament to do it for them.[79] There were two alternative ways, the plaintiffs argued, by which a State Parliament could

included merely to ensure that the legislature would be deemed to have had the power *at all past times*, even before the CLVA was enacted. Its correct interpretation depends partly on whether the words 'at all times' attach to 'be deemed', or to 'to have had'.

[75] (1931) 44 CLR 394 at 430.
[76] *Ibid.*, 443.
[77] Loxton K.C., reported in (1931) 44 CLR 394 at 403 and 400 respectively; see also 402.
[78] (1930) 31 SR (NSW) 183 at 232.
[79] (1931) 44 CLR 394 at 406.

do this itself.[80] I will refer to these, for convenience, as 'reconstitution' and 'manner and form' respectively. Reconstitution involves altering the composition or structure of the legislature, and manner and form, the procedure by which, or the form in which, laws are passed. Reconstitution depended on the power that CLVA, s. 5 conferred on each legislature to alter its own constitution, quite independently of the proviso that follows and qualifies that power, whereas manner and form depends on the proviso.

It is worth noting that, by relying exclusively on these two alternatives, the plaintiffs conceded that the power conferred by CLVA, s. 5 was, in itself, a 'continuing' one. They did not argue that it was a 'self-embracing' power that could be used to abolish or diminish itself, independently of the manner and form proviso.[81] As Dixon J. put the point, '[c]onsidered apart from the proviso, [s. 5] could not reasonably be understood to authorize any regulation, control or impairment of the power it describes. It does not say that the legislature may make laws respecting its own powers including this power'.[82] The two alternatives the defendants put forward were intended to show that s. 7A was consistent with the power being a continuing one. I will discuss reconstitution first.

A   Reconstitution

The plaintiffs argued that a referendum requirement could be made binding by changing the composition of the legislature itself, so that for particular purposes, it would consist of the King, the two Houses and the electors speaking by referendum.[83] If s. 7A had done this, the defendants' main objection would be rebutted: the legislature would be shown to retain, undiminished, the continuing power conferred by CLVA, s. 5, and to be able to repeal s. 7A at any time – except that, for this particular purpose, the legislature would consist of the King, the two Houses and the electors. On this construction of s. 7A, the electors were not external to the legislature, with the ability to veto Bills passed by the two Houses; they were, instead, an internal, constitutive element of it. The 'full power' was untouched and intact, but the power-holder was reconstituted.

---

[80] They are clearly distinguished at (1931) 44 CLR 394 at 407–8 (argument of counsel for Trethowan), in the judgment of Rich J., *ibid.*, at 418, and in the plaintiffs' submissions before the Privy Council at [1932] AC 526 at 530.

[81] This is modern terminology invented by H.L.A. Hart, *The Concept of Law* (2nd edn) (Oxford: Clarendon Press, 1994), ch. 7, s. 4.

[82] (1931) 44 CLR 394 at 430–1.

[83] (1930) 31 SR (NSW) 183 at 191.

It was agreed on all sides that a State Parliament could change its own composition, either by abolishing one of its existing Houses or by adding a new House or other decision-making body.[84] This was indisputable, given that such Parliaments had power to change their own constitutions, and that s. 9 of the Constitution Statute expressly defined 'the legislature' so as to include not only the legislature as originally constituted, but 'any future legislature which may be established' through the powers of amendment conferred by s. 4 of the Statute and by the Constitution Act itself.

In the Supreme Court, Ferguson J. suggested that the same was true even of the United Kingdom Parliament. The principle that Parliament cannot shackle its own legislative power, he said:

> does not mean … that it is beyond the power of the King, with the assent of the Lords and Commons, to pass an Act today which it is impossible for the King, with the assent of the Lords and Commons, to repeal tomorrow. Tomorrow there may be no Lords and Commons, or rather, those two estates may not compose the Parliament of tomorrow. What I conceive to be the true rule is that the sovereign Legislature of today, however constituted, cannot pass a law which the equally sovereign Legislature of tomorrow, however it may be constituted, cannot repeal.[85]

He thought the same reasoning applied to the New South Wales legislature, although he did not clearly apply it to the facts, and towards the end of his judgment, seems to rely on manner and form rather than reconstitution.[86]

In the High Court, Dixon J. also hinted that reconstitution was in principle possible:

> The power [in CLVA, s. 5] to make laws respecting its own constitution enables the legislature to deal with its own nature and composition … Laws which relate to its own constitution … must govern the legislature in the exercise of its powers, including the exercise of its power to repeal those very laws.[87]

He also said that if the British Parliament were to require the assent of the electors before any part of a particular Act could be repealed, and that requirement were later ignored, 'the Courts might be called upon to consider whether the supreme legislative power in respect of the matter had in truth been exercised in the manner required for its authentic expression and by the elements in which it had come to reside'.[88] But he

---

[84] See, e.g., *ibid.*, 227 (Long Innes J.).   [85] *Ibid.*, 207; see also 210.
[86] *Ibid.*, 210–11.   [87] (1931) 44 CLR 394 at 430.   [88] *Ibid.*, 426.

went on to decide the case on the basis of manner and form, rather than reconstitution.

Notably, even McTiernan J., who powerfully dissented in the High Court, did not reject the reconstitution argument outright. In setting out his conclusions, he said:

> the submission of the Bill to repeal sec. 7A to the electors would be neces-sary if the electors have been made a part of a Legislature which thereupon became the only authority competent to repeal sec. 7A. In my opinion sec. 7A has not that result.[89]

Whether or not s. 7A did have that result depended on the answers to two contentious questions: (a) whether or not a State Parliament could be constituted differently for different purposes, with the constituent power granted by CLVA, s. 5 being divided accordingly, and (b) whether or not s. 7A was most plausibly interpreted as doing this.

As for (a), the defendants argued that there could be only one State legis-lature in existence at any one time, so that if the electors were to be made part of the legislature for passing some laws, they had to be made part of it for all purposes.[90] McTiernan J. accepted this argument, on the ground that the many references to 'the legislature' or 'the Parliament' of the State, in the Constitution Statute, the CLVA, and the State and Commonwealth constitutions, were all references to the same body, which exercised gen-eral, plenary legislative power within the State.[91] In the Supreme Court, Long Innes J. accepted that the legislature could be constituted differ-ently for different purposes, but insisted that the constituent power had to remain vested in the legislature as constituted for ordinary pur-poses: the power conferred by s. 4 of the Constitution Statute was neces-sarily possessed by 'the legislature' as defined by s. 9 of the Statute, and an alternative legislature *ad hoc* did not fall within that definition.[92] If the electors were not made part of the legislature for general purposes, they remained outside the legislature that retained full constituent power, and any requirement that they must assent to constituent legislation would be invalid for disabling that legislature from exercising its power.[93] Long Innes J. thought that the same reasoning applied to the power vested in the 'representative legislature' by CLVA, s. 5, which was defined by CLVA, s. 1 as 'severally ... the authority, other than the Imperial Parliament or Her Majesty in Council, competent to make laws for any colony'.[94]

---

[89] *Ibid.*, 446.   [90] (1930) 31 SR (NSW) 183 at 195.   [91] (1931) 44 CLR 394 at 447–8.
[92] (1930) 31 SR (NSW) 183 at 230.   [93] *Ibid.*, 231.   [94] *Ibid.*, 230–2.

The majority in the Supreme Court chose to ignore these powerful arguments. In the High Court, Rich J. simply denied that there was any reason to define 'the legislature' as whatever legislature was competent to legislate on general matters. The legislative body could consist of different elements for the purpose of legislation on different matters, and the constituent power conferred by CLVA, s. 5 could be divided accordingly.[95]

As for (b), the defendants argued that s. 7A had neither the intention nor the effect of making the electors part of the legislature.[96] They were on solid ground here, because s. 7A does not expressly alter the definition of the legislature, and indeed, it uses the term 'the legislature' several times, plainly referring to the legislature as ordinarily constituted.[97] Sub-section (3) refers to Bills passing through 'both Houses of the legislature' before being submitted to the electors (who are nowhere described as being part of the legislature), and goes on to state that the referendum is to be held on a day to 'be appointed by the legislature'; sub-s (4) then refers to the vote being taken 'in such manner as the legislature prescribes'. Moreover, as Owen J. pointed out, the word 'manner' in sub-s (1) indicates that the section was intended to lay down the manner for passing legislation.[98] There is no foothold whatsoever within the terms of s. 7A, or in the Parliamentary debates that preceded its enactment, for the argument that it was intended to change the composition of the legislature by including the electors within it. Nor is there any foothold for an argument that the section has this effect by necessary implication. There is no good reason to think that, just because the electors are required to assent to a Bill before it is passed, they have been made part of the legislature.[99] This is because there is nothing nonsensical about requiring that a body external to the legislature must assent to legislation before it can be enacted. Section 128 of the Commonwealth Constitution does not (notwithstanding Rich J.'s apparent suggestion to the contrary)[100] make the electors part of the national Parliament for the purpose of constitutional amendment. Nor do referendum requirements in other jurisdictions have such an effect.

---

[95] (1931) 44 CLR 394 at 419–20.
[96] (1930) 31 SR (NSW) 183 at 195.
[97] This was recognised by Gavan Duffy J.: (1931) 44 CLR 394 at 412.
[98] (1930) 31 SR (NSW) 183 at 215; see also *ibid.*, 219. But at 218–19, His Honour implied that s. 7A could also be regarded as reconstituting the legislature: '[I]t is also a law respecting the constitution of the Legislature; it introduces an element (the vote of the people) into the Constitution itself'.
[99] Long Innes J. is therefore wrong to suggest otherwise, at *ibid.*, 228.
[100] (1931) 44 CLR 394 at 420.

The reconstitution argument in this statutory context was plainly fanciful – a contrived rationalisation of a pre-determined conclusion – which is no doubt why, in the High Court and the Privy Council, only Rich J accepted it.[101] Because the argument was not authoritatively endorsed or rejected, it remains to be decided whether or not a State Parliament can alter its own composition by making the electors a constituent part of it for particular purposes only. In other words, issue (a) above remains undecided.[102]

B   Manner and form

The second legal justification the plaintiffs offered for the referendum requirement was that it amounted to a 'manner and form' by which laws 'respecting the constitution, powers or procedure of Parliament' had to be passed, and therefore was valid and binding by virtue of the proviso to CLVA, s. 5. This was more plausible than the reconstitution gambit.

The defendants had a powerful argument in response, although to their detriment, they did not distinguish it clearly from a weaker argument. The powerful argument was that, because s. 5 of the CLVA declared that the legislature 'shall have' a 'full power', the proviso had to be construed so as to be consistent with the legislature's continued possession of that power; therefore, the words 'manner and form' could not include a requirement that wholly or partially deprived the legislature of the power.[103] Since s. 7A provided that Parliament could not pass certain laws without the assent of an external body (the electors), it was in substance a law that partially deprived the legislature of the power.[104] Although s. 7A itself expressly purported to prescribe the 'manner' by which the specified laws had to be passed, this was not a manner by which *the legislature* had to exercise *its* power to pass such laws. Instead, it was a manner by which the legislature *together with an external body* had to exercise *their shared* power to pass laws. It was therefore not within the scope of the proviso.

The weaker argument was that, partly for this reason, and also because CLVA, s. 5 used the word 'passed' rather than 'enacted', the proviso was

---

[101] Note also that the Commonwealth Attorney-General supported the plaintiffs' manner and form argument, but not their reconstitution argument: see 'Case for the Intervenant'.

[102] Gavan Duffy C.J. thought that Parliament might, in principle, be able to alter its composition either for general or for particular purposes, but had not done so here: (1931) 44 CLR 394 at 413.

[103] *Ibid.*, 444–5.   [104] *Ibid.*, 442.

confined to procedures or forms within the legislature itself, and excluded any requirement that had to take place outside it. According to this argument, only if the proviso were construed in this way would it be fully consistent with the legislature retaining its full power intact.

The majority in the Supreme Court failed to come to grips with either argument. Street C.J., with whom James J. concurred, simply asserted that he had reached the contrary conclusion: 'in truth all that sub-section 6 of s. 7A does is to provide a special procedure' for passing laws, which did not 'shackle and control the present Parliament': 'insistence upon the observance of a special form of procedure ... is a matter of manner and form'.[105] The only substantive argument he offered in defence of this view was one of policy.[106] Ferguson J. declared that 'the Legislature has full power to alter [s. 7A] by repealing sub-section (6)', although it had to follow the 'manner' prescribed by the sub-section[107] – simply ignoring the apparent inconsistency between the former proposition and the latter. Owen J. reasoned that s. 7A provided the 'manner' by which the laws in question had to be passed, partly because s. 128 of the Commonwealth Constitution describes its referendum requirement as the 'manner' by which constitutional amendments must be passed[108] – seemingly oblivious to the fact that the whole point of s. 128 is to deny the federal Parliament full power to amend the Constitution.[109]

In the High Court, Starke J. was even more deaf to the plaintiff's argument, asserting that '[t]he greater the constituent powers granted to the legislature, the clearer, it seems to me, is its authority to fetter its legislative power, to control and make more rigid its constitution'[110] – as if CLVA, s. 5 were merely a transitory provision, conferring a power that could be used to diminish or even abolish itself.

There was an effective rebuttal of the weaker of the defendants' two arguments. The plaintiffs argued that the historical context in which

---

[105] (1930) 31 SR (NSW) 183 at 202–3.

[106] See text to n. 133, below.

[107] (1930) 31 SR (NSW) 183 at 211; see also 206–7: 'There is no dispute as to the power of Parliament to pass the repealing Bill; the only question ... is as to the stages through which it must pass'.

[108] Ibid., 219.

[109] In argument before the High Court, Dixon J. suggested that s. 128 of the Commonwealth Constitution might itself be a law with respect to 'manner and form' which was binding because of CLVA, s. 5: (1931) 44 CLR 394 at 404. But this is clearly untenable, partly because s. 128 governs all constitutional amendments, and not merely those 'respecting the constitution, powers or procedure' of the Commonwealth Parliament. McTiernan J.'s account of s. 128 is clearly preferable: ibid., 444.

[110] Ibid., 423–4.

CLVA, s. 5 had been enacted showed that a manner and form requirement could prescribe action outside the legislature itself. They referred to a letter of the Law Officers within the then Colonial Office concerning the enactment of the CLVA.[111] This showed that the purpose of the proviso in s. 5 was to ensure that pre-existing requirements for colonial law-making would remain binding, notwithstanding the confirmation that colonial legislatures had 'full power' to alter their own constitutions. These pre-existing requirements included requirements of special majorities, including two-thirds majorities, within the legislature; reservation of Bills for the Queen's personal assent; and the tabling of Bills before both Houses of the Imperial Parliament. The last of these requirements had 'nothing to do with any of the units of the Legislature' – it was a 'form' required to be satisfied in the making of law even though it concerned matters 'happening in regard to units not part of the legislature'.[112] In the High Court, Rich and Dixon J.J. found this point to be decisive.[113] '[T]he law governing the reservation of Bills and the laying of copies before both Houses of the Imperial Parliament were matters prominently in view when s. 5 was framed. It is evident that these matters are included within the proviso', and this ruled out '[a]n interpretation which restricts the application of the words of the proviso to conditions occurring, so to speak, within the representative legislature'.[114]

The problem is that, while this effectively rebuts the weaker of the defendants' two arguments, it simply fails to address the stronger one. There is an obvious qualitative difference between a requirement that a Bill must be laid before an outside body such as the Imperial Parliament, pending the royal assent, and a requirement that it must be positively approved by an outside body such as the electorate. The former requirement does not deprive the legislature itself of the power of enactment: it merely gives members of the Imperial Parliament notice of the Bill. They might seek to persuade Ministers to advise the monarch not to assent to it, or they might propose Imperial legislation to override it, but since the monarch is part of the colonial legislature, and the Imperial Parliament is able to override colonial laws, none of this is inconsistent with the State legislature retaining full power of enactment. The latter requirement, on the other hand, is plainly inconsistent with the legislature retaining its full power of enactment. So the defendants' stronger argument – that even if a manner and form requirement can require some action outside the

---

[111] (1931) 44 CLR 394 at 407 and 409 respectively.
[112] *Ibid.*, 409.   [113] *Ibid.*, 418–19 (Rich J.), 432 (Dixon J.).   [114] *Ibid.*, 432 (Dixon J.).

legislature, it cannot deprive the legislature of its full power to legislate – stands unanswered.

The High Court majority and the Privy Council went on to adopt a sweeping, unqualified interpretation of 'manner and form'. Rich J. said that:

> In my opinion the proviso to sec. 5 relates to the entire process of turning a proposed law into a legislative enactment, and was intended to enjoin the fulfilment of *every condition* and compliance with *every requirement* which existing legislation imposed on the process of law-making.[115]

Dixon J. agreed:

> The more natural, the wider and the more generally accepted mean-ing includes within the proviso *all the conditions* which the Imperial Parliament or that of the self-governing State or Colony may see fit to prescribe as essential to the enactment of a valid law.[116]

Starke J. took the same view, quoting Berriedale Keith's statement that '*[a]ny rule whatever* which has been laid down by any legislative authority with regard to the mode of modifying the constitution is a fetter on the freedom of the Dominion Parliament which it cannot break save in the way appointed by the Act imposing the fetter'.[117]

The Privy Council endorsed Rich J.'s definition, and stated that the words of the proviso were 'amply wide enough' to cover a referendum requirement.[118]

The problem with this very broad interpretation is that it enables the proviso to be used to restrict or even extinguish the legislature's con-stituent power, rather than merely to regulate its exercise. Dixon J., at least, acknowledged that manner and form requirements could qualify or control the legislature's 'full power' to make laws respecting the mat-ters specified by CLVA, s. 5 only to a limited extent: they 'cannot do more than prescribe the mode in which laws respecting these matters must be made'.[119] But if the so-called 'mode' in which such laws must be made can require the assent of a body external to the legislature, then the 'full power' can in effect be taken from the legislature and given to a larger law-making entity of which the legislature is merely a part.

---

[115] *Ibid.*, 419; emphasis added.
[116] *Ibid.*, 432–3; emphasis added.
[117] Keith, *Imperial Unity and the Dominions*, pp. 389–90, quoted by Starke J.: (1931) 44 CLR 394 at 424; emphasis added.
[118] (1931) 47 CLR 97 at 106 and 104 respectively.
[119] (1931) 44 CLR 394 at 431.

The defendants objected that if the assent of the electorate, as a body outside the legislature, could be required, then logically, so could the assent of other external bodies such as private associations or corporations, or some other condition making it virtually impossible for laws to be passed. As Ferguson J. recounted the submission, it was urged 'that Parliament might with equal force claim the right to provide that the repealing Bill should be submitted to the Tattersall's Club, or that three years should elapse after its introduction before it should finally become law'.[120]

Ferguson J. dismissed this objection, in a passage appealing to the orthodox defence of legislative sovereignty:

> [U]nder any reading of the constitution it is conceded that the Legislature might do things quite as drastic. It might lawfully abolish one House or Parliament, or possibly both, create a third house, or thirty, extend the franchise to every man and child in the State old enough to hold a pencil, restrict it so that nobody should have a vote or sit in Parliament except young women between fifteen and eighteen, or provide that after the next dissolution there should be no further election for twenty years … All that means is that there is nothing in the constitution forbidding the Legislature to do insane things. One would not expect to find such a provision there. The constitution of every free civilised community is based on the assumption that the body to which it commits the power of making its laws may be trusted to bring to the exercise of that power a reasonable degree of sanity. If at any time that trust should prove to be misplaced, then the State would be in very evil case, and would be hard put to it to find a way of escaping disaster.[121]

This may underestimate the possibility of a Parliament seeking to tie its hands to protect the interests of an external body. A private corporation, entering into an agreement with the government involving the investment of a vast sum of money for the sake of long-term returns, might demand legally binding constraints to prevent the agreement being unilaterally changed either by a future government or by Parliament. Although it would be unwise, it might not be 'insane', for Parliament to seek to meet that demand and enact such constraints.[122] But more importantly, Ferguson J.'s response simply misses the point of the defendants' objection, which is one of logic rather than prophecy. It is not a prediction that Parliament is likely to impose such constraints, but rather, a *reductio*

---

[120] (1930) 31 SR (NSW) 183 at 202 and 208.   [121] *Ibid.*, 208–9.
[122] Two Australian cases in which this was subsequently argued to have happened are *Commonwealth Aluminium Corporation Pty. Ltd* v. *Attorney-General (WA)* [1976] Qd R 231, and *West Lakes Ltd* v. *South Australia* (1980) 25 SASR 389.

ad absurdum, which points out that if a referendum requirement is consistent with the 'full power' granted by CLVA, s. 5, then logically, so is a requirement that a private corporation must assent to legislation. If no logical distinction can be drawn between these requirements, then the absurdity of the latter demonstrates the impermissibility of the former.

Street C.J. also dismissed the defendants' objection: '[t]he suggestion of extravagant possibilities does not in my opinion serve any useful purpose', and it was unnecessary to determine how far Parliament could go in providing that laws should be immutable.[123] One might have thought that logical analysis was a useful purpose. In the High Court, the objection was just ignored, even though it was clearly and forcefully argued.[124] The Privy Council declined to consider hypothetical cases, on the ground that it only needed to decide the precise point in issue, and could consider other cases if and when they arose.[125]

Five decades later, King C.J. of the South Australian Supreme Court ventured an answer to the objection:

> When one looks at extra-Parliamentary requirements, the difficulty of treating them as relating to manner and form becomes greater. It is true that Dixon J in *Trethowan's* case … gave 'manner and form' a very wide meaning … *Trethowan's* case … however, concerned a requirement that an important constitutional alteration be approved by the electors at a referendum. Such a requirement, although extra-Parliamentary in character, is easily seen to be a manner and form provision because it is confined to obtaining the direct approval of the people whom the 'representative legislature' represents … A provision requiring the consent to legislation of a certain kind, of an entity not forming part of the legislative structure (including in that structure the people whom the members of the legislature represent), does not, to my mind, prescribe a manner or form of lawmaking, but rather amounts to a renunciation pro tanto of the lawmaking power. Such a provision relates to the substance of the lawmaking power, not to the manner or form of its exercise.[126]

What this makes clear is that the defendants and dissenting judges in *Trethowan* were right that, as a general rule, a requirement that an external body must assent to legislation cannot be regarded as a legitimate manner and form requirement, because it partially deprives the legislature of its power. The majority judges' broad interpretation of the proviso

---

[123] (1930) 31 SR (NSW) 183 at 202.
[124] See the account of Loxton K.C.'s argument in *Sydney Morning Herald*, 21 January 1931, p. 17.
[125] (1931) 47 CLR 97 at 104.
[126] *West Lakes Ltd* v. *South Australia* (1980) 25 SASR 389 at 397–8.

is therefore wrong: it just cannot be the case that 'every requirement', 'every condition', 'any rule whatsoever', and 'all the conditions' to which a State legislature might subject future law-making, amount to binding 'manner and form' requirements.

The majority judges must be regarded as having, in effect, created an exception to this general rule, so as to permit the imposition of referendum requirements. But there was no logical basis in the words of CLVA, s. 5 for this exception: that provision gave full, continuing, constituent power *to the legislature*, and not to the broader 'legislative structure', including the electorate, of which the legislature is merely the apex. Admittedly, the exception is laudable as a matter of political principle, despite its logical deficiency.

C   *Political principle and legal logic*

Lang accused the Australian courts of distorting the law due to political bias.[127] Years later, the Canadian scholar Edward McWhinney criticised the majority judges for engaging in 'a piece of *ad hoc* decision-making ... designed to counter the (according to general opinion today) rather incompetent and arrogant administration that happened to hold office in the State of New South Wales at that time'.[128] But these criticisms are too harsh. No doubt the judges were influenced by a desire to protect one of the few institutions (the Upper House) able to check a Premier widely regarded – even within his own Party – as dictatorial and dangerous.[129] But their decision also advanced three broader political principles of undeniable appeal: constitutional stability, direct popular sovereignty and self-determination. A requirement that fundamental constitutional changes must be put to the people serves the first two principles; permitting a State legislature to impose such a requirement, without needing the Imperial Parliament's assistance, serves the third. This is not to say that there are no countervailing principles.[130]

---

[127] Attributed to Lang by Boyce K.C., Premier Stevens and others, according to *Sydney Morning Herald*, 1 June 1932, p. 11.

[128] E. McWhinney, 'Trethowan's Case Reconsidered' *McGill Law Journal* 2 (1955–56) 32 at 37.

[129] For conflicting views within Labor itself, see G. Freudenberg, *Cause for Power: The Official History of the New South Wales Branch of the Australian Labor Party* (Leichhardt: Pluto Press, 1991), chs. 7 and 8.

[130] McTiernan J. offered a rather feeble response to the invocation of political principle. To the plaintiffs' argument that the State Constitution would be defective if Parliament

The majority judges, in all three courts, appear to have been influenced more by these political principles than by 'strict legalism' and logical analysis.[131] McTiernan J's dissent is superior in technical legal terms, even to Dixon J.'s subtle ruminations. It is of course true that in law, pure logic is often sterile, and must then be guided by underlying principles. But it is doubtful that the principle of direct popular sovereignty can be found within, or underlying, CLVA, s. 5. As for the other two principles, recourse to underlying principles does not provide a legal warrant for rewriting legal provisions that at best give only partial expression to them.

The majority judges seem to have taken a creative, 'statesman-like' approach, remoulding s. 5 for the sake of good government, and quietly brushing legal technicalities under the carpet. Consider, for example, their tendency to assert conclusions while ignoring powerful counter-arguments, as in the case of Rich J.'s uncritical endorsement of the feeble reconstitution argument, and the general refusal to consider 'hypothet-ical cases'. This is especially true of the Privy Council's cursory and high-handed disposal of the complex issues raised: its published opinion is full of assertions but, as Richard Latham observed, 'hardly amounts to a statement of reasons for judgment at all'.[132] Starke J.'s judgment is even more perfunctory. It does not follow that the majority judges' decision was wrong in a moral or political sense: one of the most fascinating ques-tions in legal theory is the extent to which judges are morally justified in changing the law, for a good cause, while giving the appearance of merely interpreting it.

could not impose a referendum requirement itself, and had to request the Imperial Parliament to do so, he replied:

Whether such a request would indicate a greater defect in the Constitution than a request for power to enable the Legislature to cut the knot of legislative provisions for two or more referenda, so that it could act as it deemed expe-dient in an emergency which could not in its judgment permit of the delay involved in taking the referendum or referenda, by which some existing law or new law had been fortified against repeal or amendment, is a speculation which will not decide the issue in this appeal: (1931) 44 CLR 394 at 449.

For a more powerful response, see M.J. Detmold, *The Australian Commonwealth: A Fundamental Analysis of Its Constitution* (Sydney: Law Book Co., 1986), pp. 208 and 212–6. Note also the 'conceptual difficulty' raised by Gummow J. in *McGinty v. Western Australia* (1996) 186 CLR 140 at 297, which applies to the events in *Trethowan's* case as described in the text to n. 19, above.

[131] The words in quotation marks are, of course, Dixon's, in O. Dixon, 'Address Upon Taking the Oath of Office as Chief Justice', in *Jesting Pilate, And Other Papers and Addresses* (Woinarski, ed.) (Melbourne: Law Book Co., 1965), 245 at p. 247.

[132] R.T.E. Latham, *The Law and the Commonwealth* (Oxford: Oxford University Press, 1949), p. 566.

Some of the judges openly acknowledged their attraction to basic political principles. While denying that the Court was concerned with the wisdom or expediency of s. 7A, Street C.J. said that:

> Parliament in its wisdom might well think that there were possible changes of so important and so far reaching a character that a special procedure ought to be followed before they could become law, and it might think that in respect of some of such changes the need for hastening slowly was such that the provision for a special manner of procedure should not be liable to be repealed by a simple Act passed in the ordinary way ... [A] proposal of so far reaching and so momentous a character as that for the substitution of a unicameral system for the bicameral system ... is one which Parliament might not unreasonably consider of such importance that a special form of procedure should be made compulsory ... A provision of this kind [is] introduced into the Constitution as a safeguard against hasty changes in the composition of the Legislature ...[133]

Rich J. in the High Court said much the same thing.[134] Ferguson J. emphasised self-determination, asking why New South Wales should not have the right, if it chose, to adopt a referendum requirement similar to that in the Commonwealth Constitution.[135] Dixon J.'s disapproval of confining 'a constitutional provision basal in the development of the self-governing Colonies' to 'matters of procedure' may also reflect a concern with self-determination.[136]

Dixon J. avoided any comment on the merits, preferring to couch his reasoning in strictly legal terms. It is impossible to believe, however, that he was not influenced by the desirability of requiring fundamental constitutional changes to be approved by the electors. In 1935, he described the 'discovery' of this means of requiring a referendum to alter a State constitution as possibly 'the most important legal development of the time'. He depicted it as a modern reconciliation and demarcation of the equally fundamental but competing principles of the supremacy of Parliament and the rule of law:

> The law existing for the time being is supreme when it prescribes the conditions which must be fulfilled to make a law. But on the question of what may be done by a law so made, Parliament is supreme over the law.[137]

The problem with this analysis is, as we have seen, that the majority judges' decision to uphold the validity of s. 7A was not consistent with

---

[133] (1930) 31 SR (NSW) 183 at 203.   [134] (1931) 44 CLR 394 at 420–1.
[135] (1930) 31 SR (NSW) 183 at 211.   [136] (1931) 44 CLR 394 at 432.
[137] O. Dixon, 'The Law and the Constitution', in *Jesting Pilate, And Other Papers and Addresses* (Woinarski, ed.) (Melbourne: Law Book Co., 1965), 38 at 50.

Parliament remaining 'supreme over the law'. Given this logical flaw in his analysis, which he was too astute not to have discerned, it seems that even Dixon J. delivered a 'quasi-political decision, based on a far-sighted view of ultimate constitutional policy, of the type with which the Supreme Court of the United States in its greatest periods has made us familiar'.[138]

V Aftermath and consequences

The Legislative Council had survived, but was reformed in 1933, by legislation approved by a narrow margin at a referendum held in accordance with s. 7A. Membership of the Council was restricted to 60 members with twelve year terms, to be chosen at a joint sitting of the two Houses of Parliament. Provision was made for deadlocks between the Houses to be capable of resolution by referendum. Lang strenuously opposed this legislation, but even the Federal Labor Party supported it.[139] A.B. Piddington, a legal associate of Lang's, unsuccessfully sought injunctions to prevent the Bills receiving the royal assent, on the ground that s. 7A had not been properly followed.[140] Whether the survival of the Council was an unmixed blessing remained, of course, open to debate. In 1955, one commentator observed that after fourteen years of continuous Labor government, the Council had become 'a haven for retired politicians and Union officials'.[141] It survived a further attempt at abolition in 1960.[142] Since then, partly because of the experience in Queensland, support for Upper Houses on the ground that they are vital to a system of constitutional checks and balances has strengthened.

The Queensland Parliament quickly took advantage of the decision in *Trethowan* to insert a referendum requirement into its Constitution Act. Ironically, the device used in New South Wales to protect the Upper House from abolition was used in Queensland for the opposite purpose.

---

[138] Latham, *The Law and the Commonwealth*, p. 564 (although not with reference to *Trethowan*).

[139] Clune and Griffith, *Decision and Deliberation*, pp. 324–30; Morrison, 'Dominion Office Correspondence', 338–9.

[140] *Piddington v. Attorney-General* (1933) 33 SR (NSW) 317. See also the sequel: *Doyle v. Attorney-General* (1933) 33 SR (NSW) 484. The main argument was that by requiring Bills to be 'submitted to' the electors, s. 7A required that copies of the Bills be distributed to them. See Clune and Griffith, *Decision and Deliberation*, pp. 330–2. This was the same Piddington who had been appointed to the High Court by the Hughes Labor government in 1913, but, in the face of fierce criticism from the Bar, resigned before hearing any cases.

[141] McWhinney, 'Trethowan's Case Reconsidered', 41, n. 34.

[142] See *Clayton v. Heffron* (1960) 105 CLR 214.

The Upper House had been abolished there in 1922, and in 1934, the new provision inserted into the constitution proscribed its re-establishment absent a referendum.[143] (This supplied an answer to a point that Evatt had raised in the 1920s, when he warned that abolition of the Legislative Council might be futile, because a future Parliament could just as easily re-establish it.)[144] Several other states later adopted referendum requirements, to protect a variety of constitutional provisions.[145]

The legal foundation for these and other law-making requirements changed in 1986. The Australia Act 1986 (UK and Cth) repealed the CLVA with respect to Australia, although s. 6 re-enacted the substance of the manner and form proviso. The intention was undoubtedly, in part, to preserve the effect of the decision in *Trethowan*. Therefore, even if the interpretation given to the words 'manner and form' in that case was legally erroneous, as I have argued, it must now be regarded as having received legislative endorsement by their unqualified re-enactment in s. 6.[146] Consequently, the majority judgments in *Trethowan* remain the foundation for the law on 'manner and form' in Australia.

Professional reaction to the decision was mixed. Commonwealth Attorney-General Sir John Latham rightly described it as 'a landmark in the constitutional history of the Empire'.[147] Berriedale Keith, unsurprisingly, claimed that '[i]t is plain indeed that the meaning of the proviso to the [Colonial Laws Validity] Act of 1865 was exactly to cover such an action as was intended by the Act of 1929, despite the ingenuity with which the contrary view was argued'.[148] But this is extremely dubious, given the traditional British commitment to legislative supremacy and constitutional flexibility, which prevailed at the time the CLVA was enacted, and the purpose of that Act, which was to empower rather than limit colonial legislatures.[149] That is why legal officers in Britain were initially puzzled

---

[143] Constitution Act Amendment Act 1934 (Qld) s. 3.

[144] Crockett, *Evatt, A Life*, p. 60.

[145] See P. Hanks, P. Keyzer and J. Clarke, *Australian Constitutional Law, Materials and Commentary* (7th edn) (Sydney: LexisNexis Butterworths, 2004), pp. 315–6.

[146] Kirby J. was therefore right to say that: 'It is now too late to correct the judicial decisions that construed the proviso to s. 5 as an authority to fetter the constituent and legislative powers of Australia's State Parliaments': *Attorney-General (WA) v. Marquet* (2003) 217 CLR 545 at 609 [194].

[147] Quoted in *Sydney Morning Herald*, 1 June 1932, p. 11.

[148] A.B. Keith, *The Constitutional Law of the British Dominions* (London: Macmillan, 1933), p. 106; repeated in A.B. Keith, *The Dominions as Sovereign States* (London: Macmillan, 1938), p. 169.

[149] Hence Sir Victor Windeyer's observation that the result in *Trethowan's* case would have surprised those whose actions led to its enactment: V. Windeyer, 'Responsible

by the decision. In Treasury, R.R. Sedgwick described the High Court's decision as 'very surprising'.[150] H. Grattan Bushe, a senior officer in the Dominions Office who was intimately involved in the events, observed that:

> I find it difficult to follow the decision. A subordinate Parliament can be bound by a superior Parliament, but how can a subordinate Parliament, acting in matters which are within its sovereignty, bind its successors? It is very curious to see that they have relied upon section 5 of the Colonial Laws Validity Act, (which was meant to enfranchise Colonial Legislatures) as having a restrictive effect.[151]

But the decision in *Trethowan* helped change the traditionalists' ingrained habits of thought. It inspired new theories concerning the doctrine of parliamentary sovereignty and the ability of Parliaments to bind themselves.[152] Dixon J. had agreed with Ferguson J. that even the British Parliament might be able to reconstitute itself for special purposes, or lay down binding requirements as to manner and form.[153] Many judges and scholars have quoted Dixon J.'s dictum that, even in Britain itself, if a referendum requirement were ignored, 'the Courts might be called upon to consider whether the supreme legislative power in respect of the matter had in truth been exercised in the manner required for its authentic expression and by the elements in which it had come to reside'.[154] This stimulated Richard Latham and Ivor Jennings, in the 1930s, and other academic lawyers subsequently, to think afresh about such issues.[155] They applied the concepts of reconstitution and manner and form to the British Parliament, and other Parliaments not subject to the CLVA. Some asked why, even if a Parliament were 'sovereign' in the sense that it could not limit its substantive law-making power, it should not be able to change its own structure, or the procedure or form by which it had to exercise that power. They could see no good reason why it could not, perhaps especially when, as in the case of the British Parliament, its structure and procedures were determined by common law or custom rather than a

---

Government – Highlights, Sidelights and Reflections' *Journal of the Royal Australian Historical Society* 42 (1957) 257 at 283–4.

[150] Memo, 23 December 1930, DO 35/400 11156/10.

[151] Minute, 18 March 1931, DO 35/400 1156/11.

[152] P. Oliver, *The Constitution of Independence: The Development of Constitutional Theory in Australia, Canada, and New Zealand* (Oxford: Oxford University Press, 2005), pp. 72, 82 and 87.

[153] See Ferguson J.'s dictum at text to n. 85, above.

[154] (1931) 44 CLR 394 at 426.

[155] Oliver, *The Constitution of Independence*, ch. 4.

superior written law. It is perhaps ironic that *Trethowan* sparked thinking along these lines, given that it was obviously a case in which a Parliament's substantive power *had* been limited. But other scholars went further, and concluded that, since any Parliament's law-making power was conferred and governed by law, there was no reason in principle why it could not use its constituent power to change that law, even if the effect were to limit its own power rather than merely to regulate its exercise. Their view, to use modern terminology, is that a Parliament's constituent power could be 'self-embracing' rather than 'continuing'.[156]

Remarkably, even Evatt quickly came to accept Dixon J.'s view that, to enhance the rule of law, courts should enforce requirements imposed by one Parliament upon law-making by its successors. Indeed, he thought that they should find a way to do so even if s. 5 of the CLVA were inapplicable. '[I]t is of the essence of self-government', he said, 'that there must be power to render similar constitutional safeguards [similar to s. 7A] legally effective. It may be that, [even] without the Colonial Laws Validity Act, provisions such as the Privy Council discussed in *Attorney-General for New South Wales* v. *Trethowan* may be deemed legally effective'.[157] Elsewhere, he recommended that 'once a Dominion is given complete power to determine the form of the Dominion Constitution [i.e., is released from the CLVA] ... there should be implied a power to adopt a form of Constitution which is binding. In other words, if it is a 'Constitution' at all, it should, by definition, bind the Legislature for the time being ...'.[158]

> [L]egal thought seems no longer to debar Parliament itself from setting up a Constitution which, by reason of its very nature as such, is intended to restrict the liberty of the legislative, as well as of all other organs within the appropriate constitutional unit ... In such circumstances it would become the duty of the Judiciary to enforce the terms of the Constitution ... [Not] all Courts of justice will prefer the power of the existing Legislature to the supremacy of the law. Bacon's dogma will hardly be allowed to stand in the way of modern notions of constitution making and constitution breaking.[159]

'Bacon's dogma' – that 'a supreme and absolute power cannot conclude itself, [and] neither can that which is in nature revocable be made fixed' – had earlier been quoted by the Solicitor-General in explaining

---

[156] Hart, *The Concept of Law*, ch. 7, s. 4.
[157] H.V. Evatt, 'Constitutional Interpretation in Australia' *University of Toronto Law Journal* 3 (1939) 1 at 20.
[158] Evatt, *The King and His Dominion*, p. 215.
[159] *Ibid.*, pp. 309–10.

his opinion that s. 7A was not binding.[160] Evatt had certainly changed his tune.

In *Harris* v. *Minister of Interior* (1952), the concept of reconstitution was invoked by the South African Supreme Court in holding that self-entrenched provisions of the South African Constitution were valid and binding, even though the CLVA was not applicable. Indeed, the concept was expanded to include the idea that procedural requirements as well as structural elements can form part of the definition or constitution of 'Parliament', which Parliament itself can change, although only as so defined.[161] This case, together with *Trethowan*, had such an impact on constitutional theory throughout the Commonwealth that by 1976, a leading commentator plausibly asserted that, even within Britain itself, 'the great majority of modern constitutional lawyers' had come to favour the new 'manner and form' theory.[162]

---

[160] See text to n. 20, above.

[161] *Harris* v. *Minister of Interior* [1952] (2) SA 428, esp. at 463–4 (Centlivres C.J.). See D.V. Cowen, 'Legislature and Judiciary' *Modern Law Review* 15 (1952) 282 at 287 and 289–90.

[162] G. Winterton, 'The British Grundnorm: Parliamentary Sovereignty Re-examined' *Law Quarterly Review* 92 (1976) 591 at 604.

7

Requirements as to procedure or form
for legislating

I Introduction

One of the most important questions not settled by the doctrine of parliamentary sovereignty is whether, and how, Parliament can make the legal validity of future legislation depend on compliance with statutory requirements as to procedure or form.[1] A requirement as to procedure is a requirement that Parliament follow a particular procedure in order to enact legislation of a certain kind. A requirement as to form is a requirement that such legislation take or include some particular form (for example, a particular form of words). Such requirements might be designed to protect important legislation from inadvertent or ill-considered amendment or repeal, by prompting more careful or extensive deliberation within Parliament than is required to enact ordinary legislation. They might also serve other purposes, such as: (a) to ensure that a bill likely to be controversial is brought to public attention; (b) in the case of requirements as to form, to ensure that Parliament expresses its intentions with unmistakable clarity in order to avoid subsequent misunderstandings; or (c) to differentiate between the respective functions of the two Houses in a bicameral system.

In this chapter I will argue that legally binding and judicially enforceable requirements as to procedure or form are consistent with parliamentary sovereignty, provided that they do not control or restrict the substantive content of legislation, or make it so difficult for Parliament to legislate that its power to do so is diminished. The second qualification, admittedly, gives rise to questions of degree. But provided that these qualifications are satisfied, such requirements are consistent with Parliament retaining full, continuing power to change the substance of the law however and whenever it sees fit.

[1] In this chapter the word 'Parliament' will be used to refer not only to the United Kingdom Parliament, but to any Parliament with respect to which the questions under discussion might arise.

My argument will differ in several respects from those put by proponents of the so-called 'new view' of parliamentary sovereignty, such as W. Ivor Jennings, Richard Latham and R.F.V. Heuston. First, I will not rely on Jennings' idea that (a) the common law is the source of Parliament's legislative authority and of the existing 'manner and form' requirements that govern its exercise; and (b) Parliament can change the common law, including these requirements.[2] Secondly, I will not rely on Latham's idea that the ultimate *grundnorm* of the British constitution is 'simply the sum of those principles which command the ultimate allegiance of the courts'.[3] Thirdly, I will not rely on Commonwealth cases such as *Trethowan* v. *Attorney-General (NSW)*,[4] which Jennings, Latham and Heuston pressed into service as authorities for Parliament having power to change 'manner and form' requirements.[5] They paid insufficient attention to the need to ensure that changes to such requirements do not diminish Parliament's continuing sovereign power.

To avoid confusion, I will try to avoid the term 'manner and form' except in a specific context. That term, which appears in s. 5 of the Colonial Laws Validity Act 1865 (Imp) and s. 6 of the Australia Acts 1986 (UK and Cth), has become widely used since the decision in *Trethowan*.[6] There, the High Court of Australia gave the term such a broad interpretation that it was held to include a referendum requirement. A requirement that legislation can be passed only with the assent of a body outside Parliament, whether it is a private body or the electorate as a whole, cannot be regarded as merely a requirement as to the procedure by which Parliament must exercise *its* power to change the law. This is because such a requirement takes power away from Parliament, rather than merely specifying the way in which it must exercise its power. It subjects Parliament's power to the veto of an external body.[7] In this chapter, the term 'procedure or form' rather than 'manner and form' will be used, to emphasise that we are concerned with requirements that govern the method by which Parliament must exercise

---

[2] W.I. Jennings, *The Law and the Constitution* (5th edn) (London: University of London Press, 1959), pp. 151–63. For further discussion, see Chapter 5, Section III, Part B(2), above.

[3] R.T.E. Latham, *The Law and the Commonwealth* (Oxford: Oxford University Press, 1949), p. 525.

[4] (1931) 44 CLR 97.

[5] Jennings, *The Law and the Constitution*, pp. 153–4, Latham, *The Law and the Commonwealth*, pp. 525–34, R.F.V. Heuston, *Essays in Constitutional Law* (London: Stevens & Sons, 1961), pp. 9–16.

[6] (1931) 44 CLR 97.

[7] See the discussion in Chapter 6, Section IV, Part B, above.

its full, continuing power to enact legislation without diminishing that power.

II   Alternative and restrictive requirements: *Jackson's* case

It is important to draw a distinction between three different kinds of legislative procedures. Procedures of the first kind might be called 'ordinary' or 'standard' procedures: these are the procedures routinely used to enact ordinary legislation. Those of the second kind have been called, in Australia, 'alternative' procedures: they establish an alternative procedure for enacting legislation, either in general or of a special kind, which Parliament is permitted but is not obligated to use. Alternative procedures are usually established to deal with deadlocks between the two Houses of a bicameral Parliament, enabling the assent of the Upper House to be dispensed with if certain conditions are satisfied. Procedures of the third kind have been called 'restrictive' procedures: they establish a special procedure for enacting legislation of a particular kind that is more onerous – more 'restrictive' – than the ordinary procedure, and they purport to be mandatory, in that such legislation cannot validly be enacted by the ordinary procedure.[8]

The Parliament Acts 1911 and 1949 (UK) establish an alternative procedure. It is not mandatory: Parliament may still enact any legislation by its ordinary procedure. But if that proves too difficult to use, due to a deadlock between the two Houses, Parliament has provided that it may also act through the alternative procedure.

The difference between alternative and restrictive procedures is important. The famous Commonwealth 'manner and form' cases – such as *Trethowan's* case,[9] *Harris* v. *Minister of the Interior*[10] and *Bribery Commissioner* v. *Ranasinghe*[11] – all concerned restrictive procedures. These are problematic because, by requiring legislation to be enacted by a more onerous procedure, they make it more difficult (and might make it almost impossible) for Parliament to legislate. To that extent, Parliament's substantive power to change the law – and therefore its legislative sovereignty – is diminished or even destroyed. For example, requiring certain laws to be approved in a referendum makes it impossible for Parliament by itself to enact those laws: its power to do so is subordinated to the veto of an external body.

---

[8] For this terminology, see P. Hanks, *Constitutional Law in Australia* (2nd edn) (Sydney: Butterworths, 1996), p. 92.

[9] (1931) 44 CLR 97.   [10] [1952] (2) SA 428.   [11] [1965] AC 172.

Alternative procedures do not raise the same problem. They cannot plausibly be argued to restrict Parliament's substantive power to legislate, because they leave the ordinary legislative procedure intact and always available.[12] No matter how difficult an alternative procedure may be to use – how narrow its ambit or how onerous its preconditions – it does not restrict Parliament's legislative power overall. To the contrary, it could be said to expand Parliament's practical ability to legislate, by providing an alternative procedure that might prove successful when the ordinary procedure has failed. The right way to think about how Parliament is 'limited' by such a procedure is this: the procedure does not limit Parliament's law-making powers or its practical ability to exercise them; instead, it expands that ability, but only to a limited extent.[13]

Consider the difference this makes to questions such as whether or not Parliament can be 'bound' by any requirements that form part of special legislative procedures. If they are restrictive procedures, then Parliament is obligated to follow them, which may have very significant consequences for its sovereign power to legislate. But if they are merely alternative procedures, Parliament can only be 'bound' by their requirements if it chooses to take advantage of them. Parliament might be bound to use restrictive procedures to exercise its law-making power, but is never bound by alternative procedures to do so.

In *Jackson* v. *Attorney-General*,[14] some of the judges considered whether Parliament could use the alternative procedure provided by the Parliament Acts to bypass the limitation in s. 2(1) of the Parliament Act 1911 (UK), which in authorising 'any Public Bill' to be passed by that procedure, expressly excludes bills to extend the maximum duration of Parliament beyond five years. Until the 1911 Act is amended in that respect, 'duration bills' can only be passed by the ordinary legislative procedure with the assent of the House of Lords. But there are no express words that also prevent a public bill to remove that limitation from being passed by the alternative procedure: to use the terminology developed in 'manner and form' cases, the exclusion of duration bills is not 'self-entrenched'. Could the alternative procedure be used to repeal the exclusion, without the assent of the Lords, and then be used to pass a duration bill? A majority of the judges – in my view correctly – said that it could

---

[12] C. Munro, *Studies in Constitutional Law* (2nd edn) (London: Butterworths, 1999), p. 164.

[13] See J. Allan, 'The Paradox of Sovereignty: Jackson and the Hunt for a New Rule of Recognition?' *King's Law Journal* 18 (2007) 1 at 12–14.

[14] [2005] UKHL 56.

not, on the ground that this would be contrary to a clear implication of the express words of s. 2(1).[15]

It has been argued, to the contrary, that in this respect Parliament cannot bind itself, and therefore 'it is unclear how the 1911 Act could have any greater status than subsequent amending statutes'.[16] Alison Young suggests that, if the majority in *Jackson* are correct, s. 2(1) of the 1911 Act is 'entrenched' in that it binds future Parliaments.[17] If Parliament must use its ordinary legislative procedure to remove the exclusion from s. 2(1), it is 'bound' to comply with 'a specific manner and form'.[18]

But this is surely misconceived. Parliament is free to amend or repeal s. 2(1) at any time, either expressly or by implication. That it must use its ordinary legislative procedure to do so does not mean that it has succeeded in 'binding itself' to use a 'specific manner and form'. Parliament has not imposed its ordinary legislative procedure upon itself; the requirement that all three elements of Parliament must approve legislation is a product of custom that has existed since medieval times. What Parliament has done is to enact a less onerous alternative to the ordinary procedure, while leaving the ordinary procedure unaffected. Young's argument amounts to saying that Parliament cannot establish an alternative procedure that is easier to use than the ordinary one for some legislation only: it can only establish such a procedure for all legislation, because otherwise it would be 'binding itself' to use the ordinary procedure to pass any legislation excluded from the alternative one. Indeed, it amounts to saying that if Parliament does establish an alternative legislative procedure that bypasses the House of Lords, but attempts to exclude some kinds of legislation from its scope, the attempted exclusion can be ignored (and expressly or impliedly repealed) by the House of Commons and Her Majesty in the same way that Parliament itself can ignore (and impliedly repeal) any attempt to limit its powers merely by enacting legislation inconsistent with the limitation.

When the argument is taken this far, its flaws become obvious. There is no similarity at all between Parliament attempting to restrict its substantive law-making powers by requiring itself to use a legislative procedure

---

[15] *Ibid.*, paras. 59, 79, 118, 122, 164 and 175.
[16] M. Plaxton, 'The Concept of Legislation: *Jackson* v. *Her Majesty's Attorney General' Modern Law Review* 69 (2006) 249 at 257. See also Young, *Parliamentary Sovereignty*, pp. 193–4.
[17] Young, *Parliamentary Sovereignty*, p. 194.
[18] *Ibid.* See also the illuminating discussion in R. Ekins, 'Acts of Parliament and the Parliament Acts' *Law Quarterly Review* 123 (2007) 91 at 109–10.

that is more onerous than its ordinary procedure, and Parliament partially expanding its practical ability to exercise its powers by permitting itself to use an alternative procedure that is less onerous than its ordinary one, for some but not all legislation. In the former case, the attempt to restrict its substantive powers can subsequently be ignored by Parliament; in the latter case, Parliament's decision to expand its powers only to a partial extent cannot be subsequently ignored by the House of Commons and Her Majesty. A bill not assented to by the House of Lords cannot become an Act of Parliament unless it is passed in accordance with the Parliament Acts. Thus, if the House of Commons and Her Majesty, without the assent of the Lords, were to attempt to pass an Act outside the requirements of those Acts, it would not be an Act of Parliament. This would not be an instance of Parliament itself attempting to, and being prevented from, enacting law.[19]

It seems to have been accepted by all parties and judges involved in *Jackson's* case that the alternative procedure provided by the Parliament Act 1911 (UK) was valid. But Parliament's ability to enact an alternative procedure does not entail that it can enact restrictive procedures. This is because by definition the former cannot, but the latter might, diminish its sovereign power to legislate. Partly for this reason, everything said in *Jackson's* case in relation to the possibility of the British Parliament enacting binding restrictive procedures must be classified as *obiter dicta*.[20] The question of whether Parliament can enact mandatory requirements as to procedure or form remains open.

III Policy considerations

To see why it may sometimes be desirable for a Parliament to use requirements as to procedure or form to regulate its legislative activity, it may be useful to start with an analogy.

Before going to the Antarctic for twelve months I tell a friend, who will be sending me packages of food, that I do not want any chocolate because it is bad for my health, and I ask her never to send me any food that contains chocolate because if it is accessible I cannot resist it. Seven months later I write to her from the Antarctic and ask her to send me several packets of a particular brand of biscuits. She knows that they contain

---

[19] Ekins, 'Acts of Parliament', 109.
[20] See T. Mullen, 'Reflections on *Jackson v. Attorney General*: questioning sovereignty' *Legal Studies* 1 at 11.

chocolate, but does not know whether I know it. She therefore does not know whether I have changed my mind and intend to override my earlier request, or whether I acted in ignorance of the biscuits' chocolate content, in which case I myself, if fully informed, would want her to refuse my request. Let us assume that although she receives messages from me, she cannot send any to me, and therefore cannot seek clarification of my current state of mind. She wishes to act as my 'faithful agent', and fully accepts my 'supremacy' in the matter.[21] But whether or not she should send the biscuits to me is still an open question.

In deciding what to do, she should weigh up the consequences. If my initial request was based on medical advice that I have a life threatening allergy to chocolate, she will know that I am very unlikely to have changed my mind, and will conclude that I have requested the biscuits in ignorance. Alternatively, if that request was based merely on a desire to lose some weight, she may think it possible that after seven months in the Antarctic I have exceeded that goal, and now want to end my diet. However, she may also reasonably think that if I had changed my mind about eating chocolate, I would have expressly said so, to avoid confusing her. My failure to expressly override the initial request may itself be treated as evidence that the later request was a mistake due to ignorance.

I could have prevented this uncertainty from arising by initially directing her not to send me anything that includes chocolate unless, in the future, I expressly override that directive. If the potential consequences of a mistake are extremely serious, I might want to eliminate any possibility of mistakes by insisting that she not send me chocolate unless I use a very specific form of words that establishes beyond doubt that I have changed my mind. This would be similar to a mandatory requirement as to the form of legislation, which requires that a certain form of words must be used as a pre-requisite for a statutory provision, deemed by a court to be contrary to some earlier provision, to be valid and efficacious.[22] In less serious cases, I might not want my future requests to be frustrated by technicalities: I might prefer my initial directive to be able to be overridden by any unequivocal indication of my intention to do so, regardless of the particular form of words I use. In other words, I risk making mistakes whatever I do. I might prefer my friend to act on the

---

[21] Terms used in the American literature on statutory interpretation: see Chapter 9, Section I'.
[22] A 'notwithstanding clause', such as that set out in s. 33 of the Canadian Charter of Rights and Responsibilities, is a kind of 'form' requirement: see Chapter 8.

basis of a strong presumption that I have not changed my intentions, but remain open to any unequivocal evidence that I have, rather than to adopt a more rigid and possibly obstructive approach by insisting that I use a particular form of words, which I might later forget to use. I might want my friend to act on the basis of 'necessary implication' as well as explicit words. Mandatory requirements as to procedure or form, and interpretive presumptions, can serve the same purpose, but in different ways. The differences will be discussed in the next section.

The point is that I may have a *standing commitment* that I want to protect from my own ignorance or negligence in these ways. I do not want to abdicate my ability to change my commitments, or to decide for myself what they entail. But I do want to protect myself from the consequences of certain kinds of mistakes, by authorising my agents to ignore my future instructions or requests unless they have sufficient evidence to conclude that I have not made such a mistake. My ability rationally to control my own destiny may be enhanced if I can effectively do this. If I cannot, my long-term objectives may be defeated by inadvertence or accident.

A Parliament, too, can have standing commitments, and it can be plausibly argued that an ability to protect those commitments by empowering courts to correct certain kinds of mistakes is not only consistent with, but can enhance, its sovereignty. As I have argued previously, a legislature is sovereign provided that its law-making authority is not limited in any substantive respect, even if it is bound to exercise its authority according to requirements of a purely procedural or formal kind. Indeed, a legislature is more rather than less sovereign if it has the ability to subject itself to such requirements, which enhances rather than detracts from its ability to control its deliberative and decision-making processes. If the courts were prepared to enforce these requirements, by invalidating any statute enacted contrary to them, Parliament might no longer be fully sovereign in Dicey's sense. But it would still be fully sovereign in the more important sense of being free to change the substance of the law however and whenever it should choose.[23] I therefore argued that Dicey's definition of parliamentary sovereignty should be revised as follows:

> [A] legislature has sovereign law-making power if its power to change the law is not limited by any norms, concerning the substance of legislation, that are either judicially enforceable, or written, relatively clear, and set out in a formally enacted legal instrument, even if it is governed

---

[23] J. Goldsworthy, *The Sovereignty of Parliament, History and Philosophy* (Oxford: Clarendon Press, 1999), p. 15.

by judicially enforceable norms that determine its composition, and the procedure and form by which it must legislate. Furthermore, its sovereign power is a continuing one even if it includes power to change the norms that govern its own composition, procedure, and form of legislation, provided that it cannot use that power to unduly impair its ability to change the substance of the law however and whenever it chooses.[24]

This superior definition is inconsistent with the doctrine of implied repeal. That doctrine is often thought to be essential to the doctrine of parliamentary sovereignty,[25] but no good reason for this view is apparent. It is essential to Parliament's sovereignty that it is able to amend or repeal its own earlier statutes however and whenever it chooses. But why must it be able to do so by implication, as opposed to being required in some cases to do so by using express words? A Parliament that is able to impose such a requirement on itself is empowered to protect itself from its own inadvertence. Perhaps the worry is that, if a Parliament were permitted to bind itself in this modest way, there would be no logical reason to forbid it from binding itself as to matters of substance. But there is a logical reason: the need to preserve its substantive power to change the law whenever and however it wants. A requirement as to form that it must do so expressly does not limit that substantive power.[26] Nor do very mild procedural requirements.

IV   Distinguishing requirements as to procedure or form from interpretive presumptions

Interpretive presumptions are presumptions that legislation was not intended by Parliament to have some particular consequence, and should therefore be interpreted – if possible – as not having it unless the presumption is rebutted by evidence of sufficient strength that Parliament did intend that consequence. These presumptions were, until recently, ostensibly concerned to ensure that before the courts interpret legislation as impinging on important principles or rights, they are quite sure that Parliament intended it to do so. It is not sufficient that Parliament probably intended it: reasonable doubts about its intention should be resolved

---

[24] *Ibid.*, p. 16.
[25] See A. Kavanagh, *Constitutional Review under the UK Human Rights Act* (Cambridge: Cambridge University Press, 2009), pp. 297 and 315.
[26] On this point I am in agreement with Sir John Laws in 'Constitutional Statutes' *Statute Law Review* 29 (2008) 1 and 8. But, I disagree with his view that only the common law can subject Parliament to an express repeal requirement.

against impingement. The strength of such presumptions can vary, but they are usually said to require that the requisite intention either be spelt out in express words or be 'necessarily implied'. The relevance of clear extra-textual evidence of such an intention does not seem to have been settled.[27]

A requirement as to procedure or form is: (a) prescribed by a constitution or by legislation; (b) usually formulated with some specificity; and (c) usually interpreted as mandatory, in the sense that legislation passed in violation of it is invalid *ab initio*.[28] Interpretive presumptions, on the other hand are: (a) created by the courts as well as by ordinary legislation; (b) rarely as specific as requirements as to procedure or form;[29] and (c) not mandatory, in that the consequence of a failure to satisfy them is not invalidity, but an interpretation of the legislation as not having the consequence in question.

There is another important difference between requirements as to procedure or form, and interpretive presumptions. The former but not the latter are enforced regardless of Parliament's intentions in enacting the later law. Assume, for example, the existence of a mandatory requirement as to procedure or form that is designed to protect some important principle from inadvertent amendment or repeal. The requirement then takes on a life of its own, in the sense that legislation purporting to amend or repeal that principle, but passed contrary to the requirement, will be invalid even if it is quite clear that the amendment or repeal was not inadvertent. With interpretive presumptions, on the other hand, legislative intention is crucial, at least according to their orthodox rationale. Interpretive presumptions are not supposed to be used to defeat Parliament's intention, provided that intention has been made quite clear. Therefore, if relevant

---

[27] To ensure that Parliament's intention to interfere with certain rights is known with sufficient certainty, it may be reasonable to adopt a rule that requires express words or necessary implication. But like other rules, this one might be over-inclusive, if Parliament's intentions can sometimes be clearly established by means other than express words or necessary implication, such as statements made in parliamentary debates. The risks of error might be grounds for excluding such evidence where protected rights are at stake, even if it might sometimes be persuasive in such cases and is generally admitted in other cases. For a possible example, see *Re Bolton, ex parte Beane* (1987) 162 CLR 514, discussed in J. Doyle and B. Wells 'How Far Can the Common Law Go Towards Protecting Human Rights?' in P. Alston (ed.), *Promoting Human Rights Through Bills of Rights: Comparative Perspectives* (Oxford: Oxford University Press, 1999), pp. 57–8.

[28] But some procedures have been held to be 'directory': see *Clayton v. Heffron* (1960) 105 CLR 214.

[29] See the discussion in Hon J.J. Spigelman, 'Principle of Legality and the Clear Statement Principle' *Australian Law Journal* 79 (2005) 769, esp. at 779.

evidence of Parliament's intention, including legislative history, clearly shows that it did intend to impinge on some important principle, that should be enough to overcome a presumption to the contrary, even if the intention is neither spelt out by express words nor necessarily implied by them. Otherwise, it would have to be conceded that the presumption has some other rationale, and is really, in effect, a mandatory requirement as to form.

Requirements as to procedure or form may in this respect go further than necessary: they will successfully prevent inadvertent amendments and repeals, but may sometimes frustrate advertent ones. Interpretive presumptions, on the other hand, may not always go as far as necessary: they may not prevent some inadvertent amendments or repeals, if Parliament has inadvertently used words that cannot be interpreted in any other way.

As we have seen, interpretive presumptions, and requirements as to form, such as that express words or even a particular verbal formula must be used to amend or repeal legislation, can serve similar purposes.[30] Indeed, it is sometimes unclear whether a statutory directive is intended to operate as a mandatory requirement as to form, which is a precondition to the validity of subsequent legislation, or as a mere interpretive presumption.

For example, in the *South Eastern Drainage Board* case,[31] a provision that appeared to impose a mandatory requirement as to form was construed as merely directing the interpretation of future legislation. Section 6 of the Real Property Act 1886 (SA) provided that 'no law, so far as inconsistent with this Act, shall apply to land subject to the provisions of this Act, nor shall any future law, so far as inconsistent with this Act, so apply unless it shall be expressly enacted that it shall so apply notwithstanding the provisions of the Real Property Act 1886'. The High Court of Australia interpreted this section as directing the interpretation of future legislation, rather than as imposing a 'manner and form' requirement for validity. Dixon J. said that s. 6 'is a declaration as to what meaning and operation are to be given to future enactments, not a definition or restriction of the power of the legislature'. It followed that, even if the 'notwithstanding' formula were not used, if a later enactment contained clear language that was impossible to reconcile with the earlier Act, that language had to be put into effect. 'For

---

[30] For example, T.R.S. Allan, 'Legislative Supremacy and the Rule of Law: Democracy and Constitutionalism' *Cambridge Law Journal* 44 (1985) 111.
[31] *South Eastern Drainage Board* v. *Savings Bank of South Australia* (1939) 62 CLR 603.

the later enactment of the legislature must be given effect at the expense of the earlier.'[32] Given the wording of the provision in question, this seems a dubious interpretation; it was influenced by Dixon J.'s opinion that the alternative interpretation would have given rise to constitutional objections that could not have been intended.[33]

It is also possible for what purport to be interpretive presumptions to be treated as, in effect, mandatory requirements as to form. Recently, the orthodox rationale of interpretive presumptions has been questioned, and other rationales suggested. In *R* v. *Secretary of State for Home Department; Ex parte Simms*, Lord Hoffman justified the presumptions partly on the orthodox ground that legislators may have adopted general or ambiguous words without noticing, and therefore without intending, the full consequences of their literal meaning. But he also said that 'Parliament must squarely confront what it is doing and accept the political costs.'[34] Lord Bingham observed extra-judicially that the presumptions are important because:

> if … the executive as the proponent of legislation wants to introduce a provision that would strike ordinary people as unfair or disproportionate or immoral, the need to spell out that intention explicitly on the face of the bill must operate as a discouragement, not last because of the increased risk of media criticism and parliamentary and popular resistance.[35]

This rationale has little to do with legislative intention: it would be more appropriate as a reason for imposing a mandatory requirement as to form. If the 'presumptions' are treated as requiring express words, even when Parliament's intentions are clear – given either necessary implication or legislative history – then they will amount to requirements as to form.

There is no doubt that interpretive presumptions can either be recognised by the courts or created by Parliament. Parliament has done so, for example, by enacting the Human Rights Act 1998 (UK). The difficult question is whether Parliament can go further and subject itself to mandatory requirements as to procedure or form. If the courts themselves now treat interpretive presumptions as, in effect, requiring express words before they will accept that a statute overrides 'fundamental' common law rights, or 'constitutional' statutes, they are hardly well placed to deny that Parliament can subject itself to a similar requirement.[36]

---

[32] *Ibid.*, 625.   [33] See n. 61 below.   [34] [2002] 2 AC 115 at 131.
[35] Lord Bingham of Cornhill, 'Dicey Revisited' *Public Law* 39 (2002), 48.
[36] In *Thoburn's* case, Laws L.J. spoke of interpretive presumptions as if they were requirements as to form, but Alison Young has argued that he is best understood as treating

V   Beyond the stereotypes: the variety of requirements as to procedure or form

When we think about provisions governing the 'manner and form' of legislation, we habitually contemplate a few stereotypes: provisions requiring a referendum, a special majority in Parliament, or express amendment and repeal. These are all restrictive procedures, as distinct from ordinary and alternative procedures (as previously defined).[37] But constitutions can include other provisions that purport to regulate the passage of legislation, which rarely attract attention in this context.[38] It might illuminate the issues if we take these into account, and ask whether they are or could be legally binding, and if so why. Our penchant for stereotypes may have led us to overlook some important considerations.

In Australian state constitutions, these other provisions include standard quorum requirements for the transaction of business in each House, standard voting rules that determine whether presiding officers have a deliberative or merely a casting vote, and special rules concerning the initiation and passage of finance (appropriation and taxation) bills. The latter typically provide that such bills must originate in the Lower House, after being recommended to it by the Governor; that they may be rejected but not altered by the Upper House, although it may request that the Lower House make certain kinds of amendments; that annual Appropriation Bills deal only with appropriation (a requirement as to form), and so on.[39]

Are provisions such as these, dealing with matters such as quorums, the voting rights of presiding officers, and the manner in which finance bills must be initiated, formulated and amended, legally binding? Are they, or could they be made, judicially enforceable? Could the United Kingdom Parliament enact legally binding procedures along similar lines? If the answer to all these questions is 'yes', could these parliaments go further, and enact other mandatory requirements as to procedure or form?

---

them as interpretive: see A. Young, *Parliamentary Sovereignty and the Human Rights Act* (Oxford: Hart Publishing, 2009), pp. 40–5. Sir John's recent article 'Constitutional Guarantees' *Statute Law Review* 29 (2009) 1 suggests that she is wrong. Indeed, he acknowledges that the adoption of his view would involve a change in the rule of recognition of statutes as valid laws: *ibid.*, 9.

[37] See Section II, above.

[38] An exception is Hanks, *Constitutional Law in Australia*, p. 100, text to n. 44.

[39] See, e.g., Constitution Act 1975 (Vic), ss. 62–65.

VI   Validity, enforceability and bindingness

To answer the first question – whether these provisions are legally binding – we need to ask what 'legally binding' means. There is a difference between legal validity and judicial enforceability.

For example, some of the provisions regarding finance bills in Australian constitutions expressly provide that they are, and others have been held to be, non-justiciable.[40] But they are nevertheless legally valid: the parliaments that enacted them had legal power to do so, and they do not violate any higher or superior law. Indeed, if a provision were not legally valid, it would be pointless to ask whether it is justiciable: the question of justiciability can arise only if the provision is legally valid.

But are these provisions legally 'binding' as well as valid? The answer depends on what is meant by 'binding'. In the most obvious sense of the term, which connotes judicial enforceability, they are not. But in another, weaker sense of the term, they are. They impose legal obligations that are clearly intended to govern the conduct of the two Houses of Parliament. Indeed, one of the justifications for regarding them as non-justiciable is that they can be 'enforced' by the Houses themselves, their members and presiding officers.[41] If, for example, the Upper House initiated a finance bill, the Lower House would be entitled to refuse to consider it on the ground that it violated a legal – indeed, a constitutional – requirement. The Lower House would be asserting that the Upper House is bound by that requirement, despite the fact that it is non-justiciable.

The 'remedies' or 'sanctions' available to the Lower House would be 'political' rather than judicial. The House would refuse to act on a bill passed by the Upper House contrary to constitutional requirements. In that respect, non-justiciable provisions are like constitutional conventions. But they are unlike constitutional conventions in that they have been validly enacted in statutory form. Moreover, expectations and demands that they be complied with are based partly on their status as valid laws, and not just on their merits as politically desirable practices or

---

[40] Section 46(9) of the Constitution Acts Amendment Act 1899 (WA) provides that 'Any failure to observe any provision of this section shall not be taken to affect the validity of any Act ...' See also s. 64, of the Constitution Act 1934 (SA). As to s. 54 of the Commonwealth Constitution, see *Northern Suburbs General Cemetery Reserve Trust* v. *Commonwealth* (1993) 176 CLR 555 at 578 per Mason C.J., Deane, Toohey and Gaudron J.J., and 585 per Brennan J.

[41] Richard Ekins has pointed out in correspondence that the Houses, and their members and officers, also enforce non-justiciable laws of contempt of Parliament and parliamentary privilege.

customs. If someone asked why the Lower House should not add extraneous provisions to appropriation bills, or why the Upper House should not initiate or amend such bills, it could forcefully be said in reply that this would violate not only long-standing practices and sound political principles, but the written constitution itself.

According to A.V. Dicey's definition of 'law' as 'any rule which will be enforced by the courts', these provisions are not laws.[42] But as I have argued at length elsewhere, there are good reasons to reject that definition:

> [A]s we conceive of law, what distinguishes legal norms from purely customary or moral norms is that the former belong to a system of norms that is administered by governmental institutions ... Some legal systems include constitutional rules that are 'non-justiciable' – not enforceable by their courts – but are nevertheless generally regarded by legal officials as laws binding other institutions of government ... Non-justiciable rules should be regarded as laws only if, other than not being judicially enforceable, they are indistinguishable in form and function from other rules that are unquestionably laws. That condition is satisfied if they are expressed in written, canonical form, in formally enacted legal instruments, such as constitutions; are expected to be obeyed by legal institutions other than courts; are in fact generally obeyed by those institutions; and, despite borderline problems of vagueness and ambiguity, are sufficiently clear that some possible actions of those institutions would plainly be inconsistent with them. Provided that the rules satisfy these criteria, there is no good reason to refuse to call them laws. They belong to the system of norms that is administered by legal institutions as a whole.[43]

Standard quorum requirements would no doubt also be held to be non-justiciable, on the ground that a judicial enquiry into voting within a House could not have been intended because it would violate parliamentary privilege. In the United States, quorum requirements have been held to be, in effect, non-justiciable, because the 'enrolled bill' rule has been applied.[44] In Australia, no quorum requirement has, to my knowledge, been the subject of litigation. Indeed, it is apparently common practice for quorum requirements to be ignored when legislation before a House is routine and uncontroversial. Such requirements become significant only if a member present sees fit to draw the presiding officer's attention to 'the state of the House'.[45] This suggests that parliamentarians regard such

---

[42] A.V. Dicey, *Introduction to the Study of the Law of the Constitution* (10th edn) (London: Macmillan, 1959), p. 40.
[43] J. Goldsworthy, *The Sovereignty of Parliament*, pp. 11–12.
[44] *Marshall Field & Co v. Clark* (1892) 143 US 649.
[45] Conversation with Mr Ken Coghill, former Speaker of the Victorian Legislative Assembly.

requirements as directory rather than mandatory, at least in the sense that 'substantial' rather than strict literal compliance is acceptable. On the other hand, presumably they would not claim that such requirements are in no sense legally binding. As valid statutory provisions, they can only be amended by statute, whereas if they were not legally binding, each House would be legally entitled to ignore them, and adopt Standing Orders inconsistent with them. In other words, the Houses would be in the same position as the Houses in Westminster, where quorums are governed not by statutory provisions, but by Standing Orders under the control of each House itself. It seems, then, that even though standard quorum requirements are regarded as directory and/or non-justiciable, they are legally binding in a weaker sense of the term.

The point is that requirements as to procedure or form can be legally valid, and legally binding in a weak but meaningful sense of the term, even if they do not impose judicially enforceable preconditions for the validity of legislation. This applies also to requirements enacted by the Westminster Parliament. Consider Richard Ekins' powerful argument that the requirements of the Parliament Acts 1911 and 1949 (UK) are non-justiciable, partly because s. 3 of the 1911 Act ousts the jurisdiction of the court, by providing that a certificate of the Speaker under the Act is conclusive and may not be questioned in any court.[46] Even if Ekins is right, it does not follow that the requirements of the Parliament Acts are not legally valid and binding.

VII   Sources and limits of the validity and enforceability of requirements as to procedure and form

Although provisions in Australian constitutions dealing with finance bills are usually regarded as directory and/or non-justiciable, this is a matter of statutory interpretation. It should therefore be possible for them to be made mandatory and justiciable by the use of explicit statutory wording. Indeed, some state constitutions provide that any provision in an Appropriation Act dealing with any matter other than appropriation 'shall be of no effect'.[47] It also seems possible for a standard quorum requirement to be made justiciable: an express provision to that effect would surely overcome the usual objection that a judicial enquiry into voting within a House would violate parliamentary privilege. A parliament can choose to relinquish any of its privileges.

---

[46]   Ekins, 'Acts of Parliament', 113.
[47]   Constitution Act 1902 (NSW), s. 5A(3); Constitution Act 1934 (Tas), s. 40.

There are *obiter dicta* in *Attorney-General (WA) v. Marquet*[48] that imply the opposite: that Australian requirements as to procedure or form can be judicially enforceable only if they fall within the scope of s. 6 of the Australia Act (UK and Cth) ('AA'), which applies only to the passage of legislation respecting the constitution, powers or procedure of the parliament. Since finance bills do not relate to these subject-matters, it would follow that the usual requirements governing the introduction, form and amendment of such bills cannot be made judicially enforceable; an express provision deeming them to be mandatory preconditions for the legal validity of financial legislation would be ineffectual. For the same reason, quorum requirements could only be made judicially enforceable in the case of bills dealing with the parliament's own constitution, powers and procedure, and not other bills.[49] And the same would be true of other rules of procedure, such as those governing voting by presiding officers.

These conclusions are implausible, for reasons that may also apply to the powers of the Westminster Parliament. To see why, it is useful to start with quorum requirements. There is no good reason to think that standard requirements, of the very undemanding kind that are typical of Australian state constitutions, cannot under current constitutional arrangements be made judicially enforceable across the board. This is because there is no good reason to doubt that they are legally valid, even if they are not currently judicially enforceable. And if they are valid, what reason could there possibly be to deny that a state Parliament has authority to require its courts to enforce them?

These requirements are legally valid, and can therefore be made legally enforceable, because: first, state parliaments have a plenary legislative power that surely includes power to prescribe procedures for their own decision-making; and secondly, that power is not subject to any legal restriction that would invalidate standard quorum requirements. Precisely the same reasons apply to the Westminster Parliament.

Starting with legislative power, AA, s. 2(2) provides that state parliaments have power to make laws for the peace, order and good government of their states. This is a plenary power, which AA, s. 6 plainly assumes includes power to make laws respecting their own procedures

---

[48] (2003) 202 ALR 233, at 251 per Gleeson C.J., Gummow, Hayne and Heydon J.J., and 279 per Kirby J.

[49] Section 6 of the AA states that 'a law ... made by the Parliament of a State respecting the constitution, powers or procedure of the Parliament of the State shall be of no force of effect unless it is made in such manner and form as may from time to time be required by a law made by that Parliament'.

(since it refers to the enactment of a law 'respecting the ... procedure of the Parliament'). This was clearer still under the previous regime of the Colonial Laws Validity Act 1865 (Imp) ('CLVA'), which the Australia Acts repealed in relation to Australia. Section 5 of the CLVA expressly conferred power on each colonial legislature 'to make laws respecting the ... procedure of such legislature'. In *Trethowan's* case, Dixon J. said that this 'power to make laws respecting its own procedure enables it to prescribe rules which have the force of law for its own conduct'.[50] This seems undeniable, for what would be the point of conferring power on a legislature to make laws respecting its own procedure, if those laws could not be given the full force of law: that is, if they could not be made judicially enforceable? That is why the requirements of alternative legislative procedures have been enforced by Australian courts independently of the 'manner and form' proviso in s. 5 of the CLVA.[51]

The Westminster Parliament, also, surely possesses the ability to enact procedures for its own decision-making as part of its sovereign legislative power. As Richard Ekins has pointed out, no legal requirements – statutory or common law – currently govern its ordinary legislative procedures: each House determines its own internal procedures through its Standing Orders.[52] But it is hard to find good reasons to deny that Parliament as a whole has the power to replace Standing Orders with legislative requirements. As Ekins has argued, Parliament's power to determine the decision-making procedures by which it is to be taken to have acted is the reason why the Parliament Acts 1911 and 1949 (UK) are legally valid and effective.[53] It does not, of course, logically follow that Parliament could also impose requirements on the internal proceedings of each House. But to deny that it could, it would be necessary to argue that Parliament's sovereign power is limited by immutable fundamental custom, which not only prevents Parliament from limiting its sovereign power to legislate, but also prevents it from controlling the internal decision-making procedures that govern its exercise of that power. In other words, it would be necessary to argue that immutable fundamental custom dictates that the two Houses must always have unfettered discretion to regulate their own internal procedures. That would surely be a surprising restriction on Parliament's sovereign power to legislate, since it could not be justified by the overriding need to preserve of that power.

---

[50] *A.G. for NSW* v. *Trethowan* (1931) 44 CLR 394 at 429–30.
[51] E.g., *Clayton* v. *Heffron* (1960) 105 CLR 214.
[52] Ekins, 'Acts of Parliament', 103.   [53] *Ibid.*

All these Parliaments should therefore be regarded as having power to enact procedural requirements. But it does not follow that this power is unlimited: that any and every procedure they might choose to enact would be legally valid, and could be made judicially enforceable. The power is subject to one legal restriction: neither the Westminster Parliament, nor an Australian state parliament, can destroy or diminish its continuing plenary power. In the case of the Westminster Parliament, this is the continuing sovereign power that it possesses according to the customary rule of recognition that underpins the constitution as a whole. In the case of Australian state parliaments, it is the power conferred on them formerly by s. 5 of the CLVA, and today by AA, s. 2(2). This is also a 'continuing' power: because AA, s. 15 denies that state parliaments can amend or repeal the AA, their power under s. 2(2) necessarily survives any attempt on their part to destroy or diminish it.[54]

It follows that the validity of a restrictive procedure might be successfully challenged on the ground that, in substance, it violates this limit to the power used to enact it. It has frequently been recognised that a procedural requirement could be so difficult – perhaps even impossible – to comply with, that in substance it would amount to a fetter on parliament's power to legislate.[55] Imagine, for example, a requirement that certain legislation can only be enacted if passed on two occasions, separated by an election, by a 100 per cent majority of all members of both Houses. Such a requirement would make it virtually impossible for the Parliament to legislate. If a state Parliament purported to impose such a requirement on the enactment of future legislation, it would be rendered invalid due to inconsistency with s. 2 of the AA, the source of the parliament's continuing plenary power. If the Westminster Parliament purported to do so, it could be impliedly repealed – and therefore ignored – by a subsequent Parliament. Arguably, this entails that such a requirement would also be invalid in Britain, because it would not bind the only body it purported to bind.

Standard quorum requirements do not make it difficult to pass legislation. Indeed, they are designed to make the passage of legislation easy, by requiring as few as one quarter or one third of the members of a House to be present. Since they do not infringe this, or any other restriction on a parliament's power to prescribe its own procedures, there is no good

---

[54] J. Goldsworthy, 'Manner and Form in the Australian States' *University of Melbourne Law Review* 16 (1987) 403 at 411.
[55] *Ibid.*, 409–10, 417–25 and 420, n. 79.

reason to deny that they are legally valid and could be made legally enforceable. The same goes for requirements concerning voting by presiding officers. These requirements are examples of what, in earlier work, I have called 'pure procedures or forms': requirements as to the procedure or form of legislation that do not in any way diminish Parliament's substantive power.[56]

It might be objected that, when the judges in *Marquet's* case suggested that s. 6 of the AA provides the only foundation for the enforcement of 'manner and form' requirements in Australia, they did not have in mind standard requirements, such as quorum rules, that apply to legislation in general. They were thinking, instead, of restrictive procedures that apply only to particular, narrow categories of legislation.

That might indeed be what they had in mind. We do tend to distinguish between procedural requirements that are routine and easy to comply with, and those that are unusual and more demanding. And we tend to assume that the former are legally unproblematic, whereas the latter need the support of some special rule or principle, such as the provision in AA, s. 6 that makes some 'manner and form' requirements enforceable. But is there any good reason to draw such a distinction? The continuing plenary or sovereign power of a Parliament is not limited to the enactment of requirements as to procedure or form that apply to legislation in general. There is no good reason to think that the power does not extend to the enactment of special requirements that apply only to particular categories of legislation. Nor is there any good reason to think that the relevant limit to that power – which invalidates any requirement that in substance diminishes or destroys the Parliament's continuing plenary power – tracks the distinction between general and special requirements. The issue is whether a requirement diminishes or destroys the parliament's continuing plenary power, not whether it is a general or special requirement. A general requirement that violates that limit should be held invalid, and a special requirement that does not violate it should be held valid.

To see this, imagine that a special quorum requirement of an absolute majority of members of one or both Houses of an Australian state Parliament were required for a specific category of legislation regarded as particularly important. There is surely no good reason to assume that this special requirement could be made judicially enforceable only if AA, s. 6 applied, but that if it were made the standard quorum requirement, applicable to all legislation, it could be made judicially enforceable regardless of s. 6. It makes no sense to think that whether or not AA, s. 6 is needed to make such a requirement judicially enforceable, depends on whether or not the requirement is the standard, as opposed to a special, requirement for legislating.

The tendency to assume that standard requirements are legally unproblematic – legally valid and at least potentially judicially enforceable – is a consequence of our habit of thinking about 'manner and form' in terms of a few stereotypes. Once we free ourselves of that habit, we can see that if standard requirements are legally unproblematic, it is because they do not diminish Parliament's continuing substantive power to legislate. And we can then see that special requirements might be legally unproblematic for precisely the same reason. Consider, once again, the special requirements that govern finance bills. They clearly have no detrimental effect on Parliament's substantive power to enact such bills. They merely differentiate between the functions of the two Houses. There is no good reason to deny either that they are legally valid, or that they could be made judicially enforceable.

If that is so, then arguably an absolute majority requirement could also be valid and judicially enforceable independently of AA, s. 6. It is somewhat more demanding than the standard requirement of a bare majority, provided that a quorum is present. But the crucial question is whether it infringes the relevant limit to Parliament's power to enact procedural requirements, which invalidates requirements that destroy or diminish Parliament's continuing plenary power. Surely an absolute majority requirement does not infringe that limit. The purpose of the standard quorum requirement is not to make it possible for legislation to be passed that is supported only by a minority of members in a House. It assumes that, when political parties are properly managed by their whips, a quorum of members summoned to vote will be sufficiently representative of the membership as a whole that a majority of those present will accurately reflect the views of an absolute majority. The purpose is to avoid the inconvenience of that absolute majority having to attend. The practical difference is merely attendance, not the extent of overall support for the legislation in question. But in relation to proposed legislation of sufficient importance, there is no good reason of principle why, if an absolute majority supports the legislation, it should not be required to attend and be counted, to dispel any possible doubt that it exists. The passage of legislation is, after all, the principal business for which members are elected. Party discipline is sufficiently strong that this is not an onerous exercise: any member whose absence from the House results in a failure to secure an absolute majority is subject to severe criticism from his party leaders and colleagues. The better view is that such a requirement does not diminish Parliament's substantive power to pass the legislation in question.[57]

The same reasoning applies to requirements as to form, that require express words or even a particular verbal formula in order to amend or repeal an earlier law. It is essential to a parliament's plenary power that it be able to amend or repeal its own earlier statutes. But why must it be able to do so by implication, as opposed to being required in some cases to do so by using express words? As previously argued, if a Parliament can require that an important statute be changed only by express words, or even a specific 'literary form', rather than by mere implication, it can prevent itself from changing that statute accidentally, by enacting a less important statute that its members do not realise is inconsistent with the more important one. Parliament can ensure that future legislators must be given clear notice of any proposal to change the statute, without restricting their ability to change it.[58]

It was noted earlier that in the *South-Eastern Drainage Board* case, the Australian High Court interpreted s. 6 of the Real Property Act 1886 (SA) as governing the interpretation of future legislation, rather than as imposing a 'manner and form' requirement as a precondition of validity.[59] The Court was strongly influenced by a supposed constitutional principle, stated by Evatt J., that 'the legislature of South Australia has plenary power to couch its enactments in such literary form as it may choose. It cannot be effectively commanded by a prior legislature to express its intention in a particular way.'[60] Evatt J. was guided by the earlier statement of Maugham L.J. in *Ellen Street Estates* v. *Minister of Health*, namely: 'The legislature cannot, according to our Constitution, bind itself as to the form of subsequent legislation, and it is impossible for Parliament to enact that in a subsequent statute dealing with the same subject matter there can be no implied repeal.'[61]

---

[57] For an argument to the contrary, see G. Taylor, *The Constitution of Victoria* (Sydney: Federation Press, 2006), pp. 483–4.

[58] See Section III, above.

[59] *South Eastern Drainage Board* v. *Savings Bank of South Australia* (1939) 62 CLR 603 at 625.

[60] *Ibid.*, 633. Alternatively, Dixon J. may have thought that on any other view, s. 6 would not have any effect because the subject-matter of the later law did not concern the 'constitution, powers or procedure of the legislature', as required by s. 5 of the Colonial Laws Validity Act 1865 (UK) (and today, s. 6 of the Australia Act 1986 (Cth) (UK)).

[61] *Ellen Street Estates Ltd* v. *Minister of Health* [1934] 1 KB 590 at 597.

Evatt J. was certainly wrong about Australian state legislatures, which were, and still are, explicitly authorised to subject themselves to requirements as to the 'manner and form' by which future legislation must be enacted.[62] And what is a requirement that a particular verbal formula must be used in legislation, if it is not a requirement as to the 'form' of the legislation?[63] But even in the case of the Westminster Parliament, which is not expressly authorised by a higher law to enact requirements as to 'manner and form', it is – as I have suggested – difficult to find any good reason why it should not have the power to require that special legislation be amended or repealed only by express words. The oft-quoted judicial statements to the contrary, in *Ellen Street Estates*[64] and *Vauxhall Estates* v. *Liverpool Corporation*,[65] are merely *obiter dicta*, because in the relevant statute Parliament had not purported to control the making of future legislation.[66]

The preceding reasoning therefore applies equally to the Westminster Parliament. Its sovereign power should be regarded as including power to regulate by statute its own internal decision-making procedures, subject only to the overriding requirement that its continuing sovereign power to legislate may not be destroyed or diminished. If it has the power to give legislative force to its ordinary law-making procedures, including its ordinary quorum requirements, and to make them judicially enforceable – and surely it does – then it has the power to 'bind' itself at least to that extent. The crucial question, then, is not whether Parliament can 'bind' itself, but whether it can do so in a way that destroys or diminishes its continuing sovereign power to legislate. Only requirements as to procedure or form that would have that consequence should be regarded as beyond its power to prescribe.

---

[62] Originally by s. 5 of the Colonial Laws Validity Act 1865 (UK); today by s. 6 of the Australia Act 1986 (Cth) (UK).

[63] However, manner and form requirements can only govern the future enactment of laws 'respecting the constitution, powers, or procedure' of the state parliament in question, and so in *South-East Drainage Board*, Dixon and Evatt J.J. were still right to deny that the requirement in the Real Property Act 1886 (SA) was a binding manner and form requirement within the scope of s. 5 of the CLVA.

[64] [1934] 1 KB 590 (CA).

[65] [1932] 1 KB 733 (Div Ct).

[66] P. Oliver, *The Constitution of Independence, The Development of Constitutional Theory in Australia, Canada, and New Zealand* (Oxford: Oxford University Press, 2005), pp. 9, 70–1, 98 and 306–7.

VIII   Is the 'manner and form' provision in s. 6 of the Australia Act redundant?

In the case of Australian state parliaments, it might be objected that, if procedural requirements can be valid and judicially enforceable independently of AA, s. 6, that section is redundant. Various responses are possible. The most obvious is that express provision was made for 'manner and form' requirements in AA, s. 6, and previously in s. 5 of the CLVA, to enable the judicial enforcement of some requirements that to some extent *do* diminish a state parliament's continuing power to legislate. The requirement of a referendum is the most obvious example. Logically, such a requirement diminishes the substantive power of a Parliament to legislate, because it is unable to enact specified legislation without the assent of an outside body (the electorate). In effect, this outside body is given a power to veto such legislation. It would be impossible to justify a referendum requirement along the lines set out in the previous section: it is not a requirement as to 'procedure or form' that has no impact on parliament's substantive power. Indeed, as shown in Chapter 6, Dixon J.'s reasoning in *Trethowan's* case was for this reason unpersuasive.[67] Gavan Duffy and McTiernan J.J., in dissent, argued more convincingly that the referendum requirement effectively shackled parliament's power to enact of its own motion the legislation in question.[68] Nevertheless, Dixon J.'s view prevailed, and *Trethowan's* case today stands as an unquestioned authority on the point. Section 6 of the AA was undoubtedly enacted partly to ensure that pre-existing manner and form requirements would continue to be legally binding, notwithstanding the declaration in s. 2(2) of the AA that every state Parliament has plenary legislative power with respect to its state. By re-enacting the words of the manner and form proviso in s. 5 of the CLVA, which had been authoritatively interpreted in *Trethowan's* case, s. 6 of the AA must have been intended to preserve intact the authority of that decision, ensuring *inter alia* both that pre-existing referendum requirements remain legally binding, and that new ones can be validly enacted and judicially enforced (although only in relation to laws respecting Parliament's constitution, powers or procedure). It follows that s. 6 of the AA is far from redundant, because a referendum requirement could not plausibly be justified as an example of 'pure procedure or form'.

[67]   See Chapter 6, Section IV, Part B, above.   [68]   *Ibid.*

Standard requirements governing quorums and (generally speaking) the voting rights of presiding officers do not destroy or diminish a parliament's continuing plenary power, and therefore could be made judicially enforceable independently of s. 6 of the AA. The same goes for the special requirements that commonly govern the passage of finance bills. A requirement of an absolute majority should also be valid and enforceable for the same reason. So, too, should requirements that any change to some pre-existing law must be effected by express provision, rather than by implication.[69] These special requirements cannot plausibly be regarded as diminishing Parliament's substantive power to change the law in question.

Super majority requirements, such as a requirement of a two-thirds or three-quarters majority, are more problematic.[70] They should not be regarded as purely procedural, and therefore should not be held binding independently of s. 6 of the AA. In effect, they give a minority of members the power to veto legislation. They do diminish parliament's substantive power, because they make it considerably more difficult for it to legislate. This limit on parliament's power to enact procedures or forms should be strictly construed. Whether or not s. 6 of the AA should be held capable of making super majority requirements binding is another matter. In *Trethowan's* case, the High Court adopted a broad interpretation of the words 'manner and form', extending them well beyond what I have called 'pure procedures and forms'.[71]

IX   Reconstitution

Referendum requirements are difficult to reconcile with the continuing plenary or sovereign power of a parliament. The two most common ways of attempting reconciliation are: firstly, to argue that the referendum requirement is merely a 'manner and form' by which laws must be passed, which does not limit parliament's substantive power to pass them; and secondly, to argue that the requirement changes the composition of Parliament by adding to it an additional element – the electorate as a whole – while leaving its powers unaffected.

Objections to the second alternative in the Australian context have been explained in Chapter 6.[72] If the 'reconstitution' argument were made

---

[69] E.g., s. 85(5) of the Constitution Act 1975 (Vic).
[70] Note that an absolute majority requirement is a special but not a super majority requirement.
[71] See Chapter 6, above.
[72] Chapter 6, Section IV, Part A, above.

in the United Kingdom, it would be even less plausible. There, 'Parliament' is defined by ancient custom as the House of Commons, the House of Lords and the monarch. Parliament thus defined undoubtedly has power to legislate with respect to how each of these three components is constituted. It was settled in the late seventeenth century, for example, that Parliament can control the succession to the throne. Parliament has frequently made legislative changes to the composition and mode of election of the House of Commons. And it is accepted as having a similar power with respect to the House of Lords, which would enable it to change that House into an elected body.

But if Parliament were to subject its power to enact certain kinds of legislation to the veto of the electorate, voting in a referendum, it would in substance severely restrict that portion of its power. Such a radical change would require a change in the fundamental rule of recognition – in the customary consensus among senior legal officials – that underpins the British constitution. The necessity for such a change could not be evaded by formalistic word magic – by labelling the change a 'reconstitution' of Parliament itself, rather than a limitation of its powers. The reality of such a radical change in legal authority cannot be concealed, and debate about its profound philosophical and political implications evaded, by semantic game-playing.

X   Conclusion

It is necessary to choose between two theories of the validity and justiciability of statutory requirements as to procedure or form.

According to the first theory, such requirements are only enforceable by virtue of some 'higher' or 'superior' law such as s. 6 of the AA. In the Australian states, this theory would have the unfortunate consequence that a large number of existing and possible future requirements are only justiciable in relation to legislation respecting the constitution, powers or procedure of a state parliament. This consequence affects special requirements, applicable to particular categories of legislation, that are more onerous than the general requirements that govern ordinary legislation. These special requirements include not only the usual suspects, such as referendum and super majority requirements, but also uncontroversial requirements that currently govern the passage of finance bills. Since finance bills do not concern parliament's constitution, powers or procedure, these requirements cannot – according to this theory – be made judicially enforceable. But the crux of my argument is that logically, this unfortunate consequence also affects general requirements that apply to ordinary legislation. According to this theory, even routine requirements prescribing quorums, and the voting rights of presiding officers, could be made judicially enforceable only in relation to legislation respecting a parliament's constitution, powers or procedure.

In the United Kingdom, the first theory entails that Parliament cannot make any procedural requirements binding, not even the ordinary procedures that are currently set out in Standing Orders. An inability to give legislative force to its own decision-making procedures would be a debilitating incapacity for a supposedly sovereign parliament. This theory is also inconsistent with the assumptions of all parties, and the House of Lords, in the *Jackson* case.

I have argued that the first theory is counter-intuitive, undesirable and groundless, in the sense that there are no good legal or policy reasons for it.

According to the second theory, which I have advanced, statutory requirements of a purely procedural or formal nature, which do not diminish parliament's continuing, substantive power to legislate, do not need the support of a 'higher law' such as AA, s. 6. A parliament's continuing, plenary power surely includes power to make laws respecting its own decision-making procedures and legislative forms, as long as they do not in any way diminish the continuing plenary power itself. No special, independent support, such as that provided by a 'higher law', is needed, because there is no principled objection that it is needed to overcome.

A provision such as AA, s. 6 is only needed to support a requirement, such as a referendum requirement, that does to some extent diminish a parliament's plenary power. Despite the fact that referendum requirements have that effect, one was held to be valid and enforceable in *Trethowan's* case, and by re-enacting the relevant words of s. 5 of the CLVA, s. 6 of the AA must have been intended partly to perpetuate the authority of that decision. It follows that onerous requirements of that kind can only be judicially enforceable (and indeed, legally valid) in relation to the passage of legislation respecting a state parliament's own constitution, powers or procedure. But routine general requirements such as quorum rules, and innocuous special requirements such as those that currently govern finance bills, are valid and can be made judicially enforceable independently of s.6. And if that is true, then other special requirements that do not in any way diminish parliament's substantive power, such as requirements of an absolute majority, or of express rather than implied repeal, are also valid and enforceable independently of s. 6.

These conclusions of the second theory apply equally to the Westminster Parliament. A referendum or other requirement that diminishes Parliament's sovereignty could only be made binding and justiciable if there were a radical change to the customary rule of recognition that underpins Britain's unwritten constitution. But Parliament should be permitted to bind itself to comply with purely procedural or formal requirements, which do not diminish its substantive power to legislate, even if this would also require a (much less radical) change to the rule of recognition.

The conclusion that a requirement of express words, or even of a particular verbal formula, to amend or repeal legislation, is a requirement as to form that could be made binding and justiciable, is very significant. A 'notwithstanding' clause such as the one set out in s. 33 of the Canadian Charter, providing that a statute inconsistent with human rights protected by an earlier law can have a valid operation only if it uses a particular verbal formula that expresses parliament's intention to override those rights, is a requirement as to form. Section 33 is limited in scope, and by no means preserves the law-making powers previously enjoyed by Canadian parliaments.[73] Nevertheless, it provides a model of legislative override that could be expanded in some future attempt to reconcile parliamentary sovereignty with more robust judicial enforcement of constitutional rights. For example, the Human Rights Act 1998 (UK) could be amended to authorise courts to invalidate any legislation inconsistent with the rights it protects, except for legislation expressly declaring Parliament's intention to amend or repeal them, or to override actual or possible judicial interpretations of them. Since judicial review under the Canadian Charter is often classified as 'strong' judicial review, equivalent to review under the United States Constitution, it may seem paradoxical that the inclusion of a 'notwithstanding' clause might be sufficient to make it consistent with parliamentary sovereignty.[74] Questions of judicial review, legislative override and democracy are considered in more depth in the next chapter.

---

[73] See Chapter 8 for more detailed discussion.
[74] For this classification, see G. Huscroft, 'Constitutionalism From the top Down' and A. Petter, 'Taking Dialogue Theory Much Too Seriously' *Osgoode Hall Law Journal* 45 (2007) 91 and 147 respectively.

8

Judicial review, legislative override, and democracy

I The 'notwithstanding clause'

Section 33 of the Canadian Charter of Rights famously provides that Canadian legislation 'may expressly declare ... that the Act or a provision thereof shall operate notwithstanding a provision included in section 2 or sections 7 to 15 of this Charter'. This 'notwithstanding' or 'override' clause enables legislatures to override those specified sections of the Charter, and the rights they protect, although only for renewable five-year periods.[1]

Section 33 is said to have been 'included in the *Charter* for the very purpose of preserving parliamentary sovereignty on rights issues'.[2] But this exaggerates its effect. It is limited in scope, and by no means preserves the law-making powers previously enjoyed by Canadian parliaments. It does not authorise the amendment or repeal of any provisions of the Charter; it does not authorise the override of all Charter rights; and it authorises override only for five-year periods.

Many supporters of the Charter have strongly criticised s. 33 on the predictable ground that it is incompatible with the main purpose of constitutionally entrenching rights.[3] As they see it, that purpose is to protect rights from being overridden by legislation – in other words, to prevent precisely what s. 33 expressly permits. On their view, what the Charter purports to grant with one hand, it takes away with the other. While posing as a constraint on the power of the majority to override the rights of individuals and minorities, it explicitly authorises the majority to do just that (in relation to the rights specified).

---

[1] It does not apply to other sections that protect democratic rights, mobility rights and language rights.

[2] P.W. Hogg, A.A.B. Thornton and W.K. Wright, 'A Reply on "*Charter* Dialogue Revisited"' *Osgoode Hall Law Journal* 45 (2007) 193 at 201.

[3] See criticisms quoted in M. Mandel, *The Charter of Rights and the Legalization of Politics in Canada* (2nd edn) (Toronto: Thompson Educational Publishing, 1994), pp. 88–9 and 96.

Section 33 has been eloquently defended by other supporters of the Charter, who reject this criticism as too simplistic. There are basically two ways of defending the clause. One is to argue that a legislature might sometimes be justified in overriding Charter rights in order to protect some competing right or interest, of greater weight in the circumstances, which is not mentioned in the Charter. But the Charter itself already provides for this possibility: s. 1 explicitly states that Charter rights are 'subject ... to such reasonable limits prescribed by law as can be demonstrably justified in a free and democratic society'. In this regard, those who drafted the Charter wisely avoided the impression conveyed by the American Bill of Rights (but seldom taken seriously by the courts) that the rights it protects are absolute and indefeasible. It follows that s. 33 was not needed to permit legislatures to subordinate protected rights to other rights or interests.[4]

The real problem that s. 33 was designed to overcome has to do with judicial interpretations of Charter provisions, including s. 1. This leads to the second way of defending the section, which is to argue that its real purpose must have been to enable legislatures to override judicial interpretations or applications of Charter rights with which they reasonably disagree.[5] This defence of s. 33 is admittedly difficult to reconcile with its wording, which gives rise to difficulties discussed later in this chapter.[6]

This defence has the potential to overcome not only the criticisms of s. 33 made by Charter supporters, but also the objections of those who oppose the Charter on the ground that it is undemocratic. That is not surprising. Section 33 has been described as a uniquely Canadian compromise of two rival constitutional models – the American model of strong judicial review, and the British model of parliamentary sovereignty.[7] Whether it is a genuine compromise is, of course, open to question. Geoffrey Marshall has protested that '[i]t is not so much a compromise as a capitulation' of proper rights protection to parliamentary

---

[4] L.E. Weinrib argues that the purpose of s. 33 is to enable legislatures to override rights when this cannot be justified under s. 1: 'Learning to Live With the Override' *McGill Law Journal* 35 (1990) 541 at 567–9. But any use of s. 33 that could not in principle (leaving aside judicial versus legislative judgment) 'be demonstrably justified in a free and democratic society' would surely be very difficult to justify at all.

[5] See, e.g., P.H. Russell, 'Standing Up For Notwithstanding' *Alberta Law Review* 229 (1991) 293.

[6] See Section IV, below, and T. Kanaha, 'Understanding the Notwithstanding Mechanism' *University of Toronto Law Journal* 52 (2002) 221 at 233–6.

[7] Russell, 'Standing Up', 294.

sovereignty.[8] Others take the opposite view, complaining that in practical terms it has not succeeded in curbing the undemocratic supremacy of the courts.[9] Perhaps the fact that it has satisfied neither side indicates that it is, indeed, an effective compromise.

Ideally, such a compromise would combine the most attractive features of both models, while discarding their most objectionable features.[10] For example, the most powerful and popular argument against the judicial enforcement of constitutional rights maintains that it is undemocratic for unelected judges to invalidate laws enacted by a democratically elected legislature. But given s. 33, judicial enforcement of the Charter can be argued to add a further check or balance to the political process without diminishing its fundamentally democratic character. On this view, s. 33 is part of a broader constitutional scheme that encourages a 'dialogue' between legislatures and courts, in which the latter are rarely guaranteed the 'final say'.[11] The Charter permits an appeal from the rough-and-tumble of politics to a 'forum of principle', but s. 33 confers a right of final appeal back to a consequently more informed and conscientious legislature.[12] What objection could be made, if the legislature retains the final say? As Peter Hogg has concluded: 'So long as the last word remains with the competent legislative body ... much of the American debate over the legitimacy of judicial review is rendered irrelevant.'[13]

One purpose of this chapter is to ask if Hogg is right. As we will see, Canadian legislators are loathe to use s. 33; indeed, a constitutional convention against its use may have formed everywhere except in Quebec. This is one reason why judicial review under the Charter is widely regarded as functionally equivalent to 'strong' judicial review in the United States.[14] And if it is equivalent, then presumably Charter review is

---

[8] G. Marshall, 'Taking Rights For An Override: Free Speech and Commercial Expression' *Public Law* 4 (1989) at 11.

[9] F.L. Morton and R. Knopff, *The Charter Revolution and the Court Party* (Ontario: Broadview Press, 2000).

[10] Russell, 'Standing Up'.

[11] P.W. Hogg and A.A. Bushell, 'The Charter Dialogue Between Courts and Legislatures' *Osgoode Hall Law Journal* 35 (1997) 75. See also Kanaha, 'Understanding the Notwithstanding'.

[12] See, e.g., R. Knopff and F.L. Morton, *Charter Politics* (Ontario: Nelson Canada, 1992), esp. pp. 205–6 and 225–33.

[13] P.W. Hogg, *Constitutional Law of Canada* (Ontario: Carswell, 1997), 36.10–36.11.

[14] See G. Huscroft, 'Constitutionalism From the top Down' and A. Petter, 'Taking Dialogue Theory Much Too Seriously' *Osgoode Hall Law Journal* 45 (2007) 91 and 147 respectively. But see to the contrary K. Roach, 'Dialogue or Defiance: Legislative Reversals of Supreme

equally vulnerable to objections based on the denial or abdication of the supremacy of democratically elected legislatures. If so, Hogg is wrong.

But even if he is right, his claim is not that s. 33 completely disarms critics of the Charter. Another, equally important purpose of this chapter is to ask how much of the American debate is rendered irrelevant. This requires distinguishing between different objections that have been made to the judicial enforcement of constitutional rights, and asking which of them applies notwithstanding a notwithstanding clause. In particular, it requires distinguishing rights-based from consequentialist justifications of democracy, and corresponding objections to the judicial enforcement of rights. It is possible that a clause such as s. 33 overcomes rights-based objections, because it preserves the democratic right to make the final decision, but does not overcome consequentialist objections.

These issues are relevant to the possible strengthening of human rights protection in Britain along the lines mentioned at the end of the previous chapter. It was suggested that the Human Rights Act 1998 (UK) could be amended to require courts to invalidate any legislation inconsistent with the rights it protects, except for legislation that expressly declares Parliament's intention to amend or repeal them, or to override actual or possible judicial interpretations of them. I have argued that this would be consistent with the doctrine of parliamentary sovereignty, because Parliament would retain full substantive power to change the law however and whenever it should choose. It would have bound itself only with respect to the form of the legislation needed to do so.[15] But the Canadian debate suggests that if Parliament never dared to exercise that power, this arrangement might still be vulnerable to objections based on majoritarian conceptions of democracy.

II   The rights-based objection to constitutional rights

A leading contemporary critic of constitutional rights is Jeremy Waldron. His main criticism has consistently been that the judicial enforcement of such rights is inconsistent with the democratic right of ordinary people to participate on an equal basis in public decision-making. Waldron describes this right of participation as 'the right of rights', because it is

Court decisions in Canada and the United States' *International Journal of Constitutional Law* 4 (2006) 347, and P.W. Hogg, A.A.B. Thornton and W.K. Wright, 'A Reply on *Charter Dialogue Revisited*', at 199–202.

[15] Chapter 7, Section VII, above.

the rights-theorists' solution to the problem of authoritatively resolving disputes about rights.[16] He describes his critique as 'rights-based' because it is ultimately based on this 'right of rights'.[17]

Waldron himself has summarised his critique as follows:

> If we are going to defend the idea of an entrenched Bill of Rights put effect-ively beyond revision by anyone other than the judges, we should try and think what we might say to some public-spirited citizen who wishes to launch a campaign or lobby her MP on some issue of rights about which she feels strongly ... [W]e have to imagine ourselves saying to her: 'You may write to the newspaper and get up a petition and organize a pressure group to lobby Parliament. But even if you ... orchestrate the support of a large number of like-minded men and women, and manage to prevail in the legislature, your measure may be challenged and struck down because your view of what rights we have does not accord with the judges' views. When their votes differ from yours, theirs are the votes that will prevail.' It is my submission that saying this does not comport with the respect and honour normally accorded to ordinary men and women in the con-text of a theory of rights.[18]

Waldron's argument is explicitly based on a premise that is inapplicable to most of the Canadian Charter.[19] He is concerned only with rights that are 'put effectively beyond revision [that is, amendment] by anyone other than the judges'. In *Law and Disagreement* he puts the point in this way: 'a constitutional constraint is less unreasonable ... the greater the oppor-tunity for altering it by processes of constitutional amendment. We need to bear in mind, however, that such processes are usually made very dif-ficult; indeed, their difficulty ... is precisely definitive of the constraint in question.'[20] This is not quite right, because s. 33 shows that there can be other ways of overcoming or relaxing constitutional constraints than by constitutional amendment. Section 33 does not give Canadian legisla-tures any power to amend the Charter, but does enable them to free them-selves from most of its constraints. Consequently, where those constraints are concerned, it is not the case that when the judges' votes differ from

---

[16] J. Waldron, *Law and Disagreement* (Oxford: Clarendon Press, 1999), p. 254.

[17] J. Waldron, 'A Right-Based Critique of Constitutional Rights' *Oxford Journal of Legal Studies* 13 (1993) 18; Waldron, *Law and Disagreement*, pp. 214–25 and 249–54.

[18] Waldron, 'A Right-Based Critique', 50–1. Note that all the main arguments made in *Law and Disagreement* were prefigured in this article.

[19] Earlier in the same article, Waldron makes it clear that he is concerned with constitution-ally 'entrenched' rights, which are 'immune' from legislative change, and therefore 'dis-able' the legislature and the citizens it represents: *ibid.*, 27. He also notes that his concern is with 'American-style' judicial review: *ibid.*, 19.

[20] Waldron, *Law and Disagreement*, p. 275.

those of the public-spirited citizen and her like-minded supporters, the judges' votes necessarily prevail. We should not say to her: 'When their votes differ from yours, theirs are the votes that will prevail.'[21] The public-spirited citizen can get up a petition, and lobby the legislature to override the judges. She only needs to persuade a majority of legislators to do so. And her ability to do so will depend mainly on her ability also to persuade a majority of her fellow citizens to strongly endorse her views. In Canada, after the Supreme Court invalidated the statutory prohibition of abortion, 'the aroused and losing group went immediately to the parliamentary lobby to press for legislative redress' – but it found that there was insufficient 'inclination on the part of the politicians to use the override'.[22]

Consider another of Waldron's arguments. Discussing the popular thesis that judicial enforcement of constitutional rights can enhance the quality of public debates about those rights, and therefore the character of democratic politics, he replies:

> The idea that civic republicans and participatory democrats should count this as a gain is a travesty. Civic republicans and participatory democrats are interested in *practical political deliberation*, which is not just any old debating exercise, but a form of discussion among those who are about to participate in a binding collective decision. A star-struck people may speculate about what the Supreme Court will do next on abortion or some similar issue; they may even amuse each other, as we law professors do, with stories about how we would decide, in the unlikely event that we were elevated to that eminent tribunal. The exercise of power by a few black-robed celebrities can certainly be expected to *fascinate* an articulate population. But that is hardly the essence of active citizenship. Perhaps such impotent debating is nevertheless morally improving … But independent ethical benefits of this kind are … not the primary point of civic participation in republican political theory.[23]

This reply is based on the assumption that public discussion of judicial decisions concerning constitutional rights is politically impotent: since a constitutional amendment is rarely politically feasible, those decisions are usually conclusive for practical purposes. But if s. 33 of the Charter can be invoked, that assumption is simply inoperative. Public discussion is not politically impotent.

---

[21] Waldron, 'A Right-Based Critique', 50–1.

[22] P.H. Russell, 'Canadian Constraints on Judicialization from Without' *International Political Science Review* 15 (1994) 165 at 171, quoted in M. Tushnet, 'Policy Distortion and Democratic Debilitation: Comparative Illumination of the Counter-majoritarian Difficulty' *Michigan Law Review* 94 (1995) 245 at n. 151.

[23] Waldron, *Law and Disagreement*, p. 291.

Opponents of judicial review usually respond by pointing out that s. 33 is very rarely used, because it is too politically dangerous. But the most likely reason for legislators not using the override is that the electorate is unlikely to trust their judgment about constitutional rights more than the judges' judgment. And surely that is the electorate's democratic prerogative, which Waldron would be bound to respect. It would not be open to him to object that an ingenuous electorate is likely to be deceived by the specious objectivity of constitutionalised rights, or dazzled by the mystique of the judiciary – by a naïve faith in judges' expert legal skills, superior wisdom, and impartiality. That objection would reflect precisely the same lack of faith in the electorate's capacity for enlightened self-government that motivates proponents of constitutionally entrenched rights. They fear that a majority of voters, motivated by ignorance, prejudice or passion, might trample on the rights of minorities or individuals. Waldron objects that ordinary people should not be presumed to be ignorant, prejudiced or intemperate, because that would be inconsistent with the basis of their having rights in the first place. '[S]ince the point of any argument about rights has to do with the respect that is owed to [the ordinary] person as an active, thinking being, we are hardly in a position to say that our conversation takes his rights seriously if at the same time we ignore or slight anything he has to say about the matter.'[24] But if a majority's opinions about the rights even of minorities and individuals are entitled to respect, surely their opinions about the exercise of one of their own rights – to political participation – is entitled to even more respect, because in that case there is even less danger of ignorance or prejudice. We are concerned here with the 'right of rights' of a majority of ordinary people collectively to make final decisions about rights, if necessary by endorsing a use of the override clause. It would be inconsistent for Waldron to base the right to political participation on the capacity of ordinary people for intelligent and conscientious moral deliberation, but then to doubt that capacity when it comes to deliberating about the use of an override clause. If a majority of ordinary people strongly prefer that an override not be used, because in relation to rights they trust judges more than legislators – or perhaps even more than themselves – how can the rights-based theorist say they are wrong?

This question touches on the Human Rights Act 1998 (UK), which authorises judges to declare legislation to be incompatible with protected rights, but not to invalidate it. The government and Parliament are legally

---

[24] *Ibid.*, p. 251.

free to decide whether or not the legislation should consequently be amended or repealed. It is sometimes suggested that this freedom is illusory, because it is not politically feasible to ignore a judicial declaration of incompatibility.[25] But even if this is the case, it does not follow that the judiciary has been given power to trump the democratic process. The democratic process determines what is or is not politically feasible. The same would be true if the Human Rights Act were to be amended along the lines previously suggested.[26]

Someone might be tempted to respond to this argument along much the same lines that Waldron takes in refuting a very different argument. That different argument is this: if a bill of rights has been adopted democratically, with the support of a majority of the people, then judicial invalidation of statutes for violating those rights is perfectly democratic because the people have authorised it. Waldron replies that if the people chose to establish a dictatorship, it would not follow that the dictatorship was democratic – it would only follow that democracy had been extinguished democratically. He suggests that the democratic adoption of a bill of rights 'amounts to exactly that: voting democracy out of existence, at least so far as a wide range of issues of political principle is concerned'.[27] Could a similar reply be made here – that a routine reluctance to use an override clause to trump judicial decisions is in effect a democratic abdication of democratic rights?

There is clearly a difference between relinquishing or disabling one's power to make certain kinds of decisions, and declining – even routinely – to exercise it. For example, in constitutional law there is a crucial difference between, on the one hand, a legislature irrevocably transferring its powers to another body, and on the other, its delegating those powers while retaining its ability at any time to override its delegate or even cancel the delegation. It is possible to distinguish between many different arrangements, including: (1) the permanent surrender of power; (2) the indefinite surrender of power, subject to the possibility of reclaiming it by onerous means such as a constitutional amendment; (3) the temporary surrender of power to a delegate for a fixed period, followed by its resumption or fresh delegation to the same or some other delegate; and (4) the delegation of power, whether indefinite or temporary, subject to

[25] E.g., A. Kavanagh, *Constitutional Review Under the Human Rights Act* (Cambridge: Cambridge University Press, 2009), pp. 281–9 and 322–4.

[26] See the final paragraph of the previous section.

[27] Waldron, 'A Right-Based Critique', 46.

the retention of power at any time to override the delegate and/or cancel the delegation by non-onerous means.

Democracy is surely compatible with arrangements (3) and (4), even if this is doubtful in the case of (2). Indeed, modern representative democracies resemble (3): the electorate confers legislative power on elected officials for more or less fixed periods, retaining only the power occasionally to decide whether to extend their terms or replace them.[28] We do not generally regard this as undemocratic. Nor do we regard as undemocratic the delegation of extensive law-making power to unelected officials, provided that elected officials retain the power to override them. Much modern law-making consists of regulations made by executive governments, which elected legislatures can scrutinize before they come into operation, and disallow if they see fit. Even if it were the case that legislatures seldom disallow such regulations, that would not in itself demonstrate a diminution of democracy.

It follows that we regard democracy as based on a *right* to participate *indirectly*, rather than a *duty* to participate *directly*, in public decision-making.[29] A right, by definition, does not have to be exercised; otherwise, it would be a duty rather than a right.[30] Of course, a right can be accompanied by a duty to exercise it. In Australia, for example, voters have a legal duty to exercise their right to vote. But a rights-based theorist should surely argue against the imposition of such duties. Rights are maximised if they coexist with rights *not* to exercise them. In countries where voters do not have a duty to vote, for example, some voters deliberately refuse to vote in order to express their disapproval of the candidates or the political process. Their right not to vote reflects a broader freedom not to participate in processes they find distasteful. It follows from all this that a rights-based theorist is not well placed to object to the infrequent exercise of a democratic right to override judicial decisions.

So an override clause is not subject, merely because it is rarely used, to an objection similar to Waldron's rebuttal of the 'democratic' justification of entrenched constitutional rights. This point can be taken one

---

[28] This resembles (3) because the electorate is usually unable to exercise legislative power itself, and therefore cannot resume it. It is restricted to choosing those who will exercise the power on its behalf.

[29] Except in Australia, where compulsory voting in both elections and constitutional referendums in effect imposes a duty to participate both indirectly and directly in different decision-making processes.

[30] Of course, a right can be accompanied by a duty: in Australia, the right to vote is accompanied by a duty to exercise it.

step further. The existence of an override clause rebuts Waldron's rebuttal. He objects that judicial enforcement of a bill of rights is undemocratic even if the bill was adopted democratically. His objection assumes that by adopting a bill of rights, the democratic process more or less permanently transferred to the judiciary the power of ultimate decision-making with respect to those rights. But to the extent that judicial decisions can be overriden, that assumption is inapplicable, and the objection therefore baseless. The transfer of power to the judges is more like a delegation of power to make decisions that can be overridden by the legislature, just as it can override the exercise of powers it has delegated to the executive. The 'democratic' justification of entrenched constitutional rights then stands undefeated.

III   Goal-based objections to constitutional rights

According to Waldron, '[i]f there is a democratic objection to judicial review, it must also be a rights-based objection'.[31] But that is surely wrong. Democracy has been defended on many grounds other than rights, such as perfectionist and consequentialist grounds (which I will collectively call goal-based grounds). For example, it has been argued that widespread participation in public debate and decision-making, in which all are treated as equals, helps develop important civic virtues: it lessens feelings of powerlessness, and improves self-confidence and self-respect; it promotes education, a broadening of horizons, and an appreciation of other points of view; and by doing so, it fosters co-operation and compromise, a sense of responsibility to the community, and a more willing acceptance of group decisions.[32]

Representative democracy may be more conducive to the realisation of these benefits than direct democracy. A system in which decisions can only be made by representatives of the people, after debating contentious issues face to face, rather than by the people themselves in a mass plebiscite, encourages due deliberation before decision-making. The presence of legislators representing all affected interests makes it more likely that pertinent information will be duly considered, and participation in debate requires legislators to listen carefully to one another, even if only to sharpen their rebuttals. Since prejudice

---

[31] Waldron, *Law and Disagreement*, p. 282.
[32] For a critical discussion of arguments of this sort, see W. Nelson, *On Justifying Democracy* (London: Routledge & Kegan Paul, 1980).

and intolerance tend to diminish when people engage in dialogue with one another, representative democracy is thought to promote mutual respect, moderation and compromise.[33] Moreover, legislators must build coalitions with one another if they are to be effective: all majorities are groupings of minorities that have joined forces, either in a political party, a coalition of parties, or a temporary alliance. It is taken for granted that political power is impermanent, and that opponents defeated today might turn the tables tomorrow. This adds to the impetus towards moderation, for two reasons: first, the frequent necessity to sacrifice parochial and extreme demands in order to build the necessary coalitions; and second, the fear of backlash if one's temporarily defeated adversaries should gain the upper hand in the future.[34] As Martin Diamond has put it,

> The discovery that one's grossest demands are absurdly impossible of achievement can lead to an enlightened kind of self-interest, a habitual recognition of the indisputable needs of others and a general sobriety about the general requirements of society. And something still worthier can happen. As the extremes of selfishness are moderated, the representative can become free to consider questions affecting the national interest on their merits.[35]

It is sometimes argued that the realisation of these benefits is jeopardised when politics is 'judicialised' by the enforcement of constitutional rights through litigation. 'Democratic debilitation', a term coined by Mark Tushnet, is a useful label for many ways in which, it has been alleged, such litigation might damage both the process and spirit of representative democracy.[36] Democratic debilitation can affect either legislatures, the electorate, or both. Moreover, predictions of debilitation are sometimes difficult to reconcile with one another. For example, some expect the judicialisation of politics to engender apathy and irresponsibility among legislators and the electorate, whereas others anticipate an aggravation of political extremism and intolerance, which is hardly a symptom of apathy.

---

[33] This may seem to be belied by the frequent angry and contemptuous exchanges between legislators in Australian parliaments. But it is often surmised that these are histrionics, because outside the media limelight the same legislators are respectful and even friendly towards one another.

[34] I owe the ideas in this paragraph to R. Knopff, 'Populism and the Politics of Rights: The Dual Attack on Representative Democracy' *Canadian Journal of Political Science* 31 (1998) 683 at 689–94.

[35] M. Diamond, *The Founding of the Democratic Republic* (Itasca: F.E. Peacock Publishers, 1981), p. 78, quoted in Knopff, 'Populism and the Politics of Rights', 691.

[36] Tushnet, 'Policy Distortion'.

The argument for apathy and irresponsibility goes something like this. First, legislators might be inclined to devote less attention to the compatibility of proposed legislation with protected rights, if the matter is likely to be litigated in the courts anyway. They might become reckless as to compatibility or, worse still, 'pass the buck' to the courts, and shirk responsibility for unpopular decisions they would otherwise have to make. Secondly, frequent resort to litigation to advance claims of rights might divert vital funds and energies from grass-roots political mobilization, and even victory in the courtroom could engender political impotence due to complacency. Constitutional challenges are 'conducted via technocratic representation, i.e. lawyers, who only demand fund-raising from their clientele, not advice, not meetings, marches or votes. A victory in the courts may still leave a broke and apathetic rump organisation behind, not one capable of moving forward any further.'[37] Thirdly, if political debate is subsumed by constitutional debate, couched in legalistic jargon and formulae, lay-people (including legislators) may come to be regarded, and to regard themselves, as incompetent to participate.[38] Consequently, they might lose interest in the debate. Fourthly, the loss of ultimate responsibility for how questions about rights are decided might make the electorate more politically enervated, apathetic, or even irresponsible. James Bradley Thayer famously urged judicial restraint partly because an excessive readiness to overrule the legislature might gradually diminish 'the political capacity of the people' and its sense of moral responsibility.[39]

The argument for extremism and intolerance has been put most eloquently by leading Charter critics F.L. Morton and Rainer Knopff. They argue that when judges can enforce rights, political antagonists become more inclined to resolve disagreements through litigation, rather than

---

[37] H. Glasbeek, 'A No-Frills Look at the Charter of Rights and Freedoms, or How Politicians and Lawyers Hide Reality' *Windsor Yearbook of Access to Justice* 9 (1989) 293 at 344. For strong evidence of this in the US, see G. Rosenberg, *The Hollow Hope; Can Courts Bring About Social Change?* (Chicago: University of Chicago Press, 1991), pp. 12, 282, 313–14 and 339–41. On the other hand, Rosenberg also reports that courtroom victories can galvanise the opposition into strenuous political efforts to overturn them: pp. 155–6, 138–9 and 341–2.

[38] This may also impoverish political debate, by confining it to a procrustean bed of constitutional formulae. As Waldron suggests, it is healthier to discuss issues of principle directly and freely, 'rather than having to scramble around constructing those principles out of the scraps of some sacred text, in a tendentious exercise of constitutional caligraphy': Waldron, *Law and Disagreement*, pp. 220 and 289–90.

[39] See P. Kurland (ed), *John Marshall* (Chicago: University of Chicago Press, 1967), pp. 85–6.

respectful discussion with one another in a search for compromise. This aggravates and polarises disputes, by inflating policy claims that are open to reasonable disagreement, into moral absolutes that brook no opposition. The rhetoric of rights encourages the assumption that there is a single, correct answer to contentious questions of social policy, resistance to which is wrong or even illegitimate, and should therefore be permanently overridden. 'The courtroom process is inescapably about claiming the uncompromisable trumps known as rights, and it thus encourages participants to speak the language of extremism both in and out of the courtroom.'[40] Morton and Knopff summarize their objection to the Charter as follows:

> To transfer the resolution of reasonable disagreements from legislatures to courts inflates rhetoric to unwarranted levels and replaces negotiated, majoritarian compromise politics with the intensely held policy preferences of minorities. Rights-based judicial policymaking also grants the policy preferences of courtroom victors an aura of coercive force and permanence that they do not deserve. Issues that should be subject to the ongoing flux of government by discussion are presented as beyond legitimate debate, with the partisans claiming the right to permanent victory. As the moralist of rights displaces the morality of consent, the politics of coercion replaces the politics of persuasion. The result is to embitter politics and decrease the inclination of political opponents to treat each other as fellow citizens ...[41]

Although these two arguments, for apathy and irresponsibility, and for extremism and intolerance, are not obviously compatible, they are reconcilable. It might be hypothesised that the majority of legislators and citizens – who occupy the broad 'middle ground' of politics – will become more apathetic and irresponsible, while those closer to the ends of the political spectrum will become more zealous and intolerant of their opponents. This might happen if a policy status quo, established by the moderate majority, strikes a compromise between two passionately opposed minorities. If one minority persuades a court to overturn that status quo in its favour, members of the moderate majority might not think it worth the effort required to overturn the judicial decision, given that their views were not passionately held in the first place. Their reluctance to do so might be reinforced by lack of confidence in their competence to dispute the complex legalistic reasoning of judges presumed to possess special expertise about constitutional rights. On the other hand, the opposed

---

[40] Knopff, 'Populism and the Politics of Rights', 702.
[41] Morton and Knopff, *The Charter Revolution*, p. 166.

minority, outraged by their adversaries' courtroom victory, might mount a furious effort to reverse it, escalating the political struggle between these groups and aggravating their mutual animosity. According to Mary Ann Glendon, this was precisely what happened in the aftermath of the abortion decision in *Roe* v. *Wade*.[42]

> American experience suggests that the real danger represented by regular invalidation of legislation on constitutional grounds is not that elected representatives will rise up in anger against the courts. On the contrary, legislators are often relieved at being able to say that their hands are tied by the courts, especially where controversial matters are concerned. One danger is, rather, of atrophy in the democratic processes of bargaining, education, and persuasion that takes place in and around legislatures. Another is that by too readily preventing compromise and blocking the normal political avenues for change, courts leave the disappointed majority with no legitimate political outlet … Public debate about abortion in Europe has not put an end to controversy. But it is not marked by the degree of bitterness, desperation, and outrage that occasionally erupts into violence in the United States.[43]

Although Canadian legislatures can override judicial decisions, they may fail to do so for the very reasons just described. Apathy or political inertia on the part of the moderate majority, and the increased intransigence of the opposed minorities, can make it impossible to assemble the necessary numbers. That is how Morton and Knopff explain the failure of Canadian legislatures to make better use of s. 33 to override unpopular judicial decisions.[44] But their argument also suggests that on the odd occasions when legislatures do employ s. 33, the political process is likely to be further embittered by howls of outrage from the defeated minority, whose self-righteousness would have been inflated by vindication in the courts.[45] Whatever the outcome, on this view, the flames of extremism are likely to be fanned.

Morton and Knopff's analysis is contested by Peter Hogg, who claims that in Canada, judicial enforcement of rights has generated a 'dialogue' between courts and legislatures that has actually enhanced the democratic process.[46] He has systematically examined legislative responses to

---

[42] *Roe* v. *Wade* (1973) 410 US 113.
[43] M. A. Glendon, 'A Beau Mentir Qui Vient De Lion: the 1988 Canadian Abortion Decision in Comparative Perspective' *Northwestern University Law Review* 83 (1989) 569 at 588.
[44] Morton and Knopff, *The Charter Revolution*, pp. 163 and 165.
[45] See *ibid.*, pp. 155–7, on the 'moral inflation' encouraged by the rhetoric of rights.
[46] See P.W. Hogg, 'The *Charter* Revolution: Is It Undemocratic?' *Constitutional Forum* 12 (2001/2002) 1.

judicial decisions invalidating legislation under the Charter, and concludes that in most cases new legislation was passed that accomplished the legislature's original objective consistently with the courts' interpretation of relevant Charter rights.[47] If so, then at least in these cases, the claim that Charter successes tend to induce defeatism and apathy among moderate majorities, and thereby entrench the views of extremist minorities, would seem to be falsified.[48] Morton and Knopff concede that legislatures often fail to respond to Charter decisions because they concern moral questions that are 'not a priority for the government, the opposition parties, or the majority of voters', and that '[w]hen the policy is central to the government's program, the government should have little difficulty mustering the political will to respond effectively'.[49] This suggests that the main stumbling block to effective legislative responses is not general political apathy caused by the Charter, but relative indifference about particular issues that is independent of it. Moreover, legislators would surely be more willing to use s. 33 if they did not fear that doing so would be unpopular with voters. Carefully designed surveys of public opinion in Canada indicate that in the abstract, more than two-thirds of the Canadian public prefer the courts, rather than legislatures, to have the final say in relation to Charter rights. This proportion declines, particularly among francophones, when people consider the question in the context of specific issues such as laws controlling trade unions or assisting poor people; but it remains over fifty per cent.[50] This has been attributed partly to the diminished moral authority of Canadian legislatures, due to their lack of adequate internal checks and balances.[51] This does not suggest apathy among voters, but rather, a positive distrust of their elected legislators. And who can confidently say that this distrust is undeserved?

Hogg's 'dialogue' theory, and analysis of legislative responses to judicial decisions that underlies it, have been challenged.[52] It is beyond the

---

[47] See P.W. Hogg and A.A. Bushell, 'The Charter Dialogue Between Courts and Legislatures' *Osgoode Hall Law Journal* 35 (1997) 75.

[48] Hogg goes so far as to suggest that Morton and Knopff's two examples of legislative inertia are in fact examples of dialogue: Hogg, 'The *Charter* Revolution', pp. 6–7; contra, Morton and Knopff, *The Charter Revolution*, pp. 162–5.

[49] Morton and Knopff, *The Charter Revolution*, pp. 164 and 165.

[50] Predictably, politicians are much more inclined to favour legislatures, and lawyers to favour courts. See P.M. Sniderman, J.F. Fletcher, P.H. Russell and P.E. Tetlock (eds.), *The Clash of Rights, Liberty, Equality, and Legitimacy in Pluralist Democracy* (New Haven: Yale University Press, 1996), pp. 163–7.

[51] Knopff and Morton, *Charter Politics*, p. 232.

[52] See, e.g., C. Manfredi and J.B. Kelly, 'Six Degrees of Dialogue: A Response to Hogg and Bushell' *Osgoode Hall Law Journal* 37 (1999) 513; C. Manfredi, *Judicial Power and the*

scope of this chapter to attempt to settle that debate, or the broader question of the impact of judicial enforcement of Charter rights on Canadian political culture. That would require gathering and interpreting empirical evidence of changes in the behaviour and motivations of citizens and legislators throughout the country, involving very difficult questions of cause and effect. For present purposes, the important point is that when a bill of rights includes a comprehensive override clause, it survives Waldron's rights-based objection. The question of its compatibility with democratic values then depends on sociological evidence that is inevitably impressionistic and contestable.

IV   The desuetude of s. 33

Even if Morton and Knopff are right, it is natural to ask why s. 33 has not been effective in preventing or at least minimising the democratic debilitation that they report. When judicial interpretations of rights are conclusive (subject only to constitutional amendment), it is easier to appreciate how democracy might be debilitated. But the whole point of an override clause is to ensure that the judges do not have the final word. Precisely because it enables them to be overridden, such a clause has the potential to stimulate robust and potent political debate, among both legislators and the electorate, about questions of rights that may be or have been decided by judges. In doing so, it could 'encourage a more politically vital discourse on the meaning of rights and their relationship to competing constitutional visions than what emanates from the judicial monologue that exists in a regime of judicial supremacy'.[53]

There is general agreement that s. 33 has failed to fulfill that potential in Canada. This is partly because it is widely believed that the clause has been used only once outside Quebec, and not at all since 1988.[54] In a recent thorough study, Tsvi Kanaha has demonstrated that it has in fact been used more often than this, but the fact remains that it has been used very rarely.[55] Kanaha also shows that the use of the clause has often failed to generate, among the electorate, the 'politically vital discourse on the

---

Charter; Canada and the Paradox of Liberal Constitutionalism (2nd edn) (Ontario: Oxford University Press, 2001), pp. 177–9; P. Hogg and A.A. Thornton, 'Reply to "Six Degrees of Dialogue"' *Osgoode Hall Law Journal* 37 (1999) 529.

[53] Manfredi, *Judicial Power and the Charter*, p. 191.   [54] *Ibid.*, p. 5.

[55] T. Kanaha, 'The Notwithstanding Mechanism and Public Discussion: Lessons From the Ignored Practice of Section 33 of the Charter' *Canadian Public Administration* 44 (2001) 255.

meaning of rights' that its supporters had anticipated, although he fails to consider the extent to which legislators have engaged in such discourse before using it.

The clause has been invoked so rarely that arguably '[s]omething like a convention against its use may have emerged, precisely because the political costs of invoking the power turned out to be too great'.[56] Just as conventions develop through regular practice evolving into prescriptive custom, the less s. 33 is used, the more its use is likely to be disapproved of.[57] In 1998, the Premier of Alberta withdrew a proposal to use s. 33, explaining that '[i]t became adundantly clear that to individuals in this country the Charter of Rights and Freedoms is paramount and the use of any tool ... to undermine [it] is something that should be used only in very, very rare circumstances'.[58] This attitude apparently extends to many legislators. Michael Mandel reports that when Prime Minister Mulroney condemned s. 33, after Quebec's perceived abuse of it, his speech 'led to the usual declarations by opposition members of their sincere hatred for the clause, and even a challenge to the Prime Minister to abolish it'.[59] Grant Huscroft concludes bluntly that s. 33 is now 'unused, and all but unusable' and is therefore 'simply irrelevant'.[60]

It is not clear why s. 33 has been so rarely used. Morton's and Knopff's explanation has already been discussed.[61] Howard Leeson hypothesises that it is the result of a combination of factors: the unwillingness of legislators to 'take on' the judiciary because of its superior popularity among the general public; the professionally ingrained and career-oriented tendency of government lawyers, who advise the responsible minister, to recommend deference to the courts; a preference for less drastic legislative responses of the kind discussed by Hogg, with override relegated to weapon of last resort; and a sense of futility given that an override expires after five years, unless it is renewed.[62] But two other reasons, not mentioned by Leeson, are often suggested.

---

[56] Tushnet, 'Policy Distortion', 296, citing A. Heard, *Canadian Constitutional Conventions: The Marriage of Law and Politics* (Toronto: Oxford University Press, 1991), p. 147.
[57] Howard Leeson, 'Section 33, the Notwithstanding Clause: A Paper Tiger?' *Choices* 6(4) (2000) 20 (Institute for Research on Public Policy).
[58] Quoted in Manfredi, *Judicial Power and the Charter*, pp. 187–8.
[59] Mandel, *The Charter of Rights*, p. 95.
[60] G. Huscroft, 'Constitutionalism From the Top Down', at 96.
[61] Text to n. 42, above.
[62] Leeson, 'Section 33', pp. 18–19.

One is the wording of s. 33. It authorises Canadian legislatures to declare that their enactments 'shall operate notwithstanding a provision included in [the specified sections] of this Charter'. The power is thus posed as a power to override the Charter itself, rather than disputed judicial interpretations of the Charter. This must make its use very difficult to justify. When the judiciary disagrees, or is expected to disagree, with the legislature as to the 'true' meaning and effect of Charter provisions, the legislature cannot ensure that its view will prevail without appearing to override the Charter itself. And that is vulnerable to the politically lethal objection that the legislature is openly and self-confessedly subverting constitutional rights. Indeed, Waldron argues that precisely because s. 33 places legislatures in this predicament, it does not render his democratic objection to constitutionally entrenched rights inapplicable to the Canadian Charter.[63]

There is surely no need for an override clause to convey that impression, which, at least from the legislature's point of view, is erroneous. Section 33 has always been defended on the ground that, since rights are not absolute, but must often give way to other rights and interests, what they require in particular cases is often a subject of reasonable disagreement; and that there is no good reason to assume that when judges and legislators disagree, the former are necessarily correct.[64] It is unfortunate that this justification is not reflected in the wording of the section itself. Knopff and Morton complain that '[i]t is surely eloquent testimony to the power of legalism that the Charter provision most obviously embodying non-legalistic scepticism of judicial power was phrased in legalistic language. The form and content of section 33 are mutually contradictory, and the former symbolically undermines the latter!'[65] But an override clause could conceivably be drafted differently, to authorise the legislature to declare that a statute or statutory provision shall be deemed by the courts to be consistent with specific, nominated rights. In a healthy democracy, responsible legislators would feel free to override actual or anticipated judicial interpretations of constitutional rights that, after careful and conscientious reflection, they do not agree with. That, after all, is a

---

[63] J. Waldron, 'Some Models of Dialogue Between Judges and Legislators', in G. Huscroft and I. Brodie (eds.), *Constitutionalism in the Charter Era* (Canada: LexisNexis Butterworths, 2004) pp. 7 and 34–9; J. Waldron, 'The Core of the Case Against Judicial Review' *Yale Law Journal* 115 (2006) 1347 at 1357, n. 34.

[64] See Russell, 'Standing Up'.

[65] Knopff and Morton, *Charter Politics*, pp. 179–80.

power exercised by the judges themselves, when they overrule previous judicial decisions that they have come to regard as erroneous. They do not treat their predecessors, or expect their successors to treat them, as infallible oracles.

A related obstacle inherent in the wording of s. 33 is its limitation of any override to renewable five-year periods.[66] Overrides are thereby treated as short-term expedients, no doubt because they are described as overriding the Charter itself. If judicial interpretations of rights, rather than the rights themselves, were treated as overridden, there would be less reason to impose such a limit. That would remove an additional disincentive to using the clause. It is difficult enough for a legislature to summon the political will to use it once, let alone twice or thrice, and a one-off use may not seem worth the effort.

A second reason for the apparent desuetude of s. 33 concerns the history of its use. It was first used by the Quebec legislature to insert a notwithstanding clause into all of its statutes then in force. This sweeping and indiscriminate use of the clause was upheld by the Supreme Court of Canada in *Ford* v. *Quebec (Attorney-General)*,[67] notwithstanding contrary expectations about its proper use, and respectable arguments in favour of a narrower interpretation.[68] This confirmed the worst fears of those who had originally objected to the clause,[69] although Hiebert observes that it 'did not evoke widespread public condemnation'.[70] The section was next used by the legislature of Saskatchewan, to protect a statute ordering public employees to end a strike, which was vulnerable to challenge on the ground that it violated freedom of association. This use of s. 33 did not incur any voter backlash, and may even have assisted the government's successful bid for re-election.[71] But subsequently, Quebec used the section to protect a law prohibiting the use of English in public signs. This was extremely unpopular throughout the rest of Canada, and probably sabotaged the Meech Lake Accord that was being negotiated at the time.[72] Quebec's use of the section was widely interpreted as subordinating individual rights (of Anglophones) to majoritarian preferences (of Francophones), which

---

[66] I am grateful to Grant Huscroft for emphasising this point in comments sent to me.
[67] [1988] 2 SCR 712 (Can).
[68] Manfredi, *Judicial Power and the Charter*, p. 184.
[69] *Ibid.*
[70] J. Hiebert, *Limiting Rights; The Dilemma of Judicial Review* (Canada: McGill-Queen's University Press, 1996), p. 139.
[71] Knopff and Morton, *Charter Politics*, p. 30.
[72] Hiebert, *Limiting Rights*, pp. 140–1; Mandel, *The Charter of Rights*, p. 92.

seemed to confirm the view that the protection of individual rights could be safely entrusted only to the courts. Prime Minister Mulroney immediately condemned s. 33 as a 'fatal flaw' that made the Charter 'not worth the paper it was written on'.[73] As a result, it 'became virtually impossible to defend the use of section 33 outside of Quebec';[74] 'section 33 has now, except for the francophone majority in Quebec, generally assumed the mantle of being constitutionally illegitimate'.[75]

This was arguably the result of fortuitous events in Canadian history, rather than a general law of political dynamics. Quebec's perceived abuse of the section made s. 33 virtually unusable before it had been given a 'fair go'. 'The opposition to any use of the notwithstanding clause', argues Manfredi, 'is [partly] the product of historical accident … Canadians experienced a use of section 33 that they found objectionable before the Supreme Court rendered a politically unpopular Charter decision.'[76] Moreover, s. 33 could have been either drafted so to deter Quebec's perceived abuse of it, or interpreted in the *Ford* case so as to invalidate that abuse.[77] In either case, s. 33 might have been saved from its current ignominious fate.

It is still possible that s. 33 will be resuscitated sometime in the future. It has been argued that the obstacle posed by its wording is not insurmountable because, first, regardless of formalities, the general public is sufficiently intelligent to realise that the legislative intention is to override a judicial interpretation of the Charter rather than the Charter itself, and secondly, because the legislature can clearly state that intention in a statutory preamble.[78] Furthermore, '[o]nly the fact that public opinion outside Quebec has not been deeply disturbed by decisions of the Court has so far kept the override locked up and out of sight'.

> Make no mistake about it: if conflict between the judicial and legislative branches in Canada ever approached the intensity and duration of the conflict that occurred in the United States during the Lochner era (1905–1937) or during, and just after, the Warren Court (1953–1973) (and that continues to this day with respect to abortion), the current reluctance by

---

[73] Quoted in W.A. Bogart, *Courts and Country: The Limits of Litigation and the Social and Political Life of Canada* (Toronto: Oxford University Press, 1994), p. 311.

[74] Manfredi, *Judicial Power and the Charter*, p. 187.

[75] Hiebert, *Limiting Rights*, p. 139.

[76] Quoted in Tushnet, 'Policy Distortion', 296.

[77] *Ibid.*, 299.

[78] P.W. Hogg, A.A. Bushell Thornton and W.K. Wright, 'Charter Dialogue Revisited – Or "Much Ado About Metaphors"' *Osgoode Hall Law Journal* 45 (2007) 1, 35.

Canadian politicians to use the override would disappear. Indeed, the use of the override by Quebec to protect its French language policy is a reliable indication of what would happen elsewhere in the country if a cherished policy were threatened by the Court.[79]

V Conclusion

If a bill of rights were to include a comprehensive override clause, the question of its compatibility with democratic values could not be settled by appealing to Waldron's 'right of rights' – the right to participate on an equal basis in the final determination of public policy. This is because the override clause would preserve that right. Instead, the question is whether, despite the existence of the override clause, judicial enforcement of constitutional rights would corrode 'the habits and temperament' that are necessary for democracy to thrive.[80] This could only be resolved by sociological evidence of differences in political culture that would be extremely difficult both to collect and to interpret.

In principle, an override clause such as s. 33 should help legislators resist the democratic debilitation that might otherwise attend the legalization of rights. The failure of Canadian legislatures to make more use of their override clause is something of a puzzle. It may be due to factors peculiar to Canada, especially the ways in which the clause was drafted, interpreted and allegedly abused by Quebec. Amendments to s. 33, which cannot be discussed here, have consequently been proposed in the hope of reinvigorating it.[81] If, even in Canada, there is still hope that a differently worded override clause might be put to better use, the same must be true of other countries. In Australia, the Constitutional Commission observed in 1988 that 'Canadian experience in the use of such a power is no safe guide to how such a power might be used in Australia ... There is no knowing how Australian governments might seek to utilise a legislative override power.'[82]

On the other hand, it is possible that the drafting and early usage of s. 33 were not the crucial factors, and that no over ride clause – regardless of its wording – would have proven politically useable. The major obstacle

---

[79] P.W. Hogg, A.A.B. Thornton and W.K. Wright, 'A Reply on "*Charter* Dialogue Revisited"' *Osgoode Hall Law Journal* 45 (2007) 193 at 201.

[80] Morton and Knopff, *The Charter Revolution*, pp. 149 and 151.

[81] See, e.g., Manfredi, *Judicial Power and the Charter*, pp. 192–3 and Hiebert, *Limiting Rights*, p. 142.

[82] Final Report of the Constitutional Commission (Canberra: Australian Government Publishing Service, 1988), vol.1, pp. 494, para. 9.222 and 495 para. 9.224.

to the more frequent use of the clause might lie 'less in the existing section 33 than in the perspective of oracular legalism. To the extent that judicial pronouncements are seen as the very embodiment of the constitution, rather than as debatable interpretations of it, the use of section 33 will be seen as illegitimate.'[83]

On this view, legislators, the electorate, or both, are the victims of a kind of false consciousness. They are deluded by the specious objectivity of constitutional rights, and a naïve faith in judges' capacity to discern their true import by virtue of superior legal expertise, wisdom and impartiality.

It is beyond the scope of this chapter to assess this claim, which in the absence of careful empirical research into public attitudes, presumably rests on anecdotal and impressionistic evidence. Legislators and voters show little sign of being overawed by 'oracular legalism' when seemingly lenient sentences imposed by judges on criminals are subjected (as they often are) to voluble public criticism. But perhaps matters are different where constitutional rights are concerned. In the absence of sufficient evidence to assess the claim, some general points can nevertheless be made.

As previously observed, there are two obstacles to rights-based democrats making such a claim. First, even if legislators and the electorate are deluded, their democratic right to the final say remains intact. Secondly, alleging such a delusion is difficult to reconcile with the basis of that right: namely, the presumption that ordinary people are sufficiently intelligent, knowledgeable and virtuous to deserve it.[84]

The first of these obstacles does not prevent goal-based democrats from alleging that legislators or the electorate are deluded in this way. From their perspective, the mere preservation of the democratic right to the final say is not the crucial issue. More important are the beneficial consequences that flow from its frequent exercise, and these may be jeopardised if – for whatever reason – it is exercised rarely.

But the second obstacle is not so easily avoided. Goal-based democrats regard the cultivation of intelligence, knowledge and virtue throughout the community as one of the main beneficial consequences of democracy.

---

[83] Knopff and Morton, *Charter Politics*, p. 231; Waldron, 'The Core of the Case', 1357, n. 34; G. Huscroft and P. Rishworth, "You Say You Want a Revolution": Bills of Rights in the Age of Human Rights', in D. Dyzenhaus, M. Hunt and G. Huscroft, eds., *A Simple Common Lawyer; Essays in Honour of Michael Taggart* (Oxford: Hart Publishing, 2009) pp. 123, 145; A. Petter, 'Taking Dialogue Theory Much Too Seriously' (*Osgoode Hall Law Journal* 45 (2007) 147 at 161–2.

[84] See text to n. 24, above.

Nevertheless, democracy would not be viable unless there was a considerable fund of these qualities to start with. Therefore, even goal-based democrats should have considerable faith in the inherent intelligence, knowledge and virtue of the electorate. Two points follow. First, if there are alternative explanations for a popular opinion, one dismissing it as a delusion, and the other accepting it as reasonable and possibly even justified, then goal-based democrats should accept the second explanation unless there is very clear evidence of the alleged delusion. Secondly, they should also be confident that their fellow citizens have sufficient intelligence to enable any delusion to be readily dispelled by the dissemination of accurate information. Both points apply to the apparent opinions of ordinary Canadians that their rights are better protected by judges than by legislators, and that the override clause should rarely be used.

It is dangerous for any democrat to allege that the electorate is deluded in this way. If the electorate can be duped by the claim that a small group of people possess superior expertise or wisdom, and persuaded to defer unquestioningly to the judgments of that group, then perhaps they might defer as readily to demagogues as to judges.[85] But that would strengthen the case in favour of constitutional rights.

---

[85] I owe this way of putting the point to Kristen Walker.

9

Parliamentary sovereignty and statutory interpretation

I Introduction

How statutes are interpreted is crucial to the implementation of the doctrine of parliamentary sovereignty. The doctrine maintains that every statute that Parliament enacts is legally valid, and therefore that all citizens and officials, including the courts, are legally obligated to obey it.[1] The courts' legal obligation is therefore to interpret and apply every statute in a way that is consistent with Parliament's legal authority to enact it, and their corresponding obligation to obey it.[2] In a small number of cases, what is called 'interpretation' might be tantamount to disobedience under cover of a 'noble lie'. But if that were to become more routine, and generally condoned by the other branches of government, Parliament would no longer be sovereign.

Statutory interpretation is central to debates about many specific issues discussed in the next chapter. The nature and justification of the ultra vires doctrine in administrative law, the protection of common law principles by 'presumptions' of legislative intention, the judicial response to statutes in cases such as *Anisminic*[3] and *Factortame*,[4] all raise questions about the relationship between statutory interpretation and parliamentary sovereignty. But the topic of this chapter is statutory interpretation in general, including in Australia and New Zealand as well as in Britain, and not in cases to which the Human Rights Act 1998 (UK) applies.

There are two possible methods of investigating how the doctrine of parliamentary sovereignty helps determine the way in which statutes should be interpreted. The first is normative and deductive. It involves

---

[1] I ignore here some complications discussed elsewhere, such as disapplication of statutory provisions inconsistent with laws of the European Community: see Chapter 10, Section III, Part C, below.
[2] R. Ekins, 'The Relevance of the Rule of Recognition' *Australian Journal of Legal Philosophy* 31 (2006) 95 at 103.
[3] *Anisminic Ltd* v. *Foreign Compensation Commission* [1969] 2 AC 147, [1969] 2 WLR 163.
[4] *R* v. *Secretary of State for Transport, ex parte Factortame Ltd (No 2)* [1991] 1 AC 603 (HL).

starting from the doctrine of parliamentary sovereignty as an abstract principle, and attempting to deduce from it norms that judges should follow when interpreting statutes. The second method is descriptive and inductive. Given that the doctrine of parliamentary sovereignty has been a fundamental part of the law for a long time, and assuming that most judges have for the most part conscientiously adhered to it, one might simply describe the ways in which they do in fact interpret statutes and, by induction, distil those norms that seem attributable to that doctrine. These two methods should converge on similar conclusions, thereby corroborating one another. If not, either the deductive method has gone astray, or judicial practice has departed from its proclaimed rationale.

In using the second method, and examining actual judicial practices, there is no need to confine one's attention to countries such as Britain and New Zealand, where the doctrine of parliamentary sovereignty has been accepted in its fullest sense. Even in Australia, which has written constitutions, it is commonly said that there are no limits to what a Parliament can do other than those expressly or impliedly imposed by those constitutions. In other words, the legislative authority of Australian Parliaments is not legally constrained by moral rights, common law principles, or natural law. Therefore, within their respective constitutional boundaries, they are as sovereign as the United Kingdom Parliament.[5] It follows that, as long as no question of constitutional invalidity arises, statutory interpretation should be governed by the principle of parliamentary sovereignty in exactly the same ways as in Britain and New Zealand.

Indeed, much the same is also true of statutory interpretation in the United States. Of course, American legislatures are not fully sovereign, because they do not possess legally unlimited legislative authority. But, like Australian Parliaments, their authority is limited only by their national and state constitutions. The judges have no authority to hold a statute void except on the ground that it violates a constitutional provision. In *Calder* v. *Bull*, when Justice Chase suggested that American courts might have authority to hold statutes void for violating extra-constitutional principles, Justice Iredell strongly disagreed.[6] As a leading constitutional

---

[5] J. Goldsworthy, *The Sovereignty of Parliament: History and Philosophy* (Oxford: Clarendon Press, 1999), p. 1.
[6] *Calder* v. *Bull* 3 US (3 Dall.) 385 at 398 (1798) (Iredell J., concurring).

law treatise explains: 'In form, the Supreme Court has adopted the views of Justice Iredell ...;'[7] 'the philosophy that the Justices would overturn acts of other branches only to protect specific constitutional guarantees has been the formal guideline of the Supreme Court at every stage in its history.'[8]

In his *Commentaries on American Law*, Chancellor Kent wrote: '[T]he principle in the English government, that the Parliament is omnipotent, does not prevail in the United States; though, if there be no constitutional objection to a statute, it is with us as absolute and uncontrollable as laws flowing from the sovereign power, under any other form of government.'[9] After summarising the British doctrine of parliamentary sovereignty, Roscoe Pound wrote, 'Except as constitutional limitations are infringed, the same doctrine obtains in America.'[10] Supreme Court dicta corroborate that proposition:

> The words of the statute being clear, if it unjustly discriminates ... or is cruel and inhuman in its results, as forcefully contended, the remedy lies with Congress and not with the courts. Their duty is simply to enforce the law as it is written, unless clearly unconstitutional.[11]

In 1983, the Supreme Court re-affirmed that a statute's 'wisdom is not the concern of the courts; if a challenged action does not violate the Constitution, it must be sustained'.[12] Even Douglas Edlin – a strident critic of this rule of legislative supremacy – concedes that 'almost all American

---

[7] Ronald D. Rotunda and John E. Nowak, *Treatise on Constitutional Law: Substance and Procedure* (3rd edn) (St Paul Minn.: Thomson/West, 1999), § 15.1.

[8] *Ibid.*, § 15.5.

[9] James Kent, *Commentaries on American Law* (10th edn) (Boston: Little, Brown & Co., 1860), p.503; see also Thomas M. Cooley, *A Treatise on the Constitutional Limitations Which Rest Upon the Legislative Power of the States of the American Union* (Boston: Little, Brown & Co., 1868), pp. 87–9 (describing the plenary powers of Congress as bounded only by the Constitution).

[10] Roscoe Pound, 'Common Law and Legislation' *Harvard Law Review* 21 (1908) 383 at 392.

[11] *Chung Fook* v. *White* (1924) 264 US 443 at 446; 44 S Ct 361 at 362; 68 L Ed 781. See also *Common School Dist. No 85* v. *Renville County* (1965) 141 Minn. 300 at 304; 170 NW 216 at 218: '[t]he wisdom or propriety of the statute is not a judicial question ... A statute may seem unwise, it may seem unjust ... but that view of the law, in the absence of some conflict with the Constitution, cannot be made the basis of a refusal by the courts to enforce it.'

[12] *I.N.S.* v. *Chadha* (1983) 462 US 919 at 944; 103 S Ct 2764 at 2780; 77 L Ed 2nd 317. See also *Tennessee Valley Authority* v. *Hill* (1978) 437 US 153 at 194–5; 98 S Ct 2279 at 2303; 57 L Ed 2nd 117.

judges' accept it.[13] As Kent Greenawalt explains, '[a] constitutional mark-
ing of some domains as off limits represents a conscious choice to leave
remaining domains to legislative authority'.[14] That is why, according to
Robert Summers:

> [American] constitutional law provides that, in matters of valid legisla-
> tion, the legislature is supreme. That is, the legislature's meaning is sup-
> posed to control, not the substantive political views of the judiciary. This
> principle of legislative supremacy is expressly or implicitly embedded in
> the federal and state constitutions.[15]

The principle of legislative supremacy has played a pivotal role in recent
American debates about statutory interpretation.[16] It is often expressed in
terms of courts being 'faithful agents' of the legislature.[17]

It seems likely that something like the principle of legislative supremacy is binding on judges in most legal systems. The very concepts of
'legislature' and 'judiciary' imply that the legislature, as lawmaker, has
an authority to make laws – even if it is constitutionally limited – that
the judiciary, as mere interpreter and enforcer, is bound to respect and
obey. If the judiciary were entitled to rewrite those laws, it would share the
legislative power and would be, at least in part, a legislature itself. In other
words, a principle of legislative supremacy is virtually entailed by the distinction between legislative and judicial functions, even in legal systems
in which a 'separation of powers' is not constitutionally entrenched.[18]

Taking this point one step further – perhaps one step too far – it could
be argued that, in this context, the very concept of 'interpretation' requires
respect for legislative supremacy; that any judicial method of treating

---

[13] D. Edlin, *Judges and Unjust Laws* (Ann Arbor: University of Michigan Press, 2008), p. 51.

[14] Kent Greenawalt, *Legislation: Statutory Interpretation – Twenty Questions* (New York:
Foundation Press, 1999), p. 23.

[15] Robert S. Summers, 'Statutory Interpretation in the United States', in D. Neil
MacCormick and Robert S. Summers (eds.), *Interpreting Statutes: A Comparative Study*
(Aldershot: Dartmouth, 1991), 407 at p. 450.

[16] See, for example, W. Eskridge, 'Spinning Legislative Supremacy' *Georgia Law Review* 78
(1989) 319; D. Farber, 'Statutory Interpretation and Legislative Supremacy' *Georgia Law
Review* 78 (1989) 281; E.O. Correia, 'A Legislative Conception of Legislative Supremacy'
Case W Res L Rev. 42 (1992) 1129; E.M. Maltz, 'Rhetoric and Reality in the Theory of
Statutory Interpretation: Underenforcement, Overenforcement, and the Problem of
Legislative Supremacy' *BUL Rev* 71 (1981) 767.

[17] See, for example, J. Manning, 'Textualism and the Equity of the Statute' *Columbia Law
Review* 101 (2001) 1 at 6–7 and 9–22.

[18] In *Duport Steels Ltd* v. *Sirs* [1980] 1 WLR 142 Lord Diplock said: 'the British constitution, though largely unwritten, is firmly based upon the separation of power; Parliament
makes the laws, the judiciary interprets them' (at 157B).

statutes that flouts the principle of legislative supremacy could not accurately be called 'interpretation'.[19]

Consider the following example from Germany. In the *Soraya* case, the Federal Constitutional Court had to decide whether or not compensation could be awarded for non-material (such as emotional) injury resulting from violations of the right to personality. The relevant section of the Civil Code allowed such compensation only in cases 'determined by the law', but German Courts had been awarding it in cases not determined by the law. The Constitutional Court upheld this practice by reading an unwritten exception into the Code. It said:

> The law is not identical with the whole of the written statutes. Over and above the positive enactments of the state power there can be 'ein Mehr an Recht' [a surplus of law] which has its source in the constitutional legal order as a holistic unity of meaning, and which can operate as a corrective to the written law ... [E]valuative assumptions which are imminent in the constitutional legal order, but are not, or are only incompletely, expressed in the texts of written statutes, [may] be elucidated and realized in [judicial] decisions ... It must be understood that the written statute fails to fulfil its function of providing a just solution for a legal problem. The judicial decision then fills this gap ...[20]

Even in Germany, this kind of reasoning is controversial.[21] But it would never be found in judgments of courts in the British Commonwealth or the United States. I do not mean that they never perform surgery on statutes; the point is that they rarely openly acknowledge that they are doing so.[22] The difference is that there is no firm commitment to legislative supremacy in German legal practice or theory. There is, instead, 'a fundamental conflict between two conceptions of legal argumentation', namely, 'constitutionalism', which holds that the judiciary should implement constitutional values in this fashion, and 'legalism', which urges much greater judicial restraint and respect for legislative judgments.[23] Moreover, it is significant that the reasoning in cases such as *Soraya* is not

---

[19] Such a claim is controversial. Joseph Raz, for example, treats 'interpretation' as embracing quite radical judicial 'development' of the law: see J. Goldsworthy, 'Raz on Constitutional Interpretation' *Law and Philosophy* 22 (2003) 167.

[20] *Soraya*, BverfGE 34, 269 (287), quoted in R. Alexy and R. Dreier, 'Statutory Interpretation in the Federal Republic of Germany' in MacCormick and Summers (eds.), *Interpreting Statutes*, p. 80.

[21] Alexy and Drier, 'Statutory Interpretation', pp. 80, 94, 107 and 112–13.

[22] A statute is sometimes 'read down' in order to avoid inconsistency with a constitutional provision, but the reasoning of the German Court appears to go much further than that.

[23] Alexy and Dreier, 'Statutory Interpretation', p. 117.

called 'interpretation', but rather 'gap-filling'. The concept of interpretation is confined to decisions within the lexical meaning of the provision in question, whereas decisions that go beyond or against that meaning are classified as gap-filling. *Soraya* involved what is called gap-filling '*contra legem*' – against the statute.[24] So perhaps this corroborates my suggestion that there is an internal, conceptual relationship between 'interpretation' and respect for legislative supremacy.

It is undeniable that legal interpretation is often partly creative. The word 'interpretation' is used in the common law world to denote two different processes. One involves *revealing* or *clarifying* the meaning of a legal text, a meaning that despite being previously obscured was possessed by the text all along. The other process involves *constructing* the meaning of a text, by modifying it or adding to it meaning that it did not previously possess.[25] To mark this distinction, the second, creative process is sometimes called 'construction' rather than 'interpretation'.[26] It might have assisted analytical clarity had the common law courts, like their German counterparts, used terminology that more clearly distinguished between the clarifying and creative processes. But they have not, and since popular use of the term 'interpretation' encompasses both processes, it might be better to distinguish between 'clarifying interpretation' and 'creative interpretation'.

Extremist theories of legal interpretation acknowledge only one of these processes, and ignore the other. Extreme 'formalist' theories, now disparaged as 'fairy tales', acknowledge only clarifying interpretation, as if legal texts, however poorly drafted, contain at least latent answers to every question, which merely await judicial discovery. Extreme 'realist' theories acknowledge only creative interpretation, as if legal texts possess no meaning at all until an interpreter breathes life into them. Both extremist theories are implausible, especially the second one. A law necessarily means something – nothing meaningless can be a law – and its meaning is part of what it is. A law must therefore have some meaning or (if it is ambiguous) meanings that pre-exist judicial interpretation. Otherwise it could not guide behaviour until judges interpreted it. Indeed, it could not *be law* until they had interpreted it. If meaningful laws could only exist after and as a result of judicial interpretation of texts, then the judges

---

[24] *Ibid.*, 78 f., 81, 93, 97, 98 and 114.

[25] R. Dickerson, *The Interpretation and Application of Statutes* (Boston: Little Brown, 1975), pp. 2–5.

[26] K. Whittington, *Constitutional Interpretation: Textual Meaning, Original Intent, and Judicial Review* (Lawrence: University Press of Kansas, 1999), pp. 5–9.

would be the real and only lawmakers. Law would be like baseball as seen by the umpire who supposedly said 'it ain't nothin' 'til I call it'. Although there are theorists who may have maintained something like this extreme sceptical view, it is absurd. After all, if the texts produced by judges to explain their interpretations can be meaningful, without further interpretation (which they must, to avoid an infinite deferral of meaning), then so can the legal texts the judges start with.[27]

Courts engage in both clarifying and creative interpretation, sometimes in the course of interpreting the same provision. But they rarely acknowledge this, possibly because they prefer to maintain the formalist façade that all interpretation is aimed at clarifying pre-existing meaning. An interpretation can partly reveal or clarify meaning that was there all along, and partly add to or modify it if that is necessary or desirable. Adding meaning might be necessary if the revealed meaning of the provision is insufficiently determinate to dispose of an issue that judges must decide. It might be ambiguous, vague, contradictory, insufficiently explicit, or even silent as to that issue. A court, after all, cannot wash its hands of a dispute that has been properly brought before it, and leave the parties to fight it out in the street. Modifying meaning might also be desirable, in strictly limited circumstances: for example, if the revealed meaning of the provision is plainly inconsistent with or incapable of fulfilling its purpose, due to drafting errors or other mistakes or omissions. 'Judicial statecraft' may then be justified in order to repair or rectify the provision.

But even though interpretation is sometimes partly creative, there may be limits to the kinds of creativity that can be classified as genuinely interpretive rather than legislative. Creativity that infringes the principle of legislative supremacy arguably crosses that conceptual boundary, and becomes what Roscoe Pound called 'spurious interpretation'.[28] The examples of creativity mentioned in the previous paragraph, on the other hand, are both consistent with that principle. However, I do not want to push this point too strongly. The important question is not a conceptual one concerning the meaning of the word 'interpretation'. Rather, it is how courts do or should treat statutes in a legal system that vests authority in

---

[27] It has often been noted that any assertion that texts do not have meanings is incoherent, because it asserts that it itself is meaninglessness; in other words, it asserts that it does not assert anything. See A. Altman, *Critical Legal Studies, a Liberal Critique* (Princeton: Princeton University Press, 1990), pp. 90–4; F. Schauer, *Playing By the Rules* (Oxford: Clarendon Press, 1991).

[28] R. Pound, 'Spurious Interpretation' *Columbia Law Review* 6 (1907) 379.

the legislature to make laws, which the courts are required faithfully to apply.

II The indispensability of legislative intentions

The doctrine of parliamentary sovereignty does not hold that the will of Parliament is legally binding. It holds that statutes enacted by Parliament are legally binding. The will of Parliament is legally binding only insofar as it is communicated by means of a formally enacted statute. This is vital to the rule of law, since citizens cannot be expected to conform their behaviour to legislative desires that have not been publicly promulgated. But arguably it is equally vital to the successful exercise of legislative sovereignty: in the absence of a generally accepted, well understood and reliable means for a legislature to communicate its will, there would be a much greater risk of subordinate officials and citizens misunderstanding or pretending to misunderstand it.

For these reasons it is sometimes said that the 'words of the statute, and not the intent of the drafters, are the "law"'.[29] But it would be a huge mistake to think that clarifying interpretation is concerned only with the conventional semantic meanings of those words, to the exclusion of all other evidence of legislative intention. That would be to adopt a wooden literal approach, which for all sorts of reasons is simply not viable. The pre-existing meaning of a statute cannot be confined to the conventional meanings of its words: it is necessarily enriched by additional evidence of Parliament's intentions in enacting them. Furthermore, creative interpretation – which, by definition, must operate well beyond the confines of literalism – should in some cases be guided by extra-textual evidence of Parliament's intentions. That is to say, some version of intentionalism is indispensable.

Those who deny that there is any such thing as 'legislative intention', and call it a 'fiction', seldom practise what they preach. When they put theory aside and actually read statutes, they usually revert to some version of intentionalism. Lord Steyn, for example, commences one lecture by announcing that his 'main thesis' is 'that the intent of the framers of a [legal] text is irrelevant to interpretation'.[30] Yet later in the same article, he

---

[29] F. Easterbrook, 'The Role of Original Intent in Statutory Construction' *Harvard Journal of Law and Public Policy* 11 (1988) 61.

[30] J. Steyn, 'Interpretation: Legal Texts and Their Landscape' in B.S. Markesinis (ed.), *The Clifford Chance Millennium Lectures; The Coming Together of the Common Law and the Civil Law* (Oxford: Hart Publishing, 2000) pp. 79 and 81.

himself relies on the notion of legislative intention: he argues that a court might be justified in regarding the Scotland Act 1998 as 'constitutional in character', on the ground that 'the intention was that there should be a durable settlement in favour of Scotland'.[31]

Self-proclaimed sceptics about the existence or relevance of legislative intentions often insist on the relevance of 'context'. Lord Steyn, for example, explicitly disavows any commitment to literalism, and insists that statutes must be 'construed against the contextual setting in which they come into existence'.[32] 'After all', he adds, 'a statement is only intelligible if one knows under what conditions it was made.'[33] Now, this is indeed undeniable, but why? Surely it is because information about the circumstances in which a statement was made illuminates the intentions or purposes of the speaker or writer. For what other reason could contextual information possibly be relevant? At one point Lord Steyn says that the context may include information concerning the 'major purposes' of the statute.[34] But strictly speaking, statutes like other inanimate objects do not have purposes: only the people who use them do. To attribute a purpose to a statute is to attribute the purpose to the enacting legislature. A purpose is a kind of intention, and it is self-contradictory to dismiss legislative intentions as fictions but to keep talking about statutory purposes.

It is sometimes argued that collective bodies such as legislatures simply cannot have intentions: only individuals or small groups of individuals (such as the sponsors or drafters of statutes) can have intentions, but they cannot be attributed to the legislature as a whole. To see why this is not plausible, it is necessary to take the argument seriously (which those who make it rarely do), and consider what it would be like to attempt to understand a statute without treating it as expressing any intentions. Its meaning would have to be derived solely from the conventional semantic meanings of its words and conventional rules of grammar. It would have to be treated just like a series of numbers, letters, punctuation marks and spaces created by chimpanzees banging randomly on keyboards, which by coincidence form meaningful words and sentences according to those linguistic conventions.[35]

---

[31] *Ibid.*, p. 89.   [32] *Ibid.*, p. 81.   [33] *Ibid.*, and also p. 86.   [34] *Ibid.*, p. 86.

[35] Heidi Hurd is unusually candid in this regard. Having denied that legislatures can have intentions, and concluded that statutes can therefore have only literal meanings (or what philosophers call 'sentence meanings'), she concedes that statutes are 'like the often-hypothesized novel typed by random chance by the thirteen-thousandth monkey chained to a typewriter: meaningful ... despite not having been produced as a communication by

Those who deny that a legislature can have intentions might object that this is an unfair caricature of their position, because they fully realise that a statute reflects the intentions of some subset of people involved in the legislative process, such as its sponsors and drafters. The problem is that they deny that these intentions can be attributed to the legislature itself, on the 'constitutional' ground that they cannot be shown to have been adopted or endorsed by the legislature as a whole. It follows that these intentions cannot contribute to the meaning of the statute, since it is an act of the legislature as a whole. The statute must therefore be treated *as if* it expresses no intentions at all.

Consider how bizarre it would be to treat a statute as if it did not give expression to any intentions at all. Take these examples:

(1) Section 8(1) of the Road Traffic Act 1972 (UK) provided that in certain circumstances any person 'driving or attempting to drive' a vehicle could be required to take a breath test. The defendant drove through a red light, stopped, and changed seats with his passenger. He was then asked to take a breath test, although by then he was clearly not 'driving or attempting to drive' the vehicle. (Indeed, that would arguably have been true even if he had remained in the driver's seat.) The court held that he was nevertheless required to take the test.[36]

(2) Section 8(1) of the Food and Drugs Act 1955 prohibited the sale of 'any food intended for, but unfit for, human consumption'. Some children asked for lemonade, were given corrosive caustic soda, and drank some of it. Read literally, s. 8(1) did not apply: the vendor had not sold the children food unfit for human consumption, because caustic soda is not food. But the apparent purpose of the provision was to protect the public from harmful products being sold *as* food, and it was interpreted accordingly.[37]

(3) Rule 14(2) of the Magistrates' Courts Rules 1968 (UK) stated that at the conclusion of the evidence for the complainant, 'the defendant may address the court'. It did not provide that the court must listen to the defendant's address. Nevertheless, this was held to be implied.[38]

(4) An Alberta bylaw required that 'all drug stores shall be closed at 10 p.m. on each and every night of the week'. It would be consistent

---

anyone for anyone': H. Hurd, 'Sovereignty in Silence' *Yale Law Journal* 99 (1990) 945 at 966.

[36] See F.A.R. Bennion, *Statutory Interpretation* (2nd edn) (London: Butterworths, 1992), pp. 668–9, discussing *Kaye* v. *Tyrrell* (1984) *The Times*, 9 July.

[37] *Meah* v. *Roberts* [1978] 1 All ER 97 at 98–100 and 104–6 (Q.B.); see also Bennion, *Statutory Interpretation*, pp. 611–12 (discussing *Meah*).

[38] Bennion, *Statutory Interpretation*, p. 30.

with a literal interpretation of these words for a drug store to close promptly at 10 p.m., and then reopen a short time later. But the Supreme Court of Alberta properly rejected an argument to that effect on the ground that only a lawyer could have suggested it.[39]

(5) A statute that penalized noncompliance with automatic traffic signals did not include any express exception in cases where the signals had malfunctioned due to mechanical failure. Nevertheless, the court held that such an exception was implied.[40]

As soon as we read these statutory provisions, we know at least something about the intentions that motivated their enactment. That initial knowledge is just simple common sense, based partly on shared cultural understandings, given the assumption that members of Parliament are sensible people trying to achieve rational (even if controversial) objectives.[41] Radical non-intentionalism, which denies that legislatures *ever* have ascertainable intentions (other than to enact statutes), is implausible partly because it entails that common sense cannot play that role. On the other hand, anyone who concedes that common sense can sometimes illuminate a legislature's intentions or purposes would have to concede that other extra-textual evidence might also do so.

Whenever we read statutory provisions, we naturally – irresistibly – understand them as having been designed to achieve some purpose, even if only at an abstract and not very helpful level. This is so even though that purpose may have been initially developed and proposed by the executive government, and the design provided mainly by parliamentary counsel. By virtue of its having enacted the statute, we reasonably take Parliament to have approved both the purpose and the design – perhaps with modifications made by amendments – even if the statute's words fail to give effect to either with perfect clarity and comprehensiveness. We do not, and possibly could not if we tried, divorce our understanding of the enacted words from our understanding of the evident purpose and design that led to their enactment.[42]

---

[39] *Rex* v. *Liggetts-Findlay Drug Stores Ltd* [1919] 3 WWR 1025 at 1025; see also J. Bell and G. Engle, *Statutory Interpretation* (3rd edn) (London: Butterworths, 1995), pp. 67–8 (discussing *Liggetts-Findlay*).

[40] *Turner* v. *Ciappara* (1969) VR 851; see also Bennion, *Statutory Interpretation*, p. 699 (discussing *Turner*).

[41] See Pound, 'Spurious Interpretation', 381.

[42] This understanding of statutes is proposed and developed by Richard Ekins in his D. Phil Thesis, *The Nature of Legislative Intent* (University of Oxford, 26 March 2009),

Our understanding of statutory meaning would be severely impoverished if all evidence of legislative intention, including common sense, had to be disregarded. It is also much more likely to be absurd. The object of clarifying interpretation cannot be the literal meaning of a statute, because it is much less substantial than the meaning that can be fleshed out by common sense, contextual and other extra-textual evidence of Parliament's intentions. The literal meaning is therefore much more likely to be insufficiently determinate to resolve disputes, and to need fleshing out through the exercise of judicial creativity. Literalism is also not viable as a basis for creative interpretation, which supplements or modifies the meaning of a statute. I will consider clarifying and creative interpretation separately.

A   Clarifying interpretation

(1)   Ambiguity and ellipsis

Ambiguity, both semantic and syntactic, is one reason why literal meanings are often too thin and indeterminate to be serviceable. The phenomenon is so well known that examples are superfluous. The point is that ambiguities in literal meanings are often resolved by additional evidence of the speaker's intentions, such as evidence supplied by the context in which the words were uttered. Ambiguities proliferate if such evidence is excluded, or the very idea of the speaker having an intention is dismissed as a fiction.

Another reason is what we might loosely call ellipsis. In law, as in everyday life, what we say or write is often elliptical in the sense that we omit details that we expect our audience to know already. If I say 'Everyone has gone to Paris' I expect to be understood as saying that every member of some contextually defined group has gone to Paris, not that everyone who has ever lived has done so. When I ask the bus driver 'Do you go to Blackburn?' I am asking whether he drives the bus to Blackburn as part of its scheduled route, not whether he ever goes there when he is off duty. Many philosophers of language now regard literal meanings as 'typically quite fragmentary and incomplete, and as falling far short of determining a complete proposition even after disambiguation'.[43] Consider a sign next

to be published in the near future. His preliminary views are sketched in 'The Relevance of the Rule of Recognition' *Australian Journal of Legal Philosophy* 31 (2006) 95, esp. at 108–13.

[43] D. Sperber and D. Wilson, 'Pragmatics', in F. Jackson and M. Smith (eds.), *The Oxford Handbook of Contemporary Philosophy* (Oxford: Oxford University Press, 2005), 468 at p. 477. See also A. Marmor, 'The Immorality of Textualism' *Loyola University Law Review* 38 (2005) 2063.

to an escalator that says: 'Dogs must be carried on the escalator'. Read literally, this could be taken to mean that no-one may ride on an escalator without at least two dogs in one's arms, or that no-one may carry dogs anywhere except on an escalator. But those literal meanings are obviously too absurd to have been intended. We therefore understand the sign to mean something much richer, such as this:

> Anyone who is accompanied by a dog, and wishes to travel on the escalator, must pick up the dog and hold it in his or her arms, and not allow it to stand directly on the steps of the escalator.[44]

Although those who draft legal texts attempt to be clear, precise and comprehensive, many ellipses can be found in legal texts if we look closely enough. This is partly because it is so difficult to pack into them everything that is needed to express completely and exactly what is intended. It is also because it is unnecessary and would even be counter-productive: when context supplies the missing ingredients, ellipses contribute to brevity without reducing clarity or precision. Cases (3) and (4), above, are arguably among many examples that could be given.[45]

Ambiguities and ellipses are usually resolved by common sense, contextual or other evidence of the speaker's intended meaning. If all that evidence had to be ignored, indeterminacies and gaps in meaning would have to be filled in by the interpreter. If a statutory provision, read literally, were ambiguous or incomplete, then a literalist approach would require the judges to choose how to resolve the problem. As a result, indeterminacies would greatly increase, as would the need for judicial creativity to resolve them. Literalism would thereby diminish the utility of statutes as authoritative guides for conduct; it would leave many more questions to be answered, and disputes to be resolved, by judicial creativity after expensive and time-consuming litigation. It would accord less authority to legislatures and more to judges. It would allow judges to impose their own preferred meaning on a statute rather than to accept the meaning intended by the legislature, whenever the legislature has failed to enact words whose literal meaning expresses its intended meaning completely and precisely.

This is why literalism has long been a byword for a narrow, formalistic and obstructive approach to interpretation. Legislatures inevitably fail to express themselves with perfect clarity and total comprehensiveness.

---

[44] N.E. Simmonds, 'Between Positivism and Idealism' *Cambridge Law Journal* 50 (1991) 308 at 311–12.
[45] See text to nn. 38 and 39, above.

Limiting the meaning of legislation to the literal meanings of its words often frustrates their intentions or purposes. It enables the proverbial 'coach-and-four' to be driven through a tax Act, frustrating the public interest it was designed to serve. It enables conservative judges to thwart tax laws, labour laws, or other progressive legislation enacted by a reformist legislature. By the same token, of course, it enables reformist judges to obstruct laws enacted by conservative legislatures. But judges cannot apply principles of interpretation selectively, depending on whether they approve or disapprove of the political complexion of the legislature. Principles of interpretation must be purchased wholesale, not retail.

Ellipsis poses a greater difficulty for literalism than ambiguity, because an ellipsis does not necessarily give rise to any indeterminacy that must be resolved by judicial creativity. If literalists are compelled to understand the statement 'Everyone has gone to Paris' to mean 'Everyone who has ever lived has gone to Paris' – and surely they are – there is no indeterminacy that creativity is required to cure. Instead, there is an absurdity that must stand unless the statement is corrected. Absent a correction by the speaker, it could only be corrected by the interpreter. If an ellipsis in a statutory provision makes its literal meaning absurd, the provision must – in effect – be amended by the judges.

(2)   Presuppositions

Another reason why literalism often has absurd consequences is the ubiquitous dependence of meaning on background assumptions. I will dwell on this because it is vital to the subsequent analysis of several important issues.

The words we use usually provide merely the bare bones of what we mean, which can only be properly understood if many background assumptions are grasped. If they are not taken for granted, almost anything we say is open to being misunderstood in unpredictable and bizarre ways. If I order a hamburger in a restaurant, and carefully list all the ingredients that I want, I do not think it important to specify that they should be fresh and edible, and the meat not too cold. If I thought about this at all, I would expect it to be taken for granted. Even if I did specify those conditions, I would not think to add that the hamburger should not be encased in cube of solid lucite plastic that can only be opened by a jackhammer.[46] My order implicitly requires a hamburger that can be immediately eaten without great difficulty. If, on going out at night, I insist

---

[46] J. Searle, 'Literal Meaning', in his *Expression and Meaning* (Cambridge: Cambridge University Press, 1979), 117 at p. 127.

that my son stay at home and study, I do not think to add that he may leave if the house catches fire, or if he receives a message that I have collapsed and been rushed to hospital. Nor would I later think he had disobeyed me if he did leave in those circumstances. Even if I had no conscious intentions regarding these very unlikely and unanticipated circumstances, I could truly say that I did not intend my instruction to apply to them. That is because our conscious intentions, as well as the words we use to convey them, can only be properly understood in the light of many background assumptions.[47] My instruction is implicitly subject to an indeterminate number of qualifications that I may not even have thought of, let alone expressed.

As the philosopher John Searle has argued, no matter how many of these qualifications I expressly include, there will be others I cannot anticipate. This is because, first, many of the crucial background assumptions are 'submerged in the unconscious and we don't quite know how to dredge [them] up',[48] and secondly, for every assumption spelled out, others would spring up on which the meaning of the expanded utterance would depend.[49] Each assumption depends for its full meaning on others, which together constitute a vast and complex network of beliefs and values that are generally not consciously adverted to, let alone articulated in language. If it were possible to make all of them explicit, the result would be so prolix and convoluted that it would be very difficult even to read, let alone to understand.[50] What Martinich says of conversation is true of communication generally: 'the words the participants utter are merely the surface that simultaneously outlines and conceals the underlying substance of communication and meaning'.[51]

This background network of assumptions may not be consciously adverted to by either the speaker or the hearer of an utterance. It would therefore be inappropriate to say that speakers intend to communicate them, even indirectly. They are presupposed by communications rather than implied by them. But it does not follow that speakers' intentions are

---

[47] For a fuller analysis, see J. Goldsworthy, 'Implications in Language, Law and the Constitution', in G. Lindell (ed.), *Future Directions in Australian Constitutional Law* (Sydney: Federation Press, 1994), 150 at p. 160–1.

[48] J.R. Searle, *Intentionality* (Cambridge: Cambridge University Press, 1983), p. 142.

[49] Searle, 'Literal Meaning', 126; Searle, *Intentionality*, p. 148; J.R. Searle, 'The Background of Meaning', in J. Searle, F. Keifer and M. Bierwisch (eds.), *Speech Act Theory and Pragmatics* (Holland: Reidel, 1980), p. 228.

[50] See A.P. Martinich, *Communication and Reference* (Berlin: de Gruyter, 1984), p. 45; M. Dascal, *Pragmatics and the Philosophy of Mind I* (Amsterdam: John Benjamins, 1983), p. 86; and Bennion, *Statutory Interpretation*, p. 427.

[51] Martinich, *Communication and Reference*, p. 78.

irrelevant. When we say that something is presupposed by an utterance in the sense that it is taken for granted, we are saying that the speaker took it for granted. Texts considered as objects completely independent of speakers cannot sensibly be said to take anything for granted.[52] Those who reject intentionalism in legal interpretation in effect banish this essential infrastructure of communication from consideration. As Adam Kramer explains:

> [C]ommunication is based upon a process of pragmatic inference. Under this process, one can intend what goes without saying and what does not cross one's mind. A communicator intends the background of social norms and his goals and principles within which he (non-consciously) formulated his utterance. These norms and goals and principles are thus intended to be used to determine issues that are underdetermined by the express utterance. This is not a fiction … it is the way communication and the mind works.[53]

The inevitable dependence of meaning on background assumptions that are taken for granted is true of legal documents, including statutes. Although those who draft such documents usually attempt to be very explicit, some degree of dependence on assumptions is inescapable. Many things must be taken for granted: 'the express words of every Act have the shadowy accompaniment of a host of implicit statements'.[54] These include what courts take to be simple common sense, which is why the 'Golden Rule' requires that provisions sometimes be interpreted non-literally in order to avoid patent absurdities.[55] They may also include pre-existing legal principles. As Francis Bennion explains, it is impossible for a drafter to explicitly restate all the ancillary legal considerations which may be necessary for the proper operation of an Act. Any statute 'relies for its effectiveness on [an] implied importation of surrounding legal principles and rules'.[56] Indeed, he goes so far as to claim that 'virtually the whole

---

[52] The background assumptions on which communication depends cannot be reduced to social conventions that are universally applicable and independent of particular contexts. See J. Goldsworthy, 'Marmor on Meaning, Interpretation, and Legislative Intention' *Legal Theory* 1 (1995) 439 at 461–3.

[53] A. Kramer, 'Implication in Fact as an Instance of Contractual Interpretation' *Oxford Journal of Legal Studies* 63 (2004) 384 at 385.

[54] Bennion, *Statutory Interpretation*, p. 3; see also *ibid.*, pp. 361–2 and 364; see also J. Bell, 'Studying Statutes' *Oxford Journal of Legal Studies* 13 (1993) 130 at 133.

[55] Bennion, *Statutory Interpretation*, p. 407.

[56] *Ibid.*, p. 727. See also Dickerson, *The Interpretation and Application of Statutes*, p. 29, and as to the drafting and interpretation of criminal laws, Lord Diplock in *R* v. *Miller* [1983] 2 AC 161 at 174.

body of the law is imported, by one enactment or another, as implied ancillary rules'.[57]

This is why *mens rea* is usually held to be implicit in statutes creating new criminal offences that include no express reference to it. Stephen J. said that it is simply assumed.[58] It is also why Lord Denning once held that the British North America Act 1867 (UK) did not disturb a pre-existing royal proclamation, which was 'an unwritten provision which went without saying'.[59] All the common law presumptions used in statutory interpretation can arguably be justified on this ground, the context provided by the general law implicitly limiting language that, read literally, would be over-inclusive.[60] They include the presumption that statutes are not intended to extend beyond territorial limits, to be retrospective, or to override fundamental common law freedoms. Judges are therefore often justified in claiming that, by interpreting statutory language restrictively, so that it does not disturb common law principles, they are giving effect to Parliament's implicit intention. Even in the case of unusual and unanticipated circumstances that fall within the literal meaning of a provision, and with respect to which the legislature had no conscious intention at all, it can make sense to say that it did not intend the provision to apply to them. As Aileen Kavanagh acknowledges:

> ... the orthodox justification for applying the statutory presumptions is the fact that, in general, legislators know, or can be taken to know, that their legislation will be interpreted and understood in light of them. They are part of the known background against which Parliament legislates and of which it should be aware.[61]

This provides one possible explanation of the decision in the celebrated American case of *Riggs* v. *Palmer*, concerning a murderer who claimed the right to inherit under his victim's will.[62] The New York statute dealing with the validity and effect of wills did not expressly exclude murderers from inheriting, but the state's Court of Appeals held that it should be interpreted in the light of the common law principle that no-one may

---

[57] Bennion, *Statutory Interpretation*, p. 728.
[58] *R* v. *Tolson* (1889) 23 QBD 168 at 187; see also Lord Diplock in *Sweet* v. *Parsley* [1970] AC 132 at 162–3.
[59] *R* v. *Secretary of State for Foreign and Commonwealth Affairs, ex parte Indian Association of Alberta* [1982] QB 892 at 914.
[60] For many examples, see Bennion, *Statutory Interpretation*, Parts XVI, XVII, XXIII and XXIV.
[61] A. Kavanagh, *Constitutional Review Under the UK Human Rights Act* (Cambridge: Cambridge University Press, 2009), p. 99.
[62] (1889) 115 NY 506, 22 NE 188.

profit from his own wrong, and therefore as excluding inheritance in the circumstances. The decision is arguably justified by a 'tacit general legal assumption'.[63] In a similar English case, the High Court held that a statutory provision granting widows a pension did not benefit a widow convicted of the manslaughter of her husband. Lord Lane C.J. said that the lack of any specific provision to that effect was 'merely an indication ... that the draftsman realised perfectly well that he was drawing this Act against the background of the law as it stood at the time'.[64]

When statutes are 'read down' to have a narrower application than a literal reading would warrant, so that common law freedoms are preserved, the only justification that is consistent with parliamentary sovereignty depends on the presumption that the legislature intended not to interfere with those freedoms or, at least, did not intend to interfere with them. If legislative intentions are really fictions, this justification is a camouflage that conceals judicial amendment. And if judges can legitimately amend statutes to make them consistent with common law freedoms, why should they not amend statutes to make them consistent with other common law principles, or to improve them in other ways? What principled limit to a power of judicial amendment could provide a substitute for rebuttable presumptions of legislative intention? It might be suggested that the common law, rather than Parliament's intention, both justifies and limits the judicial power of amendment. But if that were the case, the common law would be superior to statute law – a reversal of constitutional orthodoxy – and the power would not be effectively limited, because the judges can change the common law.

The literal meaning of a provision is often qualified to give effect to unstated intentions, purposes or values, when these can be reasonably regarded as implicit background assumptions that the legislature took for granted, and would have expected interpreters to take for granted. In such cases we can still regard the judicial interpreter as engaged in a cognitive process, clarifying the true meaning of the statute, which happens to differ from its literal meaning.[65]

The pioneering philosopher H.P. Grice famously attempted to explain the process of reasoning that we use in inferring implications from one another's utterances. Even when implications are grasped intuitively,

[63] Dickerson, *The Interpretation and Application of Statutes*, p. 108, n. 14; Bennion, *Statutory Interpretation*, pp. 532–3.
[64] *R v. Chief National Insurance Commissioner, ex parte Connor* [1981] QB 758, 765; see also *Re Sidgworth* [1935] Ch 89 and *Re Royse* [1985] Ch 22 at 27 per Ackner L.J.
[65] See Goldsworthy, 'Implications in Language, Law and the Constitution'.

without any conscious process of reasoning, he argued that the intuition springs from an unconscious reasoning process. He took linguistic communication to be a rational enterprise governed by an overarching Principle of Co-operation, which speakers and hearers must both respect if communication between them is to succeed. The substance of this principle is 'Do whatever is necessary to achieve the purpose of your talk; do not do anything that will frustrate that purpose.' He identified a number of more specific 'maxims of conversation' that help speakers to communicate. These maxims, of 'quantity', 'quality', 'relation' and 'manner', call for (respectively) informativeness (but also brevity), truthfulness, relevance to some supposed interest of the hearer, and clarity.[66]

The phenomenon of background assumptions or presuppositions can be accommodated by Grice's theory. The maxim of quantity requires speakers to say as much as but no more than is required for effective communication. Speakers who say more than that waste their audience's time and effort as well as their own, and risk boring, patronising and confusing their audience, thereby violating the maxim of manner. It follows that no mention should be made of matters that one's audience can be relied on to take for granted. And of course, no mention *can* be made of matters that one takes for granted oneself. Presuppositions are inferred as a consequence of the assumption that speakers have complied with the maxims, and therefore not bothered to state the obvious.

B Creative interpretation

Sir Rupert Cross observed that judges have a 'limited power' in effect to alter statutory words that would otherwise be unintelligible, absurd, or totally incompatible with the rest of the statute.[67] The court must repair or rectify the statute by undertaking some 'embroidery' to supplement or qualify its express provisions. He noted that many judges preferred not to admit that they were engaged in rectification of the statutory words.[68] But it would be more truthful to acknowledge that they do occasionally modify a statute's meaning to correct a legislative mistake or oversight.[69]

---

[66] H.P. Grice, *Studies in the Way of Words* (Cambridge, Mass: Harvard University Press, 1989), chs. 2 and 3.

[67] Bell and Engle, *Statutory Interpretation*, pp. 49 and 93.

[68] *Ibid.*, p. 98.

[69] These observations about 'purpose' and 'mistake' are somewhat loose. Professor Jim Evans has persuasively argued that the Courts should only correct a mismatch between the express provision and the immediate practical judgment or reason underlying it. See J. Evans, 'Reading Down Statutes', in R. Bigwood (ed.), *The Statute, Making and Meaning*

One example is the correction of drafting errors, which can result in the literal meaning of a provision being quite different from its obviously intended meaning, sometimes even absurdly different. When it is obvious that this has happened, and also obvious what the legislature intended to provide, the courts may be prepared to overlook the error and give effect to the intention. The legislature is deemed to have succeeded in communicating its intention despite its clumsy mode of expression. But literalists must have great difficulty justifying the judicial correction of a drafting error. The provision must be understood as if some word or words were either added to or subtracted from it. But how could this be justified, except on the basis that it is necessary to give effect to what the provision was obviously intended to mean? Indeed, how could one even identify a drafting error, except by comparing what the legislature enacted with what it obviously intended to enact? If the concept of legislative intention is discarded, or all extra-textual evidence of intention disregarded, only the words of the provision are left. The idea that the wording is mistaken could then mean only that the interpreter regards it as undesirable. But how could interpreters be allowed to rewrite a provision on the ground that they regard it as undesirable? That would be to confer on them an unbounded power of amendment, because there would be no way to distinguish correcting drafting errors from making other improvements.

Another example of creative interpretation is the correction of omissions in the design of a statute. Legislatures sometimes fail to anticipate and expressly provide for some unusual circumstance or unexpected development; there is no background assumption or presupposition that covers it; and creative interpretation is needed to help the statute achieve its purpose, or avoid damage to other standing commitments of the legislature. Cases (1), (2) and (5) above may be examples, although (5) is arguably an example of an implicit, background assumption.[70]

Consider, for example, the judicial attribution of implications to statutes. The courts usually require that implications be 'necessary' ones. Two different kinds of 'necessity' can be found in the case-law on implications, whether statutory or contractual.[71] One is a kind of 'psychological necessity': it concerns whether or not interpreters are, as it were, compelled to

---

(Wellington: LexisNexis, 2004), p. 123. This is compatible with my argument, since that practical judgment or reason can be regarded as a kind of purpose.

[70] See text to nn. 36, 37 and 40, above.

[71] Discussed in Goldsworthy, 'Implications in Language, Law and the Constitution', 168–70. See also E. Peden, *Good Faith in the Interpretation of Contracts* (Sydney: LexisNexis Butterworths, 2003), pp. 60–71.

acknowledge a supposed implication because it is so obvious as not to be reasonably deniable. This has been called the 'obviousness test'.[72] Thus, it has sometimes been asked whether the court was 'necessarily driven' to the conclusion that some term was implied;[73] or whether 'the force of the language in its surroundings carries such strength of impression in one direction, that to entertain the opposite view appears wholly unreasonable'.[74] The 'officious bystander' test in contract law seems to be a version of this approach: it requires that an implication must be so obvious that the contracting parties, had they been asked by an officious bystander whether it was included, would have testily replied 'of course!'[75] The second kind is 'practical necessity' (or in contract law, 'business efficacy'): it concerns whether or not an alleged implication is practically necessary to enable some or all of the provisions of a legal instrument to achieve their intended purposes.[76] This might be called the 'practical efficacy' test.

I have argued elsewhere that the obviousness test should be preferred to the practical efficacy test as the test for genuine implications, by which I mean implications that are truly there to be discovered.[77] Since it is possible for a provision that is essential to the practical efficacy of a legal instrument to have been omitted due to any number of possible mistakes by its drafters, its practical efficacy cannot by itself show that it was included by implication. Sometimes, what we have said or written turns out to be deficient: genuine implications do not magically spring up to protect us from our mistakes. In some cases, therefore, the practical efficacy test really serves to justify the judicial repair or rectification of legal instruments, to save them from drafting omissions that would otherwise prove fatal to their efficacy.

This may explain the idiosyncratic legal terminology that describes terms being 'implied into' or 'read into' legal instruments. Terms that are

[72] Goldsworthy, 'Implications in Language, Law and the Constitution', 168; Peden, *Good Faith*, pp. 61–3.

[73] *Hamlyn* v. *Wood* (1891) 2 QB 488 at 494 (Kay L.J.), quoted with approval by Lord Atkinson, speaking for the Judicial Committee of the Privy Council, in *Douglas* v. *Baynes* (1908) AC 477 at 482. See also *Nelson* v. *Walker* (1910) 10 CLR 560 at 586 (Isaacs J.), and H. Lucke, 'Ad Hoc Implications in Written Contracts' *Adelaide Law Review* 5 (1973) 32 at 34.

[74] *Worrall* v. *Commercial Banking Co. of Sydney Ltd* (1917) 24 CLR 28 at 32.

[75] Goldsworthy, 'Implications in Language, Law and the Constitution', 161; Peden, *Good Faith*, pp. 60–1.

[76] The version found in contract law is called the 'business efficacy' test: see Starke, Seddon and Ellinghaus, *Cheshire & Fifoot's Law of Contract* (6th edn) (Sydney: Butterworths, 1992), pp. 212–13. As for statutes, see *Slipper Island Resort Ltd* v. *Minister of Works & Development* [1981] 1 NZLR 136 at 139.

[77] Goldsworthy, 'Implications in Language, Law and the Constitution', 168–70.

genuinely *implied by* a text are *inferred from* it, not *implied into* or *read into* it: the latter are oxymoronic expressions that, in trying to have it both ways, defy ordinary English. They presumably function as euphemisms, by blurring the difference between the discovery of genuine implications, and the insertion of pretended ones. If judges are really inserting terms into an instrument to ensure that it can achieve its purposes, they should say so.[78]

Adding a term to a statute is consistent with constitutional orthodoxy if its intended purpose is obvious, and the added term is necessary for it to fulfil that purpose. If so, no damage is done either to the principle of parliamentary sovereignty, because the court is guided by Parliament's purpose, or to the rule of law, because that purpose is ascertainable by reasonable interpreters. The court exercises the kind of equitable judgment described by Aristotle, who argued that when general laws would operate unjustly in unusual circumstances, they should be corrected according to 'what the legislator himself would have said had he been present and would have put in his law had he known'.[79]

This is not to deny that analytical difficulties remain unresolved. For example, how should we distinguish between background assumptions that are presupposed by an utterance, without having been in the speaker's conscious mind, and matters that the speaker has neglected to address and which are neither expressed nor presupposed by the utterance? If the speaker has not consciously thought of either one, what is the difference? It cannot be that in the former case we know the view he would have taken if he had consciously considered the matter, but in the latter case we do not. It is possible to know what view someone would have formed if he had considered some matter, without it being presupposed by the view he has in fact formed and expressed.

The real difference seems to be that, in the case of presuppositions, it would probably have made no difference if the speaker had consciously thought of the matter: he would still have expressed no view, on the ground that it was too obvious to require expression. That is why 'obviousness' is superior to 'practical efficacy' as the test for genuine implications.

---

[78] Chief Justice James Spigelman of the New South Wales Supreme Court denies that terms can be legitimately added to statutes, and disapproves of the expression 'reading into' because it suggests the opposite: see the lucid summary of views he has expressed in several cases, in his *Statutory Interpretation and Human Rights* (St Lucia: University of Queensland Press, 2008), ch. 3, esp. pp. 132–4.

[79] Aristotle *Nichomachean Ethics*, vol. 10, 1137b22–24.

Every speaker unconsciously engages in a split-second cost-benefit calculation to determine whether or not some point should be expressly mentioned, based on an assessment of whether – given cultural norms and other knowledge of their intended audience – it is likely to be taken for granted; its importance; whether it is easily inferable from other matters that will be expressly mentioned; the benefits in terms of brevity and efficiency of not expressing the point; and the possible costs of miscommunication if it turns out that it should have been expressed.[80] The audience engages in a similar analysis in deciding whether the speaker is likely to have expected them to take the point for granted.

III   Evidence of legislative intention

A statute does not mean whatever Parliament intended it to mean. It is a commonplace that the meaning people intend to communicate can differ from the meaning they succeed in communicating. People can intend to say or imply something but fail to do so, and conversely, they can say or imply something they did not intend. If we are told that we have misunderstood someone's utterance, we often defend ourselves by replying 'I now realise what she meant to say, but that's not what she did say', or 'He may not have intended to say that, but he did'. The object of interpretation is the statute actually enacted, not some other statute that members of Parliament may have mistakenly believed they were enacting.

British and British Commonwealth courts were traditionally reluctant to consult extrinsic evidence of legislative intention, such as official reports of parliamentary debates, partly because a law is supposed to be something that can be readily understood by those who are subject to it, or at least by their legal advisers, rather than something whose meaning depends on esoteric information.[81] The courts' traditional evidential limitations may have been too restrictive, but some limit to evidence of legislative intentions is crucial to the rule of law. The law can only provide a useful framework for social interaction if its meaning is made public, or at least readily ascertainable; moreover, inflicting penalties or other costs for a failure to comply with uncommunicated intentions is obviously unfair.[82] In addition, an evidential limitation reflects a sound principle that we also

---

[80] Kramer, 'Implication in Fact', 387–8.

[81] This was not the only reason: evidence of what was said in parliamentary debates was also regarded as unreliable, and as unprofitably adding to the time and expense of litigation.

[82] See T.R.S. Allan, 'Legislative Supremacy and the Rule of Law: Democracy and Constitutionalism' *Cambridge Law Journal* 44 (1985) 111 at 117–18 and 122–14.

use in everyday life. The full meaning of what people say to us depends partly on what we know about their intentions; but it does not depend on esoteric information such as what they confide only to their spouses or write in their private diaries. The meaning of an utterance depends partly on what its intended audience knows, or can reasonably be expected to know, about the speaker's intentions, but not on concealed intentions.[83] In the case of statutes, the courts have therefore distinguished between whatever hidden intentions the legislature may have had, and those intentions it has communicated by the statute it has enacted, given readily available knowledge of its context and purpose. While the former are irrelevant, the latter may be crucial. That is why, when interpreting a statute, judges often take into account the circumstances when it was made and what it was intended to achieve, when these are, or were when it was made, matters of common knowledge.[84]

We can summarise all this, somewhat inexactly, by saying that the meaning of a statute is what the legislature appears to have intended it to mean, given evidence of its intention that is readily available to its intended audience. This seems consistent with Lord Hoffmann's dictum that the intention of Parliament normally amounts to 'the interpretation which the reasonable reader would give to the statute read against its background'.[85]

It is not altogether clear who the 'intended audience' of a statute is. The courts have always held that the meaning of statutory provisions may depend on specialised knowledge possessed by lawyers: for example, knowledge of the technical legal meaning of particular words or phrases, or of pre-existing deficiencies in the law that the provisions were intended to remedy. It is not the case, therefore, that they have admitted as evidence of legislative intention only matters known by the general public. It is as if they have treated lawyers as the 'intended audience', or at least lay-people only through the medium of professional legal advice. A law is supposed

---

[83] See J. Goldsworthy, 'Moderate versus Strong Intentionalism: Knapp and Michaels Revisited' *San Diego Law Review* 42 (2005) 669.

[84] See, e.g., P.B. Maxwell, *On the Interpretation of Statutes* (London: W. Maxwell & Son, 1875), pp. 20–1; P. Langan, *Maxwell on the Interpretation of Statutes* (12th edn) (London: Sweet & Maxwell, 1969), pp. 47–50; E. Driedger, *Construction of Statutes* (2nd edn) (Toronto: Butterworths, 1983), pp. 149–51; J.F. Burrows, 'Statutory Interpretation in New Zealand', reprinted in N.J. Singer, *Sutherland Statutory Construction* (5th edn) (1992) vol. 2A, 647 at 658; Bell and Engle, *Statutory Interpretation*, pp. 143–4; G. Devenish, *Interpretation of Statutes* (South Africa: Juta & Co., 1992), pp. 127–9 and 130–3; D. Gifford, *Statutory Interpretation* (Sydney: Law Book, 1990), pp. 117–19.

[85] *R (Wilkinson)* v. *Inland Revenue Commissioners* [2006] All ER 529 at [18].

to be something that can be readily understood by those who are subject to it, but sometimes it may be necessary to consult a lawyer.

Lord Steyn among others draws a distinction between the 'subjective' intentions or 'individual views' of legislators, on the one hand, and the 'objective meaning' of the statute they enacted, on the other.[86] But legislative intentions are not necessarily individual, private and subjective: they can be shared, publicly ascertainable, and, in that sense, objective. As we have seen, 'objective meaning' is determined partly by context only because context provides evidence of subjective intentions.[87] It is, nevertheless, possible to draw a distinction between objective meaning and subjective intentions, by relying on the requirement that evidence of a speaker's subjective intentions is relevant to the meaning of her utterance only if it is readily available to her intended audience. The intentions themselves are, necessarily, subjective, but relevant evidence of them must be publicly accessible and, in that sense, objective.

Lord Steyn is perfectly right to insist that 'a legal text has a public character, and … it must be read in the light of publicly available evidence'.[88] But a good deal of evidence of legislative intentions is publicly available, so the rule of law is not violated if it is taken into account. As examples of obvious drafting errors show, the evidence often consists of simple common sense and shared cultural understandings. That is why the courts are usually willing to take judicial notice of the circumstances when the statute was passed, and its purpose, insofar as these are or were at the time either commonly known or readily ascertainable by legal advisers.[89] This is evidence that Lord Steyn himself emphasises may be crucial, in establishing the mischief that the statute was intended to cure.[90]

It is beyond the scope of this essay to attempt a detailed account of the methods by which legislative intentions can be determined.[91] As to whether statements made in Parliament should be admissible as evidence of legislative intention or purpose, principled arguments can clearly be made either way. I will not rehearse them here, but merely note that, in principle, both alternatives can be argued to be consistent with legislative

---

[86] Steyn, 'Interpretation: Legal Texts and Their Landscape', 80, 81 and 85.

[87] See text to nn. 32–34, above.

[88] Steyn, 'Interpretation: Legal Texts and Their Landscape', 89–90.

[89] See n. 84, above.

[90] Steyn, 'Interpretation: Legal Texts and Their Landscape', 81.

[91] Useful discussions can be found in Dickerson, *The Interpretation and Application of Statutes*, ch. 7; K. Greenawalt, *Twenty Questions*, chs. 8–12; and J. Evans, *Statutory Interpretation; Problems of Communication* (Auckland: Oxford University Press, 1988), ch. 12.

supremacy. In that respect, the important question is whether such state-ments are likely to provide reliable evidence of the intention of Parliament as a whole. This, in turn, depends partly on how the evidence is likely to be used. Statements made in Parliament can be used as evidence of the contemporaneous meanings of words, and of the general purposes of a statute, particularly if they are numerous, rarely contradicted, made by representatives of diverse political interests, and corroborated by other evidence of intention. In the United States, so-called 'purposivists' and 'textualists' are locked in debate about the relevance of what they call legislative history to statutory interpretation. Both sides accept the prin-ciple that the courts must act as 'faithful agents' of the legislature – which is the principle of legislative supremacy – but they differ as to how that obligation is best fulfilled. The textualists distrust the reliability of legis-lative history as evidence of the intent of the legislature as a whole.[92] Any principle of interpretation can, of course, be misapplied or abused. The question is whether courts can be trusted to use legislative history with due sensitivity to the methodological problems involved.

Of course, there are other objections to the use of legislative history, based on the rule of law and on efficiency, rather than legislative suprem-acy. For example, the relative inaccessibility of legislative history to the general public, and even to many legal advisers, raises doubts about how it can possibly inform the public meaning of a statute. As one who shares these doubts, I am not reassured by the observation that for the general public, Hansard is no more esoteric or inaccessible than the All England Law Reports.[93] For a start, judicial decisions are readily available to legal advisers, and are summarised in many accessible textbooks and other sec-ondary sources. To everything that has already been written about this, one point can be added. The relevance of extrinsic evidence of legislative intention may differ, depending on whether a court is engaged in clarifying or creative interpretation. If the meaning of a statutory provision is inde-terminate, and judicial creativity is needed to resolve the indeterminacy, public reliance on the text is a weak objection to legislative history being consulted, because there is no determinate meaning that can be relied on.

It must be acknowledged that, in many cases of prima facie uncer-tainty about the meaning of statutory provisions, it will not be possible

---

[92] See J. Manning, 'Textualism and the Equity of the Statute', *Columbia Law Review* 101 (2001) 1 at 6–7 and 9–22.
[93] I. Loveland, 'Redefining Parliamentary Sovereignty? A New Perspective on the Search for Meaning in Law' *Parliamentary Affairs* 46 (1993) 319.

to dispel the uncertainty by establishing Parliament's intention, because there will be insufficient evidence of it. In these cases the uncertainty will have to be resolved by judicial creativity. It must also be acknowledged that, in some other cases, admissible evidence of Parliament's intention may justify attributing an intention to it that (unbeknown to the interpreter) it did not in fact possess. That is an inescapable hazard of the interpretive enterprise. We do not have direct, unmediated access to anyone's intentions – we only have evidence of them, and the evidence can sometimes mislead.

IV   Alternatives to intentionalism

We have seen that statutory provisions often cannot be interpreted and applied literally, because the consequences of doing so would be so unreasonable that no legal system could tolerate them. Intentionalist theories offer one way of avoiding these consequences. If that approach is rejected, not many alternatives are available. This can be shown by considering various justifications of the decision in *Riggs* v. *Palmer*,[94] concerning whether a murderer could be prevented from inheriting under his victim's will, despite the relevant statute being silent on the subject.

Intentionalists can offer two different justifications of the decision. One is that, although the legislators had no conscious intention concerning murderers inheriting, it was reasonable to understand the statute in the light of a tacit, background assumption that was taken for granted.[95] The second is that the court engaged in 'equitable' rectification along Aristotelian lines, adding to it a qualification needed to prevent damage to an important principle that the legislature itself would probably have wanted to avoid had it adverted to the matter.[96]

If the very idea of a legislature having ascertainable intentions or purposes is rejected, what alternative justifications are available?

A   Judicial override

One is to accept that statutes should be interpreted literally, but deny that they should always be applied accordingly. This would be possible if courts were entitled to amend, override or disobey statutes. Some legal theorists

---

[94] (1889) 115 NY 506, 22 NE 188, discussed at pp. 241–2, above.
[95] See Section II, Part A(2), above.
[96] See Section II, Part B, above.

have suggested that the courts may, indeed, sometimes do this. The issue has been discussed in the context of the debate between H.L.A. Hart and Lon Fuller, concerning whether the meaning of a statutory rule depends partly on its purpose. Fuller defended the claim that it does, partly by relying on examples in which literal interpretations lead to unreasonable or absurd results.[97] Some of Hart's defenders have replied that Fuller's point goes to the application of rules, rather than to their meaning. There are different versions of this reply.

Andrei Marmor once argued, in effect, that arguments like Fuller's show that judges may sometimes have to disobey the law. He wrote that they confuse 'the question of what *following a rule consists in* (which interested Hart), with that of *whether a rule should be applied in the circumstances*'. Whether a rule should or should not be applied in the circumstances depends on its moral content and that of the legal system in question. According to Marmor, it does not follow that the rule cannot be understood without reference either to its purposes or to moral considerations.[98]

But this exaggerates and aggravates the problem. It turns a humble problem of statutory interpretation into a challenge to judicial fidelity to law. Judicial disobedience of the law is generally thought to be an extreme remedy, to be reserved for truly extraordinary situations in which a law is so morally outrageous that the reasons why judges should almost always obey the law are outweighed or overridden. Run-of-the-mill cases of statutory interpretation in which a literal reading would have unreasonable consequences are problematic, but must they be treated as posing such a grave moral dilemma? Is there really no way that judges can deal with them except by violating their judicial oaths and disobeying the law? A less spectacular solution would surely be preferable.

Frederick Schauer has offered a different version of the same reply, according to which judges have legal authority to decline to apply statutes. Like Marmor, he denies that Fuller's argument shows that the meaning of a rule depends on its purpose; it shows, instead, that judges should sometimes refuse to follow a rule if doing so would be absurd or unjust.[99] Moreover, he claims that the Anglo-American legal tradition authorises

---

[97] L. Fuller, 'Positivism and Fidelity to Law: A Reply to Professor Hart' *Harvard Law Review* 71 (1958) 630 at 662–9.
[98] Andrei Marmor, *Interpretation and Legal Theory* (Oxford: Clarendon Press, 1992), pp. 136–7.
[99] Frederick Schauer, *Playing by the Rules: A Philosophical Examination of Rule-Based Decision-Making in Law and in Life* (Oxford: Clarendon Press, 1991), pp. 209–10.

judges to do so. For example, he denies that the statutory rules considered in *Riggs* v. *Palmer* were unclear. This was not a hard case in the sense of not being clearly covered by the existing rules: the events in question plainly fell within the scope of the relevant statute.[100] The problem was that the statutory rules provided an answer that was 'socially, politically, or morally hard to swallow'. According to Schauer, American practice, and less pervasively English practice, empowers the judge to override or revise such rules.[101]

Schauer differs from Marmor by describing this judicial power to override or revise statutes as a legal rather than an extralegal power. But this explanation of the decision in *Riggs* is inconsistent with the explanation given by the court itself. As Jeremy Elkins has pointed out, 'the court went out of its way to argue that it was interpreting the Statute of Wills, rather than displacing it'.[102] Ronald Dworkin has also observed that none of the judges denied that if the statute, properly interpreted, gave the inheritance to the murderer, then they were bound to let him have it. 'None said that in that case the law must be reformed in the interests of justice.' The judges' disagreement was about 'what the statute required when properly read'.[103]

In addition, Schauer's explanation of the decision is vulnerable to a constitutional objection. According to the American principle of legislative supremacy, courts are legally required to obey any statute that is constitutionally valid. Statutes are not subordinate to judge-made common law principles; if there is any inconsistency between them, the common law principles rather than the statute must give way. This is certainly the position in Britain, whose constitution is based on the doctrine of parliamentary sovereignty. And we have seen that the principle that statutory law is superior to common law is equally well established in the United States.[104] American statutes are subject to constitutional guarantees, some of which are famously 'open ended' and have been interpreted extremely broadly. But that provides no support for the entirely different proposition that the courts may overturn or amend statutes that are inconsistent with ordinary common law principles, such as that people should not profit from their own wrongs.

---

[100]   *Ibid.*, pp. 200 and 209.
[101]   *Ibid.*, p. 210; on *Riggs* v. *Palmer*, see *ibid.* at pp. 189–90, 200 and 203.
[102]   Jeremy Elkins, 'Frederick Schauer on the Force of Rules', in Linda Meyer (ed.), *Rules and Reasoning: Essays in Honour of Fred Schauer* (Oxford: Hart Publishing, 1999), 79 at p. 90.
[103]   R. Dworkin, *Law's Empire* (Cambridge Mass.: Harvard University Press, 1986), p. 16.
[104]   See Section I, above.

New legislation is sometimes depicted as being enveloped and enmeshed by common law principles, which the courts use to subdue and domesticate it.[105] But that is consistent with constitutional orthodoxy only up to a point. A statute can legitimately be 'read down' to accommodate common law principles as long as it is reasonable to presume that Parliament intended this, or would have intended it if the particular facts had been drawn to its attention. As I have acknowledged, courts may sometimes go so far as to change the meanings of statutory provisions. But that this is consistent with constitutional orthodoxy only if it serves the legislature's purposes in ways that would presumably meet with its approval. The courts thereby remain subordinate to the legislature, acting like agents faithfully carrying out the presumed will of their principal, subject to rule of law requirements.[106]

B   Constructivism

A second alternative to intentionalism consists of 'constructivist' theories of interpretation, according to which the purposes and meanings attributed to statutes are, to a substantial extent, constructed by the judges who interpret them. Constructivists agree that the meaning of a statutory provision cannot sensibly be confined to the literal meaning of its words. But since it cannot be enriched by evidence of the legislature's intentions or purposes (which are either non-existent or indiscernible), it must be enriched by something else, such as the moral principles of the community as a whole, or 'true' moral principles.

Ronald Dworkin in *Law's Empire* expounded the most influential version of constructivisim. He rejected what he called 'conversational' interpretation, based on the 'speaker's meaning' theory which holds that the meaning of ordinary speech is determined partly by the speaker's mental state.[107] In the case of statutes and written constitutions, that theory was confounded by 'a catalogue of mysteries', including the identity of 'the speaker' and the mental state that contributes to meaning.[108] Instead, these laws had to be interpreted constructively.

---

[105] See, e.g., Joseph Raz, *Ethics in the Public Domain: Essays in the Morality of Law and Politics* (Oxford: Clarendon Press, 1994), p. 359.

[106] See text to n. 17, above. Something like this analogy is usefully developed in Richard A. Posner, *The Problems of Jurisprudence* (Cambridge Mass., Harvard University Press, 1990), pp. 269–73. By rule of law requirements, I mean that the will of the legislature must be publicly ascertainable from the words it enacted, understood in the light of contextual evidence that is readily available to its intended audience.

[107] Dworkin, *Law's Empire*, p. 50 and 315.

[108] *Ibid.*, p. 315; see also p. 348.

Constructive interpretation, of art or social practices, for example, is also essentially concerned with purposes, but the relevant purposes are supplied by the interpreter rather than the author. Constructive interpretation is 'a matter of imposing purpose on an object or practice in order to make of it the best possible example of the form or genre to which it is taken to belong'.[109] The law should therefore be interpreted so as to make it 'the best that it can be'. This requires that interpretations of the law give due weight to the principle of integrity, which requires the state or community to act on a single, coherent set of principles.[110] Judges must 'identify legal rights and duties, so far as possible, on the assumption that they were all created by a single author – the community personified – expressing a coherent conception of justice and fairness'.[111]

Dworkin attempts to accommodate actual judicial practice, such as the way in which judges 'constantly refer to the various statements congressmen and other legislators make, in committee reports or formal debates, about the purpose of an act'.[112] He claims that his theory of constructive interpretion provides a better account of actual judicial practice than the speaker's meaning theory.[113] The 'doctrine celebrated in judicial rhetoric', that statutory meaning depends partly on the legislature's intentions, is really Dworkin's own principle of adjudicative integrity.[114]

Constructive interpretation does not depend on the actual intentions or mental states of any person or group, not even those of a majority of citizens embodied in the community's conventional or popular morality.[115] Actions, purposes, faults and responsibilities are attributed to corporations and institutions, including the state itself, by 'supposing' or 'assuming' that they are persons who can be committed to principles in something like the way real people can be. The community does not really have an independent metaphysical existence: it is 'a creature of the practices of thought and language in which it figures', treated 'as if ... [it] really were some special kind of entity distinct from the actual people who are its citizens'.[116] Constructive interpretation aims to identify a coherent set of principles that best explains and justifies all the decisions that have been taken in the name of the community. Integrity requires the judge 'to construct, for each statute he is asked to enforce, some justification that fits and flows through that statute and is, if possible, consistent with other

---

[109] *Ibid.*, p. 52.   [110] *Ibid.*, p. 166.   [111] *Ibid.*, p. 225.   [112] *Ibid.*, p. 314.
[113] *Ibid.*, p. 316.   [114] *Ibid.*, p. 337.   [115] *Ibid.*, pp. 335–6 and 168–9.
[116] *Ibid.*, pp. 171 and 168 respectively, emphasis added.

legislation in force'.[117] Such an interpretation, which must embrace other statutes as well, made at different times by legislators with different political convictions, is likely to differ from an interpretation of one statute considered alone.[118]

Conversational interpretation is concerned with speaker's meanings at the time the statute was passed. Only original intentions are pertinent: 'an appeal to changed opinion must be an anachronism, a logically absurd excuse for judicial amendment'.[119] By contrast, Dworkin's constructivism is concerned with the community's present, rather than its past, commitments.[120] The primary aim of the interpreter is to identify a set of principles that justifies, not the statute's original enactment, but its current place within the law as a whole. The object is to identify a coherent conception of justice and fairness that best explains and justifies the contemporary community's commitment to its laws, including that statute.

Thus, in *Riggs* v. *Palmer*, the express provisions of the Statute of Wills are understood to be subject to an implied exclusion of the murderer of a testator from inheriting, not because of the 'speaker's meaning' theory that 'those who adopted the statute did not intend murderers to inherit', but instead, 'because *we* think the case for excluding murderers from a general statute of wills is a strong one, sanctioned by principles elsewhere respected in the law' (that people should not be permitted to profit from their own wrongs).[121]

Michael Moore has also defended a constructivist theory of statutory interpretation. He agrees that literalism is untenable, and that statutes must be interpreted in the light of their purposes. But, like Dworkin, he denies that these can be purposes of the enacting legislature, because it had no mental states that are both useful and discoverable.[122] Determining the purpose or function of a statute requires recourse to 'real values': it involves 'constructing the morally best purpose for a statute, and construing it by reference to that purpose'.[123] 'Purpose' means not 'intent' but 'function': the function that the statute serves in a just society.[124]

---

[117] *Ibid.*, p. 338.   [118] *Ibid.*, pp. 349–50.   [119] *Ibid.*, p. 349.   [120] *Ibid.*, p. 225.
[121] *Ibid.*, p. 352, emphasis in original.
[122] *Ibid.*, 386. See also Michael S. Moore, 'The Semantics of Judging' *Southern California Law Review* 54 (1980) 151 at 263–5.
[123] Michael S. Moore, 'A Natural Law Theory of Interpretation' *Southern California Law Review* 58 (1985) 277 at 354.
[124] Moore, 'A Natural Law Theory', 397.

Moore's approach is reminiscent of Dworkin's view that judges should strive to make statutes 'the best that they can be'; according to Moore, they should seek the morally best purposes that 'fit' the statute, in the sense that a rational legislature could have enacted it in order to pursue those purposes.[125] But the 'fit' requirement is flexible; if judges are unable to 'fit' a morally acceptable purpose onto the literal meaning of a statute's words, they can stretch or even overrule that meaning in order to achieve their objective. In deciding what a statutory word means, a court 'ought to balance off its linguistic intuitions against its ethical intuitions about what, in rules of this sort, the word *ought to mean*'.[126]

> There may be no set of acceptable purposes for a particular statute that a judge could find intelligibly promoted by it unless he greatly stretches his linguistic intuitions. Only then does he become self-conscious of his necessarily creative role.[127]

Riggs can again be used as an example.[128] When the Statute of Wills is subjected to Moore's 'purposive interpretation', moral values are used to help determine its meaning, by qualifying or modifying its literal meaning to produce a result consistent with the purposes that the judges believe it morally ought to serve. Thus, despite its literal meaning, it is interpreted as not allowing murderers to inherit under their victims' wills.

But are there any limits to the extent to which the meaning of a statute's actual words can be bent, stretched or overridden? According to the orthodox, intentionalist justification of non-literal interpretation, the scope for modifying literal meanings is limited by the presumed intentions and purposes of the legislature. But Moore's purposive interpretation is subject to no such limit. Does his argument permit a court to decide that a statute morally ought to serve some valuable purpose, and then 'interpret' it so that it does, no matter what it actually says?

There are moral reasons – namely, 'rule of law' values – for not straying too far from the literal meaning of a statute.[129] Judges must weigh these values against the moral values that would be promoted by overriding the literal meaning. It would seem to follow that the literal meaning might sometimes prevail, even if it has unjust consequences. On the other hand, Moore says that there is no case 'in which the linguistic intuitions are so

---

[125] Moore, 'The Semantics of Judging', 259–60 and 293–4.
[126] *Ibid.*, 278.
[127] *Ibid.*, 294; see also Moore, 'A Natural Law Theory', 385.
[128] Discussed in Moore, 'Semantics of Judging', 277–8.
[129] *Ibid.*, 321 and 385; see also *ibid.*, 313–20 for a description of the rule of law virtues.

strong that the ethical intuitions might not be determinative the other way'.[130] If it is necessary to avoid extreme injustice, 'a judge may "overrule" the ordinary meaning by acknowledging that this is a term of art in the law, guided by the law's special purposes and not by ordinary meaning'.[131] He also claims that judges must always ask a final, 'safety-valve' question concerning the justice of applying the statute.[132] He acknowledges that this might lead to overruling the statute as enacted.[133] His constructivist approach to interpretation therefore turns into invalidation if this is needed as a last resort in order to achieve justice.

Trevor Allan also defends what he calls 'robust constructivism' involving 'a "constructive" notion of legislative intention'.[134] Unlike Dworkin and Moore, Allan concedes that Parliament does have intentions of relevance to interpretation.[135] But the 'true (or legal) meaning' of a statute is 'constructed in the light of the background values we treat as fundamental'.[136] 'The relevant intention is essentially metaphorical'; it is 'attributed [to Parliament] rather than (in any straight-forward sense) discovered'.[137] It is a product of interpreting the text of the statute and its 'apparent purpose' in the light of settled common law principles of fairness and legality.[138] Even 'purpose' is partly 'constructed': the statute is taken to embody the purposes of the 'ideal legislator'.[139] 'The true or legal meaning of a provision is the sense that best reflects the various requirements of political morality, all fairly taken into account'; 'legal outcomes that would be widely thought unjust or inexpedient will be excluded'.[140] 'A statute ultimately means what the courts decide it ought to mean in particular instances.'[141]

Like Michael Moore, Allan argues that the graver the threat posed by a statute's words to a fundamental right, the more a court is justified in

---

[130] *Ibid.*, 278. [131] Moore, 'A Natural Law Theory', 385.

[132] *Ibid.*, 386–7. [133] *Ibid.*

[134] T.R.S. Allan, 'Legislative Supremacy and Legislative Intent: A Reply to Professor Craig' *Oxford Journal of Legal Studies* 24 (2004) 563 at 567–8 and 570 (on Dworkin). He distinguishes his theory from Dworkin's, and acknowledges Dworkin's change of position post-*Law's Empire*, in T.R.S. Allan, 'Legislative Supremacy and Legislative Intention: Interpretation, Meaning, and Authority' *Cambridge Law Journal* 63 (2004) 685 at 694 (although at 700 he seems to prefers the theory in *Law's Empire*).

[135] Allan, 'Legislative Supremacy and Legislative Intention: Interpretation, Meaning, and Authority', 694.

[136] *Ibid.*, 695. [137] *Ibid.*, 693 and 692.

[138] Allan, 'Legislative Supremacy and Legislative Intent: A Reply to Professor Craig', 568.

[139] 'Legislative Supremacy and Legislative Intention: Interpretation, Meaning, and Authority', 690 and 694.

[140] *Ibid.*, 695 and 696. [141] *Ibid.*, 690.

adopting a strained interpretation of them: 'a suitably elastic interpretation can, in all the circumstances, properly be accepted'.[142] 'In practice, almost anything is "possible" when the requirements of justice are sufficiently pressing.'[143] Therefore, 'a robust constructivism ... can accomplish everything that striking down can achieve'.[144] As for *Riggs* v. *Palmer*, it 'does not matter, for any practical purpose, whether we regard the Statute of Wills as rendered inapplicable by overriding common law principle or whether we treat the statute as containing, on its true construction, an implied exception to its literal terms'.[145]

C   Criticism of constructivism

Constructivist theories purport to justify a judicial power to 'construct' statutory meaning that is constitutionally unacceptable. The very idea that judicial interpreters 'construct' meaning shows that it is a power amounting, at minimum, to co-authorship of the statute. It is a power to subordinate the words chosen by the legislature (and, if they exist, its intentions and purposes) to moral values chosen by the judges. The legislature is no longer the sole author of the statute it enacts: no matter what it provides, the content of the statute will be determined partly by values 'read into it' by the judges. The meaning of a statute, Allan declares, is 'the joint responsibility of Parliament and the courts'.[146]

As Richard Ekins has argued, it is difficult to see how constructivism can be reconciled with the fundamental notion that Parliament has authority to make law. The theory treats Parliament as merely providing raw material, in the form of words, which the judges combine with other material to construct law.[147] Putting the same point another way,

> The courts are enjoined to interpret each statute as a purposive communication – but not a communication from real legislators. Instead the statute should be read as though it were a communication from the judge to himself, via the thought experiment of the ideal legislator.[148]

[142] Allan, 'Legislative Supremacy and Legislative Intent: A Reply to Professor Craig', 580.
[143] Allan, 'Legislative Supremacy and Legislative Intention: Interpretation, Meaning, and Authority', 707.
[144] Allan, 'Legislative Supremacy and Legislative Intent: A Reply to Professor Craig', 581.
[145] Allan, 'Legislative Supremacy and Legislative Intention: Interpretation, Meaning, and Authority', 699.
[146] *Ibid.*, 689, n. 13.
[147] R. Ekins, 'The Relevance of the Rule of Recognition' *Australian J Legal Philosophy* 31 (2006) 95, 100.
[148] *Ibid.*, 106.

This is a recipe for frustrating or usurping Parliament's authority, rather than respecting and facilitating it.[149]

Some versions of constructivism may be more extreme than others. Dworkin makes some room for the principle of legislative supremacy; although constructive interpretation tries to satisfy the demands of integrity, by making every statute consistent with the moral principles that underpin the law as a whole, he acknowledges that in some instances this might be impossible. If a particular statute cannot be made consistent with those principles, legislative supremacy requires that it nevertheless be enforced.[150]

But as propounded by Moore and Allan, there are no limits to the ability of constructivist judges to modify or qualify a statute in order to avoid injustice as they see it. Admittedly, Moore concedes that adherence to literal meanings is supported by 'rule of law values', which include 'the principle of democracy' – the principle that '[b]ecause legislatures represent the majority's wishes better than courts do, democracies' legislatures should have their wishes carried out by a judge even if that judge disagrees with the wisdom of such wishes'.[151] This is the principle of legislative supremacy. But the judges have power to weigh the rule of law values against substantive moral values. The difference between constitutional orthodoxy and Moore's position is therefore clear. According to him, the principle of legislative supremacy is merely one of a number of principles that judges are entitled to subordinate to other, substantive moral values that they deem to be of greater weight. The degree of deference to be accorded the legislature is ultimately a matter for them, and no-one else, to decide. That decision will inevitably depend on the weight they attribute to the substantive moral values they would prefer the legislature's enactments to serve. It is not clear whether Dworkin's theory is, ultimately, any different in this respect.

Moore and Allan frankly acknowledge that in extreme cases, constructive interpretation might distort the plain or intended meaning of a statute so severely that the statute as enacted is, in effect, overridden or invalidated.[152] Invalidation is interpretation, as they define it, pushed to the limit. From the co-authorship that is inherent in all constructive interpretation, the judiciary at that point comes out on top. Allan asserts that the judicial practice of interpreting statutes restrictively, in order to

---

[149] *Ibid.*, 103.   [150] R. Dworkin, *Law's Empire*, 268 and 401.

[151] *Ibid.*, 315.   [152] Moore, 'A Natural Law Theory', 386–7; Allan, 17.

protect important common law principles, is 'radically inconsistent with a notion of unlimited legislative supremacy'.[153]

It is difficult to imagine a constructivist theory of interpretation that does not dispense with, or severely dilute, legislative supremacy. That must be the consequence of any theory that authorises the judges to change the actually intended meaning of a statute in order to comply with extraneous moral values they regard as paramount.

Constructivism claims to provide the best description, or 'interpretation', of actual judicial practice. This is a dubious claim, given the ubiquity of judicial references to legislative intention. In *Law's Empire*, Dworkin is forced to argue that 'the doctrine celebrated in judicial rhetoric', that statutory meaning depends partly on legislative intentions, is in reality his own principle of adjudicative integrity.[154] If so, it is odd that the judges have concealed that principle behind such misleading rhetoric. He is also compelled to provide a convoluted rationalisation of the common judicial practice of consulting reports of legislative committees, and statements made by legislative sponsors of statutes, when interpreting them. The rationalistaion maintains that these reports and statements are 'themselves acts of the state personified', which the principle of integrity requires to be accommodated by a coherent theory of the community's principled commitments.[155] There is no need for such gymnastics if, as I have argued, Dworkin's scepticism about the existence of legislative intentions is misconceived. Orthodox intentionalism remains the most straight-forward and persuasive account of the judges' actual interpretive practices.

Perhaps this is why, in his more recent work, Dworkin has embraced a version of intentionalism, based on the speaker's meaning theory that he repudiated so emphatically in *Law's Empire*.[156] He now frequently uses 'the familiar model of ordinary speech', and examples of it, to explain and illuminate statutory and constitutional meaning.[157] '[J]ust as our judgment about what friends and strangers say relies on specific information about them and the context in which they speak,' he says, 'so does

---

[153] T.R.S. Allan, *Law, Liberty and Justice: the Legal Foundations of British Constitutionalism* (Oxford: Clarendon Press, 1993), p. 17.

[154] R. Dworkin, *Law's Empire*, 337.

[155] *Ibid.*, 342–3.   [156] See n. 107, above.

[157] See, e.g., Dworkin, 'Comment on Scalia', 116–17; R. Dworkin, 'Arduous Virtue of Fidelity: Originalism, Scalia, Tribe and Nerve' *Fordham Law Review* 65 (1997) 1249 at 1255–6; and R. Dworkin, *Freedom's Law; The Moral Reading of the American Constitution* (New York: Oxford University Press, 1996), pp. 292–3.

our understanding of what the framers said'.[158] In particular, it relies on our understanding of 'semantic' intentions, as opposed to 'expectation' intentions. Semantic intentions are what people intend to say by uttering certain words on a particular occasion, while expectation intentions are what they intend, expect or hope will be the consequence of uttering them.[159] These two kinds of intentions differ, because people may hold erroneous beliefs about the consequences, including the proper application, of what they say.

> Any reader of anything must attend to semantic intention, because the same sounds or even words can be used with the intention of saying different things. If I tell you ... that I admire bays, you would have to decide whether I intended to say that I admire certain horses or certain bodies of water. Until you had, you would have no idea what I had actually said even though you would know what sounds I had uttered ... We do not know what Congress actually said [in a statute] ... until we have answered the question of what it is reasonable to suppose, in all the circumstances including the rest of the statute, it intended to say in speaking as it did.[160]

'[A] text is not just a series of letters and spaces: It consists of propositions', and '[w]e decide what propositions a text contains by assigning semantic intentions to those who made the text'.[161]

> History is therefore plainly relevant. But only in a particular way. We turn to history to answer the question of what they intended to *say*, not the different question of what *other* intentions they had. We have no need to decide what they expected to happen, or hoped would happen, in consequence of their having said what they did ...[162]

Moreover, Dworkin insists that in deciding what law-makers intended to say, an interpreter is not confined to the 'acontextual meaning of the language they used'.[163] He approves of an example, supplied by Michael McConnell, of a constitutional provision in which the framers appear to have used general language to enact a rule much more limited than its acontextual meaning would suggest. The 'ex post facto' clause in Article

---

[158] Dworkin, *Freedom's Law*, p. 10.
[159] R. Dworkin, 'Comment on Scalia', in A. Scalia, *A Matter of Interpretation; Federal Courts and the Law* (Princeton: Princeton University Press, 1997), 115 at pp. 116 and 119.
[160] Dworkin, 'Comment on Scalia', p. 117.
[161] Dworkin, 'Arduous Virtue of Fidelity', 1260.
[162] Dworkin, *Freedom's Law*, p. 10.
[163] Dworkin, 'Reflections on Fidelity' *Fordham Law Review* 65 (1997) 1799 at 1815–16.

I, section 9 of the United States Constitution, states that 'no … ex post facto law shall be passed'. According to McConnell, the framers were persuaded, after they had adopted those words, that in law – as distinct from everyday usage – the words 'ex post facto law' were restricted to criminal laws, which led them to insert a separate clause prohibiting the retrospective impairment of contractual obligations.[164] Dworkin agrees that, based on what McConnell says, it is much more plausible to interpret the words in a restricted, rather than an unrestricted, way, and that this 'illustrates, therefore, the pertinence of history to the construction of semantic as well as expectation intention'.[165]

That Dworkin's approach has changed since *Law's Empire* is shown by the very different justification of the decision in *Riggs* v. *Palmer* that he now favours. As we have seen, Dworkin in *Law's Empire* rejected the 'speaker's meaning' justification for the decision.[166] But now, Dworkin offers this justification for it:

> I continue to think that the majority reached the right decision, in *Riggs* v. *Palmer*, in holding that, according to the better interpretive reconstruction, those who created the Statute of Wills did not intend to say something that allowed a murderer to inherit from his victim … It is a perfectly familiar speech practice not to include, even in quite specific instructions, all the qualifications one would accept or insist on: all the qualifications, as one might put it, that 'go without saying'.[167]

He adds that this justification of *Riggs* and similar cases is based on 'a convincing explanation for the speech acts in question'.[168] But explaining a speech act in terms of the speaker's intentions is what the speaker's meaning theory is all about![169]

V   Conclusion

Statutory interpretation is not as mysterious as some theorists would have us believe. Parliament has legal authority to make laws that the courts are legally obligated to obey. Parliament exercises its authority by using

---

[164] M. McConnell, 'The Importance of Humility in Judicial Review: a Comment on Ronald Dworkin's "Moral Reading" of the Constitution' *Fordham Law Review* 65 (1997) 1269 at 1280, esp. n. 54.

[165] Dworkin, 'Reflections on Fidelity', 1806.

[166] Dworkin, *Law's Empire*, pp. 351–2; see n. 121, above.

[167] Dworkin, 'Reflections on Fidelity', 1816.   [168] *Ibid.*, 1816.

[169] For more detailed discussion of the complexities of Dworkin's more recent work on interpretation, see J. Goldsworthy, 'Dworkin as an Originalist' *Constitutional Commentary* 17 (2000) 49.

language to communicate its will in much the same way that language is used in everyday life. The interpretation of statutes is a specialised case of linguistic interpretation in general, and many of the principles developed by the courts are explicitly formulated analogues of principles that we use intuitively in everyday life.[170] As two Australian judges put it, '[t]he fundamental object of statutory construction in every case is to ascertain the legislative intention ... The rules [of interpretation] ... are no more than rules of common sense, designed to achieve this object.'[171]

For many centuries, the common law has recognised that the object of all interpretation 'is to determine what intention is conveyed either expressly or by implication by the language used', or in other words, 'to give effect to the intention of the [law-maker] as that intention is to be gathered from the language employed having regard to the context in connection with which it is employed'.[172] This has often been said to be 'the *only rule*', or 'the fundamental rule of interpretation, to which all others are subordinate'.[173] This is a rule that leading cases and textbooks on statutory interpretation in Britain, Australia, Canada and the United States have affirmed for a very long time.[174] Indeed, it can be found at least as far back as the fifteenth century: Chrimes reports that it 'was certainly established by the second half of the fifteenth century', and by Henry VII's reign was 'sufficiently established to be clearly stated several times from the bench'.[175]

---

[170] This thesis is most comprehensively defended in G. Miller, 'Pragmatics and the Maxims of Interpretation' *Wisconsin Law Review* (1990) 1179. For strong support, see D. Pearce and R. Geddes, *Statutory Interpretation in Australia* (3rd edn) (Sydney: Butterworths, 1988), pp. 15 and 63. See also F. Bowers, *Linguistic Aspects of Legislative Expression* (Vancouver: University of British Columbia Press, 1989), pp. 8–9.

[171] *Cooper Brookes (Wollongong) Pty Ltd* v. *F.C.T.* (1981) 35 ALR 151 at 169–70 per Mason and Wilson JJ.

[172] Maxwell, *On the Interpretation of Statutes*, p. 1; *Attorney-General* v. *Carlton Bank* [1899] 2 QB 158 at 164 per Lord Russell.

[173] Respectively, *Sussex Peerage Case* (1844) 8 ER 1034 at 1057 per Tindall C.J.; *Amalgamated Society of Engineers* v. *Adelaide Steamship Co. Ltd* (1920) 28 CLR 129 at 161 per Higgins J.

[174] Maxwell, *On the Interpretation of Statutes*, p. 1; *Halsbury's Laws of England* (4th edn) Vol. 44, para. 522; Bennion, *Statutory Interpretation*, pp. 345–7; Langan, *Maxwell on the Interpretation of Statutes*, p. 28; H. Black, *Handbook on the Construction and Interpretation of the Laws* (St. Paul, Minn.: West Pub. Co., 1896), 35ff.; Singer, *Sutherland Statutory Construction*, 22–3; Driedger, *Construction of Statutes*, pp. 105–6; P.A. Cote, *The Interpretation of Legislation in Canada* (2nd edn) (Quebec, 1991) at pp. 4–5.

[175] S.B. Chrimes, *English Constitutional Ideas in the Fifteenth Century* (New York, 1966 reprint), p. 294. See also P. Hamburger, *Law and Judicial Duty* (Cambridge, Mass.: Harvard University Press, 2008), pp. 52–8. Many early authorities which consistently attest to the crucial role of legislative intention in statutory interpretation are

When the fundamental principle of statutory interpretation is ignored, as it too often is, many of the particular maxims and presumptions of interpretation can seem like a jumble, or worse, a series of mutually contradictory directives, able to be selectively marshalled to support whatever interpretation is preferred on policy grounds.[176] But once it is understood that the clarification of a statute's meaning requires taking account of all admissible evidence of legislative intention (that is or was readily available to the legislature's intended audience), then it should be appreciated that there can be a wide variety of evidence, that some items of evidence may contradict others, and that a final judgment requires weighing them against one another. The difficulty of the task should not impugn its authenticity.

It is entirely reasonable to presume that Parliament did not intend to act absurdly or unjustly, or to violate established rights. This, too, has been recognised for centuries.[177] But the presumption is defeasible. William Blackstone said that if a statute would otherwise lead to 'absurd consequences, manifestly contradictory to common reason ... the judges are in decency to conclude that this consequence was not foreseen by the Parliament, and therefore they are at liberty to ... *quo ad hoc* disregard it'. On the other hand, 'if the Parliament will positively enact a thing to be done which is unreasonable, I know of no power that can control it ...'[178] More recently, Francis Bennion expressed the same idea:

> If the result of a literal construction appears absurd or mischievous, the court must ask itself whether Parliament really meant it. There is a presumption that Parliament does not intend to do anything that will produce an absurd result. If the court thinks that what it considers to be

---

cited in R. Berger's excellent collection of early English sources, '"Original Intention" in Historical Perspective' *George Washington Law Review* 54 (1986) 296 at 299–308; see also R. Berger, 'The Founders Views – According to Jefferson Powell' *Texas Law Review* 67 (1989) 1033 at 1059–65.

[176] The classical statement of this view is K. Llewellyn, 'Remarks on the Theory of Appellate Decision and the Rules or Canons About How Statutes Are to be Construed' *Vanderbilt Law Review* 3 (1950) 395. In his list of the canons of interpretation, Llewellyn does not include the principle that statutes should be interpreted according to the intentions of the legislature. This is surprising, given that in the very next article, Charles Curtis reports that '[w]e have, almost all of us, I think, been brought up in the belief that the interpretation of legal documents consists essentially in a search for the intention of the author', and that this 'familiar doctrine is current as well as orthodox': C. Curtis, 'A Better Theory of Legal Interpretation' *Vanderbilt Law Review* 3 (1950) 407 at 407 and 408.

[177] Hamburger, *Law and Judicial Duty*, pp. 54–6.

[178] W. Blackstone, *Commentaries on the Laws of England*, vol. 1, 91 (spelling modernised).

absurd was really and truly contemplated by Parliament, and was deliberately intended, then the court must defer to that.[179]

The crucial point is that all this turns on the ideas of legislative intention and purpose. When judges interpret provisions non-literally in order to give effect to Parliament's presumed intentions or purposes, they are still acting as Parliament's faithful agents. If we were to jettison the ideas of intention and purpose, it would be much more difficult both to justify and to limit a judicial power to interpret non-literally. All non-literal interpretation would be creative rather than cognitive, guided by the judges' values (including 'common law values') rather than Parliament's. The judges would then have effective supremacy over statute law, and legislative power superior to that of Parliament itself, since they always have the 'last word' at the point of application of the law. That would amount to even more power than the 'dual' or 'bi-polar' sovereignty that some English judges have recently claimed on behalf of the judiciary.[180]

[179] Bennion, *Statutory Interpretation*, p. 338.
[180] See Goldsworthy, *The Sovereignty of Parliament*, p. 2.

10

Challenging parliamentary sovereignty: Past, present and future

I Introduction

Some critics portray the doctrine of parliamentary sovereignty as a myth that conceals the true nature of constitutionalism in Britain and other common law jurisdictions.[1] In reality, they say, Parliament and the courts are engaged in a 'collaborative enterprise', with sovereignty divided between them;[2] or the constitution is ultimately based on a common law 'principle of legality' which the courts, rather than Parliament, have ultimate authority to interpret and enforce.[3]

Sometimes the critics really seem to be suggesting that the constitution is evolving inexorably in this direction. In fact, there are at least four different claims they might be making, which are not all mutually compatible. The first is that Parliament was never sovereign: that the doctrine of parliamentary sovereignty was always mistaken as a matter of law. The second is that, even if Parliament is accepted as sovereign today, this is a relatively recent deviation from a venerable constitutional tradition that should now be restored. The third is that even if Parliament was once sovereign, recent developments mean that it no longer is. The fourth is that even if Parliament was and still is sovereign, times are rapidly changing, and it is unlikely to retain sovereignty for much longer. Those who make the second, third or fourth claim often argue that parliamentary sovereignty is a doctrine of judge-made common law, which the courts may therefore unilaterally curtail. That argument has already been refuted.[4]

In this chapter, the critics' claims about the past, present and future of parliamentary sovereignty will be examined.

---

[1] E.g. Philip A. Joseph, 'Parliament, the Courts, and the Collaborative Enterprise' *King's College Law Journal* 15 (2004) 321 at 333.
[2] *Ibid.*, 334; A. Kavanagh, *Constitutional Review Under the UK Human Rights Act* (Cambridge: Cambridge University Press, 2009), p. 414.
[3] S. Lakin, 'Debunking the Idea of Parliamentary Sovereignty: the Controlling Factor of Legality in the British Constitution' *Oxford Journal of Legal Studies* 28 (2008) 709.
[4] See Chapter 2, above.

II The past

A Doctor Bonham's *case and the common law tradition*

In a recent book defending 'common law constitutionalism', Douglas Edlin seems to make the second claim (despite rhetoric that is often more sweeping): that although Parliament is generally regarded as sovereign today, this is a relatively recent deviation from a constitutional tradition that should now be restored.[5]

Edlin frankly concedes that parliamentary sovereignty 'dominates English legal minds today'[6] and might seem to have 'become irretrievably imbedded in the collective psyche of the English legal community';[7] that an 'attenuated role of common law courts [is] assumed by current English legal practice';[8] and that the English judiciary is 'wholly captivated and captured by the dogma of absolute parliamentary supremacy'.[9] Almost the only support in current English judicial thinking that he cites for his strong version of common law constitutionalism is the courts' treatment of privative clauses, exemplified in the *Anisminic* case,[10] and Lord Steyn's reasoning in *Simms*, which Edlin discusses at length.[11] He says that these cases 'show that the burgeoning of parliamentary sovereignty has not swept from the English legal landscape' older common law principles.[12] Yet Edlin concedes that Lord Steyn's reasoning is 'exceptional' and 'extra-ordinary'; that he did not claim any judicial power to overrule statutes; and that 'most English judges' would still agree with Lord Hoffman's more restrained approach.[13] Surprisingly, Edlin does not cite the unprecedented obiter dicta questioning parliamentary sovereignty of Lords Hope and Steyn in *Jackson* v. *Attorney-General*,[14] which would have provided him with better ammunition.

Edlin therefore concedes that he must demonstrate that what he calls 'common law review' of the legality of statutes can be 'introduced' into and 'adapt even to the English legal environment',[15] which will

---

[5] Douglas E. Edlin, *Judges and Unjust Laws, Common Law Constitutionalism and the Foundations of Judicial Review* (Ann Arbor: University of Michigan Press, 2008).

[6] *Ibid.*, p. 174.   [7] *Ibid.*, p. 178; see also p. 173.   [8] *Ibid.*, p. 175.   [9] *Ibid.*, p. 183.

[10] *Anisminic* v. *Foreign Compensation Commission* v. *Secretary of State for the Home Department, ex parte Simms* [2000] 2 AC 115, discussed in Section III, Part B, below.

[11] Edlin, *Judges and Unjust Laws*, pp. 159–61, 178 and 186 (on *Anisminic*), and 178–87 (on *Simms*).

[12] *Ibid.*, p. 194.   [13] *Ibid.*, pp. 182, 183 and 186–7.

[14] *R (Jackson)* v. *Attorney-General* [2006] 1 AC 262.

[15] Edlin, *Judges and Unjust Laws*, pp. 10 and 169.

require 'overcoming the doctrine of ... legislative supremacy as ... currently understood by English lawyers and judges' through a 'process of reconceptualization'.[16] Changes in judicial attitudes are necessary, and also sufficient, since 'legislative supremacy is based finally on the attitudes of judges rather than on the pronouncements of Parliament'.[17]

His argument for change is that English lawyers should recover 'their birthright', 'England's authentic common law heritage', and 'accept the mantle of [their] common law ancestry', which supposedly recognised that judges are capable of reviewing the compatibility of legislation with the rule of law.[18] The changes he calls for are 'not revolutionary ... [o]r if they are, then they represent a reactionary revolution ... [which] would return England's legal system to its roots'.[19] Yet the only historical support he provides for this claim is his 'strong' interpretation of Sir Edward Coke's famous dictum in *Dr Bonham's* case, whose 'progeny' supposedly include Lord Steyn's judgment in *Simms*.[20] Edlin describes his reading of Coke's dictum in *Bonham* as '*the* historical and theoretical basis for judicial review of legislation according to common law principles ...'[21] He later states that this was '*the first* judicial pronouncement of the authority of common law courts to review legislative ... acts to ensure compliance with common law principles',[22] although he is able to supplement it only with American cases.[23]

Edlin's interpretation of Coke is contradicted by the most careful and thorough recent examinations of Coke's language, which have confirmed (albeit for different reasons) that he did not intend to assert a judicial power to invalidate statutes.[24] Moreover, Edlin admits that even on his

---

[16] *Ibid.*, pp. 170 and 177.   [17] *Ibid.*, p. 187.   [18] *Ibid.*, pp. 176, 183 and 187.   [19] *Ibid.*, p. 177.

[20] *Ibid.*, p. 184. At pp. 74–9, Edlin also discusses a dictum of Lord Mansfield in *Omychund v. Barker* (1744) 1 Atk 22; 26 Eng Rep 15. But that dictum provides no support for judicial review of legislation.

[21] Edlin, *Judges and Unjust Laws*, p. 7 (emphasis added).

[22] *Ibid.*, p. 27 (emphasis added).

[23] Notably, Edlin fails to respond to the evidence and arguments in Chapter 2 of this book, although an earlier version of it was previously published in a book edited by him: J. Goldsworthy, 'The Myth of the Common Law Constitution', in D. Edlin (ed.), *Common Law Theory* (Cambridge: Cambridge University Press, 2007), ch. 8.

[24] I. Williams, '*Dr Bonham's Case* and "Void" Statutes' *Journal of Legal History* 27 (2006) 111; P. Hamburger, *Law and Judicial Duty* (Cambridge Mass: Harvard University Press, 2008), ch. 8 and Appendix I. R. Helmholz, 'Bonham's case, Judicial Review and the Law of Nature' (2009) *J. of Legal Analysis* 325. Hamburger disagrees with Williams at *ibid.*, p. 625, n. 7. Edlin (*Judges and Unjust Laws*, ch. 5) presents arguments to the contrary, but fails to refer to Williams (Hamburger's book was not available to him), or to undertake anything like their detailed comparative analysis of the contemporaneous use of words

reading of Coke's judgment, (a) the precedents there cited provided only 'tenuous support' for Coke's views;[25] and (b) Coke's supposed attempt to establish judicial review of statutes was 'defeated' by subsequent events in England.[26] Even if Edlin's now discredited interpretation of Coke were correct, it is very difficult to see how the failed attempt of a single judge to promote judicial review of statutes, which had only tenuous support in precedent, could characterise 'England's authentic common law heritage'.[27]

B   The Parliament of Scotland before the Union

I previously disputed the well-known dictum of Lord Cooper in *MacCormick* v. *Lord Advocate*, that the doctrine of parliamentary sovereignty 'is a distinctively English principle which has no counterpart in Scottish constitutional law', and that there was no good reason to think that the new Parliament of Great Britain, created by the Act of Union 1707, 'must inherit all the peculiar characteristics of the English Parliament but none of the Scottish Parliament'.[28] This dictum is still occasionally cited on the assumption that Lord Cooper's dictum was soundly based. Iain McLean and Alistair McMillan, for example, have recently asserted that the dictum 'seems unanswerable. At least in relation to Scotland, [Dicey's theory] is neither descriptively correct nor normatively defensible.'[29] In *Jackson* v. *Attorney General*, Lord Hope referred to 'the English principle of the absolute legislative sovereignty of Parliament', mentioned the dicta of Lord Cooper and other Scottish judges discussing this and the effect of the Act of Union, and concluded that 'here too it may be said that the concept of a Parliament that is absolutely sovereign is not entirely in accord with reality'.[30]

such as 'void' or of the precedents cited by Coke. Some of Edlin's arguments are refuted by Williams, e.g. concerning the views of contemporaneous critics of Coke: compare Edlin at p. 73 with Williams at pp. 126–7.

[25]   Edlin, *Judges and Unjust Laws*, pp. 67 and 71.

[26]   *Ibid.*, p. 58.

[27]   See n. 18, above. Admittedly, Edlin also cites two other judicial dicta often taken to support the 'strong' reading of Coke in *Dr Bonham's* case: *ibid.*, 237, n. 111.

[28]   *MacCormick* v. *Lord Advocate* [1953] SC 396 at 411; discussed in J. Goldsworthy, *The Sovereignty of Parliament, History and Philosophy* (Oxford: Clarendon Press, 1999), pp. 165–73.

[29]   I. McLean and A. McMillan, 'Professor Dicey's Contradictions' *Public Law* (2007) 435 at 441.

[30]   *Jackson* v. *Attorney General* [2005] UKHL 56; [2006] AC 262 at [104]; see also [159] per Baroness Hale.

McLean and McMillan ignore my own previous effort to show that the Diceyan theory is descriptively accurate and normatively defensible, even in relation to the pre-1707 Scottish Parliament and the constitutional effect of the Act of Union.[31] They might be more interested in the conclusions of a Scottish historian, Julian Goodare, who has written extensively on the nature of the authority of the Scottish Parliament before 1707. Here is his conclusion:

> Parliament in its full sense – that is, estates and crown – was very much a sovereign body. It had not always been one, but it became one in the course of the sixteenth century. Traditional accounts of the Scottish Parliament have often said that it was not sovereign, but this is wrong. What I mean by sovereignty is the exercise of untrammelled power by a government.[32]

This conclusion is restated, and the extensive evidence and argument for it set out in full, in *The Government of Scotland 1560–1625*, where Goodare asserts that in Scotland before 1707 'parliamentary sovereignty was well understood and rigorously adhered to'.[33]

On the other hand, J.D. Ford regards Goodare's thesis as 'impressive but ultimately unpersuasive'.[34] Ford cites cases in which Scottish judges decided: (a) that statutory provisions had fallen into desuetude due to contrary popular usage, although this appears to have been occasionally controversial and sometimes difficult to distinguish from statutory interpretation;[35] or (b) that a statute had not come into force because it had not been accepted by the people, although the judges could also declare that, in the public interest, the statute would be enforced in future.[36] The significance of these cases is difficult to evaluate. They do not suggest that Parliament's authority was limited by fundamental laws, but rather that its statutes had to have some influence on public behaviour in order to be recognised as legally efficacious. It is not clear whether, when statutes were held not to have such an influence, this was

---

[31] Goldsworthy, *The Sovereignty of Parliament*, pp. 165–73.

[32] J. Goodare, 'Scotland's Parliament in its British context 1603–1707', in H.T. Dickinson and M. Lynch (eds.), *The Challenge to Westminster; Sovereignty, Devolution and Independence* (East Lothian: Tuckwell Press, 2000), 22 at p. 24.

[33] J. Goodare, *The Government of Scotland 1560–1625* (Oxford: Oxford University Press, 2004), p. 86.

[34] J.D. Ford, 'The Legal Provisions in the Acts of Union' *Cambridge Law Journal* 66 (2007) 106 at 136, n. 137.

[35] J.D. Ford, *Law and Opinion in Scotland During the Seventeenth Century* (Oxford: Hart Publishing, 2007), pp. 322–4, 326 and 428.

[36] *Ibid.*, pp. 326–7.

due merely to public ignorance, or in some cases, also to public resistance. Hopefully, further research will clarify these matters. Ford also cites the opinion of the eminent seventeenth-century lawyer Sir George MacKenzie, that Parliament was bound by fundamental laws, but adds that whether MacKenzie thought that judges could review the validity of statutes is much less clear.[37] Ford quotes a report of a decision in 1622, in which the Lords of Session are said to have held that 'acts of Parliament cannot be annulled or reduced but in subsequent parliaments and by no inferior judges …'[38]

C *The philosophical origins of parliamentary sovereignty*

Many critics of the doctrine of parliamentary sovereignty claim that it derives from a Hobbesian or Austinian theory of law that is now known to be erroneous.[39] By implication, Parliament could not have been sovereign before these theories held sway. These theories portray law as a body of commands, backed by threats, issued by a sovereign with sufficient power to enforce compliance if necessary. According to both, a sovereign's power cannot be conferred, or limited, by human law (as distinct from the higher law of God or nature), because that power is the source of, and therefore is necessarily superior to, human law. They regard this as a necessary truth about human law, wherever it exists. But there are differences between the two theories: for example, Austin acknowledged that subjects might have a moral obligation to disobey the sovereign's commands if they violate the laws of God, whereas Hobbes, regarding social order as imperative, insisted on obedience except in extreme cases where this would imperil a subject's own life.

The legal theories of Hobbes and Austin have indeed long been discredited. Most legal positivists now follow H.L.A. Hart, and think of legal systems as being based on fundamental rules of recognition, rather than on the extra-legal power of a sovereign. In my earlier book, I showed that the doctrine of parliamentary sovereignty can easily be understood accordingly. It is not a matter of eternal truth, compelled by logic. Whether any particular legal system includes a doctrine of

---

[37] *Ibid.*, p.478.   [38] Quoted in *ibid.*, 479, n. 29.
[39] Edlin, *Judges and Unjust Laws*, pp. 173–4 and 177–8; The Hon. E.W. Thomas, 'The Relationship of Parliament and the Courts' *Victoria University of Wellington Law Review* 5 (2000) 9; Joseph, 'Parliament, the Courts and the Collaborative Enterprise', 321, 333 and 345; Rt Hon. Dame Sian Elias, 'Sovereignty in the 21st Century: Another Spin on the Merry-go-round' *Public Law Review* 14 (2003) 148, 150 and 151.

legislative sovereignty depends on its own distinctive rule (or rules) of recognition.[40] It is simply wrong to say that '[f]or sovereignty theorists, the constitution must be founded on supremacy of one sort or another'.[41]

But it follows from this that some other doubts about the doctrine are misconceived. It has been suggested that the doctrine is incompatible with the modern realisation that whoever the law-makers may be, rules are required to specify the manner and form by which they legislate, to enable the community to distinguish between real and pretended laws.[42] It is true that Austin's theory has difficulty accommodating manner and form requirements. But there is no such difficulty if parliamentary sovereignty is regarded as grounded in rules of recognition.[43] It is true that the courts must identify and uphold these rules, but this does not entail that they may also hold Parliament to be subject to deeper, substantive principles, such as that of democracy.[44] This simply does not follow.[45] It is possible for rules of recognition to consist entirely of purely formal and procedural rules, law-making in accordance with them being unlimited by any rules or principles of substance.[46]

Historically, parliamentary sovereignty has stronger roots in Lockean than in Hobbesian political theory. In the late seventeenth and eighteenth centuries, Hobbes's theory was not very popular even among Tories, who thought it bordered on atheism, let alone among Whigs. Yet the Whigs, inspired by Locke and like-minded writers, were initially more strongly committed to parliamentary sovereignty than the Tories, many of whom preferred to think that the royal succession, and certain 'absolute' royal prerogatives, were not subject to parliamentary authority.

This may seem surprising, since Locke is famous for arguing that there are limits to what a legislature may legitimately do, implicit in the trust that the people have committed to it. But in Locke's theory, those limits

---

[40] As Elias suggests, the foundation of a legal system does not necessarily consist of one master rule of recognition. There might be a number of rules that 'interact and cross-refer': Elias, 'Sovereignty in the 21st Century', 151, quoting Neil MacCormick.

[41] P. Joseph, *Constitutional and Administrative Law in New Zealand* (3rd edn) (Wellington: Thomson/Brookers, 2007), p. 544.

[42] Elias, 'Sovereignty in the 21st Century', 150.

[43] Goldsworthy, *The Sovereignty of Parliament*, pp. 13–16.

[44] Elias, 'Sovereignty in the 21st Century', 151; see also 156 ('explicit analysis of constitutional principle') and 162 (on protecting the essential democratic process).

[45] See Goldsworthy, *The Sovereignty of Parliament*, pp. 253–9. Also, the judicial decisions in Australia, Canada and India that Elias refers to are all of doubtful correctness.

[46] See Chapter 7 above.

are moral rather than legal, and they are enforced not by legal remedies dispensed by courts, but by popular rebellion that dissolves the constitution. He regarded the legislature as the supreme power within the constitution, subject only to a higher power outside the constitution – the community as a whole – which, if the legislature abused its trust, could dissolve the constitution and establish a new one, in which some new legislature would be legally supreme.[47]

The truth in the widespread belief that the doctrine of parliamentary sovereignty was firmly established by the Revolution of 1688 is that the Whig theory of the constitution prevailed over that of the Tories. Within a short period, most Tories had accepted that Parliament could control the royal succession and all of the Crown's prerogatives.[48] But throughout the eighteenth century, the consensus that Parliament had legally unlimited authority was not based on the Hobbesian thesis that the supreme power within any state has a right to virtually absolute obedience. Constitutional thought was much more sophisticated than that. The Whig theory – that in the face of tyranny, popular rebellion might be justified – was generally accepted. But it was also believed, not unreasonably, that the law itself should not recognise any limits to Parliament's authority (even though moral limits were acknowledged), or countenance rebellion in any circumstances, because of the risk that such limits would be construed too broadly, and rebellion incited too easily by demagogues.[49] It was also often observed that the moral limits to legislative authority were too vague and controversial to be legally serviceable.[50] No doubt the Whigs, when they acquired power, deliberately downplayed the right of resistance, but the Lockean theory remained intact. And this is the constitutional theory that was propounded by Blackstone.[51]

It is true that in the nineteenth century, legal philosophy in Britain came to be dominated by Austin's theory. But Austin explicitly rejected Hobbes's demand of almost absolute obedience to the established sovereign, and acknowledged that resistance to tyranny might be justified in extreme cases.[52] Dicey agreed with this,[53] but also distanced himself from Austin's general philosophy of law. Dicey astutely suggested that, rather than the doctrine of parliamentary sovereignty being derived from Austin's theory, that theory was a generalisation drawn from English law, and owed its rapid acceptance to the familiarity of English jurists with the

---

[47] See Goldsworthy, *The Sovereignty of Parliament*, pp. 151–3.
[48] *Ibid.*, pp. 159–64.   [49] *Ibid.*, pp. 173–81.   [50] *Ibid.*   [51] *Ibid.*, pp. 19 and 181–3.
[52] *Ibid.*, p. 19.   [53] *Ibid.*

already well established doctrine of parliamentary sovereignty.[54] I suspect that Dicey was right on both counts.

In claiming that the doctrine of parliamentary sovereignty owes much more to Locke than Hobbes, I am not suggesting that it was established by Locke. As I have previously argued, the doctrine has much deeper roots than late seventeenth- and eighteenth-century political theory. These roots include: the sovereignty of the medieval King; Parliament's role as the King's highest seat of judgment, in which his powers were most absolute; its standing as the highest court in the realm from which there could be no appeal; its claim to represent the collective wisdom of the entire community; distrust of the ability of the King's judges to withstand improper royal influence; the perceived need for a decision-maker able to take extraordinary measures to protect the community in an emergency; the presumed equal right of every generation to change its laws; and confidence in the capacity of Parliament's three component elements to check and balance one another.[55]

D   The 'collaborative model'

Philip Joseph claims that the doctrine of parliamentary sovereignty is a 'latter day myth' resulting from 'sleight of hand' and 'lazy thinking'.[56] 'Parliament has never been sovereign', he says. 'Sovereignty implies autocracy ... [but] [l]egislative power has never been of this nature.'[57] Parliamentary sovereignty has always been a 'perverse legal theory', which conveyed a 'skewed conception of legislative power' and misrepresented the true 'constitutional balance' between the political and judicial branches of government.[58]

But the evidence provided for this claim is very thin. Joseph is reluctant to assert that the courts currently have power to invalidate legislation. At one point, he expressly denies that the courts 'claim judicial power to strike down or disapply Parliament's legislation'.[59] He also concedes that 'the Glorious Revolution settled Parliament's right to override or qualify

---

[54] A.V. Dicey, *Introduction to the Study of the Law of the Constitution* (10th edn) (London: Macmillan, 1959), p. 72.

[55] Summarised in Goldsworthy, *The Sovereignty of Parliament*, ch. 9.

[56] *Ibid.*, p. 321.

[57] Joseph, 'Parliament, the Courts, and the Collaborative Enterprise', 321. This claim is repeated in the latest edition of Joseph, *Constitutional and Administrative Law in New Zealand* (3rd edn), p. 543.

[58] Joseph, 'Parliament, the Courts, and the Collaborative Enterprise', 345.

[59] *Ibid.*, p. 328.

judge-made principles of common law',[60] and that the courts 'defer to the political decisions of the legislature [and] avoid making judgments about legislative policy'.[61] On the other hand, he states that 'the judicial branch asserts its autonomy to uphold the rule of law',[62] and that whether Parliament can effectively abrogate fundamental rights is an 'imponderable' that 'leaves room for conjecture'. This is because the courts, while paying 'lip-service' to its power to do so, may refuse to acknowledge that it has spoken with sufficient clarity.[63] But this implies that the courts would be (nobly) lying, which is not at all the same as claiming that they have legal authority to refuse to enforce legislation that abrogates rights.

One of Joseph's major claims is that:

> Throughout English constitutional history, Parliament and the courts have exercised co-ordinate, constitutive authority . . . Theirs is a symbiotic relationship founded in political realities: Parliament and the political executive must look to the Courts for judicial recognition of legislative power, and the Courts must look to Parliament and the political executive for recognition of judicial independence.[64]

If by 'co-ordinate authority' he means authority that is equal in rank,[65] my previous book demonstrates that this historical claim is false. The courts of Westminster were not traditionally regarded as Parliament's equals: they were 'inferior courts', whose judgments were subject to appeal to the 'High Court of Parliament', the King's highest seat of judgment, in which his authority was most ample and absolute.[66] That book cites countless statements to this effect from the reign of Edward II onwards.[67] Parliament's status as the supreme power in the realm was accepted by John Locke, and was at the core of the constitutional theory of the Whigs, which triumphed in 1688.[68] Indeed, Parliament's superiority to 'inferior' courts such as King's Bench was one (but only one) of the principal reasons why its statutes were regarded as legally unchallengeable. Joseph's claim is philosophically as well as historically dubious. From the undoubted fact that parliamentary sovereignty depends (partly) on judicial recognition, it simply does not follow that Parliament and the courts possess

---

[60] *Ibid.*, p. 335.   [61] *Ibid.*, p. 334.   [62] *Ibid.*, p. 336.   [63] *Ibid.*, p. 342.

[64] *Ibid.*, p. 322. See also Joseph, *Constitutional and Administrative Law in New Zealand* (3rd edn), pp. 543–5.

[65] *Concise Oxford Dictionary of Current English* (6th edn) (Oxford: Clarendon Press, 1976), p. 224.

[66] Goldsworthy, *The Sovereignty of Parliament*, pp. 58 and 89–90.

[67] See *ibid.*, Index, p. 318, under 'Parliament, as highest court, not subject to appeal'.

[68] *Ibid.*, pp. 151 and 160.

'co-ordinate authority'. Indeed, judicial recognition of parliamentary sovereignty suggests the opposite.[69]

Joseph asserts that '[s]overeignty theorists discount any historical, constitutional role of the Courts, such as upholding the rule of law, securing the constitutional balance, or standing between the individual and the State', and also discount 'the constitutive authority of the Courts to develop the law'.[70] But there is no reason why sovereignty theorists should discount any of these things, because none of them is incompatible with parliamentary sovereignty. It should be borne in mind, however, that the notion that it is the unique or distinctive role of the courts to uphold the rule of law, secure the constitutional balance and protect the individual, is a modern one. For most of English constitutional history, Parliament was believed to play the pivotal role in all three respects.[71] But sovereignty theorists have no reason whatsoever to deny that Parliament and the courts collaborate in their endeavours to achieve good government in conformity with the rule of law.

Joseph argues that classical sovereignty theory is inconsistent with 'the constitutive law-making/law-partnership role of the Courts when they construe and apply legislation'.[72] According to him, the courts:

> ... are more actively engaged in law-creation than sovereignty theorists concede. It is a misrepresentation that the Courts receive Parliament's words, interpret them according to what Parliament is presumed (but did not *really*) intend, and apply them, without regard to the constitutional, legal or social framework. This formalist depiction reserves to the Courts a servile, patronising role.[73]

Since Joseph cites one of my own essays on statutory interpretation, I need do little more than refer readers to it.[74] The careful reader will discover that I acknowledge both the frequently creative, law-making role of the courts in interpreting statutes, and the way that judges often interpret statutes in the light of fundamental – 'constitutional', if you will – common law rights

---

[69] R. Ekins, 'The Myth of Constitutional Dialogue: Final Legal Authority, Parliament and the Courts' (2004) *Bell Gully Public Lecture*, 5 (unpublished, on file with author).

[70] Joseph, 'Parliament, the Courts, and the Collaborative Enterprise', 332 and 335.

[71] Goldsworthy, *The Sovereignty of Parliament*, Index, p. 318, under 'Parliament as incorporating checks and balances', and 'Parliament as principal guardian of liberty'.

[72] Joseph, 'Parliament, the Courts, and the Collaborative Enterprise', 322.

[73] *Ibid.*, 337.

[74] Jeffrey Goldsworthy, 'Parliamentary Sovereignty and Statutory Interpretation', in R. Bigwood (ed.), *The Statute: Making and Meaning* (Wellington: LexisNexis, 2004), p. 187. See Chapter 9, above.

and principles.[75] Joseph is right that on my account, resort to these common law rights and principles is justified only insofar as there is genuine uncertainty about Parliament's intentions, but I also accept the modern position that where basic rights and principles are at stake, it is reasonable to conclude that there is such uncertainty absent express words or necessary implication.[76] I argue that British and Commonwealth courts have always justified the common law presumptions in this way.[77] In leading cases, over many hundreds of years, 'it is almost universally asserted that the most fundamental principle of interpretation is that statutes should be interpreted according to the intention they convey, either expressly or by implication given the context [including the "constitutional" context] in which they were enacted'.[78] There is nothing 'servile' and 'patronising' in judges being guided by this principle, unless one thinks that it is servile and patronising for judges to respect the law-making authority of democratically elected legislatures, and to obey the laws they make. But in any event, the courts themselves have long embraced the principle.

Joseph seems to believe that the courts have a much more independent and creative role in interpreting statutes by virtue of their 'co-ordinate authority' as the final arbiters of what the law is. He states: 'No-one can dispute that the judiciary has final authority to determine what is or is not law';[79] '[t]he judiciary ... *is* the final authority by virtue of the judicial function'.[80] This line of thought leads him to the rather extreme conclusion that '[i]n the final analysis, Parliament's statutes ... mean what the Courts say they mean, even if judges choose to adopt self-constraining interpretations that are entirely sympathetic to the parliamentary purpose'.[81]

I do not believe, and doubt that many judges believe, that statutes mean whatever the courts say they mean. (I am also confident that Joseph does not really believe this.) Statutes are not empty shells with no meaningful content until the courts breathe life into them. They are necessarily assumed to have meaningful content that is binding on the courts as well as other legal officials and citizens. If they did not, they would not be laws. The courts' authority to 'determine what the law is', amounts to authority to ascertain that content, to clarify it when it is obscure and to supplement it when it is indeterminate. They have no authority to change that content,

---

[75] Goldsworthy, 'Parliamentary Sovereignty and Statutory Interpretation', pp. 189–93 and 206–8.

[76] *Ibid.*, p. 209.   [77] Goldsworthy, *The Sovereignty of Parliament*, pp. 250–2.

[78] Goldsworthy, 'Parliamentary Sovereignty and Statutory Interpretation', 191.

[79] Joseph, 'Parliament, the Courts, and the Collaborative Enterprise', 324.

[80] *Ibid.*, 330.   [81] *Ibid.*

except perhaps in very limited circumstances, to correct some deficiency in Parliament's expression of its obvious purpose.[82] Such authority is certainly not entailed by the fact that the interpretation adopted by an ultimate appellate court is final, in the sense of not being subject to appeal. That an institution has the final word in this sense does not mean that it is either unconstrained or infallible.[83] It may be genuinely bound by laws, including statutes, and constitutional doctrines such as parliamentary sovereignty, even if its compliance with them is not enforceable by appeal to some other institution. If Joseph believes that the courts do have authority to change the content of a statute as enacted by Parliament, regardless of Parliament's own purposes, he needs to spell out the extent of that authority, and argue for its existence, in more detail.

Joseph's sweeping claims that Parliament was never sovereign, and that the doctrine of parliamentary sovereignty is a latter-day myth, are hard to reconcile with his earlier writings. In the first edition of his book *Constitutional and Administrative Law in New Zealand*, published in 1993, he expressed the opposite opinion in no uncertain terms.[84] He asserted there that the United Kingdom and New Zealand Parliaments both possessed sovereign law-making power.[85] Moreover, he disapproved of statements to the contrary made by Sir Robin Cooke (as he then was).[86] In a sophisticated but compressed analysis of the foundations of legal authority, Joseph exploded the conceit that parliamentary sovereignty is a judicial construction, and explained that it cannot be changed either by Parliament, or by the courts, alone. '[A] broader accommodation through a Bill of Rights or some other national settlement for controlling or redefining legislative power' was required.[87] Even in the second edition of his book, published as recently as 2001, Joseph repeated most of these points.[88]

Of course, it is possible that Joseph is right in 2004, but was wrong in 1993 and 2001, about whether the United Kingdom and New Zealand

---

[82] On these limited circumstances, see Chapter 9, Section II, Part B, above. In Hart's terminology, the courts' authority is conferred by a 'rule of adjudication' rather than a 'rule of change': H.L.A. Hart, *The Concept of Law* (Oxford: Clarendon Press, 1961), pp. 93–4.

[83] Goldsworthy, *The Sovereignty of Parliament*, pp. 272–4.

[84] Philip A. Joseph, *Constitutional and Administrative Law in New Zealand* (Sydney: Law Book Co., 1993).

[85] *Ibid.*, pp. 2, 8, 12, 396, 418 and 429–31.

[86] *Ibid.*, pp. 445 and 454–6.

[87] *Ibid.*, 455–6. This is repeated in Joseph, *Constitutional and Administrative Law in New Zealand* (3rd edn), pp. 536–8.

[88] Philip A. Joseph, *Constitutional and Administrative Law in New Zealand* (2nd edn) (Wellington: Brookers, 2001), pp. 3, 16, 461, 472, 475 and 507–9.

Parliaments were ever truly sovereign. People are entitled to change their minds. Yet Joseph's earlier certainty, based on impressive research and lucid analysis, surely raises doubts about his current claim that parliamentary sovereignty is a 'latter-day myth' resulting from 'sleight of hand' and 'lazy thinking'.[89] There is considerable evidence even in his new critique that the doctrine of parliamentary sovereignty is not a 'myth'. Much of this article concerns very recent developments, which in his opinion show that Parliament, today, is not sovereign. These developments include the enactment of the Human Rights Act 1998 (UK) and the way its application is challenging orthodox understandings of statutory interpretation; the relatively recent expansion of judicial review in administrative law, and its supposed incompatibility with parliamentary sovereignty; the influence of proportionality analysis; and so on. But evidence of this kind does not show that Parliament was not sovereign in the past. Quite the contrary, insofar as Joseph acknowledges that these are recent developments, it suggests the opposite. He argues that these developments require 'new' constitutional theorising, which a conservative judiciary has not yet embraced.[90] At most, all this strongly suggests incipient change, not long-standing practice. Recent judicial innovations may require new theories, and may constitute a challenge to the doctrine of parliamentary sovereignty. But they cast very little light on the nature of parliamentary authority in the past.

III   The present and future

Defenders of parliamentary sovereignty cannot ignore constitutional change. Constitutional arrangements and understandings today are in many respects very different from those of the past. But the doctrine of parliamentary sovereignty has survived centuries of change, and has the capacity to survive many more. I will argue that the recent constitutional developments discussed by its critics are compatible with the doctrine.

If I am wrong, and one or more recent developments have undermined parliamentary sovereignty, it is crucial to identify them in order to achieve a clear understanding of the new constitutional order. For example, if legislation such as the European Communities Act 1972 (UK) or the Human Rights Act 1998 (UK) has made parliamentary sovereignty redundant, that is presumably because Parliament has somehow succeeded in binding

---

[89] Joseph, 'Parliament, the Courts, and the Collaborative Enterprise', 321.
[90] *Ibid.*, 322 including n. 4, 321–3, 327, 340, 342–5.

itself, which does not vindicate the theory of common law constitutionalism. Moreover, this would not affect parliamentary sovereignty in New Zealand, or in other Commonwealth jurisdictions where the doctrine exists in attenuated form. But other grounds for challenging parliamentary sovereignty might entail some version of common law constitutionalism, and potentially affect every common law jurisdiction.

A   *Judicial review of administrative action*

One of Joseph's central arguments is that judicial review of administrative action has for centuries been based on the courts' inherent jurisdiction as a matter of common law.[91] Joseph is here taking aim at the 'ultra vires' theory of judicial review, one of the protagonists in recent British debates over the nature and foundations of judicial review of administrative action.[92]

The ultra vires theory, championed by Christopher Forsyth and Mark Elliott, holds that judicial review of administrative action taken under statute enforces legal limits imposed by the statute itself, implicitly if not explicitly. This is supposedly because, when administrative power is conferred, and not relevantly limited, by statute, the imposition by judges of limits to that power would be tantamount to overriding the statute, in defiance of Parliament's sovereignty. This claim appears to depend on the proposition that whatever the statute itself does not prohibit, it permits, so that any limits imposed by judges on the exercise of statutory powers would necessarily be inconsistent with that permission.[93] Forsyth and Elliott now advocate a 'modified' ultra vires theory, which attributes to Parliament a tacit or implied general authorisation of the courts' creative development of the grounds of judicial review.[94]

Sir John Laws, writing extra-judicially, described the ultra vires theory as 'a "fig-leaf" serving to provide a façade of constitutional decency, with lip-service to the sovereign Parliament, while being out of touch with reality'.[95] The rival 'common law' theory, advanced by Paul Craig,

---

[91]   *Ibid.*, 328–33.

[92]   The debate started with C. Forsyth, 'Of Fig Leaves and Fairy Tales: The *Ultra Vires* Doctrine, the Sovereignty of Parliament and Judicial Review' *Cambridge Law Journal* 55 (1996) 122. Many of the responses this article provoked are collected in C. Forsyth (ed.), *Judicial Review and the Constitution* (Oxford: Hart Publishing, 2000).

[93]   C. Forsyth and M. Elliott, 'The Legitimacy of Judicial Review' *Public Law* (2003) 286 at 289.

[94]   See Forsyth's and Elliott's contributions in Forsyth (ed.), *Judicial Review and the Constitution*.

[95]   Qutoed by H.W.R. Wade and C.F. Forsyth, *Administrative Law* (9th edn) (Oxford: Oxford University Press, 2004), p. 39.

maintains that judicial review enforces legal limits to administrative power that have largely been laid down, and continue to be creatively developed, as a matter of common law, without any need for Parliament's imprimatur. He urges us to frankly acknowledge that the principles enforced by the courts through judicial review are creatures of the common law, rather than genuine implications of statutes.[96] He argues that subjecting administrative powers to common law principles of good administration is no more controversial than subjecting such powers to common law principles of tort.[97] In neither case is it necessary to attribute to Parliament an intention to authorise or consent to the imposition, and as long as Parliament is free to override any limits imposed by common law, it remains sovereign.[98] Craig's position follows from the basic 'rule of law' principle, that the Crown is subject to the ordinary law of the land, including the common law, unless it is granted an exemption by statute.

Trevor Allan occupies an intermediate position. He agrees with Forsyth and Elliott that 'constitutional logic' requires the grounds of judicial review of administrative action under statute to be found within the statute itself, yet he regards legislative intent as largely an artefact of judicial 'construction' (rather than an object of judicial discovery) in accordance with common law principles.[99] He also disagrees with Forsyth, Elliott and Craig by holding that Parliament's authority is limited by fundamental common law principles.[100]

The ultra vires theorists are wrong to suggest that whatever Parliament does not forbid, it permits. There are many matters with respect to which Parliament may not have formed, or communicated, any intention one way or the other, leaving the common law free to regulate them. To use terminology familiar in the jurisprudence of federal systems, concerned with the relationship between national and state laws, if the legislation of one parliament is not intended to 'cover the field', another parliament

---

[96] See the contributions of Paul Craig in Forsyth (ed.), *Judicial Review and the Constitution*.

[97] P. Craig, 'Competing Models of Judicial Review' *Public Law* 428 (1999) 433–5.

[98] P. Craig, 'Constitutional Foundations, the Rule of Law and Supremacy' *Public Law* 92 (2003) esp. at 107–10; P. Craig, 'The Common Law, Shared Power and Judicial Review' *Oxford Journal of Legal Studies* 24 (2004) 237, esp. at 249–56; P. Craig and N. Bamforth, 'Constitutional Analysis, Constitutional Principle and Judicial Review' *Public Law* 763 (2001) esp. at 768–71.

[99] T.R.S. Allan, 'Legislative Supremacy and Legislative Intent: A Reply to Professor Craig' *Oxford Journal of Legal Studies* 24 (2004) 563, and 'Legislative Supremacy and Legislative Intention: Interpretation, Meaning, and Authority' *Cambridge Law Journal* 63 (2004) 685. See the discussion in Chapter 9, Section IV, Part B, above.

[100] Allan, 'Legislative Supremacy and Legislative Intent: A Reply to Professor Craig', 582.

may legislate with respect to the same subject-matter.[101] If so, it is hard to see why judges may not develop the common law in relation to that subject-matter. The ultra vires theorists have yet to respond effectively to this criticism, but they do insist that even principles of tort can justifiably be imposed on statutory authorities only if Parliament's tacit authorisation or consent can be presumed.[102]

On the other hand, it seems unlikely that the grounds of judicial review can all be justified in the same way. The ultra vires theory is undoubtedly well suited to what used to be called 'simple' ultra vires: the absence of the statutory power that was purportedly exercised. It may also be able to explain some of the other grounds. As we have seen, judicial interpretations of statutory provisions that supplement or qualify their literal meanings are sometimes justified by the idea of implicit or background assumptions.[103] When Parliament confers power on an administrator, does it really need to spell out that the power is to be exercised without bias, in good faith, for the purposes for which it has been conferred, on the basis of at least a scintilla of evidence, and within the bounds of rationality? Surely the courts are justified in treating such limits to the exercise of administrative power as presuppositions that are taken for granted.

Admittedly, this justification might not fit all the grounds of review, or at least, not completely. An alternative possible justification relies on the idea that judges may sometimes 'embroider' a statute, by filling in details, and supplementing or qualifying its provisions, to ensure that it achieves its purposes without damaging other important objectives or principles to which the legislature is committed.[104] Aronson, Dyer and Groves have proposed something like this understanding of the case law.[105] The intimate, almost inextricable relationship, in a particular case, between the grounds of review and the provisions and purposes of the statute in question, suggest that this may be a better account of judicial creativity than the idea that the courts have developed independent, common law

---

[101] T. Endicott, 'Constitutional Logic' *University of Toronto Law Journal* 53 (2003) 201; A. Halpin, 'The Theoretical Controversy Concerning Judicial Review' *Modern Law Review* 64 (2001) 500, esp. at 501–6.

[102] M. Elliott, 'Legislative Intention Versus Judicial Creativity? Administrative Law as a Co-operative Enterprise', in Forsyth (ed.) *Judicial Review and the Constitution*, pp. 347–8, above.

[103] See Chapter 9, Section II, Part A(2).

[104] *Ibid.*, Section II, Part B, above.

[105] M. Aronson, B. Dyer and M. Groves, *Judicial Review of Administrative Action* (3rd edn) (Sydney: Lawbook Co., 2004), pp. 101–2.

grounds of review. Yet Craig's common law theory might be the most plausible explanation of some other grounds of review.

We have, then, many possible explanations of the grounds of review to choose from, and they may not all be justifiable on the same basis. But judicial review is not unique in raising these difficult theoretical questions. Consider, again, the decision in *Riggs* v. *Palmer*, concerning the murderer who claimed the right to an inheritance under his victim's will.[106] Although the New York statute dealing with wills did not expressly exclude murderers from inheriting, the state's Court of Appeals held that it did exclude them, by interpreting it in the light of the common law principle that no-one may profit from his own wrong. This decision has been explained in terms similar to each of the various theories of judicial review that have been mentioned:

(1) Although the legislators had no conscious intention concerning murderers inheriting, it was reasonable to understand the statute in the light of tacit, background assumptions that can be taken for granted.[107] This is equivalent to Forsyth's and Elliott's 'modified' ultra vires theory.

(2) The judges engaged in 'equitable' interpretation along Aristotelian lines, adding to it a qualification needed to prevent damage to an important principle that the legislature itself would probably have chosen to avoid had it addressed the question.[108] This is related to Aronson's, Dyer's and Groves' theory.

(3) The legislature had no relevant intention one way or another; but precisely for that reason, it did not purport to 'cover the field', and left room for the operation of independent, common law principles.[109] This is similar to Craig's theory.

(4) The judges attributed to the legislature an artificial, 'constructive' intention, based on common law principles, that helped to make the statute 'the best that it can be' (to use one of Dworkin's expressions).[110] This is equivalent to one aspect of Allan's theory.[111]

---

[106] (1889) 115 NY 506, 22 NE 188.

[107] R. Dworkin, 'Reflections on Fidelity' *Fordham Law Review* 65 (1997) 1799 at 1816. See also Chapter 9, Section IV, end of Part C, above.

[108] See, for example, Jim Evans's theory of equitable exceptions: J. Evans, 'Reading Down Statutes', in R. Bigwood (ed.), *The Statute; Making and Meaning* (Wellington: LexisNexis, 2004), p. 123.

[109] D. Farber, 'Courts, Statutes, and Public Policy: the Case of the Murderous Heir' *Southern Methodist University Law Review* 53 (2000) 37.

[110] R. Dworkin, *Law's Empire* (Cambridge, Mass: Belknap Press, 1986), pp. 351–2.

[111] See Trevor Allan's discussion of Riggs in Allan, 'Legislative Supremacy and Legislative Intention: Interpretation, Meaning, and Authority', 696–703.

(5) In effect, the decision subordinated the statute, and the will of the legislature, to common law principles (contrary to the American doctrine that the legislature is supreme as long as it does not violate limits imposed by the state or national Constitution).[112] This is equivalent to another aspect of Allan's theory.[113]

The most important point is that in the case of judicial review, there is no good reason to accept (5). I would also reject (4), on the ground that it reduces to (5). This is because, if legislative intentions are not real, but artificial 'constructs' that are essentially fictions, then we must pierce through the fiction to ascertain the underlying reality – which must be (5) (since all the other alternatives depend to some extent on legislative intentions being real).

As for (1), (2) and (3), the right choice will probably vary, depending on the particular ground of review in question. Although the choice is of analytical interest, it may be of little practical importance. What is of great practical importance is whether, by interpreting a statute as subject to some unexpressed qualification, a court is being faithful to Parliament's purposes, insofar as these have been clearly communicated, or whether it is really overriding them, and the statute, to give effect to its own policy preferences. There appears to be no good reason to think that this is generally true of the judicial review of administrative decision-making. One exception may be the courts' treatment of some privative clauses that purport to oust their jurisdiction to review administrative action.

B   The Anisminic case

Many critics have claimed that the *Anisminic* case[114] is flatly inconsistent with parliamentary sovereignty, because the House of Lords, in effect, refused to obey Parliament's command that decisions of the statutory authority in question were not to be judicially reviewed.[115] Two responses

---

[112] A. Marmor, *Interpretation and Legal Theory* (Oxford: Clarendon Press, 1992), pp. 136–7; F. Schauer, *Playing By the Rules: a Philosophical Examination of Rule-Based Decision Making in Law and Life* (Oxford: Clarendon Press, 1991), pp. 209–10; both critically discussed in Chapter 9, Section IV, Part A, above.

[113] T.R.S. Allan, 'Legislative Supremacy and Legislative Intention: Interpretation, Meaning, and Authority', 699, quoted in Chapter 9, Section IV, end of Part B, above.

[114] *Anisminic Ltd* v. *Foreign Compensation Commission* [1969] 2 AC 147, [1969] 2 WLR 163.

[115] For example, H.W.R. Wade and C.F. Forsyth, *Administrative Law* (7th edn) (Oxford: Oxford University Press, 1994), p. 737; Thomas, 'The Relationship of Parliament and the Courts', 27.

can be made. The first is that even Trevor Allan, no friend of parliamentary sovereignty, has justified the decision in that case on the orthodox ground of presumed legislative intention. He said that '[i]t is quite as reasonable to suppose that Parliament intended the courts to superintend the Foreign Compensation Commission, as regards the extent of its jurisdiction, as to suppose the contrary. Far more reasonable – it would seem almost absurd to think that Parliament intended the Commission's activities to be free from all legal control.'[116] Allan has not subsequently changed his mind.[117] And as I have previously observed, judges who presume that Parliament did not intend to violate some important common law principle 'do not deliberately flout the doctrine of parliamentary sovereignty unless they know that there is clear, admissible evidence that it did intend to do so'.[118]

Many scholars believe that judges routinely evade privative clauses by lying about Parliament's likely intention in enacting them.[119] Aronson, Dyer and Groves use the term 'disingenuous disobedience'.[120] Sir William Wade referred to 'the logical contortions and evasions' to which judges were 'driven' by privative clauses, although he added that their stance should be condoned rather than criticised.[121] Justice E.W. Thomas recommends that we candidly admit what the judges have been doing: 'I know of no rule of law or logic which would make judicial disobedience more palatable simply because it is done covertly.'[122]

Let us assume that the Court did knowingly disobey Parliament. The second possible response was outlined in my earlier book:

> It must also be admitted that in some ... cases, the judges' claim to be faithful to Parliament's implicit intention has been a 'noble lie', used to conceal judicial disobedience. But such cases are relatively rare, and the fact that the lie is felt to be required indicates that the judges themselves realise that their disobedience is, legally speaking, illicit. The lie also preserves Parliament's freedom, after reconsidering its position, to

[116] T.R.S. Allan, 'Legislative Supremacy and the Rule of Law: Democracy and Constitutionalism' *Cambridge Law Journal* 44 (1995) 111 at 127.

[117] T.R.S. Allan, *Constitutional Justice; a Liberal Theory of the Rule of Law* (Oxford: Oxford University Press, 2001), pp. 211–12.

[118] Goldsworthy, *The Sovereignty of Parliament*, p. 252.

[119] See, e.g., C. Saunders, 'Plaintiff S157: A case-study in common law constitutionalism' *Australian Journal of Administrative Law* 12 (2005) 115 at 117 and 125.

[120] Aronson, Dyer and Groves, *Judicial Review of Administrative Action* (3rd edn), p. 830.

[121] Sir William Wade, *Constitutional Fundamentals* (rev'd edn) (London: Stevens & Sons, 1989), p. 86.

[122] Thomas, 'The Relationship of Parliament and the Courts', 27.

override the judges by enacting new legislation expressing its intention more clearly.[123]

C   Britain and the European Community

An important challenge to parliamentary sovereignty is posed by the decision of the House of Lords in *R* v. *Secretary of State for Transport, ex parte Factortame Ltd (No 2)* ('*Factortame*').[124] Some provisions of the Merchant Shipping Act 1988 (UK) ('the MS Act') were 'disapplied' by the House of Lords, because the European Court of Justice had held that they were inconsistent with laws of the European Community that were operative within the United Kingdom by virtue of s. 2(1) of the European Communities Act 1972 (UK) ('the EC Act'). Section 2(4) of the EC Act states that any other enactment, past or future, 'shall be construed and have effect subject to the foregoing provisions of this section'. The practical consequence of the decision is that British legislation inconsistent with applicable EC laws will be 'disapplied' unless Parliament either: (a) makes it quite clear, by express words or necessary implication, that it specifically intends the legislation to be applied notwithstanding the inconsistency; or if this is held to be insufficient to make the legislation applicable, (b) enacts legislation formally withdrawing Britain from the European Community.

Paul Craig suggests that (a) would be insufficient to save British legislation from disapplication, because the courts are likely to rule that as long as Britain remains in the Community it 'cannot simply pick and choose which [of the Community's] norms to accept'.[125] But I will assume that (a) would be sufficient. It is the business of the government and Parliament, not the courts, to decide whether or not Britain should abide by its treaty commitments. The duty of the courts is to accept their decision, even if they regard it as undesirable on policy grounds. As we will see, (a) is arguably consistent with parliamentary sovereignty, for reasons to do with either statutory interpretation or 'pure procedure or form'.[126] But if (b) were necessary, then the EC Act would have subjected Parliament's law-making power to a limitation of substance: although Parliament would

---

[123] Goldsworthy, *The Sovereignty of Parliament*, p. 252.

[124] [1991] 1 AC 603 (HL).

[125] See P. Craig, 'Report on the United Kingdom', in A.M. Slaughter, A.S. Sweet and J.H.H. Weiler (eds.), *The European Court and National Courts; Doctrine and Jurisprudence* (Oxford: Hart Publishing, 1998), 195 at p. 204.

[126] See Chapter 7, above.

still have power to withdraw Britain from the European Community, it would no longer have power to override applicable Community laws without withdrawing Britain from the Community. That could not be explained in terms of a mere requirement as to the form of British legislation. Parliament would, indeed, have abdicated part of its sovereignty, even if it retains the power to recover it.

It is easy for a proponent of parliamentary sovereignty to justify the decision in *Factortame* on policy grounds. The inconsistency of the MS Act with EC law was inadvertent: while preparing the draft legislation, the government was advised that it was consistent with EC law, and gave an assurance to that effect when the question was raised in Parliament.[127] Parliament unknowingly had two inconsistent intentions: an intention to enact the MS Act, and an intention not to legislate inconsistently with Community laws. As explained in Chapter 7, there are good reasons why Parliament might want to authorise the courts to correct this kind of mistake, by 'disapplying' legislation that inadvertently overrides or interferes with some important existing law or principle to which Parliament is committed.[128] The decision in *Factortame* is therefore perfectly consistent with parliamentary sovereignty as a theoretical principle. But whether and if so how the decision can be reconciled with the orthodox legal understanding of parliamentary sovereignty remains subject to debate.

The decision in *Factortame* to 'disapply' statutory provisions might be inconsistent with Dicey's understanding of parliamentary sovereignty, which is still frequently quoted and relied on.[129] Dicey defined Parliament's sovereignty in terms of two criteria, one positive and the other negative. The positive criterion is that Parliament has 'the right to make or unmake any law whatever'; the negative one is that 'no person or body is recognised by the law of England as having a right to override or set aside the legislation of Parliament'.[130] If the second criterion is essential to parliamentary sovereignty, then the decision in *Factortame* probably spells the

---

[127] G. Lindell, 'The Statutory Protection of Rights and Parliamentary Sovereignty: Guidance From the United Kingdom?' *Public Law Review* 17 (2006) 188 at 195; D. Nicol, *EC Membership and the Judicialization of British Politics* (Oxford: Oxford University Press, 2001), p. 182.

[128] See Chapter 7, Section III, above.

[129] E.g., A. Young, *Parliamentary Sovereignty and the Human Rights Act* (Oxford: Hart Publishing, 2008), ch. 1; A. Kavanagh, *Constitutional Review Under the UK Human Rights Act* (Cambridge: Cambridge University Press, 2009), ch. 11.

[130] A.V. Dicey, *An Introduction to the Study of the Law of the Constitution* (10th edn), E.C.S. Wade, (ed.) (London: Macmillan, 1959), p. 40.

end of the doctrine, since it apparently involved the court overriding or setting aside, at least partially, some provisions of the MS Act.

Dicey also adhered to the doctrine of implied repeal, which is often regarded as an essential concomitant of parliamentary sovereignty.[131] The doctrine of implied repeal maintains that, since a sovereign Parliament can no more be bound by its own previous laws than by any other legal constraint, it must be at liberty to ignore those laws whenever it passes a new one. Any earlier law that is inconsistent with a new law is necessarily repealed by implication (although 'disapplied' would be a better term than 'repealed'.[132]) The decision in *Factortame* is arguably inconsistent with this doctrine, given that provisions of the later MS Act were overridden or set aside ultimately due to the authority of the earlier EC Act.

It can be argued, on the other hand, that the decision in *Factortame* is not inconsistent with either Dicey's second criterion, or the doctrine of implied repeal. One possible argument is that the decision involved the interpretation of the MS Act in the light of the EC Act, rather than disapplication of the MS Act due to inconsistency with the EC Act. That interpretive argument will be considered shortly. But it is important to bear in mind that an alternative defence of the compatibility of the decision with parliamentary sovereignty is available. This is to deny that either Dicey's second criterion, or the doctrine of implied repeal, is truly essential to parliamentary sovereignty, when it is understood conceptually or theoretically. Reasons for this denial are provided in Chapter 7, which argues that a sovereign Parliament should have power to bind itself to comply with requirements as to pure procedure or form which, by definition, do

---

[131] As for implied repeal, see Kavanagh, *Constitutional Review*, pp. 315 and 297; Craig, 'Report on the United Kingdom', 210.

[132] This is for two reasons. First, the earlier statute is 'repealed' only insofar as it is inconsistent with the later one. Therefore, if inconsistency arises only in particular circumstances, the operation of the earlier law should be unaffected – and able to be applied 'distributively' – in all other circumstances. '[I]f the provisions are not wholly inconsistent, but may become inconsistent in their application to particular cases, then to that extent the provisions of the former Act are excepted or their operation is excluded with respect to cases falling within the provisions of the later Act': *Goodwin* v. *Phillips* (1908) 7 CLR 1 at 7 (emphasis added) (Griffith C.J.). Secondly, the inconsistent provisions of the earlier statute are not, as it were, expunged from the statute book: if the later statute were to be formally repealed, the earlier one should be fully revived. For useful discussion, see E.A. Driedger, *Construction of Statutes* (2nd edn) (Toronto: Butterworths, 1983), pp. 231–5. Implied repeal due to inconsistency of statutes therefore seems identical to the invalidity of state laws, when inconsistent with Commonwealth laws, under s. 109 of the Australian Constitution.

not destroy or diminish Parliament's substantive law-making power.[133] If this view is taken, then it can be conceded that the MS Act was disapplied due to inconsistency with the earlier EC Act, the latter being interpreted as imposing a requirement as to the form of future legislation – namely, that any breach of applicable EC law must be authorised by express words clearly communicating Parliament's intention to do so – rather than as imposing a limitation of substance. This could serve as a fall-back position if the interpretive argument, which will now be explored in depth, should fail.[134] But it should be recalled that the difference between a 'procedure or form' and an 'interpretive' reading of a statutory directive is sometimes hard to draw.[135]

(1)   Implied repeal and different subject-matters

Adam Tomkins has offered two arguments to show that the decision in *Factortame* is consistent with orthodox understandings of parliamentary sovereignty and implied repeal.[136] His first argument is that in disapplying provisions of the MS Act, the court was enforcing EC law, not English law, and therefore the doctrine of parliamentary sovereignty – which is part of English law, not EC law – was unaffected. But given that Tomkins also rightly insists that the court had jurisdiction to apply EC law only because the ECA required it to do so, it was ultimately English law that the court was enforcing. Tomkins claims that even after *Factortame*, it remains the case that 'under English law [in contrast to EC law] nobody may override or set aside a statute'.[137] Yet in one sense of 'under' this is wrong, because the court was enforcing EC law 'under' the EC Act.

Tomkins's second argument is, in part, that the principle of implied repeal was unaffected by the decision because there can only be an implied repeal if two Acts deal with the same subject-matter, and the EC Act and MS Act did not do so. He cites Maugham L.J. in *Ellen Street Estates* v. *Minister of Health*, who said that 'it is impossible for Parliament to enact that in a subsequent statute *dealing with the same subject-matter* there can be no implied repeal'.[138] A similar argument has been made by

[133] See Chapter 7, Section VII, above.
[134] I here disagree with the position I previously took in J. Goldsworthy, 'Parliamentary Sovereignty and Statutory Interpretation', in R. Bigwood (ed.), *The Statute; Making and Meaning*, 187 at p. 201.
[135] Chapter 7, Section IV, above.
[136] A. Tomkins, *Public Law* (Oxford: Clarendon Press, 2003), pp. 117–19.
[137] *Ibid.*, p. 118.
[138] [1934] 1 KB 590 at 597 (emphasis added), cited by Tomkins, *Public Law*, p. 107.

Nick Barber and Alison Young, who distinguish between two different 'models' of implied repeal: the 'conflict of norms model' and the 'conflict of subject-matter model'.[139] According to the former, implied repeal is triggered by any conflict between two statutory norms; according to the latter, which Barber and Young endorse, implied repeal is triggered only when the two norms 'stand upon the same subject-matter'.[140] Tomkins, applying the second model, concludes:

> The Merchant Shipping Act and the European Communities Act did not deal with the same subject-matter. The one concerned fishing and the other concerned the legal relationship between the United Kingdom and the European Community. It is frankly preposterous to suggest that there could have been an issue of implied repeal here: what provision of the Merchant Shipping Act could be said to have impliedly repealed what provision of the European Communities Act?[141]

Advocates of the first model of implied repeal would reply that the EC Act, together with relevant EC law, in effect required the court not to apply the relevant provisions of the MS Act, whereas the MS Act – simply by virtue of being an Act of Parliament – required the court to apply them. The MS Act's inconsistency with EC law would have been of no legal consequence had it not also amounted to inconsistency with the legal force conferred on EC law by the EC Act. The answer to Tomkins' question is therefore: 'the provisions of the MS Act that are inconsistent with applicable EC laws, are also inconsistent with – and therefore impliedly repeal – the provisions of the EC Act that confer binding force on those EC laws.' Can this conclusion be evaded by adopting the 'conflict of subject-matters model'?

Many objections can be made to that model. One is that it is novel. The leading texts on statutory interpretation do not mention it, and appear instead to regard any unavoidable inconsistency between statutes as sufficient to trigger implied repeal.[142] In *Ellen Street Estates*, Maugham L.J. was the only judge to treat the subject-matter of the laws as a significant consideration, although he did not assert that implied repeal can occur only when inconsistent laws deal with the same subject-matter.

---

[139] N.W. Barber and A.L. Young, 'The Rise of Prospective Henry VIII Clauses and Their Implications for Sovereignty' [2003] *Public Law* 112 at 115.

[140] *Ibid*. For their endorsement, see 116 and 126–7.

[141] Tomkins, *Public Law*, p. 119. See also E. Ellis, 'Supremacy of Parliament and the European Law' *Law Quarterly Review* 96 (1980) 511 at 513.

[142] See, e.g., F. Bennion, *Statutory Interpretation* (4th edn) (London: Butterworths, 2002), pp. 254–5.

Secondly, there does not seem to be any good reason why, if two statutes are inconsistent, the fact that they deal with different subject-matters should prevent implied repeal. Surely it is inconsistency between two laws that gives rise to the need for implied repeal, regardless of the subject-matters they are dealing with. If one provides that *a* must do *x*, and the other that *a* must not do *x*, the fact that they do so while dealing with different subject-matters cannot help. As the inconsistency makes it impossible for a court to fully apply both laws; one must therefore prevail, and Parliament's continuing sovereignty requires that it be the later one. Why should the earlier law prevail over the later law just because they deal with different subject-matters?

Thirdly, this suggests that, if a difference in their subject-matters is significant, this must be because it indicates that the two laws are not, despite appearances, inconsistent.[143] It is clear that although two laws dealing with quite different subject-matters can conflict, a difference in their subject-matters may suggest that the laws should be interpreted so that both can operate, side by side, confined to their respective subject-matters. It is well established that a later, general law can be interpreted as impliedly qualified, so that it does not interfere with an earlier, more specific law. If Parliament in the earlier statute carefully settled a specific matter, and in the later statute provided for more general matters without any clear indication (other than arguably careless language) of having intended to disturb the earlier settlement, the later statute can be 'read down' by finding it subject to an implied qualification making it inapplicable to the specific matter. The maxim *generalia specialibus non derogant* ('general things do not derogate from special things') is generally invoked in such cases.

By much the same reasoning, a later law dealing with one subject-matter might be interpreted as impliedly qualified, so that it does not interfere with an earlier law dealing with a different subject-matter, even if the two laws would be inconsistent if construed literally. Indeed, Maugham L.J. may have mentioned subject-matters because he had in mind cases involving general and specific laws.[144] In a similar observation, Griffith C.J. of the Australian High Court clearly intended to distinguish such cases: '... where the provisions of a *particular* Act of Parliament *dealing with a particular subject matter* are wholly inconsistent with the provisions of an earlier Act dealing with the same subject matter, then the earlier Act is

---

[143] See also the full discussion in Young, *Parliamentary Sovereignty and the Human Rights Act*, pp. 45–9.
[144] Barber and Young acknowledge this in 'The Rise of Prospective Henry VIII Clauses', 116.

repealed by implication'.[145] This observation does not imply that no inconsistency between two laws dealing with different subject-matters can ever
trigger implied repeal; it implies merely that an apparent inconsistency
between a later law dealing with a general subject-matter and an earlier
law dealing with a particular subject-matter may not trigger an implied
repeal. If this is right, then the distinction between the 'conflict of norm
model' and the 'conflict of subject-matters model' of implied repeal is fallacious. Implied repeal is triggered by inconsistency between norms, but
if two norms deal with quite different subject-matters, it *may* be possible
to interpret them so as to dispel a *prima facie* inconsistency. Australian
cases dealing with alleged inconsistencies between state and federal laws
provide many examples.[146] On the other hand, if one law provides that *a*
must do *x*, and the other that *a* must not do *x*, the fact that they do so while
dealing with different subject-matters cannot help. This is a consequence
of the fact that laws dealing with different subject-matters can contradict
one another, whether or not Parliament intended or even adverted to the
contradiction.

(2)   Statutory interpretation, legislative intention,
        and legislative mistakes

The usual way to avoid implied repeal is to remove the appearance of
inconsistency between two statutes through interpretation. The question then becomes: is it possible in a case such as *Factortame* to interpret
the two statutes so that they can be confined to their respective subject-
matters, thereby avoiding inconsistency? One difficulty is that, when a
later, general statute is 'read down' to accommodate an earlier, special law,
the operation of the later, general law is otherwise unaffected. As Lord
Selborne put it, implied repeal can be avoided 'where there are general
words in a later Act *capable of reasonable and sensible application* without
extending them to subjects specially dealt with by earlier legislation ...'[147]
This is relatively easy if any impact on the earlier legislation would be, at
most, collateral damage, because the principal, intended operation of the
later legislation lies elsewhere. But what if exempting an earlier law from
the scope of the later law would render the latter incapable of a reasonable and sensible application – in other words, if the exemption cannot be
made without in effect nullifying the later law? The courts seem to have

---

[145] *Goodwin* v. *Phillips* (1908) 7 CLR 1 at 7 (emphasis added).
[146] See S. Joseph and M. Castan, *Federal Constitutional Law, A Contemporary View* (2nd
edn) (Sydney: Lawbook Co., 2006), pp. 226–41.
[147] *Seward* v. *The Vera Cruz* (1884) 10 App Cas 59 at 68.

assumed that a later law can be qualified, without impugning the sovereignty of Parliament. But can a later law be nullified?

One of the questions raised by *Factortame* is whether complete disapplication of a statutory provision, or even the statute as a whole, could in some cases follow from interpretation of that very statute. A lucid argument to this effect has been made by Geoffrey Lindell. He points out that Parliament might intend that a particular statute should come into operation only if a certain condition is satisfied (such as that the statute does not conflict with EC law); that a requirement to that effect would be effective if included in the statute itself; and that it should also be effective if enacted in a previous statute, of general and ambulatory effect, purporting to govern the operation of future legislation. Such a general and ambulatory requirement would operate as a 'standing or continuing expression of the notional will and intent of Parliament', obviating the need to include the requirement in every subsequent statute.[148] Parliament should then be deemed to adhere to that standing intention unless and until it is clearly repudiated.

Lindell's argument seems plausible to this point. But does it follow that the disapplication of a statute for non-compliance with a precondition laid down in a previous statute can plausibly be attributed to the interpretation of the disapplied statute itself? Lindell cites Lord Bridge's statement that the relevant provisions of s. 2 of the ECA had 'precisely the same effect as if a section were incorporated' in the MS Act.[149] But even if preconditions imposed by an earlier statute have much the same effect 'as if' they were expressly incorporated in the later, disapplied statute, the fact remains that they were not so incorporated. It could just as plausibly be said that a declaration in an earlier statute that all later statutes inconsistent with it are invalid, has the same effect 'as if' it were incorporated in every later statute.[150] Disapplication – which is a kind of invalidation – cannot be converted into interpretation by means of a fiction.

---

[148] Lindell, 'The Statutory Protection of Rights and Parliamentary Sovereignty', esp. at 194–5 (for an earlier version, see G. Lindell, 'Invalidity, Disapplication and the Construction of Acts of Parliament: Their Relationship With Parliamentary Sovereignty in the Light of the European Communities Act and the Human Rights Act' (1999) 2 *Cambridge Yearbook of European Legal Studies* 399, esp. at 405–7). For a similar argument, see T.C. Hartley, *Constitutional Problems of the European Union* (Oxford: Hart Publishing, 1999), pp. 172–3.

[149] Lindell, 'The Statutory Protection of Rights and Parliamentary Sovereignty', quoting *R v. Secretary of State for Transport, ex parte Factortame Ltd* [1990] 2 AC 85 at 140.

[150] Sir William Wade, 'Sovereignty – Revolution or Evolution?' *Law Quarterly Review* 112 (1996) 568 at 570.

Lindell also draws an analogy with the interpretation of a later statute according to the provisions of an Interpretation Act, which Lord Dunedin once said are 'so to speak, written into every statute'.[151] But interpreting statutory provisions according to guidelines in an Interpretation Act seems qualitatively different from refusing to apply them due to non-compliance with preconditions imposed by an earlier Act. Parliamentary counsel are presumed to be familiar with an Interpretation Act, and to craft statutory language with its guidelines in mind. Since counsel act as Parliament's assistants in drafting legislation, it is plausible to attribute to Parliament itself an expectation that its legislation be interpreted accordingly. An Interpretation Act is a bit like a code-book, which the intended recipient of a coded message uses to de-code the message only because the sender of the message is known to have used it in coding the message. It is less plausible to attribute to Parliament, when it enacts a statute, an intention that the statute be disapplied. In the case of the MS Act that was partially disapplied in *Factortame*, the government had apparently been advised that it was consistent with EC law.[152] That advice was conveyed to Parliament, when the government was asked whether there was a risk of the draft legislation being challenged in the European Court.[153] Parliament presumably acted on the mistaken assumption that there was no obstacle to the legislation coming into effective operation. It did not intend to enact legislation inconsistent with EC law. But it does not follow just from this that Parliament, when it enacted the MS Act, intended that it should be disapplied if it were found to be inconsistent with EC law. It appears that Parliament failed to entertain that possibility, or to contemplate its consequences.

One way of understanding, or reinforcing, Lindell's argument is to rely on the notion of implicit, background assumptions, which was discussed in Chapter 9.[154] Even if Parliament lacked a positive intention that its Act should be disapplied if shown to be inconsistent with EC law, it might be reasonable to attribute to it an implicit, background assumption to that effect, amounting to a standing commitment. Since (we are assuming at present) the question remains one of interpretation, rather than validity, courts must always remain open to the possibility that, in enacting a later statute, Parliament has overridden that standing

---

[151] Lindell, 'The Statutory Protection of Rights and Parliamentary Sovereignty', 195, quoting Lord Dunedin in *Re Silver Brothers Ltd* [1932] AC 514 at 523.

[152] Lindell, 'The Statutory Protection of Rights and Parliamentary Sovereignty', 195.

[153] Nicol, *EC Membership and the Judicialization of British Politics*, p. 182.

[154] Chapter 9, Section II, Part A(2), above.

commitment, at least to the extent necessary to enact the statute. In the absence of an express statement to that effect, it may be reasonable to conclude that it has not done so but, instead, has made a mistake. It is certainly reasonable where matters of such fundamental importance as Britain's membership of the European Community is concerned. Since violation of Community law by a member state could have extremely serious consequences, there are weighty reasons why Parliament might want British courts not to apply legislation that is inadvertently inconsistent with Community law – weighty reasons, in other words, why Parliament might want to authorise the courts to correct its mistakes in that regard.[155] In principle, there is no diminution of legislative sovereignty if they do so.

The court is required to decide whether or not the later Act evinces an intention to override what an earlier Act declared to be a standing commitment, concerning a matter whose fundamental importance suggests that it is very unlikely to be overridden. This is a matter of interpreting the later Act. Does it or does it not evince the unlikely intention that is required for its provisions to be operative? If not, it may embody or presuppose two incompatible intentions: an intention to enact provisions that the legislature did not understand to be inconsistent with European law, and an ongoing, implicit, standing commitment that provisions inconsistent with European law not be applied. One of these intentions must give way to the other, and a court should give priority to that which Parliament itself would most likely regard as paramount.

On the other hand, the situation in *Factortame* arguably should be distinguished from the usual 'background assumption' cases. In those cases, it can reasonably be concluded that the legislation enacted, and Parliament's intention in enacting it, should be understood in the light of background assumptions that did not need to be spelled out. Parliament did not make a mistake, because it did not need to spell out obvious background assumptions. The legislation is subject to a genuinely implied or presupposed qualification. By contrast, in enacting the legislation considered in *Factortame*, Parliament did, in effect, make a mistake.

---

[155] Admittedly, this may not have been Parliament's intention when it enacted the European Communities Act. A recent book that has investigated Parliament's original intention concludes that most members of Parliament were ignorant or confused about the nature and effect of the Act: see Nicol, *EC Membership and the Judicialization of British Politics*. If so, Parliament may not have had any coherent intention concerning the meaning of s. 2(4) of that Act. But that possibility is an inescapable hazard of the interpretive enterprise.

To return to another theme in Chapter 7, there is an alternative way of explaining an implied qualification when Parliament has made a mistake in the design of a statute. We might have to concede that there was no implicit assumption; that the legislature erred by failing to anticipate and expressly provide for some circumstance or subsequent development; and that creative interpretation is needed to avoid a result that would be inconsistent with the purpose of the statute, or with other important objectives or principles that it is reasonable to presume that the legislature would not have wanted to damage. In some cases, the court must repair or rectify the statute, by undertaking some 'embroidery' to supplement or qualify its express provisions, in order to correct a legislative oversight. As previously observed, that may be why lawyers use the peculiar terminology of qualifications being 'implied into' or 'read into' legal instruments.[156] Alison Young appears to suggest that *Factortame* is best understood in this way, as involving the Court in effect 'reading into' every future Act, including the MS Act, words that require its provisions to take effect subject to applicable EC laws.[157] (Although it is not clear whether she regards this exercise as giving effect to an implicit assumption of the MS Act, or as rectifying it.)

In many cases of rectification, Parliament either overlooked the existence of an earlier law or legal principle, or erroneously believed that the later law was consistent with it. The implied qualification gives effect to what Parliament presumably would have intended had the inconsistency with the earlier law or principle been brought to its attention. The 'implied' qualification that is 'read into' the later law really involves partial disapplication of it, to avoid a result that Parliament presumably would not have wanted.[158] This is a well established judicial technique, although it has not been used to completely disapply statutory provisions. The truly innovative consequence of the decision in *Factortame* may be the extension of this technique to complete disapplication.

Is the decision in *Factortame* best justified by the first, the second, or neither of these two explanations? According to Danny Nicol's study of the origins of the EC Act in 1972, members of Parliament (and therefore presumably Parliament itself) at that time had no clear intention as to

---

[156] Chapter 9, Section II, Part B, above.
[157] Young, *Parliamentary Sovereignty and the Human Rights Act*, pp. 44, 51, 55 and 62. On the other hand, a passage towards the bottom of p. 56 is more difficult to reconcile with continuing parliamentary sovereignty.
[158] See Chapter 9, Section II, Part B, above.

the constitutional consequences of that Act.[159] Yet we know that by the time the MS Act was passed, the government and Parliament were aware of the importance of ensuring that statutory provisions did not breach relevant EC laws. The government assured Parliament that the MS Act did not do so.[160] The government's legal advice, on which that assurance was based, turned out to be wrong. Does it follow that Parliament made a mistake, which had to be corrected by the judges 'reading into' the MS Act a qualification that was not (really) already there, although one that was consistent with Parliament's standing commitments? Or is the better interpretation of the MS Act that Parliament acted on the basis of a genuine presupposition or background assumption that EC law should not be breached, which qualified the operation of that Act?

To adopt either the first or the second explanations assumes that it can make sense to think of Parliament as having standing commitments that may not be consciously adverted to when a law is passed. For those who would dismiss that assumption as a 'fairy tale' used to preserve 'the formal veneer of legal sovereignty',[161] there is, as I previously foreshadowed, a third explanation that is also consistent with parliamentary sovereignty. This is that Parliament in the EC Act in effect subjected itself to a mild requirement as to the form of future legislation, requiring that express words be used to override applicable EC laws. This requirement does not prevent Parliament from exercising at any time its substantive power to override EC laws, but does entail that Parliament must use express words to do so, or else provisions inconsistent with those laws will be inoperative.[162]

The key difference between the third explanation, and both the first and second ones, is this: when Parliament is bound by a requirement as to form, it is bound by an earlier law regardless of whatever its later intentions may have been; on the other hand, genuine interpretation of a later law depends on a bona fide attempt to determine Parliament's intentions and standing commitments at the time it was enacted, which prevail regardless of the procedure or form that Parliament adopted.[163]

---

[159] Nicol, *EC Membership and the Judicialisation of British Politics.*

[160] Lindell, 'The Statutory Protection of Rights and Parliamentary Sovereignty', 195; Nicol, *EC Membership and the Judicialization of British Politics*, p. 182.

[161] P. Craig, 'Britain in the European Union', in J. Jowell and D. Oliver (eds.), *The Changing Constitution* (6th edn) (Oxford: Oxford University Press, 2007), 84 at p. 97.

[162] See text to n. 133, above, and Chapter 7, above.

[163] See Chapter 7, Section IV, above.

D   Judicial review under the Human Rights Act

Some critics of parliamentary sovereignty assert that it cannot be reconciled with the expanded judicial role under the Human Rights Act 1998 ('the HRA').[164] Several judges in *Jackson v. Attorney-General* expressed similar, although rather cryptic, opinions.[165] Like most commentators, I fail to see the difficulty. Parliament has enacted the HRA, and has the power to repeal it at any time. The Act gives the courts considerable latitude in interpreting statutes, but no power to disapply or invalidate them. Aileen Kavanagh provides the most sustained and powerful response to my view, which she concedes is 'widely believed, amongst both judiciary and academic commentators'. She argues that the HRA, as judicially interpreted and applied, has rendered the doctrine of parliamentary sovereignty redundant.[166]

Some of Kavanagh's arguments depend on treating Dicey's definition of parliamentary sovereignty as axiomatic.[167] For example, she holds that the HRA is a 'constitutional statute' that is partially 'entrenched' because the rights it protects are immune from the doctrine of implied repeal.[168] Alison Young has forcefully argued, to the contrary, that s. 3(1) of the HRA is not immune from implied repeal. A later Act that is inconsistent with rights protected by the HRA is not inconsistent with the courts' interpretive duty under s. 3(1), and so the question of implied repeal simply does not arise; however, a later Act that imposed a contradictory interpretive duty would impliedly repeal s. 3(1).[169] I think Young is right, but the question is of less importance if, as I have argued, parliamentary sovereignty is best regarded as not entailing the doctrine of implied repeal.[170]

Kavanagh also relies partly on Parliament being subject to 'legal limits' that arise from Britain's membership of the European Union.[171] But as she acknowledges, these international legal obligations are not part of

---

[164] Joseph, 'Parliament, the Courts, and the Collaborative Enterprise', 322; Elias, 'Sovereignty in the 21st Century', 157.

[165] *Jackson v. Attorney-General* [2005] UKHL 56 at [102] per Lord Steyn, [104]–[107] per Lord Hope, and [159] per Baroness Hale. See the comments of Tom Mullen, 'Reflections on *Jackson v. Attorney-General*: questioning sovereignty' *Legal Studies* 27 (2007) 1 at 12–13.

[166] Kavanagh, *Constitutional Review*, esp. ch. 11.

[167] *Ibid.*, p. 315.   [168] *Ibid.*, pp. 315 and 317.

[169] Young, *Parliamentary Sovereignty and the Human Rights Act*, p. 53.

[170] See Chapter 7, Section III, above.

[171] Kavanagh, *Constitutional Review*, pp. 317 and 321.

Britain's domestic legal system.[172] They are therefore irrelevant to the scope of Parliament's law-making authority as defined within that system.

In addition, she emphasises the HRA's 'legal pervasiveness and its interpretive robustness', especially the practical equivalence of the very strong methods of 'interpretation' authorised by s. 3 of the Act, and partial disapplication or invalidation.[173] She claims that the courts have construed s. 3 as authorising them to 'rectify' legislation by re-writing it, if its operation would otherwise sometimes violate protected rights. This, she suggests, is tantamount to partial disapplication of the legislation: disapplication to the extent that its operation would otherwise violate those rights. I argued in the preceding section that disapplication, when it is authorised by and (as far as legal constraints are concerned) can easily be avoided by Parliament itself, is not inconsistent with parliamentary sovereignty, even if it is inconsistent with the second of Dicey's definitional criteria.[174]

Kavanagh places more emphasis on the power in s. 4 to issue declarations of incompatibility between a statute and protected rights. She maintains that, in practice, this power is (or is becoming) 'similar to a judicial strike-down power', and therefore imposes substantial limits on Parliament's law-making functions.[175] As she sees it, a practice or convention is developing that legislation will always be changed in response to such declarations, and for a good reason: if the elected branches of government were to ignore a declaration, they would threaten the comity between them and the judiciary, and 'challenge the judges' constitutional role as the body empowered to pronounce authoritatively on the requirements of the law, including rights provisions'.[176] Therefore, a declaration is and should be 'effectively final in almost all cases'.[177]

This robustly 'constitutionalist' understanding of the moral and political obligations of the elected branches of government when handed a declaration of incompatibility is highly debatable. One might wonder why, if they should always feel obligated to accept and act on such declarations, which are therefore 'similar' to formal invalidation, the HRA did not take the more straight-forward route of giving the judges the power to invalidate. Parliament's very deliberate decision not to do so surely

---

[172] *Ibid.*, p. 321.   [173] *Ibid.*, p. 318–19.   [174] See also Chapter 7, Section III, above.

[175] Kavanagh, *Constitutional Review*, p. 287; see also pp. 285 and 289. Kavanagh says that the 'salient difference' between these powers concerns the plight of the individual litigant: *ibid.*, pp. 287 and 290.

[176] *Ibid.*, pp. 286–7.   [177] *Ibid.*, p. 288.

implies that it anticipated that it might, in some cases, be legitimate and even desirable for the elected branches to act on their own opinions, rather than those of the judiciary, as to the content of contested rights or the balance between them and other competing, weighty considerations. In a healthy democratic society, cases of clear injustice are rare; in the vast majority of cases, whether or not the law violates some basic right is open to reasonable arguments on both sides. The whole point of having a democracy is that in these debatable cases, the opinion of the majority rather than of an unelected elite should ultimately prevail. As Jeremy Waldron has argued:

> It is puzzling that some philosophers and jurists treat rights as though they were somehow beyond disagreement, as though they could be dealt with on a different plane – on the solemn plane of constitutional principle far above the hurly-burly of legislatures and political controversy and dis-reputable procedures like voting.[178]

Rights should not be treated as truths that are objectively knowable only to the supposedly apolitical legal mind, by which democratic decision-making can be dispassionately judged. Of course the majority is not always right – but then again, it is not always wrong, and the nub of the problem is that there is no impartial, objective method capable of authori-tatively determining when it is right or wrong. This does not mean that judges have no role to play. As argued in Chapter 8, allowing aggrieved litigants to seek non-binding judicial opinions about the impact of legis-lation on their rights can add a further check or balance to the political system, without diminishing its fundamentally democratic character. It permits an appeal from the rough-and-tumble of politics to a 'forum of principle', subject to a right of final appeal back to a consequently more informed and conscientious legislature. But,

> ... [i]n a healthy democracy, responsible legislators would feel free to override actual or anticipated judicial interpretations of constitutional rights that, after careful and conscientious reflection, they do not agree with. That, after all, is a power exercised by the judges themselves, when they overrule previous judicial decisions that they have come to regard as erroneous. They do not treat their predecessors, or expect their successors to treat them, as infallible oracles.[179]

---

[178] J. Waldron, *Law and Disagreement* (Oxford: Oxford University Press, 1999), p. 12.
[179] Chapter 8, at p. 219–20, above. For a more extended defence of this idea, see D. Nicol, 'The Human Rights Act and the Politicians' *Legal Studies* 24 (2004) 451, esp. at 454–5.

This view is implicit in the popular 'dialogue' model of the relationship between the courts and the elected branches of government in decision-making about rights, which Kavanagh opposes.[180]

None of this diminishes Kavanagh's main point, which is that in practice declarations of incompatibility may come to have similar consequences to judicial invalidation. She also relies on the likelihood that the HRA is already, or will soon become, politically impossible for Parliament to repeal.[181] All of this leads her to conclude that from a practical (as opposed to a 'formal') perspective, Parliament has abandoned its sovereignty. 'Parliament has the last word only in the most formal sense.'[182] She shares Mark Elliott's concern that a 'gap' has opened up between what he calls the 'theory' of Parliament's sovereign authority to legislate, and the 'reality' of its more limited political power to do so.[183] Elliott urges that this gap be closed.[184]

But it is far from clear that any such gap exists. It has always been part of the justification of sovereign power, whether monarchical or parliamentary, that the repository of the power is subject to powerful extra-legal constraints, both 'internal' (moral) and 'external' (political), which make many theoretically possible abuses of the power virtually impossible in reality. There have always been many logically possible laws that, for moral and political reasons, Parliament would never enact, the hypothetical 'blue-eyed babies' statute being one of them. Yet it has seldom been thought to follow that Parliament lacked legal authority to enact such laws. Far from being a problem for the theory of sovereignty, this 'gap' between the absence of legal constraints, and the presence of moral and political ones, is essential to its acceptability. We would not want an institution to possess sovereign power if there were no such gap – if there were no effective moral or political constraints on its exercise of power. If the gap is expanded by additional, self-imposed constraints, such as the HRA, then (many would think) so much the better.

---

[180] Kavanagh, *Constitutional Review*, pp. 128–32 and 408–11. For a defence of the dialogue model see Young, *Parliamentary Sovereignty and the Human Rights Act*, pp. 118–30.

[181] *Ibid.*, pp. 315–16.   [182] *Ibid.*, p. 324.

[183] *Ibid.*, pp. 316 and 325. See also Joseph, *Constitutional and Administrative Law in New Zealand* (3rd edn), p. 543: 'Here, theory and reality disconnect: Parliament has absolute power but some laws it cannot enact.'

[184] M. Elliott, 'Parliamentary Sovereignty and the New Constitutional Order: Legislative Freedom, Political Reality, and Convention' *Legal Studies* 22 (2002) 340; M. Elliott, 'United Kingdom: Parliamentary Sovereignty Under Pressure' *International Journal of Constitutional Law* 2 (2004) 545, *passim*.

There is no inconsistency here between 'theory' and 'reality'.[185] Parliament is legally sovereign both in theory and reality, and it is subject to moral and political constraints both in theory and reality. When Elliott complains that 'the doctrine of parliamentary sovereignty misstates the scope of the authority which, in practical political terms, Parliament possesses', he misunderstands the doctrine's purpose.[186] Its purpose is merely to make it clear that no other official or institution has legal authority to invalidate or override statutes. It does not purport to describe the scope of Parliament's likely desire and ability to enact statutes as a matter of practical politics. It makes perfectly good sense to say both: (1) that there are many things that a majority in Parliament either would never want to do, or for political reasons could never do, and (2) that it is not the courts' business to attempt to list these things, or to add the threat of judicial invalidation to the moral and political imperatives that prevent Parliament from doing them. There are good reasons for leaving the enforcement of moral and political constraints to political actors, rather than transforming them into legal constraints; for a start, this leaves room open for negotiation, compromise, and the continuing evolution of political practice and constitutional convention. If the 'gap' between Parliament's moral and political authority, and its legal authority, were closed, the courts would be authorised to decide which moral and political constraints should be judicially enforceable: in effect, this would be a blank cheque to rewrite the constitution. We would then lose a genuine and crucial 'gap', between Parliament submitting itself to political fetters, and its being subject to legal fetters imposed by judges in the name of a mythical 'common law constitution'. Tellingly, after mentioning Britain's membership of the EU, Kavanagh observes that 'there are now signs that, post-HRA, the courts are prepared openly to announce *their* ability to limit parliamentary sovereignty'.[187] Since any limits to Parliament's law-making authority imposed by the ECA and the HRA are self-imposed, it hardly follows that the courts are entitled to add further limits. The danger of arguments such as Elliot's and Kavanagh's is that they might suggest otherwise.

It is true that the practical significance of the doctrine of parliamentary sovereignty diminishes as Parliament's practical (moral and political) ability to exercise its sovereignty is reduced. As Parliament is increasingly hemmed in by practical constraints, whether or not they are self-imposed,

---

[185] Elliot, 'Parliamentary Sovereignty and the New Constitutional Order', 353.
[186] *Ibid.*, 342.   [187] Kavanagh, *Constitutional Review*, pp. 326–7 (emphasis added).

the area in which it has a practically unfettered law-making discretion shrinks. But even if it is true that the practical significance of the legal doctrine of parliamentary sovereignty has substantially diminished, and is likely to continue to diminish, this does not expose any gap between 'theory' and 'reality'.

Kavanagh's case against parliamentary sovereignty appears to rest ultimately on a version of common law constitutionalism. There is a tension in her analysis between claims that the HRA renders parliamentary sovereignty redundant, and claims that it does not give the courts distinctively new methods of interpretation, but merely 'expands' or 'enhances', 'in significant but subtle ways', methods they have traditionally used.[188] For example, she says that judges 'have always possessed (and exercised) the power to rectify statutory language, if to do so would remove an injustice or violate a fundamental constitutional principle'; therefore, 'if there are legitimacy problems about interpretation under the HRA, they apply *with equal force* to pre-HRA adjudication'.[189] She frequently claims that the traditional presumptions of statutory interpretation amount in reality to the imposition by the common law of a form of 'constitutional entrenchment' that protects fundamental rights.[190] '[T]he courts possess an inherent common law jurisdiction to protect and enforce constitutional rights, including the ability to ensure that legislation enacted by Parliament conforms to them.'[191] Admittedly, the HRA adds to the pre-existing judicial armoury the power to issue declarations of incompatibility. But Kavanagh says that 'the most profound influence of the HRA may well be in the impetus it gives the judiciary to be more explicit and more assertive about the nature of their constitutional role'.[192]

On this view, it is the court's traditional common law jurisdiction that makes parliamentary sovereignty redundant. The HRA merely reduces the courts' previous tendency 'to underplay the substantive nature' of that jurisdiction by 'maintaining fairytales'.[193] This claim warrants more careful examination.

E The common law protection of rights

For centuries, the courts have been guided by a presumption that Parliament does not intend to interfere with generally accepted principles

---

[188] For statements of the former kind, see *ibid.*, ch. 11; for claims of the latter kind, see pp. 114–16, 275–6, 280 and 309.

[189] *Ibid.*, p. 115 (emphasis added). See also p. 275.

[190] E.g., *ibid.*, pp. 306, 328 and 280.   [191] *Ibid.*, p. 336.   [192] *Ibid.*, p. 415.   [193] *Ibid.*

of morality, or with fundamental common law rights and freedoms, a presumption defeasible by express words or necessary implication. The traditional justification for these presumptions was entirely consistent with parliamentary sovereignty. Dicey himself acknowledged that the courts, when interpreting statutes, 'presume that Parliament did not intend to violate the ordinary rules of morality, or the principles of international law'.[194] As the High Court of Australia explained: 'The rationale for all such rules lies in the assumption that the legislature would, if it intended to achieve the particular effect, have made its intention in that regard unambiguously clear.'[195] Even Kavanagh, who is no friend of parliamentary sovereignty, concedes that:

> the orthodox justification for applying the statutory presumptions is the fact that, in general, legislators know, or can be taken to know, that their legislation will be interpreted and understood in light of them. They are part of the known background against which Parliament legislates and of which it should be aware.[196]

This can be put in terms of giving effect to Parliament's 'standing commitments': it is deemed to have a standing commitment to preserve basic common law rights and freedoms, which it should not be taken to have repudiated absent very clear evidence such as express words or necessary implication.[197]

Parliament's standing commitments need not be confined to those implicit in past practice; it can make them explicit, and even subscribe to new ones. The British Parliament did so when it enacted the HRA, which requires courts to interpret legislation, whenever possible, as compatible with enumerated rights. That Act could have been interpreted as going no further, apart from protecting a larger number of rights, than orthodox presumptions or canons of interpretation that protect common law rights from anything less than express or necessarily implied alteration or interference. In fact, it has been interpreted as giving British courts much greater power to rewrite legislation in order to ensure compliance with the protected rights.

Apart from this, the most obvious difference between common law and statutory presumptions is that the latter are created by Parliament

---

[194] A.V. Dicey, *An Introduction to the Study of the Law of the Constitution* (10th edn), pp. 62–3.
[195] *Bropho* v. *Western Australia* (1990) 93 ALR 207 at 215.
[196] Kavanagh, *Constitutional Review*, p. 99.
[197] See Chapter 7, Section III, above.

itself, and amount to self-avowed standing commitments. A common law presumption amounts to an attribution by the courts of a standing commitment to Parliament, and whether the attribution is accurate may be questionable. Traditional, well-established presumptions, well known to parliamentary counsel, are no longer questionable. If I know that others attribute standing commitments to me, and do nothing to disavow them, I confirm the attribution and dispel any previous doubts. But new presumptions might also be recognised by the courts. As the Australian High Court explained, if what was previously accepted as a fundamental principle or right ceases to be so regarded, the presumption that the legislature would not have intended to infringe it is necessarily undermined.[198] If so, the opposite process must also be possible. According to Sir Anthony Mason, a recent Australian case 'indicates that the courts will protect rights and interests other than those hitherto protected by the common law'.[199] The presumptions of statutory construction protect whatever rights are 'generally accepted' today as fundamental, even if they were not previously recognised by the common law.[200] It should be added, however, that if the orthodox justification of the presumptions is taken seriously, the relevant question is what rights were generally accepted as fundamental when the statute in question was enacted.

There is a widespread modern tendency to dismiss the traditional justification of the presumptions as an artificial rationalisation or polite fiction. Sir Anthony Mason has referred to the 'evident fictional character' of strong presumptive rules, fictional because 'they do not reflect actual legislative intent'.[201] It has been claimed that the common law presumptions 'no longer have anything to do with the intent of the Legislature; they are a means of controlling that intent'.[202] Kavanagh asserts that '[t]he law reports are full of (pre-HRA) cases where the courts ... refused

---

[198] *Bropho* v. *Western Australia* (1990) 93 ALR 207 at 215 per Mason C.J., Deane, Dawson, Toohey, Gaudron and McHugh J.J.

[199] Sir Anthony Mason, 'Courts, Constitutions and Fundamental Rights' in R. Rawlings (ed.), *Law, Society and Economy* (Oxford: Clarendon Press, 1997), 273 at p. 281.

[200] *Ibid.*, 281–2.

[201] Sir Anthony Mason, 'Commentary' *Australian Journal of Legal Philosophy* 27 (2002) 172 at 175. Not all judges agree, of course. Former Chief Justice Murray Gleeson stated that the presumption that Parliament does not intend to overturn fundamental freedoms 'is not based upon a fiction': The Hon Murray Gleeson, 'Legality – Spirit and Principle', *The Second Magna Carta Lecture*, NSW Parliament House, Sydney, 20 November 2003, at p. 11 (www.highcourt.gov.au/speeches/cj/cj_20nov.html).

[202] L. Tremblay, 'Section 7 of the Charter: Substantive Due Process' (1984) 18 *UBC Law Review* 201 at 242. See also Kavangh, *Constitutional Review*, p. 335.

to follow the clear implications of statutory terms where it would deny a fundamental right or cause clear injustice';[203] the 'presumed intentions' to which judges appeal are often independent of or even contrary to the legislators' actual historical intentions;[204] and in cases such as *Anisminic*, 'even clearly expressed enacted intention has been insufficient to rebut the application of certain presumptions'.[205] In reality, it is said, the courts have stubbornly protected the fundamental values of the common law from legislative interference, while acknowledging political constraints on their ability to do so.[206] John Finnis puts it this way:

> Constitutional principles and rights prevail over ordinary norms of statutory interpretation; the presumption that statutes do not overturn these rights and principles qualifies the ordinary subordination of our common law to parliamentary authority.[207]

This line of thinking leads to the conclusion that the presumptions 'can be viewed as the courts' efforts to provide, in effect, a common law bill of rights – a protection for the civil liberties of the individual against invasion by the state'.[208] As Sir Rupert Cross put it, the presumptions operate 'at a higher level as expressions of fundamental principles governing civil liberties and the relations between Parliament, the executive and the courts. They operate here as constitutional principles ...'[209] In the United States, presumptions used in statutory interpretation have been called 'clear statement rules', and their creation described as 'quasi-constitutional lawmaking'.[210] In Britain, an analogy has been drawn between the effect of interpretive presumptions, and that of 'manner and form' provisions that require express words or even a particular verbal formula in order to amend or repeal legislation of a certain kind.[211] Sir John Laws

---

[203] Kavanagh, *Constitutional Review*, p. 115.

[204] *Ibid.*, p. 98.

[205] *Ibid.*, pp. 98, n. 39 and 105.

[206] J. Burrows, 'The Changing Approach to the Interpretation of Statutes' *Victoria University of Wellington Law Review* 33 (2002) 981 at 982–3, 990–5 and 997–8.

[207] J. Finnis, 'Nationality, Alienage and Constitutional Principle' *Law Quarterly Review* 123 (2007) 417 at 417.

[208] D.C. Pearce and R.S. Geddes, *Statutory Interpretation in Australia* (5th edn) (Sydney: Butterworths, 2001), p. 131. Kavanagh cites many other expressions of this view: Kavanagh, *Constitutional Review*, pp. 97–9.

[209] J. Bell and G. Engle, *Statutory Interpretation* (3rd edn) (London: Butterworths, 1995), 166.

[210] See W. Eskridge and P. Frickey, 'Quasi-Constitutional Law: Clear Statement Rules as Constitutional Lawmaking' *Vanderbilt Law Review* 45 (1992) 593.

[211] For example, T.R.S. Allan, 'Legislative Supremacy and the Rule of Law: Democracy and Constitutionalism' *Cambridge Law Journal* 44 (1985) 111.

is typically forthright in claiming that 'we *already have* constitutional guarantees: guarantees given by the common law, entrenched by a rule that they may only be overridden by statutory measures leaving no room for doubt as to the legislative intention to effect that result'.[212] He defines 'constitutional guarantee' as 'a legal measure which … protects basic or fundamental rights against intrusion or subversion by the State', and 'that is in some sense entrenched – that is, it is proof against being changed, or abrogated, by those legal mechanisms which are deployed to change ordinary laws'.[213] He relishes 'a great irony. The common law does what on conventional doctrine Parliament cannot do: provide for an entrenched constitutional measure.'[214]

Some of these ideas found expression in the famous passage in *Ex parte Simms*, in which Lord Hoffmann said:

> Parliament can, if it chooses, legislate contrary to fundamental principles of human rights … But the principle of legality means that Parliament must squarely confront what it is doing and accept the political cost. Fundamental rights cannot be overridden by general or ambiguous words. This is because there is too great a risk that the full implications of their unqualified meaning may have passed unnoticed in the democratic process. In the absence of express language or necessary implication to the contrary, the courts therefore presume that even the most general words were intended to be subject to the basic rights of the individual. In this way the courts of the United Kingdom, though acknowledging the sovereignty of Parliament, apply principles of constitutionality little different from those which exist in countries where the power of the legislature is expressly limited by a constitutional document.[215]

Lord Bingham, writing extra-judicially, said that the presumptions are important because

> … if, as sometimes happens, the executive as the proponent of legislation wants to introduce a provision that would strike ordinary people as unfair or disproportionate or immoral, the need to spell out that intention explicitly on the face of the bill must operate as a discouragement, not last because of the increased risk of media criticism and parliamentary and popular resistance.[216]

These statements suggest that the presumptions are not really motivated by genuine uncertainty about Parliament's intentions; instead,

---

[212] Sir John Laws, 'Constitutional Guarantees' *Statute Law Review* 29 (2008) 1 at 8.
[213] *Ibid.*, 1–2.   [214] *Ibid.*, 8.
[215] *R* v. *Secretary of State for the Home Department, ex parte Simms* [2000] 2 AC 115 at 131.
[216] Lord Bingham of Cornhill, 'Dicey Revisited' [2002] *Public Law* 39 at 48.

they amount to quasi-constitutional 'manner and form' requirements, imposed by the judiciary, to enhance Parliament's accountability to the electorate. On the other hand, the statements are consistent with the more modest view that enhancing Parliament's accountability is an additional advantage of presumptions that must still be justified primarily on more orthodox grounds.

It is undoubtedly true that judges have used common law presumptions to interpret legislation more narrowly than Parliament apparently intended, thereby frustrating its objectives. Dicey noted with apparent approval that

> from the moment Parliament has uttered its will as lawgiver, that will becomes subject to the interpretation put upon it by the judges of the land, and the judges, who are influenced by the feelings of magistrates no less than by the general spirit of the common law, are disposed to construe statutory exceptions to common law principles in a mode which would not commend itself ... to the Houses of Parliament, if the Houses were called upon to interpret their own enactments.[217]

Historically, this is notorious in the case of a good deal of legislation dealing with taxation and industrial relations, and attempting to restrict judicial review of administrative decisions. The use of the presumptions by conservative judges to curtail or thwart progressive legislation is not something that judges today should be proud of. It tarnishes the image of a fearless judiciary shielding the individual from the tyranny of the state. In many cases the judges misapplied the presumptions, by using them as a polite fiction or smokescreen to conceal judicial disobedience of Parliament.[218] Should these cases now be used to support the proposition that the presumptions were really, all along, creatures of the common law, independent of and applicable contrary to Parliament's known intentions? That would be inconsistent with the doctrine of parliamentary sovereignty.

As previously argued, if the express meaning of a provision is incompatible with some right, the only way consistent with parliamentary sovereignty that it can be 'read down' to remove the incompatibility is to presume that Parliament did not intend to interfere with the right. If it clearly did intend to do so, then to read the legislation down is to rewrite or partially disapply it. If in doing that the judges are not correcting a mistake, by giving effect to one of Parliament's own standing commitments,

---

[217] Dicey, *An Introduction to the Study of the Law of the Constitution* (10th edn), 413–14.
[218] Kavangh, *Constitutional Review*, pp. 334–5.

then they are engaging in judicial legislation rather than interpretation.[219] That is something that judges are not constitutionally permitted to do. It is also to assume a power that is difficult to confine. If judges can legitimately rewrite statutes to make them consistent with a 'common law bill of rights', why should they not be able to use the same power to improve statutes in other ways? To repeat a question posed earlier: what principled limit to a power of judicial amendment could provide a substitute for rebuttable presumptions of legislative intention?[220]

We must choose between three options. First, we can continue to accept that application of the common law presumptions must be justified primarily by genuine uncertainty about legislative intentions, even if as a by-product they also enhance Parliament's political accountability to the electorate. If we choose this option, we must reject as wrongly decided those cases in which the presumptions have been used as a smokescreen to conceal judicial disobedience of Parliament. On the other hand, if we choose the second or third options, we can accept most if not all of these cases as correctly decided.

The second option is to accept Kavanagh's claim that, in reality, the courts have always possessed an 'inherent jurisdiction' to protect fundamental rights from legislative infringement or subversion. A major difficulty is that, if so, why have the courts not said so? Why have they felt the need to engage in a pretence, by hiding behind spurious 'presumptions' of legislative intention? According to Kavanagh, the 'politics of judicial lawmaking in the UK' required the courts to do this: 'given the fact that respecting the will of Parliament is thought to be one of the most fundamental principles of statutory interpretation … we should not be surprised if judges routinely say that their judgments give effect to the will of Parliament'.[221] The judges appeal to 'legislative intentions' that in reality are 'constructed' by them and used as 'a rhetorical device' to give them 'a 'cloak of respectability'.[222] 'Judicial assurances that they are loyally giving effect to Parliament's intention' have a 'beguiling effect' that obscures the reality of judicial creativity.[223] But surely this deeply felt need for concealment suggests that the courts were aware that they would have been flouting constitutional orthodoxy to openly proclaim that they were partially disapplying legislation to give effect to 'constitutional values' of their own choosing.

---

[219] See Chapter 9, Section II, Part B, above.
[220] *Ibid.*, Section II, end of Part A.
[221] Kavanagh, *Constitutional Review*, pp. 335 and 81.
[222] *Ibid.*, pp. 98, n. 38, 82 and 115.   [223] *Ibid.*, p. 115.

This leads to the third option, which is that the courts have waged a stealthy, and ultimately successful, campaign to acquire – or usurp – authority to protect 'constitutional' values of their choice, by imposing a kind of manner and form requirement on Parliament.[224] As Jeffrey Jowell more charitably puts it, '*consciously or unconsciously*, [the judges] were chipping away at the rock of parliamentary supremacy by making it increasingly difficult for Parliament to authorise the infringement of the rule of law and ... fundamental rights'.[225] When we are strongly attracted to a particular conclusion, we are sorely tempted to assess evidence selectively, and bend or stretch logic. Even if we try to resist the temptation, we may fail at the subconscious level. In other words, even if we do not lie, we may delude ourselves. This is a universal human trait, which judges share with the rest of us. If they believe that a statute would otherwise infringe rights, they may be strongly motivated to prevent the infringement through interpretation. If it is not possible to do so through orthodox methods that are consistent with parliamentary sovereignty, they may be tempted to adopt a 'spurious interpretation'.[226] This amounts to 'put[ting] a meaning into the text as a juggler puts coins, or what not, into a dummy's hair, to be pulled forth presently with an air of discovery'.[227]

To adopt either the second or third options is to lend support to the claim that, rather than being subordinate to Parliament, the judiciary now shares sovereign power with it. It might then seem legitimate for the judiciary to enlarge its share of sovereignty by adding to the constitutional values that it protects, or strengthening the method by which it protects them. For example, in a jurisdiction lacking a statutory Bill of Rights, the courts might introduce one 'through the back door', by developing a common law bill of rights that protects the same rights as a statutory bill and provides the same level of protection. Or the courts might ramp up the strength of the 'presumptions', by advancing from strict interpretation to invalidation of legislation. If the former is tantamount to partial disapplication, why not – in a sufficiently extreme case – assume the power of full disapplication? After all, that is precisely what common

[224] See the comments of J. Evans, 'Controlling the Use of Parliamentary History' *New Zealand Universities Law Review* 18 (1998) 1 at 44.

[225] J. Jowell, 'Parliamentary Sovereignty Under the New Constitutional Hypothesis' *Public Law* 562 (2006) 575 (emphasis added).

[226] R. Pound, 'Spurious Interpretation' *Columbia Law Review* 6 (1907) 379.

[227] *Ibid.*, 382.

law constitutionalists such as Trevor Allan claim that the courts, in some cases, already do.[228]

F   Constitutional statutes

Lord Justice Laws (with the agreement of Crane J.) has recently proposed a novel explanation of the effect of the European Communities Act 1972 (UK) ('the EC Act'), in authorising the judicial 'disapplication' of statutes that are inconsistent with European Community laws that it makes binding. He suggests that the EC Act is just one of a number of 'constitutional statutes' that can now be amended or repealed only by express words, and not mere implication.[229] This suggestion could be endorsed on relatively orthodox grounds: it is plausible to think that some statutes are of such constitutional importance that Parliament is very unlikely to intend to interfere with them, and should therefore be presumed not to intend to do so in the absence of clear, express words to the contrary. This is especially plausible when, as in the case of the EC Act itself, the statute expressly provides that future legislation inconsistent with it should not be applied. What is remarkable about Laws L.J.'s judgment is his repeated and emphatic claim that the basis of his suggestion is not legislative intent, but 'the common law'. Parliament, he insists, cannot bind its successors by stipulating as to the manner and form of future legislation.[230] The doctrine of implied repeal, 'which was always the common law's own creature', can only be changed 'by our own courts, to which the scope and nature of Parliamentary sovereignty are ultimately confided'.[231]

> The courts may say – have said – that there are certain circumstances in which the legislature may only enact what it desires to enact if it does so by express, or at any rate specific, provision.[232]

This amounts to a judicial power to impose upon Parliament a modest 'manner and form' requirement, a power which Laws L.J. denies that Parliament itself possesses. He asserts that the common law has imposed the requirement both to protect 'rights which should properly be classified as constitutional or fundamental', and – now – 'constitutional statutes'.[233] 'The ECA is, *by force of the common law*, a constitutional statute.'[234] This amounts to the adoption of a strong version of 'common

---

[228] See Chapter 9, Section IV, Part B, above.
[229] *Thoburn v. Sunderland City Council* [2003] QB 151 at [60].
[230] *Ibid.,* [59].   [231] *Ibid.,* [60].   [232] *Ibid.,* [60].   [233] *Ibid.,* [62].   [234] *Ibid.* (emphasis added).

law constitutionalism', the term now widely used to denote a variety of theories that attribute some kind of constitutional status to the common law.[235]

As in the case of the presumptions of statutory interpretation, there are alternative ways of justifying the idea that there are constitutional statutes that cannot be repealed by implication. One is the orthodox idea that some statutes are of such constitutional importance that Parliament is very unlikely to intend to meddle with them indirectly, as a side-effect of provisions dealing primarily with other matters. We already accept that there are fundamental common law rights that Parliament is very unlikely to intend to override, and it is just as plausible to think that there are very important statutes that it is equally unlikely to intend to override.[236] Not doubt the HRA, as Kavanagh argues, is one of them.[237] This is no doubt why Lord Wilberforce said in 1967 that he felt 'some reluctance to holding that an Act of such constitutional significance as the Union with Ireland Act is subject to the doctrine of implied repeal'.[238]

Another way of justifying the same result is Laws L.J.'s suggestion that 'the common law' – which really means the judges – has conferred this elevated status and concomitant protection upon these statutes. Kavanagh agrees with Laws, asserting that the HRA is a 'constitutional statute' that, along with fundamental common law rights, is 'constitutionally entrenched in the common law'.[239]

Alison Young has argued at length that, despite Laws L.J.'s apparent adoption of the second justification, his discussion as a whole is best interpreted as adopting the first one.[240] She concedes, however, that his actual words provide strong support for the second justification.[241] Moreover, in a recent journal article he unequivocally adopts the second one, and acknowledges that the adoption of his recommendation would involve a change in the rule of recognition of statutes as valid laws.[242]

But, as demonstrated in Chapter 2, it is simply untrue that 'the scope and nature of Parliamentary sovereignty are ultimately confided' to the

---

[235] See Chapter 2, above.
[236] See Lindell, 'The Statutory Protection of Rights and Parliamentary Sovereignty', 197–8.
[237] Kavanagh, *Constitutional Review*, pp. 293–306.
[238] *Earl of Antrim's Petition (House of Lords)* [1967] 1 AC 691, quoted in Bennion, *Statutory Interpretation* (4th edn), p. 255 s. 87, and by Kavanagh, *Constitutional Review*, p. 301.
[239] Kavanagh, *Constitutional Review*, p. 306.
[240] Young, *Parliamentary Sovereignty and the Human Rights Act*, pp. 13 and 40–5.
[241] *Ibid.*, p. 41.
[242] Sir John Laws, 'Constitutional Guarantees', esp. at 8–9.

courts.[243] It cannot truly follow from this false premise either that the doctrine of implied repeal was 'the common law's own creature', or that the courts have authority to modify the doctrine by holding that sometimes the legislature may only legislate if it does so 'by express, or at any rate specific, provision'.[244] If, as Laws L.J. insists, Parliament itself lacks authority to impose requirements as to manner or form upon its legislative power,[245] it would be very surprising if the courts had authority to do so. The first, orthodox justification of 'constitutional statutes' should be preferred.

G   Constitutional principles

It is often observed that the courts' attitude towards parliamentary authority is changing, for various reasons that include statutory innovations such as the EC Act, the HRA and devolution, and increased judicial interest in the protection of rights.[246] Paul Craig, for example, believes that the new judicial power to disapply legislation inconsistent with EC law makes the prospect of the judges assuming a similar power to disapply legislation inconsistent with rights 'less novel or revolutionary'.[247] Kavanagh, whose focus is on the HRA, agrees:

> Once we begin to refine the doctrine of parliamentary sovereignty by admitting the legitimacy of legal limits on Parliament's power, then this begs the question of what value remains in articulating these issues in terms of sovereignty at all ... [T]he immensely important obiter dicta contained in *Jackson* ... are important signposts to a subtle change in constitutional culture ... They are a signal that the judiciary no longer wishes to play a part in maintaining fairytales ... The HRA is, albeit slowly and incrementally, contributing to a change in how we understand constitutional law ... and has begun to unleash the constitutional imagination in order to reassess the theoretical foundations of UK constitutional law.[248]

The most serious challenge likely to confront the doctrine of parliamentary sovereignty in the near future is likely to arise from further development of the tendency to describe important common law principles, and now statutes, as having a 'constitutional' status that entitles them to special judicial protection.[249] Describing important principles

---

[243] *Thoburn* v. *Sunderland City Council* [2003] QB 151 at [60].
[244] *Ibid.*   [245] *Ibid.*, [59].   [246] E.g., Craig, 'Report on the United Kingdom', at 215.
[247] *Ibid.*, 218.   [248] Kavanagh, *Constitutional Review*, pp. 413–15.
[249] Joseph and Elias both advert to this phenomenon: Joseph, 'Parliament, the Courts, and the Collaborative Enterprise'; Elias, 'Sovereignty in the 21st Century', 161.

as 'constitutional' is, of course, a familiar feature of British constitutional discourse, and in itself entirely consistent with parliamentary sovereignty. Sir Robert Chambers, Blackstone's successor to the Vinerian Chair at Oxford, embraced parliamentary sovereignty whole-heartedly, but said that a particular statute 'though not illegal, for the enaction of the supreme power is the definition of legality, was yet unconstitutional', because it was 'contrary to the principles of the English government'.[250] In 1830, Henry Brougham criticised the Benthamites for denying that any sensible distinction could be drawn between the concepts of illegality and unconstitutionality: 'Cannot they comprehend how a thing may be wrong, as inconsistent with the spirit of our political system, which yet the law has not prohibited?' Statutes committing such wrongs could sensibly be condemned as 'contrary to the spirit, and dangerous to the existence, of the constitution – in one word, as *unconstitutional*. Yet ... they would be legal: for the legislature itself would have sanctioned them.'[251] This distinction, perpetuated by Austin and Dicey, survives today in the language of constitutional convention.[252] That is why Lord Wilberforce once rejected a possible interpretation of a statute on the ground that it would produce a result 'which is arbitrary, unjust, and in my opinion unconstitutional'.[253]

The problem is that the subtle distinctions encoded in this traditional terminology are increasingly liable to be misunderstood or obfuscated. The campaign to confer 'constitutional' status on a growing number of principles or rights ultimately aims at arming the judiciary to protect them from legislative interference. Sir John Laws is the leading judicial proponent of further developments in this direction.[254]

---

[250] R. Chambers, *A Course of Lectures on the English Law Delivered at the University of Oxford 1767–1773*, T.M. Curley (ed.) (Madison: University of Wisconsin Press, 1986), vol. I, p. 141.

[251] H. Brougham, 'Review of *Inquiry into the Rise and Growth of the Royal Prerogative in England*, by James Allan' *Edinburgh Review* 52 (1830) 139 and 142.

[252] J. Austin, *The Province of Jurisprudence Determined*, H.L.A. Hart (ed.) (London: Weidenfeld & Nicholson, 1954), pp. 257–8; Dicey, *Introduction to the Study of the Law of the Constitution*, pp. 24–7 and Part III. See also Goldsworthy, *The Sovereignty of Parliament*, pp. 190–2.

[253] *Vestey* v. *Inland Revenue Commissioners* [1980] AC 1148 at 1174.

[254] *Thoburn* v. *Sunderland City Council* [2003] QB 151 at [63]-[64] per Laws L.J. See *R* v. *Secretary of State for the Home Department, ex parte Simms* [2000] 2 AC 115 at 131 per Lord Hoffmann; Jeffrey Jowell, 'Beyond the Rule of Law: Towards Constitutional Judicial Review' *Public Law* 671 (2000) 675, 682 and 683; D.L. Keir and F.H. Lawson, *Cases in Constitutional Law* (4th edn rev.) (Oxford: Clarendon Press, 1959), p. 10; Lord Devlin, 'Judges as Lawmakers' *Modern Law Review* 39 (1976) 1 at 14.

> In its present state of evolution, the British system may be said to stand at an intermediate stage between parliamentary supremacy and constitutional supremacy ... Parliament remains the sovereign legislature ... But at the same time, the common law has come to recognise and endorse the notion of constitutional, or fundamental, rights.[255]

He foresees 'in the tranquil development of the common law ... a gradual re-ordering of our constitutional priorities to bring alive the nascent idea that a democratic legislature cannot be above the law'.[256] As Lord Irvine has observed, this is 'a prediction that we are only half-way on a constitutional journey and that, in the fullness of time, we will leave parliamentary supremacy behind altogether'.[257]

Laws L.J. and some other judges seem intent on building up a body of dicta, announcing the constitutional status of an uncertain number of common law principles, dicta that might, at some future time, be regarded as authority for the proposition that these principles lie beyond the reach of statute. At present, fundamental principles are protected mainly through presumptions of legislative intent, and the grounds of judicial review of administrative action. But if the concept of legislative intention is eventually discarded as a fiction, the way in which statutory language is sometimes bent or stretched to accommodate these principles might have to be explained in terms of their inherent constitutional status, thereby elevating them above statute law. We would then have a 'common law constitution' with a vengeance.

It is impossible to predict with any confidence whether or not the judiciary will try to push this far, or if it does, whether Parliament will allow it to succeed. That is no doubt why many recent critics have been reluctant to make any stronger claim than that it is 'possible' that the courts might hold that Parliament cannot abrogate fundamental rights.[258] Their reticence is presumably due partly to their realising that it is not yet clear that the courts could get away with it. But one further point should be made.

---

[255] *International Transport Roth GmbH* v. *Secretary of State for the Home Department* [2002] EWCA Civ 158; [2002] 3 WLR 344 at [71].

[256] Sir John Laws, 'Illegality and the Problem of Jurisdiction', in M. Supperstone and J. Goldie (eds.), *Judicial Review* (2nd edn) (London: Butterworths, 1997), 4.17.

[257] Lord Irvine of Lairg, 'The Impact of the Human Rights Act: Parliament, the Courts and the Executive' *Public Law* (2003) 308 at 310.

[258] Elias, 'Sovereignty in the 21st Century', 160; Thomas, 'The Relationship of Parliament and the Courts', 8; Joseph, 'Parliament, the Courts, and the Collaborative Enterprise', 342.

Judges are often keen to dispel any impression that *they* are engaged in attempting to change the constitution. Laws L.J., for example, speaks of 'the common law' coming to recognise the existence of constitutional rights.[259] In *Thoburn's* case, he observes that the traditional doctrine of sovereignty has been modified 'by the common law': 'the common law has in recent years allowed, or rather created, exceptions to the doctrine of implied repeal: a doctrine which was always the common law's own creature'.[260] This apparent attribution of change to 'the common law' as an autonomous and (even more mysteriously) active agent is intriguing. The declaratory theory of judging, which modern judges often disparage as a 'fairy tale', apparently on some occasions still has some merit or utility.

There are two possible explanations of this style of rhetoric. The cynical explanation is that judges such as Laws L.J. are ducking for cover, seeking to avoid political flak by pretending that in constitutional matters the common law somehow evolves by itself, rather than being changed by them. When judges speak as if the common law is an autonomous and active agent, and they are merely its dutiful spokesmen, they are using the common law like a ventriloquist's dummy.

But I would prefer to accept a non-cynical explanation. Earlier, I pointed out that rules of recognition, and other unwritten constitutional rules, are constituted by a consensus among senior legal officials. I also suggested that this is what people might mean, when they describe such rules as common law rules: in other words, that the rules and principles of the 'common law constitution' are customs of legal officialdom, which the judges did not create, and cannot change, unilaterally.[261] Mark Elliott has developed a similar theory, according to which Laws L.J.'s common law constitution is best understood in terms of constitutional conventions crystallising into law.[262] The existence of constitutional conventions requires consensus among legal officials, including members of the elected branches of government. If Elliott is right, the common law constitution also depends on such a consensus, and can change only if that consensus changes. If this is an accurate account of what Laws L.J. means by 'the common law', in constitutional matters, then he is not being disingenuous when he speaks as if it is at least partly independent of judicial

---

[259] See text to n. 256, above.
[260] [2002] EWHC 195 (Admin); [2002] 1 CMLR 50 at [59]-[60].
[261] See end of Chapter 2, above.
[262] Elliot, 'Parliamentary Sovereignty and the New Constitutional Order', 362–76.

opinion, and potentially subject to changes that the judiciary neither initiates nor controls. The evolution of custom is beyond any one institution's deliberate control. If so, then Laws L.J. is not a legal revolutionary at all: he is merely predicting evolutionary, consensual, and therefore uncontroversial, change.

INDEX